FOUNDATIONS OF

GENERAL TOPOLOGY

FOUNDATIONS OF
GENERAL TOPOLOGY

William J. Pervin

Department of Mathematics
The Pennsylvania State University
University Park, Pennsylvania

NEW YORK **ACADEMIC PRESS** LONDON

ACADEMIC PRESS, INC.
111 Fifth Avenue, New York, New York 10003

United Kingdom Edition published by
ACADEMIC PRESS, INC. (LONDON) LTD.
24/28 Oval Road, London NW1

LIBRARY OF CONGRESS CATALOG CARD NUMBER: 64-17796

Fourth Printing, 1972

PRINTED IN THE UNITED STATES OF AMERICA

This book is dedicated to

my parents,
my wife, and
my children.

Preface

The teaching of topology affords the instructor an opportunity not only to impart necessary mathematical content, but also to expose the student to both rigor and abstraction. This text, which grew out of lectures presented at The Pennsylvania State University, is designed to emphasize the value of careful presentations of proofs and to show the power of abstraction.

Since the axiomatic method is fundamental to mathematics, the student should become acquainted with it as early as possible. The author has presented various amounts of this material to students with quite varying backgrounds; he has attempted to make this book equally flexible. The only prerequisite is the study of some analysis; even the traditional "Advanced Calculus" should be sufficient. It should be particularly noted that no part of this text requires the material sometimes labeled "Modern Algebra."

Since it is possible to reach this level with no detailed knowledge of set theory, the first chapter presents the basic material in the most naive way (i.e., non-axiomatically). For students needing merely some review and practice in set theory, the second chapter introduces some important notions about cardinal and ordinal numbers, again in the naive sense. Well-prepared students may be started with the third chapter with only an occasional reference to the introductory chapters for notation.

In the third through seventh chapters, the fundamentals of general topology are presented in logical order progressing from the most general case of a topological space to the restrictive case of a complete metric space. The author has found it possible to cover this material in a one-semester course with well-prepared graduate students and have time left for a few of the basic topics from the latter portion of the book (such as Sections *8.1*, *8.2*, *9.3*, and *10.1*). Including the material introduced in the problems, there is more than enough material in the entire book for a two-semester course. Students who must start with the introductory chapters will cover correspondingly less of this additional material.

The proofs are given in considerable detail so that they may serve as models for the student to emulate. Only after he has had experience in giving such detailed proofs is the student prepared to omit the "obvious" steps. Although no figures are given in the text, the instructor should encourage the student to make diagrams to help his visualization. The student must be cautioned, however, that a picture is not a proof, which is the main reason for omitting them here.

The problems at the ends of the sections are both to test the student's comprehension and abilities and to introduce additional material. Those problems which are given with bibliographic references are usually too difficult for any but the best students and are intended more as suggestions for further reading and work.

Although this material is a prerequisite for the study of many fields of mathematics, here it is presented to be studied for its own sake. It is hoped that the student finishing this text will choose to continue to study and do research in the field, and the number of references has been greatly increased for his benefit.

The author has been influenced in his style of presentation by lectures by Norman Levine and the classic book by Waclaw Sierpinski. The choice of material was influenced by lectures by G. S. Young and the classic book by J. L. Kelley. The author is grateful to the many students and colleagues who have found and corrected mistakes and suggested improvements in earlier versions of this book.

Throughout the book we will use the contraction "iff" for the phrase "if and only if," and will mark the end of a proof by the symbol ∎.

W. J. P.

Contents

Chapter 5 Separation and Countability Axioms

Chapter 6 Metric Spaces

Chapter 7 Complete Metric Spaces

Chapter 8 Product Spaces

Chapter 9 Function and Quotient Spaces

CHAPTER I

Algebra of Sets

1.1 Sets and Subsets

It is not possible to define every term used in mathematics, but all of mathematics can be defined in terms of a few undefined concepts. The basic undefined notion with which we will be concerned is that of a **set**. In an attempt to clarify the intuitive notion of a set, we will note that the words "family," "collection," and "aggregate" are, and will be used as, synonyms for the word "set." Implicit in our idea of a set is the notion that an object either belongs or does not belong to any collection we call a set. The objects, or elements, which make up our sets will be referred to as **points**, even though they may have nothing to do with the geometric concept we have of points. Thus, if our set is the collection of all states in the United States, then we may say that Pennsylvania is one point of the set and that Europe is not a point of the set.

In many discussions there is a fixed set of points from which all the sets under consideration are chosen. We will refer to this totality of all points under discussion, when such a set exists, as the **universe**. Our sets would then be collections of points chosen from the universe.

If we choose the natural numbers $\{1, 2, 3, \ldots\}$ as our universe, many elementary sets may be defined. The set of all even (natural) numbers, the set of all odd numbers, the set of all prime numbers, and the set of all numbers less than or equal to four are simple examples of sets.

Clearly, in any fixed universe, a set is determined by stating a property that its elements must satisfy. If $P(x)$ is a proposition expressing a property of the point x (in the universe) which is either true or false depending on the choice of the point x, we can speak of the set of points x for which $P(x)$ is true. If we suppress any mention of the universe, we may designate this set by $\{x : P(x)\}$. The set of all even numbers could now be written $\{x : x \text{ is even}\}$. The set of all numbers less than or equal to four could be written $\{x : x \leqslant 4\}$. If there are only a few members of a set, we may also describe it by listing its elements. Thus, $\{1, 2, 3, 4\}$ is the set of all numbers less than or equal to four.

In general, we will designate points of our universe by italic lower case letters $x, y, z, \ldots$, and sets chosen from our universe by italic capital letters $A, B, C, \ldots$. To designate the fundamental logical notion of membership in a set, we will write $x \in E$ and read this as "the point x is a member of the set E," "x belongs to E," or any other equivalent phrase which fits the grammar of the sentence. The negation of this statement, "x does not belong to E," will be written $x \notin E$. For example, $2 \in \{x : x \text{ is even}\}$ but $6 \notin \{x : x \leqslant 4\}$.

Two sets A and B will be called **equal**, written $A = B$, if and only if (iff) they contain exactly the same points. In terms of our basic notion of membership, this is equivalent to saying that $A = B$ iff $x \in A$ implies and is implied by $x \in B$.

Theorem 1.1.1. *For any sets A, B, and C:*

[*Reflexive Law*] $A = A$,

[*Symmetric Law*] $A = B$ *implies* $B = A$, *and*

[*Transitive Law*] $A = B$ *and* $B = C$ *imply* $A = C$.

Proof. Each of these laws follows from a corresponding logical law. Thus, since every statement is equivalent to itself, $x \in A$ must be equivalent to $x \in A$, so that $A = A$. Similarly, since $x \in A$ being equivalent to $x \in B$ implies that $x \in B$ is equivalent to $x \in A$, the symmetric law follows. Finally, $x \in A$ being equivalent to $x \in B$, and $x \in B$ being equivalent to $x \in C$, imply that $x \in A$ is equivalent to $x \in C$, which is the transitive law. ∎

A set A is a **subset** of a set B, written $A \subseteq B$ or $B \supseteq A$, iff $x \in A$ implies that $x \in B$. We will also say that B **contains** A, and call B a **superset** of A. For the negation of $A \subseteq B$ we will write $A \nsubseteq B$.

It is important to notice that this definition does not rule out the possibility of having $A = B$ when $A \subseteq B$. Our notion of equality shows, in fact, that $A = B$ iff $A \subseteq B$ and $B \subseteq A$. If we wish to express the fact that $A \subseteq B$ but $A \neq B$, we will call A a **proper subset** of B and write $A \subset B$. We will warn the reader that many authors use the symbol $\subset$ to express both subsets and proper subsets. The proof of the following theorem will be left to the problems at the end of the section.

Theorem 1.1.2. *For any sets A, B, and C:*

[*Reflexive Law*]	$A \subseteq A$,
[*Antisymmetric Law*]	$A \subseteq B$ *and* $B \subseteq A$ *imply* $A = B$, *and*
[*Transitive Law*]	$A \subseteq B$ *and* $B \subseteq C$ *imply* $A \subseteq C$.

We have already stated that we want some set to be determined from a fixed universe by stating any property that its elements must satisfy. If we choose $P(x)$ to be the statement $x \neq x$, it is clear that $P(x)$ is true for no elements of the universe. We must, therefore, accept the collection of no elements as a set. This set will be called the **empty** or **null** set and will always be denoted by $\emptyset$.

Theorem 1.1.3. *For any set E, $\emptyset \subseteq E$.*

Proof. In order for the containment $\emptyset \subseteq E$ to be false, the statement "For all x, $x \in \emptyset$ implies that $x \in E$" would have to be false. The negation of this statement, however, is "There exists an x such that $x \in \emptyset$ and $x \notin E$." This would imply that there exists a point in $\emptyset$ which is false by the definition of the empty set. Since the containment $\emptyset \subseteq E$ cannot be false without causing a contradiction, it must be true. ∎

We must distinguish between the members and the subsets of a set. Thus, the set whose only member is x is $\{x\}$. Thus, $\emptyset \in \{\emptyset\}$, and so $\emptyset \neq \{\emptyset\}$; that is, the set $\{\emptyset\}$ is not empty because it contains something: the set $\emptyset$. In general, $x \in E$ iff $\{x\} \subseteq E$.

Exercises

1. Let the natural numbers $\{1, 2, 3, \ldots\}$ be the universe. Describe the following sets:

$A = \{x : x \text{ is even}\}$,
$B = \{x : \text{there exists a } y \text{ such that } 2y = x\}$,
$C = \{x : x > 1\}$,
$D = \{x : x = 2\}$,
$E = \{x : x \text{ is even and prime}\}$, and
$F = \{x : \text{there exists a } y \text{ such that } y + 1 = x\}$.

To which of these sets does the number 2 belong? To which does 3 belong? Which of these sets are equal? What subset relations hold between these sets?

2. Prove 1.1.2.

1.2 Operations on Sets

The **union** of two sets A and B, written $A \cup B$, is the set of all points which belong to either A or B or both. The **intersection** of two sets A and B, written $A \cap B$, is the set of all points which belong to both A and B. The **difference** between two sets A and B, or the **relative complement** of B in A, written $A \setminus B$ or $\complement_A B$, is the set of all points in A which are not in B.

Our definitions may be rewritten as follows: $A \cup B = \{x : x \in A$ or $x \in B\}$, $A \cap B = \{x : x \in A$ and $x \in B\}$, and $A \setminus B = \{x : x \in A$ but $x \notin B\}$. Some of the elementary properties of unions, intersections, and differences may be proven immediately.

Theorem 1.2.1. *For any sets A, B, and C:*

[*Commutative Laws*] $A \cup B = B \cup A,$
$A \cap B = B \cap A,$

[*Associative Laws*] $A \cup (B \cup C) = (A \cup B) \cup C,$
$A \cap (B \cap C) = (A \cap B) \cap C,$

[*Distributive Laws*] $A \cap (B \cup C) = (A \cap B) \cup (A \cap C),$
$A \cup (B \cap C) = (A \cup B) \cap (A \cup C),$

[*DeMorgan's Laws*] $C \setminus (A \cup B) = (C \setminus A) \cap (C \setminus B)$, *and*
$C \setminus (A \cap B) = (C \setminus A) \cup (C \setminus B).$

Proof. Each of these laws follows immediately from the corresponding logical law. Let us prove the second DeMorgan law as an example. A point x belongs to $C \setminus (A \cap B)$ iff $x \in C$ and $x \notin (A \cap B)$. By the logical DeMorgan law, $x \notin (A \cap B)$ iff $x \notin A$ or $x \notin B$. Using the logical distributive law, $x \in [C \setminus (A \cap B)]$ is now equivalent to $[x \in C$ and $x \notin A]$ or $[x \in C$ and $x \notin B]$, which is equivalent to $x \in [(C \setminus A) \cup (C \setminus B)]$, as desired. ∎

When there is a fixed universe X under consideration, we will abbreviate $X \setminus E$ and $\complement_X E$ by $\complement E$, and call this the (absolute) **complement** of E. Other notations used for this are E^c, E', $\sim E$, and $-E$. Notice that $\complement \varnothing = X$ and $\complement X = \varnothing$. The Law of Double Negation shows that $\complement\complement E = E$ for all sets $E \subseteq X$. With this notation we may write $A \setminus B = A \cap (\complement B)$.

The definitions of union and intersection may be extended to any finite or infinite collection of sets as follows. If $\mathscr{E}$ is an arbitrary collection of subsets of a universe, then the **union** of all the sets of $\mathscr{E}$ is the set of all points in the universe which belong to at least one set in the collection $\mathscr{E}$. We denote this union by $\bigcup \{E : E \in \mathscr{E}\}$. The **intersection** of all the sets of $\mathscr{E}$ is the set of all points in the universe which belong to all of the sets in the collection $\mathscr{E}$ and is denoted by $\bigcap \{E : E \in \mathscr{E}\}$.

When the collection $\mathscr{E}$ is finite and consists of the sets $E_1, E_2, E_3, \ldots, E_n$, we will write $\bigcup_{i=1}^{n} E_i$ or $E_1 \cup E_2 \cup \ldots \cup E_n$ for their union and $\bigcap_{i=1}^{n} E_i$ or $E_1 \cap E_2 \cap \ldots \cap E_n$ for their intersection. It is easy to show that these unions and intersections are commutative and associative, and that generalized distributive and DeMorgan laws also hold. It is consistent with the above definitions to consider the case when the family $\mathscr{E}$ is empty, and define $\bigcup \{E : E \in \emptyset\} = \emptyset$ and $\bigcap \{E : E \in \emptyset\} = X$ where X is the fixed universe.

If two sets A and B have an empty intersection, that is, if $A \cap B = \emptyset$, we say that A and B are **disjoint**. For any set E, E and $\complement E$ are disjoint sets. On the other hand, the union of E and $\complement E$ is X, the universe.

Exercises

1. Let $\mathscr{E}$ be a collection (possibly empty) of subsets of a universe X. Prove the following:

   (i) For every $E^* \in \mathscr{E}$, $\bigcap \{E : E \in \mathscr{E}\} \subseteq E^* \subseteq \bigcup \{E : E \in \mathscr{E}\}$,

   (ii) $\complement \bigcap \{E : E \in \mathscr{E}\} = \bigcup \{\complement E : E \in \mathscr{E}\}$, and

   (iii) $E^* \cap (\bigcup \{E : E \in \mathscr{E}\}) = \bigcup \{E^* \cap E : E \in \mathscr{E}\}$.

State and prove the other DeMorgan law and the other distributive law.

2. If E is a subset of the universe X, prove:

   (i) $E \cup E = E \cap E = E$,

   (ii) $E \cup \emptyset = E$, $E \cap \emptyset = \emptyset$, and

   (iii) $E \cup X = X$, $E \cap X = E$.

3. Prove that the following statements are equivalent for any two subsets $A, B \subseteq X$:

   (i) $A \cap B = A$,

   (ii) $A \cup B = B$,

   (iii) $A \subseteq B$,

   (iv) $\complement A \supseteq \complement B$,

   (v) $A \cap \complement B = \emptyset$, and

   (vi) $\complement A \cup B = X$.

4. Prove the following properties about the differences between the sets $A, B, C \subseteq X$:

   (i) $A \setminus A = \emptyset$, $A \setminus \emptyset = A$, $\emptyset \setminus A = \emptyset$, $A \setminus X = \emptyset$,

   (ii) $(A \setminus B) \setminus C = (A \setminus C) \setminus (B \setminus C)$,

(iii) $A \setminus (A \setminus B) = A \cap B$, and
(iv) $A \cap (B \setminus C) = (A \cap B) \setminus C$.

5. Define the **symmetric difference**, $A \triangle B$, of two subsets $A, B \subseteq X$ by the equation

$$A \triangle B = (A \setminus B) \cup (B \setminus A).$$

Prove the following properties of the symmetric difference:

(i) $A \triangle B = (A \cup B) \setminus (A \cap B)$,
(ii) $A \triangle B = B \triangle A$,
(iii) $A \triangle (B \triangle C) = (A \triangle B) \triangle C$,
(iv) $A \cap (B \triangle C) = (A \cap B) \triangle (A \cap C)$, and
(v) for every pair of sets $A, B \subseteq X$, there exists a set $C \subseteq X$ such that $A \triangle C = B$. Is C unique? Find some other properties of the symmetric difference.

1.3 Relations

A **relation** between two sets X and Y is a collection $\mathfrak{r}$ of ordered pairs $\langle x, y\rangle$ with $x \in X$ and $y \in Y$. If $\mathfrak{r}$ is a relation, we may write $\langle x, y\rangle \in \mathfrak{r}$ as $x \,\mathfrak{r}\, y$ and say that x is $\mathfrak{r}$-related to y.

By "ordered" pair we imply that in general $\langle x, y\rangle$ does not equal $\langle y, x\rangle$. We define equality between ordered pairs by setting $\langle x_1, y_1\rangle = \langle x_2, y_2\rangle$ iff $x_1 = x_2$ and $y_1 = y_2$. An example of a relation between the set of all points of a set X and the set of all subsets of a set X is the "belongs to" relation. Thus, the point x and the set E are in this relation iff $x \in E$.

If the sets X and Y are both the set of real numbers, we may define a relation $\mathfrak{r}$ by setting $x \,\mathfrak{r}\, y$ iff $x < y$. We may then write $\langle 2, 3\rangle \in \mathfrak{r}$ or $2 \,\mathfrak{r}\, 3$ since $2 < 3$. We are often interested in cases where the sets X and Y are equal, and we then say that $\mathfrak{r}$ is a **relation on** X. Thus, $<$ is a relation on the set of real numbers.

Since a relation is a set, we may consider the largest and smallest cases to be of interest. The relation consisting of all ordered pairs $\langle x, y\rangle$ with $x \in X$ and $y \in Y$ is called the **Cartesian product** of X and Y, written $X \times Y$. The name is clearly derived from the fact that if X and Y are both the set of real numbers, then $X \times Y$ is the Cartesian plane. A relation between X and Y may now be described as a subset of the Cartesian product of X and Y. The Cartesian product is the largest relation possible between two sets, while the empty set gives us the smallest relation between X and Y in which $x \,\emptyset\, y$ never holds.

The **domain** of a relation $\mathfrak{r}$ between X and Y is defined to be $\{x : x \,\mathfrak{r}\, y \text{ for some } y \in Y\}$, while the **range** of $\mathfrak{r}$ is defined to be

$\{y : x \mathfrak{r} y$ for some $x \in X\}$. In the case of $\mathfrak{r} = X \times Y$, the domain of $\mathfrak{r}$ is X, while the range of $\mathfrak{r}$ is Y. On the other hand, the empty relation has both its domain and its range empty.

The **identity relation**, $\mathfrak{i}_X$, on a set X is defined by setting $\langle x, y\rangle \in \mathfrak{i}_X$ iff $x = y$. This relation is sometimes called the **diagonal** due to its position in the Cartesian plane. The domain and range of $\mathfrak{i}_X$ are both X, and if the set X is understood from the context we will refer to the identity relation $\mathfrak{i}$.

The **inverse relation**, $\mathfrak{r}^{-1}$, of a relation $\mathfrak{r}$ between two sets X and Y is the relation between Y and X defined by setting $\langle y, x\rangle \in \mathfrak{r}^{-1}$ iff $\langle x, y\rangle \in \mathfrak{r}$. It is easy to see that the domain of $\mathfrak{r}^{-1}$ is the same as the range of $\mathfrak{r}$, while the range of $\mathfrak{r}^{-1}$ is the domain of $\mathfrak{r}$. If the sets X and Y are the same, then $\mathfrak{r}$ and $\mathfrak{r}^{-1}$ are both relations on X; that is, subsets of $X \times X$. If $\mathfrak{r}$ is the relation $<$ on the set of real numbers, then $\mathfrak{r}^{-1}$ would clearly be the relation $>$. In particular, $\mathfrak{r}$ is everything above, $\mathfrak{i}$ is everything on, and $\mathfrak{r}^{-1}$ is everything below the line $y = x$ in the Cartesian plane.

If $\mathfrak{r}$ is a relation between X and Y, and $\mathfrak{s}$ is a relation between Y and Z, then the **composition relation**, written $\mathfrak{s} \circ \mathfrak{r}$, is the relation between X and Z defined by setting $\langle x, z\rangle \in \mathfrak{s} \circ \mathfrak{r}$ iff there exists a point $y \in Y$ such that $\langle x, y\rangle \in \mathfrak{r}$ and $\langle y, z\rangle \in \mathfrak{s}$.

Theorem 1.3.1. *If* $\mathfrak{r} \subseteq X \times Y$ *and* $\mathfrak{s} \subseteq Y \times Z$, *then* $(\mathfrak{s} \circ \mathfrak{r})^{-1} = \mathfrak{r}^{-1} \circ \mathfrak{s}^{-1}$.

Proof. $\langle z, x\rangle \in (\mathfrak{s} \circ \mathfrak{r})^{-1}$ iff $\langle x, z\rangle \in \mathfrak{s} \circ \mathfrak{r}$ which, by definition, means that there exists a point $y \in Y$ such that $\langle x, y\rangle \in \mathfrak{r}$ and $\langle y, z\rangle \in \mathfrak{s}$. Again, these are equivalent to requiring that $\langle z, y\rangle \in \mathfrak{s}^{-1}$ and $\langle y, x\rangle \in \mathfrak{r}^{-1}$, or $\langle z, x\rangle \in \mathfrak{r}^{-1} \circ \mathfrak{s}^{-1}$. ∎

A relation $\mathfrak{r}$ on a set X is said to be **reflexive** iff $x \mathfrak{r} x$ for every $x \in X$; **symmetric** iff $x \mathfrak{r} y$ implies that $y \mathfrak{r} x$; and **transitive** iff $x \mathfrak{r} y$ and $y \mathfrak{r} z$ imply that $x \mathfrak{r} z$. A relation which is reflexive, symmetric, and transitive is said to be an **equivalence relation** on X.

The simplest example of an equivalence relation is equality $(=)$ between points of the set X. This was proven in **1.1.1**. In that case, $\mathfrak{r} = \mathfrak{i}_X$. On the other hand, the relation $X \times X$ is an equivalence relation on X in which every pair of points are related. The relation $\leqslant$ on the set of real numbers is both reflexive and transitive but is not symmetric and hence is not an equivalence relation. An equivalence relation may be described in terms of the relations introduced above.

Theorem 1.3.2. *A relation* $\mathfrak{r}$ *on a set* X *is reflexive iff* $\mathfrak{i}_X \subseteq \mathfrak{r}$; *symmetric iff* $\mathfrak{r}^{-1} = \mathfrak{r}$; *and transitive iff* $\mathfrak{r} \circ \mathfrak{r} \subseteq \mathfrak{r}$.

Proof. The first two statements are obvious. To prove the third, let us first assume that $\mathfrak{r}$ is transitive and let $\langle x, z\rangle \in \mathfrak{r} \circ \mathfrak{r}$. This means that there exists a point $y \in X$ such that $\langle x, y\rangle \in \mathfrak{r}$ and $\langle y, z\rangle \in \mathfrak{r}$. By transitivity, $\langle x, z\rangle \in \mathfrak{r}$, as desired. Conversely, if $\mathfrak{r} \circ \mathfrak{r} \subseteq \mathfrak{r}$, and if $\langle x, y\rangle \in \mathfrak{r}$ and $\langle y, z\rangle \in \mathfrak{r}$, then, because of the point y, $\langle x, z\rangle \in \mathfrak{r} \circ \mathfrak{r} \subseteq \mathfrak{r}$, and $\mathfrak{r}$ is transitive. ▮

The above theorem shows that $\mathfrak{i}_X$ is the smallest equivalence relation on a set X. The notion of **congruence** in number theory is an interesting example of an equivalence relation which is not equality. If X is the set of integers, then the relation $\mathfrak{r}$ of congruence modulo 3 is defined by setting $x \mathfrak{r} y$ iff $x - y$ is divisible by 3. We usually write this $x \equiv y \bmod 3$. It is clear that this is an equivalence relation which is not just an identity since $2 \neq 5$ but $2 \mathfrak{r} 5$. The relation of congruence modulo 3 divides up the set of integers into three disjoint subsets, $\{..., -3, 0, 3, 6, ...\}$, $\{..., -2, 1, 4, 7, ...\}$, and $\{..., -1, 2, 5, 8, ...\}$, such that two points in the same subset are $\mathfrak{r}$-related, but two points from different subsets are not $\mathfrak{r}$-related.

This idea may be generalized as follows. If $\mathfrak{r}$ is an equivalence relation on a set X, then for each point $x \in X$, the **equivalence class** of x, written $[x]$, is $\{y : x \mathfrak{r} y\}$. In our example of congruence modulo 3, it is clear that $[0] = [3] = ... = \{..., -3, 0, 3, 6, ...\}$, while $[1] = [4] = ... = \{..., -2, 1, 4, 7, ...\}$.

Since every equivalence relation is reflexive, $x \in [x]$ for every $x \in X$, and so every point of X is in some equivalence class. We will now show that an equivalence relation divides up the set X into disjoint subsets such that $x \mathfrak{r} y$ iff x and y belong to the same subset.

Theorem 1.3.3. *If* $\mathfrak{r}$ *is an equivalence relation on a set* X, *then for any* $x, y \in X$, *either* $[x] \cap [y] = \emptyset$ *or* $[x] = [y]$.

Proof. Suppose $[x] \cap [y] \neq \emptyset$; we must show that $[x] = [y]$. By our hypothesis, there exists a point $z \in [x] \cap [y]$. Now $z \in [x]$ and $z \in [y]$ so $x \mathfrak{r} z$ and $y \mathfrak{r} z$. By symmetry, $z \mathfrak{r} y$ also. By transitivity, $x \mathfrak{r} y$, and again by symmetry $y \mathfrak{r} x$. Now for any $t \in X$, $x \mathfrak{r} t$ iff $y \mathfrak{r} t$ by transitivity, and so $t \in [x]$ iff $t \in [y]$ and $[x] = [y]$. ▮

The family of all equivalence classes of a set X with respect to an equivalence relation $\mathfrak{r}$ is written $X/\mathfrak{r}$, read $X \bmod \mathfrak{r}$, and is often called the **quotient set** of X modulo $\mathfrak{r}$.

Exercises

1. In axiomatic treatments of set theory, an ordered pair, $\langle x, y\rangle$, is defined purely in terms of the notion of a set to be $\{\{x\}, \{x, y\}\}$. Prove that $\langle x_1, y_1\rangle = \langle x_2, y_2\rangle$ iff $x_1 = x_2$ and $y_1 = y_2$, using this definition.

2. Let $\mathfrak{r}$, $\mathfrak{s}$, and $\mathfrak{t}$ be relations on a set X. Prove the following properties:

(i) $(\mathfrak{r}^{-1})^{-1} = \mathfrak{r}$,

(ii) $\mathfrak{r} \circ (\mathfrak{s} \circ \mathfrak{t}) = (\mathfrak{r} \circ \mathfrak{s}) \circ \mathfrak{t}$, and

(iii) $\mathfrak{r} \circ \mathfrak{i}_X = \mathfrak{i}_X \circ \mathfrak{r} = \mathfrak{r}$.

3. If $\mathfrak{r}$ is a relation on a set X, compare $\mathfrak{r}^{-1} \circ \mathfrak{r}$ with $\mathfrak{i}_X$. If they are the same, prove it; if they are not the same, give an example of where they differ.

4. Let $\mathfrak{r}$ and $\mathfrak{s}$ be the relations on the set of real numbers defined by setting $x\,\mathfrak{r}\,y$ iff $x - 1 < y < x + 1$, and $x\,\mathfrak{s}\,y$ iff $y = -x$. Find $\mathfrak{r} \circ \mathfrak{s}$ and show which portions of the Cartesian plane are in $\mathfrak{r}$, $\mathfrak{s}$, $\mathfrak{r} \circ \mathfrak{s}$, and $\mathfrak{s} \circ \mathfrak{r}$.

5. Let $\mathfrak{r}$ and $\mathfrak{s}$ be the relations on the set of real numbers defined by setting $x\,\mathfrak{r}\,y$ iff $x^2 = y$, and $x\,\mathfrak{s}\,y$ iff $x < y$. Find $\mathfrak{r} \circ \mathfrak{s}$ and show which portions of the Cartesian plane are in $\mathfrak{r}$, $\mathfrak{s}$, $\mathfrak{r} \circ \mathfrak{s}$, and $\mathfrak{s} \circ \mathfrak{r}$.

6. Show that the properties of a relation being reflexive, symmetric, and transitive are independent in the sense that there are relations which satisfy any two of these properties but not the third. On the other hand, show that for a relation which has domain X, if the relation is symmetric and transitive on X, then it is also reflexive on X, and hence is an equivalence relation.

7. A **partition** of a set X is a collection of nonempty, disjoint subsets of X whose union is X. Show that a partition of a set X defines an equivalence relation $\mathfrak{r}$ by setting $x\,\mathfrak{r}\,y$ iff x and y belong to the same subset of the partition. Furthermore, the equivalence classes of $\mathfrak{r}$ are exactly the sets of the partition.

8. Let X be the set of all real numbers and define a relation $\mathfrak{r}$ on X by setting $x\,\mathfrak{r}\,y$ iff $x - y$ is an integer (positive, zero, or negative). Show that this is an equivalence relation, and describe the equivalence classes modulo $\mathfrak{r}$.

9. Let X be the set of all polynomials with real coefficients in the real variable x and define a relation $\mathfrak{r}$ on X by setting $p(x)\,\mathfrak{r}\,q(x)$ iff $dp/dx = dq/dx$. Show that $\mathfrak{r}$ is an equivalence relation and describe the equivalence classes modulo $\mathfrak{r}$.

10. With the same universe X as in the preceding problem, define a relation $\mathfrak{s}$ on X by setting $p(x)\,\mathfrak{s}\,q(x)$ iff the degree of $p(x)$ equals the degree of $q(x)$. Show that $\mathfrak{s}$ is an equivalence relation, and describe the equivalence classes modulo $\mathfrak{s}$. Compare the relation $\mathfrak{s}$ with the relation $\mathfrak{r}$ of the preceding problem.

11. Verify the following properties of the Cartesian product of sets where $A, B \subseteq X$ and $C, D \subseteq Y$:

(i) $(A \cup B) \times (C \cup D) = (A \times C) \cup (A \times D) \cup (B \times C) \cup (B \times D)$,

(ii) $(A \cap B) \times (C \cap D) = (A \times C) \cap (B \times D)$,

(iii) $\complement_{X\times Y}(A \times C) = (\complement_X A \times Y) \cup (X \times \complement_Y C)$, and

(iv) $(A \setminus B) \times C = (A \times C) \setminus (B \times C)$.

1.4 Mappings

A **mapping**, $\mathfrak{f}$, of a set X into a set Y, written $\mathfrak{f} : X \to Y$, is a relation between X and Y such that $\{y : x\, \mathfrak{f}\, y\}$ consists of exactly one point, written $\mathfrak{f}(x)$, for each point $x \in X$. Other terms for mappings are "function," "transformation," and "operator." We also say that $\mathfrak{f}$ takes x into $y = \mathfrak{f}(x)$.

What we have defined might well be called a **single-valued mapping**, but we will not consider any other type of relation a mapping. It is clear that the domain of a mapping of X into Y is the set X. Another way of describing the unique character of $\mathfrak{f}(x)$ is to require that $\langle x, y_1\rangle \in \mathfrak{f}$ and $\langle x, y_2\rangle \in \mathfrak{f}$ imply that $y_1 = y_2$. Two mappings $\mathfrak{f}$ and $\mathfrak{g}$ of X into Y are the same iff they are the same subset of $X \times Y$ and hence iff $\mathfrak{f}(x) = \mathfrak{g}(x)$ for every $x \in X$.

If $\mathfrak{f}$ is a mapping of X into Y, then the **graph** of $\mathfrak{f}$ is the subset of $X \times Y$ defined by $\{\langle x, y\rangle : y = \mathfrak{f}(x), x \in X\}$. Although the geometric notion of the graph is interesting, note that a mapping, as a subset of $X \times Y$, is indistinguishable from its graph.

If $\mathfrak{f} : X \to Y$ and $E \subseteq X$, we will write $\mathfrak{f}(E)$ for $\{y : y = \mathfrak{f}(x)$ for some $x \in E\}$ and call this set the **image** of E under $\mathfrak{f}$. We have thus associated with each mapping $\mathfrak{f}$ of X into Y another mapping, which we will also denote by $\mathfrak{f}$, from the family of all subsets of X into the family of subsets of Y. Some authors use the notation $\mathfrak{f}[E]$ to emphasize that this is not the same mapping as $\mathfrak{f}$, but we will assume that the reader can tell from the context which mapping is being used. We may also write $\mathfrak{f}(E)$ as $\bigcup \{\mathfrak{f}(x) : x \in E\}$.

Theorem 1.4.1. *If* $\mathfrak{f} : X \to Y$ *and* $\mathscr{E}$ *is a family of subsets of* X, *then*

(i) $\mathfrak{f}(\bigcup \{E : E \in \mathscr{E}\}) = \bigcup \{\mathfrak{f}(E) : E \in \mathscr{E}\}$;

(ii) $\mathfrak{f}(\bigcap \{E : E \in \mathscr{E}\}) \subseteq \bigcap \{\mathfrak{f}(E) : E \in \mathscr{E}\}$, *where equality need not hold*;

(iii) $A \subseteq B$ *implies that* $\mathfrak{f}(A) \subseteq \mathfrak{f}(B)$;

(iv) $\mathfrak{f}(A \setminus B) \supseteq \mathfrak{f}(A) \setminus \mathfrak{f}(B)$, *where equality need not hold*;

(v) $\mathfrak{f}(E) = \emptyset$ *iff* $E = \emptyset$; *and*

(vi) *no general containment holds between* $\mathfrak{f}(\complement_X E)$ *and* $\complement_Y \mathfrak{f}(E)$.

Proof. (i): $y \in \mathfrak{f}(\bigcup \{E : E \in \mathscr{E}\})$ iff there exists a point $x \in \bigcup\{E : E \in \mathscr{E}\}$ such that $y = \mathfrak{f}(x)$. This is equivalent to asserting that there exists a point x such that there exists a set E^* such that $x \in E^* \in \mathscr{E}$ and $y = \mathfrak{f}(x)$. This, however, is equivalent to the requirement that there exists a set $E^* \in \mathscr{E}$ such that $y \in \mathfrak{f}(E^*)$, and this means that $y \in \bigcup \{\mathfrak{f}(E) : E \in \mathscr{E}\}$.

(ii): $y \in \mathfrak{f}(\bigcap \{E : E \in \mathscr{E}\})$ iff there exists a point $x \in \bigcap \{E : E \in \mathscr{E}\}$ such that $y = \mathfrak{f}(x)$. This is equivalent to asserting that there exists a point x such that for every $E^* \in \mathscr{E}$ we have $x \in E^*$ and $y = \mathfrak{f}(x)$. This, however, implies that for every $E^* \in \mathscr{E}$, $y \in \mathfrak{f}(E^*)$, and this means that $y \in \bigcap \{\mathfrak{f}(E) : E \in \mathscr{E}\}$. It is very important to notice that one of these implications cannot be reversed. In particular, from the fact that for every $E^* \in \mathscr{E}$ we have $y \in \mathfrak{f}(E^*)$ we may conclude that for every $E^* \in \mathscr{E}$ there exists a point $x \in E^*$ such that $y = \mathfrak{f}(x)$, but we cannot reverse the order of the quantifiers because the x whose existence is asserted here may depend on the set E^* chosen. For example, let $\mathfrak{f}$ be the mapping of the set $X = \{x_1, x_2\}$ into the set $Y = \{y\}$ defined by setting $\mathfrak{f}(x) = y$ for each $x \in X$. If $\mathscr{E}$ is the family of sets $\{\{x_1\}, \{x_2\}\}$, then $\mathfrak{f}(\bigcap \{E : E \in \mathscr{E}\}) = \mathfrak{f}(\{x_1\} \cap \{x_2\}) = \mathfrak{f}(\varnothing) = \varnothing$, while $\bigcap \{\mathfrak{f}(E) : E \in \mathscr{E}\}) = \mathfrak{f}(\{x_1\}) \cap \mathfrak{f}(\{x_2\}) = \{y\} \cap \{y\} = \{y\}$. Note that for each set $E^* \in \mathscr{E}$, there is an $x \in E^*$ going into y, but for different sets E^* we must choose different x's.

(iii): Obvious.

(iv): $y \in \mathfrak{f}(A) \setminus \mathfrak{f}(B)$ iff $y \in \mathfrak{f}(A)$ and $y \notin \mathfrak{f}(B)$. This is equivalent to requiring that there exists a point $x \in A$ such that $y = \mathfrak{f}(x)$ but still $y \notin \mathfrak{f}(B)$. This implies that $x \notin B$, so we must have $x \in A \setminus B$ and $y = \mathfrak{f}(x)$, which means that $y \in \mathfrak{f}(A \setminus B)$. Again we cannot reverse all the implications because, although the point x is not in B, there might be some other point in B which does go into y under the mapping $\mathfrak{f}$. For example, let $\mathfrak{f} : X \to Y$ be the mapping defined in part (ii) above. If $A = \{x_1, x_2\} = X$ and $B = \{x_2\}$, then $\mathfrak{f}(A \setminus B) = \mathfrak{f}(\{x_1\}) = \{y\}$ while $\mathfrak{f}(A) \setminus \mathfrak{f}(B) = \{y\} \setminus \{y\} = \varnothing$. Note that, although x_1 is not in B, $x_2 \in B$ and $y = \mathfrak{f}(x_2)$.

(v): Obvious.

(vi): Let $X = \{x_1, x_2\}$, $Y = \{y_1, y_2\}$, and $\mathfrak{f}(x) = y_1$ for each $x \in X$. If $E = \{x_1\}$, then $\mathfrak{f}(\complement_X E) = \{y_1\}$ while $\complement_Y \mathfrak{f}(E) = \{y_2\}$. ∎

Although the domain of a mapping $\mathfrak{f} : X \to Y$ is the set X, the range of $\mathfrak{f}$ need not be Y. That is, $\mathfrak{f}(X) \subseteq Y$, but we may have $\mathfrak{f}(X) \neq Y$. If $\mathfrak{f}(X) = Y$, we say that $\mathfrak{f}$ is a **surjection** or **epimorphism**. More briefly, we will say that $\mathfrak{f}$ is a mapping of X **onto** Y, or that $\mathfrak{f}$ is onto.

Theorem 1.4.2. A mapping $\mathfrak{f} : X \to Y$ is onto Y iff $\mathfrak{f}(\complement_X E) \supseteq \complement_Y \mathfrak{f}(E)$ for every $E \subseteq X$.

Proof. If the containment holds for all $E \subseteq X$, then it holds for $E = \varnothing$. In this case we have $Y \supseteq \mathfrak{f}(\complement_X \varnothing) = \mathfrak{f}(X) \supseteq \complement_Y \mathfrak{f}(\varnothing) = \complement_Y \varnothing = Y$

and so $\mathfrak{f}(X) = Y$. Conversely, let us suppose that $\mathfrak{f}$ is onto. $y \in \complement_Y \mathfrak{f}(E)$ iff $y \notin \mathfrak{f}(E)$, which means that if $y = \mathfrak{f}(x)$ then $x \notin E$ or $x \in \complement_X E$. Since $\mathfrak{f}$ is onto, there exists some point $x^* \in X$ such that $y = \mathfrak{f}(x^*)$. By the implication just shown, $x^* \in \complement_X E$. Thus there exists a point $x^* \in \complement_X E$ such that $y = \mathfrak{f}(x^*)$ and so $y \in \mathfrak{f}(\complement_X E)$. ∎

If $\mathfrak{f} : X \to Y$ and $S \subseteq Y$, we will write $\mathfrak{f}^{-1}(S)$ for $\{x : \mathfrak{f}(x) \in S\}$ and call this set the **inverse image** of S under $\mathfrak{f}$. We have thus associated with each mapping $\mathfrak{f}$ of X into Y another mapping, $\mathfrak{f}^{-1}$, from the family of all subsets of Y to the family of subsets of X. Some authors emphasize the fact that $\mathfrak{f}^{-1}$ is not the arithmetic inverse by using the notation $\mathfrak{f}^{\leftarrow}$ for $\mathfrak{f}^{-1}$. The proof of the following theorem will be left to the problems at the end of the section.

Theorem 1.4.3. *If $\mathfrak{f} : X \to Y$ and $\mathscr{S}$ is a family of subsets of Y, then*

(i) $\mathfrak{f}^{-1}(\bigcup \{S : S \in \mathscr{S}\}) = \bigcup \{\mathfrak{f}^{-1}(S) : S \in \mathscr{S}\}$;

(ii) $\mathfrak{f}^{-1}(\bigcap \{S : S \in \mathscr{S}\}) = \bigcap \{\mathfrak{f}^{-1}(S) : S \in \mathscr{S}\}$;

(iii) $S \subseteq T$ *implies that* $\mathfrak{f}^{-1}(S) \subseteq \mathfrak{f}^{-1}(T)$;

(iv) $\mathfrak{f}^{-1}(S \setminus T) = \mathfrak{f}^{-1}(S) \setminus \mathfrak{f}^{-1}(T)$;

(v) $\mathfrak{f}^{-1}(S) = \emptyset$ *iff* $S \cap \mathfrak{f}(X) = \emptyset$; *and*

(vi) $\mathfrak{f}^{-1}(\complement_Y S) = \complement_X \mathfrak{f}^{-1}(S)$.

The fact that $\mathfrak{f}^{-1}$, unlike $\mathfrak{f}$, preserves the set-theoretic operations of union, intersection, containment, difference, and complement will be very important in the study of continuous mappings (see Chapter 4). We must still be careful not to assume too much about the behavior of $\mathfrak{f}^{-1}$. Although $E \subseteq \mathfrak{f}^{-1}(\mathfrak{f}(E))$ for every $E \subseteq X$, these two sets need not be equal. Again, $\mathfrak{f}(\mathfrak{f}^{-1}(S)) = S \cap \mathfrak{f}(X)$ which in general is contained in S but need not equal S. Of course, if $\mathfrak{f}$ is onto, it follows that $\mathfrak{f}(\mathfrak{f}^{-1}(S)) = S$ for every $S \subseteq Y$.

The inverse image of a set consisting of a single point is particularly important. If $\mathfrak{f}^{-1}(\{y\})$ is exactly one point for each $y \in \mathfrak{f}(X)$ we say that $\mathfrak{f}$ is an **injection** or **monomorphism**. More simply, we shall say that $\mathfrak{f}$ is **one-to-one**. It is important to note that we only consider points $y \in \mathfrak{f}(X)$, not all $y \in Y$, for otherwise we would be requiring that $\mathfrak{f}$ also be onto. It is easy to see that a mapping $\mathfrak{f}$ is one-to-one iff the images of any two distinct points are two distinct points. A mapping which is both one-to-one and onto (both a monomorphism and an epimorphism) is called an **isomorphism**.

We have already used the notation $E_1, E_2, \ldots$ to express the fact that we were dealing with a family of sets which we could distinguish by the subscript used in each case. The idea of a mapping may be used to extend this notion. If X is a set and Λ is another collection of objects, then an **indexing** of X by Λ is a mapping of Λ onto X. If $\lambda \in \Lambda$, the element of X associated with λ by this mapping will be denoted by x_λ. We may now write $X = \{x_\lambda : \lambda \in \Lambda\}$. A collection of points indexed by Λ may be denoted by $\{x_\lambda\}_{\lambda \in \Lambda}$ or even $\{x_\lambda\}$ if the indexing set Λ is either understood or unimportant in the discussion.

If $\mathscr{E}$ is a collection of sets $\{E_\lambda\}_{\lambda \in \Lambda}$, then the union of all the sets in $\mathscr{E}$, $\bigcup \{E : E \in \mathscr{E}\}$, may also be written $\bigcup \{E_\lambda : \lambda \in \Lambda\}$ or $\bigcup_{\lambda \in \Lambda} E_\lambda$, or even $\bigcup_\lambda E_\lambda$ if Λ is understood. A similar notation will be used for intersections. If, in the future, we use the phrase "for all λ," we mean for all λ in some understood or unimportant indexing set.

The Cartesian product of two sets X and Y was defined to be $\{\langle x, y\rangle : x \in X \text{ and } y \in Y\}$. This may be extended immediately to define the Cartesian product of a finite collection of sets. If $E_1, E_2, ..., E_n$ is a finite collection of sets (indexed by $\{1, 2, ..., n\}$), then the Cartesian product of these sets, denoted by $E_1 \times E_2 \times ... \times E_n$, is the collection of all ordered n-tuples $\langle x_1, x_2, ..., x_n\rangle$ where $x_i \in E_i$ for each $i = 1, 2, ..., n$. Note that each n-tuple may be considered as defining a mapping of the indexing set $\{1, 2, ..., n\}$ into the union of the sets E_i such that the value of the mapping at i, written x_i, is in the set E_i.

If $\{E_\lambda\}_{\lambda \in \Lambda}$ is a collection of sets, the **Cartesian product** of these sets, denoted by $\prod_{\lambda \in \Lambda} E_\lambda$ or $\prod \{E_\lambda : \lambda \in \Lambda\}$, is the collection of all mappings of Λ into $\bigcup_{\lambda \in \Lambda} E_\lambda$ such that the image of the mapping at $\lambda \in \Lambda$ is in the set E_λ. We will denote the individual mappings in this collection by $\langle x_\lambda\rangle_{\lambda \in \Lambda}$ where x_λ is the point in E_λ which is the image of λ.

Exercises

1. Prove Theorem **1.4.3**.

2. If $\mathfrak{f} : X \to Y$ and $E \subseteq X$, show that $E \subseteq \mathfrak{f}^{-1}(\mathfrak{f}(E))$. Give an example where the two sets are not equal. Show that they are equal if $\mathfrak{f}$ is one-to-one.

3. If $\mathfrak{f} : X \to Y$ and $S \subseteq Y$, show that $\mathfrak{f}(\mathfrak{f}^{-1}(S)) = S \cap \mathfrak{f}(X)$.

4. If $\mathfrak{f} : X \to Y$, show that $\mathfrak{f}^{-1}$ is a mapping of Y onto X iff $\mathfrak{f}$ is one-to-one and onto.

5. If $\mathfrak{f} : X \to Y$ and $\mathfrak{g} : Y \to X$, are the relations $\mathfrak{g} \circ \mathfrak{f}$ and $\mathfrak{f} \circ \mathfrak{g}$ mappings? Are they the same relation?

6. If $\mathfrak{f} : X \to Y$ and $\mathfrak{g} : Y \to X$ are such that $\mathfrak{g} \circ \mathfrak{f} = \mathfrak{i}_X$, show that $\mathfrak{f}$ is one-to-one and $\mathfrak{g}$ is onto. Show also that the converse holds; that is, if $\mathfrak{f}$ is one-to-one, then there is such a mapping $\mathfrak{g}$, and if $\mathfrak{g}$ is onto, there is such a mapping $\mathfrak{f}$.

7. If $\mathfrak{f} : X \to Y$, prove the following:

(i) $\mathfrak{f}$ is one-to-one iff $\mathfrak{f}(A \cap B) = \mathfrak{f}(A) \cap \mathfrak{f}(B)$ for all $A, B \subseteq X$.

(ii) $\mathfrak{f}$ is one-to-one and onto iff $\mathfrak{f}(\complement E) = \complement\mathfrak{f}(E)$ for every $E \subseteq X$.

1.5 Partial Orders

A relation $\mathfrak{r}$ on a set X is **antisymmetric** iff $x \,\mathfrak{r}\, y$ and $y \,\mathfrak{r}\, x$ imply that $x = y$. A relation on X which is reflexive, antisymmetric, and transitive is called a **partial order** on X. The relation $\leqslant$ on the real numbers is an example of a partial order, and a partial order will usually be denoted by the symbol $\leqslant$. If $x \leqslant y$ we will say that x **precedes** or is **smaller than** y, and y **follows** or is **larger than** x. We may also write $y \geqslant x$ for $x \leqslant y$.

The only equivalence relation on a set X which is also a partial order on X is the identity relation $\mathfrak{i}_X$. It is clear that $\mathfrak{r}$ is antisymmetric iff $\mathfrak{r} \cap \mathfrak{r}^{-1} \subseteq \mathfrak{i}$. Theorem **1.1.2** shows that inclusion ($\subseteq$) is a partial order on the family of all subsets of a set. Indeed, we have already used the notion that a set is larger than any set it contains in this sense.

If $\leqslant$ is a partial order on a set X, then there is a relation on X, which we shall always denote by $<$, which is defined by setting $x < y$ iff $x \leqslant y$ and $x \neq y$. It is clear that this relation is transitive and **irreflexive**; that is, for no $x \in X$ is it true that $x < x$. On the other hand, a transitive, irreflexive relation $<$ determines a partial order $\leqslant$ by the rule that $x \leqslant y$ iff $x < y$ or $x = y$. We will say that $<$ is the **strong relation** determined by $\leqslant$, and $\leqslant$ is the **weak relation** determined by $<$.

If $\leqslant$ is a partial order on a set X, there may exist a point $a \in X$ such that $a \leqslant x$ for every $x \in X$. Such an element is called the **first** or **smallest element** of X. Similarly, if there exists a point $b \in X$ such that $x \leqslant b$ for every $x \in X$, we say that b is the **last** or **largest element** of X. It is clear, by the antisymmetry of a partial order, that the first and last elements are unique, if they exist.

The set of natural numbers with their usual ordering by size, which we may denote by $\langle 1, 2, 3, \ldots \rangle$, has a first element, 1, but no last element. If the set of natural numbers is partially ordered as indicated by writing $\langle \ldots, 3, 2, 1 \rangle$, there is then a last element but no first element. Another partial ordering might be $\langle 1, 3, 5, \ldots; \ldots, 6, 4, 2 \rangle$ which has both a first and a last element, while $\langle ..., 5, 3, 1, 2, 4, 6, ... \rangle$ has neither a first nor a last element.

In contrast to a largest element, a **maximal element** is a point b such that $x \geqslant b$ implies that $x = b$. Thus a maximal element is one which is not less than any other element of X. **Minimal elements** are similarly defined. Clearly, if there is a largest element it will be the unique maximal element.

If E is a subset of a partially ordered set X, an element $a \in X$ such that $a \leqslant x$ for all $x \in E$ is a **lower bound** for the set E. We say that a set is **bounded below** iff there is a lower bound for the set. **Upper bounds** are similarly defined, as are sets which are **bounded above**. A set is said to be **bounded** iff it has both a lower bound and an upper bound.

In the natural ordering for the set of natural numbers, the set of all even numbers has 1 and 2 as lower bounds but no upper bounds. In the ordering $\langle 1, 3, 5, ...; ..., 6, 4, 2 \rangle$, the even numbers have all the odd numbers as lower bounds and 2 as the only upper bound.

The collection of lower bounds for a set E may have a largest member, and this element, if it exists, is called the **greatest lower bound** or **infimum** of E, written inf E. Similarly, the collection of upper bounds for E may have a smallest member, and this element, if it exists, is called the **least upper bound** or **supremum** of E, written sup E. In the natural ordering for the set of natural numbers, 2 is the infimum of the set of even numbers. In the case of the ordering $\langle 1, 3, 5, ...; ..., 6, 4, 2 \rangle$, there is no infimum to the set of even numbers even though they are bounded below.

A partially ordered set X is **order-complete** iff every nonempty subset of X which is bounded below has a greatest lower bound. Although this definition is phrased in terms of lower bounds, it is easy to show that it is equivalent to requiring that every nonempty subset which is bounded above have a least upper bound.

The natural numbers with their usual ordering are an example of an order-complete set since each nonempty subset which is bounded below clearly has a first element, which is the infimum of the subset. The rational numbers ordered by size are not order-complete, since the subset consisting of all rationals which are positive and have squares greater than 2 does not have an infimum, even though it is bounded below by 0.

Although the rational numbers are not order-complete, a most important property of the real numbers is that they are order-complete with respect to their usual ordering. In some treatments of advanced calculus (e.g., Olmsted [18, p. 23]) the completeness of the reals is made one of the axioms defining the real numbers. In other cases (e.g., Knopp [15, pp. 23-36]), the real numbers are derived from the rational numbers by some "completing" procedure. In Chapter 7 we will give a general method for "completing" a metric space which is applicable to the rationals, and so we will omit that topic here.

The natural, rational, and real numbers, with their usual orderings, have an additional property which is very important. Given any two numbers, at least one of them is less than or equal to the other. A partial ordering $\leqslant$ on a set X is a **linear** or **total order** iff either $x \leqslant y$ or $y \leqslant x$ for every pair of points $x, y \in X$. A set with a linear ordering is called a **chain**. The family of subsets of a set, ordered by inclusion, is an example of a partially ordered set which is not a linearly ordered set. Another way of characterizing a linear order $\mathfrak{r}$ is that we must have $\mathfrak{r} \cup \mathfrak{r}^{-1} = X \times X$.

Exercises

1. Show that a partially ordered set is order-complete iff every nonempty subset which is bounded above has a least upper bound.

2. Is the **power set** $\mathscr{P}(X)$, consisting of all subsets of a set X, partially ordered by inclusion ($\subseteq$)? What is the strong relation associated with $\subseteq$? What are the smallest, largest, maximal, and minimal elements in $\mathscr{P}(X)$? If we let $\mathscr{P}^*(X)$ denote the family of all nonempty, proper subsets of X, what are the smallest, largest, maximal, and minimal elements?

3. Show that we may partially order the set **C** of all complex numbers by setting $x_1 + iy_1 \leqslant x_2 + iy_2$ iff $x_1 < x_2$ or $x_1 = x_2$ and $y_1 \leqslant y_2$. Is this a linear order? Are the complex numbers order-complete with this order? Generalize this example to an order of $X \times X$, where X is any partially ordered set.

4. A **lattice** is a partially ordered set in which every pair of elements (and hence any finite set of elements) has both an infimum and a supremum. If every subset has both an infimum and a supremum, then the lattice is called **complete**. Are $\mathscr{P}(X)$ and $\mathscr{P}^*(X)$ complete lattices when ordered by inclusion? For additional information see Birkhoff [2].

CHAPTER 2

Cardinal and Ordinal Numbers

2.1 Equipotent Sets

Two sets A and B are **equipotent**, written $A \sim B$, iff there exists a one-to-one mapping of A onto B. It is clear that this relation between sets is an equivalence relation and hence divides up any collection of sets into equivalence classes. Any set which is empty or equipotent to a set of natural numbers of the form $\{1, 2, ..., n\}$ for some natural number n is said to be **finite**. All other sets will be called **infinite** sets.

Equipotence is, in some sense, a measure of the "number" of points in a set. It is natural to try to order sets according to the number of points they contain by setting $A \lesssim B$ iff A is equipotent to a subset of B. This relation is clearly reflexive and transitive. The following theorem of Bernstein shows that it is antisymmetric.

Theorem 2.1.1. *If $A \lesssim B$ and $B \lesssim A$, then $A \sim B$.*

Proof. Let $A \sim B_1 \subseteq B$ and $B \sim A_1 \subseteq A$. The one-to-one mapping of B onto A_1 sets up a one-to-one mapping of B_1 onto some subset A_2 of A_1. The theorem is now reduced to showing that if $A \sim A_2 \subseteq A_1 \subseteq A$, then $A_1 \sim A$, since we have $B \sim A_1$, and with transitivity this would imply that $B \sim A$.

Let us divide A up into the three disjoint subsets $E = A_2, F = A_1 \setminus A_2$, and $G = A \setminus A_1$. We must show that, for disjoint sets, $E \cup F \cup G \sim E$ implies that $E \cup F \cup G \sim E \cup F$.

The one-to-one mapping of $E \cup F \cup G$ onto E sets up a division of E into three disjoint subsets E_1, F_1, and G_1 which are the images of E, F, and G, respectively. By transitivity, we have $E \cup F \cup G \sim E \sim E_1$, and the corresponding mapping sets up a division of E_1 into three disjoint subsets E_2, F_2, and G_2 which are the images of E, F, and G, respectively. By induction, we continue this process.

We may illustrate the results of the successive divisions of $E \cup F \cup G$ as follows:

$$\begin{aligned} E \cup F \cup G &= F \cup G \cup (E_1 \cup F_1 \cup G_1) \\ &= F \cup G \cup F_1 \cup G_1 \cup (E_2 \cup F_2 \cup G_2) \\ &= F \cup G \cup F_1 \cup G_1 \cup F_2 \cup G_2 \cup (E_3 \cup F_3 \cup G_3) = \ldots . \end{aligned}$$

Furthermore, $E \sim E_1 \sim E_2 \sim \ldots$, $F \sim F_1 \sim F_2 \sim \ldots$, and $G \sim G_1 \sim G_2 \sim \ldots$. We may also calculate

$$\begin{aligned} E \cup F &= F \cup (E_1 \cup F_1 \cup G_1) \\ &= F \cup G_1 \cup F_1 \cup (E_2 \cup F_2 \cup G_2) = \ldots . \end{aligned}$$

Since this division process may not exhaust E, let us denote $E_1 \cap E_2 \cap E_3 \cap \ldots$ by D. We now have the following decompositions into disjoint sets:

$$E \cup F \cup G = D \cup F \cup G \cup F_1 \cup G_1 \cup F_2 \cup G_2 \cup \ldots \qquad (*)$$

$$E \cup F = D \cup F \cup G_1 \cup F_1 \cup G_2 \cup F_2 \cup G_3 \cup \ldots \qquad (**)$$

In these decompositions, sets in the same column on the right hand side of the equations are equipotent. In order to show that $E \cup F \cup G \sim E \cup F$, we choose our mapping as follows. For each $x \in E \cup F \cup G$, we find that one set in the decomposition (*) which contains x. There is some one-to-one mapping of that set onto the set below it in (**), and we take x into its image under that mapping. We have thus defined a one-to-one mapping of $E \cup F \cup G$ onto $E \cup F$. ▮

We shall show in Section **2.4** that this partial ordering is a linear order. Among the infinite sets, one is particularly important. A set which is equipotent to the set of natural numbers $\{1, 2, 3, \ldots\}$ is called **denumerable**. A set which is either finite or denumerable is called **countable**.

In order for a set E to be denumerable, there must be some one-to-one mapping of the natural numbers onto E. This means that we must be able to list the elements of the set E in an infinite sequence, thus: $E = \langle x_1, x_2, x_3, \ldots \rangle$ where x_n is the element of E which is the image of n.

Lemma. *The set of all rational numbers is denumerable.*

Proof. Let us list the positive rational numbers in an infinite number of sequences (without repetitions) according to the sizes of their denominators, thus:

$$
\begin{array}{ccccccc}
1/1, & & 2/1, & & 3/1, & & 4/1, \ldots \\
 & \nearrow & & \nearrow & & \nearrow & \\
1/2, & & 3/2, & & 5/2, & & 7/2, \ldots \\
 & \nearrow & & \nearrow & & & \\
1/3, & & 2/3, & & 4/3, & & 5/3, \ldots \\
 & \nearrow & & & & & \\
1/4, & & 3/4, & & 5/4, & & 7/4, \ldots \\
\vdots & & & & & &
\end{array}
$$

As indicated above we may now list all the positive rationals as follows: $\langle 1, 1/2, 2, 1/3, 3/2, 3, 1/4, 2/3, 5/2, 4, 1/5, \ldots\rangle$. All the rational numbers may be listed in the infinite sequence $\langle 0, 1, -1, 1/2, -1/2, 2, -2, 1/3, -1/3, 3/2, -3/2, \ldots\rangle$. ▮

The value of the above lemma is to give us a method of proof which may be generalized to give the following stronger result.

Theorem 2.1.2. *The union of a denumerable number of denumerable sets is a denumerable set.*

Proof. Let $\langle E_1, E_2, E_3, \ldots\rangle$ be a denumerable family of denumerable sets. Since each set E_n is denumerable, we may list its elements in an infinite sequence:

$$
\begin{array}{lcccccccc}
E_1 = \langle x_{11}, & & x_{12}, & & x_{13}, & & x_{14}, & \ldots\rangle \\
 & \nearrow & & \nearrow & & \nearrow & & \\
E_2 = \langle x_{21}, & & x_{22}, & & x_{23}, & & x_{24}, & \ldots\rangle \\
 & \nearrow & & \nearrow & & & & \\
E_3 = \langle x_{31}, & & x_{32}, & & x_{33}, & & x_{34}, & \ldots\rangle \\
 & \nearrow & & & & & & \\
E_4 = \langle x_{41}, & & x_{42}, & & x_{43}, & & x_{44}, & \ldots\rangle \\
\vdots & & & & & & &
\end{array}
$$

By the same procedure as in the lemma, we may list the elements in the union of the sets E_n (with possible repetitions) as follows: $\langle x_{11}, x_{21}, x_{12}, x_{31}, x_{22}, x_{13}, x_{41}, x_{32}, x_{23}, \ldots\rangle$. Upon omitting repetitions, we have the desired sequence. ▮

Theorem **2.1.2** may be used to show that the set of all algebraic numbers (roots of polynomials with rational coefficients) is also denumerable. The set of all points in the plane with both coordinates rational would also be denumerable. Since the union of two finite sets is a finite set, it is clear that the removal of a finite number of elements from an infinite set leaves an infinite set. From this we may obtain the following theorem.

Theorem 2.1.3. *Every infinite set contains a denumerable subset.*

Proof. If E is an infinite set, it is not empty, so we may choose a point $x_1 \in E$. The set $E \setminus \{x_1\}$ is still infinite, and so nonempty, and we may choose a point $x_2 \in E \setminus \{x_1\}$. The set $E \setminus \{x_1, x_2\}$ is still infinite and so nonempty, and we may choose a point $x_3 \in E \setminus \{x_1, x_2\}$. Proceeding by induction, we thus choose an infinite sequence $\langle x_1, x_2, x_3, \ldots\rangle$ of distinct points of E giving us our denumerable subset. ▮

For a discussion of the dependence of this proof on the Axiom of Choice, see Halmos [10, pp. 59-61] and Section **2.5**.

Corollary. *Every infinite set is equipotent to a proper subset of itself.*

Proof. If E is an infinite set, it contains a denumerable subset by **2.1.3**, and hence may be written $E = \langle x_1, x_2, x_3, \ldots\rangle \cup E^*$ where E^* is the subset remaining after removing the elements of the denumerable subset from E; in particular, E^* may be empty. We may now show that E is equipotent to the proper subset $E \setminus \{x_1\}$ by defining a one-to-one mapping $\mathfrak{f}$ of E onto $E \setminus \{x_1\}$ as follows: $\mathfrak{f}(x_n) = x_{n+1}$ for $n = 1, 2, 3, \ldots$ and $\mathfrak{f}(x) = x$ for $x \in E^*$. ▮

Since a finite set is never equipotent to a proper subset of itself, this theorem characterizes infinite sets and was used by Dedekind to define infinite sets. So far all the infinite sets discussed have been equipotent to the set of natural numbers; that is, denumerable. The method of proof used in the following theorem is as important as the theorem itself.

Theorem 2.1.4. *The set of all real numbers is uncountable.*

Proof. We will assume an acquaintance with the decimal notation for real numbers. We will show that the set of real numbers in the interval (0, 1) cannot be listed in a sequence, and hence is not denumerable. Suppose the real numbers in (0, 1) could be listed in an infinite sequence $\langle x_1, x_2, x_3, \ldots\rangle$. Let us expand each of these numbers into decimal form, choosing the nonterminating form where there is a choice (i.e., we use 0.4999... for 1/2 not 0.5000...). We may arrange these expansions as follows:

$$
\begin{array}{l}
x_1 = 0.x_{11}\ x_{12}\ x_{13} \dots \\
\qquad\quad \searrow \\
x_2 = 0.x_{21}\ x_{22}\ x_{23} \dots \\
\qquad\qquad\ \searrow \\
x_3 = 0.x_{31}\ x_{32}\ x_{33} \dots \\
\ \vdots \qquad\qquad\qquad\ \searrow
\end{array}
$$

By considering the numerals along the main diagonal in this array, we may construct another real number in (0, 1), say x, choosing the nth digit of x to be any numeral other than 0, 9, or x_{nn}. Since x does not have all its digits zero or all its digits nine, it is a real number in (0, 1). It is also in nonterminating form since x does not have all zeros from some point on. Hence x should appear with this decimal expansion somewhere in the above array. But x differs from the nth real in our array at the nth digit, and so x does not appear. Our assumption that we could list all the real numbers in (0, 1) in an infinite sequence has led to a contradiction, and so the set must be uncountable. The mapping $\mathfrak{f}$ defined by setting $\mathfrak{f}(x) = \tan(2x - 1)\,\pi/2$ gives a one-to-one correspondence between the reals in (0, 1) and all the real numbers, and completes the proof of the theorem. ▮

We may show by Bernstein's theorem **2.1.1** that every open, closed, or half-open interval of real numbers is equipotent to the set of all real numbers.

Exercises

1. Show that the family of all finite subsets of a denumerable set is denumerable.
2. Show that the real and the complex numbers are equipotent.
3. Show that the algebraic numbers are denumerable.

2.2 Cardinal Numbers

The equivalence relation of equipotence divides up any collection of sets into equivalence classes, and we will use the term **cardinal number** to designate the property that equipotent sets have in common. Cardinal numbers will be, in some sense, a measure of the number of points in sets. If E is a set, we write $\overline{\overline{E}}$ for the cardinal number of E. The basic property of cardinal numbers is that $A \sim B$ implies that $\overline{\overline{A}} = \overline{\overline{B}}$.

For finite sets the cardinal number is easy to describe. We shall say that any set equipotent to the set $\{1, 2, 3, \ldots, n\}$ has cardinal number n. The empty set will be said to have cardinal number 0. Thus, for finite sets, the cardinal number of a set is just how many points it contains.

Among the infinite sets, the denumerable ones will be said to have cardinal number $\aleph_0$, where $\aleph$ is the first letter of the Hebrew alphabet, and is pronounced "aleph." Sets which are equipotent to the set of all real numbers are said to have cardinal number c.

We may partially order any set of cardinal numbers by setting $\bar{\bar{A}} \leqslant \bar{\bar{B}}$ iff $A^* \lesssim B^*$, where A^* is any set equipotent to A and B^* is any set equipotent to B. Bernstein's theorem **2.1.1** shows that this is a partial ordering. We may rephrase **2.1.4** by saying that $c > \aleph_0$. Theorem **2.1.3** states that $\aleph_0 \leqslant a$ for any infinite cardinal number a. It is clear that $n < \aleph_0$, where n is any finite cardinal number.

We will now define addition for cardinal numbers in a way that generalizes the notion for finite cardinals. Note that, for finite cardinals m and n, we would obtain $m + n$ by choosing a set M with m elements, a disjoint set N with n elements, and considering how many points there would be in $M \cup N$. Similarly, if $\{a_\lambda\}$ is any collection of cardinal numbers, their **sum**, written $\sum_\lambda a_\lambda$, is the cardinal number of the set $\bigcup_\lambda A_\lambda$ where $\{A_\lambda\}$ is a collection of disjoint sets such that $\bar{\bar{A}}_\lambda = a_\lambda$ for every λ.

In order to show that the sum of cardinal numbers has been well defined, we must show that if $\{A_\lambda^*\}$ is a collection of disjoint sets such that $\bar{\bar{A}}_\lambda^* = \bar{\bar{A}}_\lambda$ for every λ, then $\bigcup_\lambda A_\lambda^* \sim \bigcup_\lambda A_\lambda$. That is, it does not matter which representative we choose for a set of cardinal number a_λ. It is clear that the sum of cardinal numbers is both commutative and associative. We will also write $a_1 + a_2 + a_3 + \ldots$ for the sum of a countable number of cardinal numbers $a_1, a_2, a_3, \ldots$.

Since the sets $\{1, 3, 5, \ldots\}$ and $\{2, 4, 6, \ldots\}$ are disjoint, have cardinal number $\aleph_0$, and have as their union the denumerable set $\{1, 2, 3, 4, \ldots\}$, we see that $\aleph_0 + \aleph_0 = \aleph_0$. An even stronger result follows from **2.1.2**: $\aleph_0 + \aleph_0 + \aleph_0 + \ldots = \aleph_0$. Similarly, since the sets $[0, 1)$ and $[1, 2)$ of real numbers are disjoint, have cardinal number c, and have as their union the set $[0, 2)$ which also has cardinal number c, we see that $c + c = c$. More generally, $c + c + c + \ldots = c$ since the sets $[n, n + 1)$ are all disjoint, have cardinal number c, and have as their union the set $\{x : x \geqslant 1\}$ which also has cardinal number c.

From these results it is clear that we cannot define subtraction for cardinal numbers, in the sense that there is no inverse to addition.

Thus, the equation $c + x = c$ has "solutions" of any finite cardinal n, $\aleph_0$, and c.

We will now define multiplication for cardinal numbers in a way that generalizes the notion for finite cardinals. Note that, for finite cardinals m and n, we would obtain mn by choosing a set M with m elements, a set N with n elements, and considering how many pairs of the form $\langle x, y\rangle$ with $x \in M$ and $y \in N$ exist. Similarly, if a and b are cardinal numbers, their **product** written ab, is the cardinal number of the set $A \times B$, where $\bar{\bar{A}} = a$ and $\bar{\bar{B}} = b$. In order to show that the product of cardinal numbers has been well defined, we must show that if $A^* \sim A$ and $B^* \sim B$, then $A^* \times B^* \sim A \times B$. That is, it does not matter which representatives we choose for sets of cardinal numbers a and b.

It is clear that the product of cardinal numbers is commutative, associative, and distributive with respect to addition. We will leave as an exercise the generalization of this definition to the product of an arbitrary number of cardinal numbers.

Theorem 2.2.1. (i) $\aleph_0\aleph_0 = \aleph_0$; (ii) $\aleph_0 c = c$; *and* (iii) $cc = c$.

Proof. (i): By definition, $\aleph_0\aleph_0$ is the cardinal number of $\{\langle x, y\rangle : x$ and y are natural numbers$\}$. Using the procedure of **2.1.2**, we may arrange this set in the following array:

$$\begin{array}{cccc} \langle 1,1\rangle & \langle 1,2\rangle & \langle 1,3\rangle & \cdots \\ \langle 2,1\rangle & \langle 2,2\rangle & \langle 2,3\rangle & \cdots \\ \langle 3,1\rangle & \langle 3,2\rangle & \langle 3,3\rangle & \cdots \\ \vdots & & & \end{array}$$

and then order it in an infinite sequence:

$$\langle\langle 1, 1\rangle, \langle 2, 1\rangle, \langle 1, 2\rangle, \langle 3, 1\rangle, \ldots\rangle.$$

(ii): By definition, $\aleph_0 c$ is the cardinal number of $\{\langle x, y\rangle : x$ is a natural number and $y \in [0, 1)\}$. The mapping $\mathfrak{f}$, defined by setting $\mathfrak{f}(\langle x, y\rangle) = x + y$, is both one-to-one and onto the set of all real numbers greater than or equal to one, and this set has cardinal number c.

(iii): By definition, cc is the cardinal number of $\{\langle x, y\rangle : x, y \in (0, 1]\}$. For each point $\langle x, y\rangle$ in this set we may expand x and y into their unique nonterminating decimal expansions and write $\langle x, y\rangle = \langle 0.x_1x_2x_3 \ldots, 0.y_1y_2y_3y\ldots\rangle$. Since $0.x_1y_1x_2y_2 \ldots$ will be a nonterminating decimal expansion of some number in (0, 1], we may define a one-to-one mapping of our set onto some subset of (0, 1]. Clearly there is a one-to-one mapping of (0, 1] onto some subset of our set, and so we may use Bernstein's theorem to complete the proof. ▮

From these results it is clear that we cannot define division for cardinal numbers, in the sense that there is no inverse to multiplication. Thus, the equation $cx = c$ has "solutions" of any finite cardinal n, $\aleph_0$, and c.

The final arithmetic operation we shall define for cardinal numbers is that of taking powers. For finite cardinals m and n, we would expect m^n to be the product of n equal factors of m. For arbitrary cardinals, we would then wish a^b to be the cardinal number of $\prod\{A_\beta : \beta \in B\}$ where the cardinal numbers of all the sets A_β are a and the cardinal number of B is b. In particular, we may choose $A_\beta = A$ for all $\beta \in B$ and write this as $\prod\{A : \beta \in B\}$.

By the definition of Cartesian products given in Section **1.4**, we may rephrase this as follows. If a and b are cardinal numbers, a^b is the cardinal number of the set of all mappings of B into A where $\bar{\bar{A}} = a$ and $\bar{\bar{B}} = b$. It is easy to show that this is a well-defined operation and that the elementary laws of exponents hold. Thus, if a, b, and c are cardinal numbers, then $a^b a^c = a^{b+c}$, $(a^b)^c = a^{bc}$, and $a^c b^c = (ab)^c$.

For finite sets, the number of subsets of a set with n elements is 2^n. This result may be generalized to infinite sets quite easily. The family of all subset of a set E is called the **power set** of E, written $\mathscr{P}(E)$.

Lemma. *If A is a set with cardinal number a, then $\mathscr{P}(A)$ has cardinal number 2^a.*

Proof. By definition, 2^a is the cardinal number of the family of all mappings of A to a set with two elements, say $\{0, 1\}$. A one-to-one mapping of this family of mappings onto $\mathscr{P}(A)$ is obtained by taking each mapping into the subset of A on which it is equal to 1. ▮

With the aid of this lemma, we may prove the following theorem of Cantor.

Theorem 2.2.2. *$2^a > a$ for every cardinal number a.*

Proof. Suppose A is a set with cardinal number a. Then 2^a is the cardinal number of $\mathscr{P}(A)$ by the lemma. The mapping of A into $\mathscr{P}(A)$ defined by taking each point $x \in A$ into the subset $\{x\} \in \mathscr{P}(A)$ shows that $A \lesssim \mathscr{P}(A)$ and so $2^a \geqslant a$. We must now show that A and $\mathscr{P}(A)$

are not equipotent. Suppose $\mathfrak{f}$ were a one-to-one mapping of A onto $\mathscr{P}(A)$. That is, for each point $x \in A$, there is associated a subset $\mathfrak{f}(x)$ of A. Let us denote by A^* the subset of A consisting of all those points x for which $x \notin \mathfrak{f}(x)$. This is a well-defined subset of A and hence a member of $\mathscr{P}(A)$. Since $\mathfrak{f}$ is a mapping onto $\mathscr{P}(A)$, there must be some point $x^* \in A$ such that $\mathfrak{f}(x^*) = A^*$. We now ask whether $x^* \in A^*$ or $x^* \notin A^*$. If $x^* \in A^*$, then by the definition of A^*, x^* is a point for which $x^* \notin \mathfrak{f}(x^*) = A^*$. On the other hand, if $x^* \notin A^*$, then $x^* \in \mathfrak{f}(x^*) = A^*$. This contradiction proves the theorem. ▮

We see from this theorem that there is no largest cardinal number. In the case of $a = \aleph_0$, this theorem yields $2^{\aleph_0} > \aleph_0$. A direct proof of that result follows from the fact that $2^{\aleph_0} = c$.

Theorem 2.2.3. $2^{\aleph_0} = c$.

Proof. By definition, $2^{\aleph_0}$ is the cardinal number of the set of all mappings of the natural numbers into the set $\{0, 1\}$. If $\mathfrak{f}$ is such a mapping, we may write $\mathfrak{f}(n) = f_n$, and thus each mapping is determined by a sequence of zeros and ones: $\langle f_1, f_2, f_3, \ldots\rangle$. With each such sequence we may associate the real number $\sum_n f_n/2^n$; that is, the real number whose binary expansion is $0.f_1f_2f_3 \ldots$. Now each real number in $(0, 1]$ has exactly one nonterminating binary expansion, while only a denumerable number of them also have a terminating binary expansion. From this it follows that $2^{\aleph_0} = c + \aleph_0 = c$. ▮

It is clear that the same argument could be made for any finite cardinal n to show that $n^{\aleph_0} = c$. A very famous unsolved problem of set theory is the question of whether there is a cardinal number strictly between $\aleph_0$ and c. The **continuum hypothesis** asserts that there is no such cardinal number. Gödel [8] has shown that if the axioms of set theory are themselves consistent, then no inconsistency will arise from the introduction of the continuum hypothesis. The **generalized continuum hypothesis** is that there is no cardinal number strictly between a and 2^a for any infinite cardinal a.

Exercises

1. Let A, A^*, B, and B^* be sets such that $A \cap B = A^* \cap B^* = \emptyset$, $A \sim A^*$, and $B \sim B^*$. Show that $A \cup B \sim A^* \cup B^*$, and hence the sum of two cardinal numbers is a well defined operation.

2. Show that $a + \aleph_0 = a$ for any infinite cardinal number a.

3. Let a, b, c, and d be cardinal numbers such that $a \leqslant b$ and $c \leqslant d$. Show that $a + c \leqslant b + d$, $ac \leqslant bd$, and $a^c \leqslant b^c$. Does $a < b$ and $c < d$ imply that $a + c < b + d$?

4. Let a, b, and c be cardinal numbers. Prove that $a^b a^c = a^{b+c}$, $(a^b)^c = a^{bc}$, and $a^c b^c = (ab)^c$.

5. Define the product of an arbitrary number of cardinal numbers and show that your definition agrees with that given for a finite product.

6. Find $\aleph_0! = 1 \cdot 2 \cdot \ldots \cdot n \cdot \ldots \cdot \aleph_0$.

7. Prove König's Theorem: If $a_\lambda < b_\lambda$ for all λ, then $\Sigma_\lambda a_\lambda < \Pi_\lambda b_\lambda$.

8. Find $c^{\aleph_0}$.

9. If f is the cardinal number of the set of all real-valued functions defined on $[0, 1]$, then $f = 2^c$.

10. If a or b is an infinite cardinal number, then $a + b = ab = \max\{a, b\}$.

2.3 Order Types

When considering ordered sets, the notion of equipotence is not sufficient, since it depends only on the sets and not their orderings. In this section we will consider an equivalence relation between ordered sets which requires that they have not only the same cardinal number, but also the same ordering. Thus, two sets X and Y, partially ordered by the relations $\leqslant_X$ and $\leqslant_Y$, respectively, will be called **similar**, written $X \simeq Y$, iff there exists a one-to-one mapping $\mathfrak{f}$ of X onto Y such that $\mathfrak{f}(x_1) \leqslant_Y \mathfrak{f}(x_2)$ iff $x_1 \leqslant_X x_2$. Such a mapping will be called a **similarity**.

It is clear that this relation is an equivalence relation between partially ordered sets, and hence divides up any collection of such sets into equivalence classes. Sets in the same equivalence class will be said to have the same **order type**. Since similar sets are equipotent, all sets of the same order type have the same cardinal number. In this way we may associate a cardinal number with each order type.

In order to show that two sets are not of the same order type, we will often make use of the obvious fact that of two similar sets, either both have a first (last) element or neither has one. We may use this fact to show that the equipotent sets $\mathbf{N} = \langle 1, 2, 3, \ldots \rangle$ and $\mathbf{N}^* = \langle \ldots, 3, 2, 1 \rangle$ are not similar, and hence do not have the same order type. We will always use ω to denote the order type of $\mathbf{N}$, the set of natural numbers with their usual ordering. The order type of the set of rational numbers, with their usual ordering, will be denote by η, while the order type of the set of real numbers, with their usual ordering, will be denoted by λ.

For finite sets, the notions of equipotence and similarity are equivalent so we will denote the order type of a set with n elements by $\boldsymbol{n}$. If A is a set with order type α, we will denote by α^* the order type of the set A^*, which is the set A with the "reverse" ordering (see $\mathbf{N}$ and $\mathbf{N}^*$ above). Thus, ω^* is the order type of $\mathbf{N}^*$.

It is natural to partially order these order types by setting $\alpha \leqslant \beta$ iff A is similar to a subset of B, where α is the order type of A and β is the order type of B. It is easy to show that this is a partial ordering of any set of order types. That this is not a linear ordering, in general, follows from the example of the order types ω and ω^*. Every subset of $\mathbf{N}$ has a first element, and each subset of $\mathbf{N}^*$ has a last element.

If α and β are order types, their **sum**, written $\alpha + \beta$, is the order type of the ordered set $\langle A, B\rangle$, where A and B have order types α and β respectively. It is to be understood that the ordered set $\langle A, B\rangle$ refers to the set $A \cup B$ ordered by the rule that every element of A precedes every element of B, while elements in A or B are ordered according to their order in A or B, respectively.

From this definition it follows that $1 + \omega$ is the order type of the set $\langle 0; 1, 2, 3, \ldots\rangle$ and so equals ω. On the other hand, $\omega + 1$ is the order type of the set $\langle 1, 2, 3, \ldots; 0\rangle$, and this set is not similar to $\mathbf{N}$ (it has a last element) and so does not have order type ω. This example shows that addition of order types is not commutative. It is obviously associative, however.

An example of a set with order type $\omega + \omega$ would be $\langle 1, 3, 5, \ldots; 2, 4, 6, \ldots\rangle$, while a set with order type $\omega^* + \omega$ would be $\langle \ldots, -2, -1, 0; 1, 2, 3, \ldots\rangle$. In general, $\boldsymbol{n} + \omega = \omega$ since we may write $\langle 1, 2, 3, \ldots, n; n+1, n+2, n+3, \ldots\rangle$, but $\omega + \boldsymbol{n} \neq \omega$ since $\langle n+1, n+2, \ldots; 1, 2, \ldots, n\rangle$ is not similar to $\mathbf{N}$. It is clear that any open interval (a, b) of real numbers has the same order type, λ, as the set of all real numbers. Examples of sets with order types $1 + \lambda$, $\lambda + 1$, and $1 + \lambda + 1$ are the intervals $[a, b)$, $(a, b]$, and $[a, b]$, respectively.

It is easy to extend the above definition to the sum of any arbitrary number of order types. We will now define multiplication for order types. The motivation for the following definition is that we may consider the product of finite numbers mn as n copies of m elements. Thus, for order types α and β, we will choose representatives A and B, and for each element in B we will place a copy of A.

If α and β are order types, their **product**, written $\alpha\beta$, is the order of the ordered set $B \times A$ given the **lexicographical** or **dictionary order**, where A and B are sets with order types α and β, respectively.

It is to be understood that in the dictionary order, $\langle x_1, x_2\rangle \leqslant \langle y_1, y_2\rangle$ iff $x_1 < y_1$, or $x_1 = y_1$ and $x_2 \leqslant y_2$.

For example, 2ω is the order type of a set consisting of ω copies of a set with two elements; i.e., it can be represented by $\langle\langle 1, a\rangle, \langle 1, b\rangle; \langle 2, a\rangle, \langle 2, b\rangle; \langle 3, a\rangle, \langle 3, b\rangle; \ldots\rangle$, where we use **N** for a set with order type ω and $\langle a, b\rangle$ for a set with order type 2. On the other hand, $\omega 2$ is the order type of a set consisting of two copies of a set with order type ω; i.e., it can be represented by

$$\langle\langle a, 1\rangle, \langle a, 2\rangle, \langle a, 3\rangle, \ldots; \langle b, 1\rangle, \langle b, 2\rangle, \langle b, 3\rangle, \ldots\rangle,$$

which is a set with order type $\omega + \omega$. This example shows that multiplication of order types is not commutative, since $2\omega = \omega \neq \omega + \omega = \omega 2$. Note that, in general, $\alpha 2 = \alpha + \alpha$ for any order type α.

Although multiplication of order types is not commutative, it is easy to show that it is associative and that the distributive law $\alpha(\beta + \gamma) = \alpha\beta + \alpha\gamma$ holds. However, the other distributive law, $(\alpha + \beta)\,\gamma = \alpha\gamma + \beta\gamma$, does not hold! For example, $(\omega + 1)\,2 = (\omega + 1) + (\omega + 1) = \omega + (1 + \omega) + 1 = \omega + \omega + 1 = \omega 2 + 1$, which is not the same order type as $\omega 2 + 1 \cdot 2 = \omega 2 + 2$ since the second order type would be represented by a set which has an immediate predecessor to the last element, while a representative of the first order type would have no such element.

It is easy to extend the above definition to the product of any arbitrary number of order types. It would also be natural to define simple powers of order types such as $\omega^2 = \omega \cdot \omega = \omega + \omega + \omega + \ldots$; which can be represented by the positive rational numbers ordered as follows:

$$\langle 1, 2, 3, \ldots; 1/2, 3/2, 5/2, \ldots; 1/3, 2/3, 4/3, \ldots; \ldots\rangle.$$

Exercises

1. If $\mathfrak{f}$ is a similarity mapping of X onto Y, then $\mathfrak{f}(x) < \mathfrak{f}(y)$ whenever $x < y$. Show that this is not true if we merely require that $\mathfrak{f}$ be "order preserving"; i.e., that $\mathfrak{f}(x) \leqslant \mathfrak{f}(y)$ whenever $x \leq y$.

2. Show that for any order types α, β, and γ:

(i) $(\alpha + \beta)^* = \beta^* + \alpha^*$,

(ii) $(\alpha\beta)^* = \alpha^*\beta^*$,

(iii) $(\alpha + \beta) + \gamma = \alpha + (\beta + \gamma)$,

(iv) $(\alpha\beta)\gamma = \alpha(\beta\gamma)$,

(v) $\alpha(\beta + \gamma) = \alpha\beta + \alpha\gamma$.

3. Show that:

(i) $\eta^* = \eta$, and $\lambda^* = \lambda$,

(ii) $\eta + \eta = \eta$, but $\lambda + \lambda \neq \lambda$,

(iii) $\eta + 1 + \eta = \eta$, and $\lambda + 1 + \lambda = \lambda$,

(iv) If $m \neq n$, then $\omega + m \neq \omega + n$ and $m + \omega^* \neq n + \omega^*$,

(v) $(1 + \lambda)\,\omega = 1 + \lambda$.

2.4 Ordinal Numbers

A partially ordered set X is **well-ordered** iff every nonempty subset of X has a first element. Examples of well-ordered sets would be any finite set, and sets of order types ωn for any finite n. Sets of order types λ, η, and ω^* are not well-ordered. It is easy to see that any well-ordered set is linearly ordered. If x and y are any two elements of a well-ordered set, the subset $\{x, y\}$ must contain a first element, and we would have either $x \leqslant y$ or $y \leqslant x$. It is also clear that every subset of a well-ordered set is itself a well-ordered set with the same ordering.

The property of being a well-ordered set is obviously possesssed by all or none of the sets of the same order type. The order type of a well-ordered set will be called an **ordinal number**. In the previous section we defined addition and multiplication of order types. It is an easy exercise to show that, if A and B are well-ordered sets, then $\langle A, B\rangle$ and $B \times A$ are well-ordered sets, and hence that addition and multiplication of ordinal numbers is well defined.

The following properties of well-ordered sets will be needed in our characterizations of ordinal numbers and our proof of comparability for them.

Theorem 2.4.1. *If $\mathfrak{f}$ is a similarity mapping of the well-ordered set X onto the subset $Y \subseteq X$, then $x \leqslant \mathfrak{f}(x)$ for all $x \in X$.*

Proof. Suppose there were elements x such that $x > \mathfrak{f}(x)$. The set of all such elements, being a nonempty subset of a well-ordered set, would have a first element, say x^*. If $\mathfrak{f}(x^*) = z$, then $x^* > z$. Since $\mathfrak{f}$ is a similarity, and hence one-to-one, $x^* > z$ implies that $\mathfrak{f}(x^*) > \mathfrak{f}(z)$, that is, $z > \mathfrak{f}(z)$. But then z is an element smaller than x^* with the same property for which x^* was defined to be the smallest. ▮

If x is an element of the well-ordered set X, then the **initial segment** of X determined by x, denoted by X_x, is the set of all $y \in X$ such that $y < x$.

Corollary. *A well-ordered set is not similar to any of its initial segments. In particular, distinct initial segments of a well-ordered set are not similar.*

Proof. If X were similar to its initial segment X_x, and $\mathfrak{f}$ were the similarity mapping, then we would have $\mathfrak{f}(x) \in X_x$ and hence $\mathfrak{f}(x) < x$, which violates the theorem. ∎

We already have partially ordered order types of well-ordered sets, and so the above corollary shows that, for ordinal numbers α and β, $\alpha < \beta$ iff A is similar to an initial segment of B, where A and B are (well-ordered) sets with order types α and β, respectively. In order to prove that this ordering is linear, we will first consider the very powerful method of transfinite induction.

We recall that one way to formulate the principle of (finite) induction is as follows. If E is a subset of the natural numbers $\mathbf{N}$ such that $\mathbf{N}_n \subseteq E$ implies that $n \in E$, then $E = \mathbf{N}$. Note that the condition $1 \in E$ is not necessary in this form of the principle, since the section of $\mathbf{N}$ determined by 1 is empty and so is contained in E. We may now generalize this principle to any well-ordered set.

Theorem 2.4.2. (Principle of Transfinite Induction). *If X is a well-ordered set, and E is a subset of X with the property that $X_x \subseteq E$ implies that $x \in E$, then $E = X$.*

Proof. If $E \neq X$, then the subset of X consisting of the elements in $X \setminus E$ would be nonempty, and would hence contain a first element x. Clearly every element of the section X_x, being smaller than x, is in E and so, by our hypothesis, $x \in E$, which is a contradiction. ∎

Our first application of this principle will be a proof of the fact that the ordinals are linearly ordered.

Theorem 2.4.3. If α and β are ordinal numbers, then either $\alpha \leqslant \beta$ or $\beta \leqslant \alpha$.

Proof. Let A and B be (well-ordered) sets with order types α and β, respectively. If either A or B is empty, the theorem is obvious. Otherwise we may associate the first element of B with the first element of A. If $a \in A$ and each element of A_a has been associated with an element of B, then either every element of B has been associated with some element of A, and we must stop, or else there would be a first element of B not yet associated with an element of A, which we then associate with a. Using the principle of transfinite induction, it is clear that the process must either stop and give a similarity between B and a section of A ($\beta < \alpha$), give a similarity between A and B ($\alpha = \beta$), or exhaust A and give a similarity between A and a section of B ($\alpha < \beta$). ▮

Corollary. *Every set of ordinal numbers is a well-ordered set.*

Proof. Suppose Φ is a set of ordinal numbers which is not well-ordered. There must then be a subset of Φ which has no first element. Since Φ is linearly ordered by the theorem, we must be able to construct a sequence of ordinals $\langle\alpha_n\rangle_{n\in\mathbf{N}}$ such that $\alpha_1 > \alpha_2 > \alpha_3 > \ldots$. Let A be a set with ordinal α_1, which is then a well-ordered set. There must be initial segments $A_{a_2}, A_{a_3}, A_{a_4}, \ldots$ whose ordinal numbers are $\alpha_2, \alpha_3, \alpha_4, \ldots$ respectively. But then $a_2 > a_3 > a_4 > \ldots$ gives us a subset of A which has no first element. ▮

The previous theorem and its corollary allow us to characterize ordinal numbers in a very concise way. Since collections of ordinal numbers are well-ordered, we may speak of initial segments of ordinals. In particular, we will denote by W_α the set of all ordinal numbers less than the ordinal number α, ordered by increasing size of the elements.

Theorem 2.4.4. *Each ordinal number α is the order type of the set W_α.*

Proof. Let A be a set of ordinal α. For each ordinal number $\beta < \alpha$, there must correspond an initial segment A_b of A. On the other hand, each element $b \in A$ determines a segment A_b which has ordinal $\beta < \alpha$. In this way we have set up a one-to-one mapping of W_α onto A. This mapping is a similarity since $\alpha_1 \leqslant \alpha_2$ implies that $A_{b_1} \subseteq A_{b_2}$, and so $b_1 \leqslant b_2$, and conversely. ▮

We may use these properties of ordinal numbers to show that the cardinal numbers are linearly ordered. In order to do this, we must make use of the well-ordering theorem proved by Zermelo [82].

Well-Ordering Theorem. *Every set can be well-ordered.*

For a proof of this theorem, see Kamke [13, pp. 112-115] or Halmos [10, pp. 67-69].

To each ordinal number α, we may associate a definite cardinal number, that of W_α. With the aid of the well-ordering theorem, we may associate with each cardinal number a nonempty set composed of those ordinal numbers with that cardinal number. Since each set of ordinals is well ordered, there is a unique first ordinal in this set. In this way we associate with each cardinal number a, a unique ordinal $\alpha(a)$, called the **initial ordinal** of a.

Theorem 2.4.5. *If a and b are cardinal numbers, then either $a \leqslant b$ or $b \leqslant a$.*

Proof. Let $\alpha(a)$ and $\alpha(b)$ be the initial ordinal numbers of a and b respectively. If A and B are (well-ordered) sets with these ordinals, then they have cardinals a and b, respectively. The well-ordered sets are comparable, however, so one of them is similar to a subset of the other. Similar sets are also equipotent, so one of the set A and B is equipotent to a subset of the other. Thus, either $a \leqslant b$ or $b \leqslant a$. ▮

As an example of an initial ordinal, ω is the initial ordinal of the cardinal number $\aleph_0$. A particularly important property of ω is that W_ω is an infinite well-ordered set, each of whose initial segments is finite. Another very important ordinal number is the **first uncountable ordinal**. If we take the set of all ordinal numbers with finite or denumerable cardinals, this set will be well-ordered, and hence have an ordinal number, which we denote by Ω. We see that W_Ω is an uncountable well-ordered set, each of whose initial segments is countable.

The cardinal number of Ω is the second smallest infinite cardinal number and is denoted by $\aleph_1$. It is clear that $\aleph_1 \leqslant 2^{\aleph_0}$, and the continuum hypothesis asserts that the two are equal. The crucial property of Ω is found in the following theorem.

Theorem 2.4.6. *If E is a countable subset of W_Ω, then there exists an element $\beta \in W_\Omega$ such that $\alpha \leqslant \beta$ for all $\alpha \in E$.*

Proof. For each $\alpha \in E$, the set $\{x : x < \alpha\}$ is countable since it is an initial segment of W_Ω. The union $\bigcup \{\{x : x < \alpha\} : \alpha \in E\}$ is then countable by **2.1.2.** ▮

Exercises

1. A set is well ordered iff it has no subset whose order type is ω^*.
2. If A and B are well-ordered sets, show that $\langle A, B\rangle$ and $B \times A$ are well ordered.
3. Every infinite well-ordered set contains a subset whose ordinal number is ω.
4. A mapping f is said to be **order-preserving** iff $f(x) \leqslant f(y)$ whenever $x \leqslant y$. Show

that the only one-to-one order-preserving mapping of a well-ordered set onto itself is the identity mapping.

5. Show that the initial ordinal of an infinite cardinal has no immediate predecessor.

6. What is the cardinal number of the set of all ordinal numbers of a given cardinal number?

2.5 Axiom of Choice

Although we are not at all interested in presenting here an axiomatic treatment of set theory, one intuitively obvious axiom deserves mention. It is clear from the definition that when we have a nonempty set, we may choose a point from that set. The same holds for any finite number of nonempty sets—we may choose a point from each one. Strangely enough, when we have an infinite number of nonempty sets, the assumption that we can always choose a point from each set leads to some very unintuitive conclusions.

Stating the principle more precisely, if $\{X_\lambda\}_{\lambda\in\Lambda}$ is a collection of nonempty sets, for each $\lambda \in \Lambda$ we may choose a point $x_\lambda \in X_\lambda$. Equivalently, we may say that there is a mapping $\mathfrak{f}$ of Λ into $\bigcup_{\lambda\in\Lambda} X_\lambda$ such that $\mathfrak{f}(\lambda) = x_\lambda \in X_\lambda$. Finally, we may state this in set-theoretic terms as follows.

Axiom of Choice. The Cartesian product of a nonempty family of nonempty sets is nonempty.

There are a few obviously equivalent ways of stating this principle, of which the following is historically important.

Zermelo's Postulate. If $\mathscr{E}$ is a family of nonempty, disjoint sets, then there exists a set E^* such that $E^* \cap E$ consists of exactly one point for every $E \in \mathscr{E}$.

The interesting thing about this axiom is not the various obviously equivalent ways in which it may be stated, but the many equivalent statements of it which do not seem to have any connection with the original form. Thus, for example, the Well-Ordering Theorem mentioned in the previous section is actually equivalent to the Axiom of Choice. Another useful statement which is equivalent to this axiom is the following, which will be used in Chapter 8.

Zorn's Lemma. If a nonempty partially ordered set X is such that every linearly ordered subset has an upper bound, then X contains a maximal element.

For a proof of this lemma assuming the Axiom of Choice and a discussion of the proof of the converse theorem, see Halmos [10, pp. 62-65].

At this point we may assume that the reader has been exposed to sufficient set theory to allow him to study profitably general topology. A few more remarks are in order, however. We note in particular that the intuitive set theory studied here also prepares the student to study some form of axiomatic set theory. The very readable book by Halmos [10] is highly recommended as a minimum.

We wish to emphasize the need for further study because the intuitive set theory we have used is actually not correct. That is, our definitions will lead to contradictions. Recalling that we would allow almost any collection of objects to form a set, we should expect that we could form the set of all ordinal numbers. The following shows that this is a self-contradictory idea.

Burali-Forti Paradox. There is no set containing all the ordinal numbers.

Proof. Suppose X is the set of all ordinal numbers. By the corollary to **2.4.3**, X is well ordered, and hence its order type, say α, is an ordinal number. Thus $\alpha \in X$. In fact, by **2.4.4**, α is the order type of $W_\alpha = X_\alpha$. But, by the corollary to **2.4.1**, a well-ordered set cannot be similar to any of its initial segments. The contradiction lies in the fact that both X and X_α have order type α. ∎

The above paradox is not the only strange result we obtain if we are too loose with our intuitive notions. Historically, one of the first such paradoxes was pointed out by Russell. He showed that a contradiction will arise from the consideration of a set of all sets. The particular paradox comes from trying to form a set X which contains those sets which do not contain themselves. It is easy to show that $X \in X$ iff $X \notin X$.

Since the purpose of this book is to give a careful treatment of general topology, not set theory, we will leave this topic with another recommendation to the student to study further in this field.

Exercises

1. The **Maximal Chain Condition** is: Every chain in a partially ordered set is contained in a maximal chain. Show that Zorn's Lemma, the Well-Ordering Theorem, the Maximal Chain Condition, and the requirement that every partially ordered set contain a maximal element are all equivalent.

2. Show that Zorn's Lemma is equivalent to the following: If a nonempty partially ordered set X is such that every linearly ordered subset has a lower bound, then X contains a minimal element.

3. Use Zorn's Lemma to show that there exists a set B of real numbers such that (i) for any finite number of elements $x_1, x_2, \ldots, x_n \in B$ and for any rational numbers $r_1, r_2, \ldots, r_n \neq 0$, we have $r_1x_1 + r_2x_2 + \ldots + r_nx_n \neq 0$; and (ii) for every $x \neq 0$, $x = r_1x_1 + r_2x_2 + \ldots + r_nx_n$ for some rationals r_i and some $x_i \in B$. Such a set B is called a **Hamel basis** for the real numbers. For an example of the use of such a basis, see Goffman [9, p. 150].

CHAPTER **3**

Topological Spaces

Introduction

Before starting an axiomatic treatment of general topology, we should first consider the source of the axioms. Ultimately, all our work will be based on the generalization and abstraction of the set of real numbers. We will assume that the reader has had an introductory course in analysis, and so is familiar with the notions of limits, continuity, compactness, and connectedness for the real numbers.

In most modern treatments of advanced calculus it is pointed out that, although all the definitions are given in terms of the metric (distance) structure of the real numbers, everything may be rephrased in terms of the open sets alone. That is, if one knows which sets are open, one can tell which mappings are continuous, which sets are compact, which sets have limit points, and so on.

In general topology we strip away not only the algebraic structure, but even the metric structure of the real numbers, and we suppose that we know only which sets are the open sets. More generally, for any abstract set we may suppose that we know which subsets are to be considered as the open sets.

The next question is: What properties of the collection of open subsets of the real numbers shall be taken to be the axioms for the collection of all open subsets in an arbitrary abstract set? We shall try to be as general as possible, and so we shall give as few axioms as possible for this collection.

The most interesting fact is that we are able to define most of the important notions of analysis and prove generalized forms of many of the important theorems of analysis if we merely require that this collection be closed under arbitrary unions and finite intersections.

3.1 Open Sets and Limit Points

A **topological space** $(X, \mathscr{T})$ is a set X of points and a family $\mathscr{T}$ of subsets of X which satisfies the following axioms:

[0.1] The union of any number of members of $\mathscr{T}$ is a member of $\mathscr{T}$. ($\emptyset \in \mathscr{T}$)

[0.2] The intersection of any finite number of members of $\mathscr{T}$ is a member of $\mathscr{T}$. ($X \in \mathscr{T}$)

The family $\mathscr{T}$ is called a **topology** for X, and the members of $\mathscr{T}$ are said to be the **open sets** of the topological space $(X, \mathscr{T})$. Two topological spaces are the same iff both the points and the family of open sets are the same in each. When the topology is clearly understood from the context, we may simply speak of the space X.

A simple topology for a set X is obtained by choosing $\mathscr{T}$ to be the family consisting of just $\emptyset$ and X. This family satisfies the axioms **[0.1]** and **[0.2]**, and hence is a topology for X. We call this topology the **indiscrete** topology for X. On the other hand, the family of all subsets of X satisfies the above axioms, and so yields a topology for X, which we call the **discrete** topology for X.

It should be noted that the special statements about $\emptyset$ and X in the above axioms are really unnecessary, since the union $\bigcup \{G_\lambda : \lambda \in \emptyset\} = \emptyset$, and the finite intersection $\bigcap \{G_\lambda : \lambda \in \emptyset\} = X$, and so $\emptyset$ and X must be open for any topology. It is useful to emphasize these facts, however, since we will often show that a family of subsets of X is a topology for X by proving that the union of any nonempty family of open sets is open, and that the intersection of any two open sets is open. In that case, we would have to specifically check that $\emptyset$ and X are open sets.

We may order the various topologies for a set X by inclusion, setting $\mathscr{T}_1 \leqslant \mathscr{T}_2$ iff $\mathscr{T}_1 \subseteq \mathscr{T}_2$. Although the union of two topologies for X need not be a topology, the intersection of any number of topologies is a topology, and so the family of all topologies for a set X forms a complete lattice. Clearly, the discrete and indiscrete topologies are the largest and smallest topologies for a set.

Another, more complicated topology may be formed by choosing as the open sets for a set X, the empty set and all complements of finite sets. That this is a topology for X follows from DeMorgan's laws. If $\complement G_\lambda$ is finite for all λ, then $\complement(\bigcup_\lambda G_\lambda) = \bigcap_\lambda(\complement G_\lambda)$ is finite, while if $\complement G_i$ is finite for $i = 1, 2, ..., n$, then $\complement(\bigcap_{i=1}^n G_i) = \bigcup_{i=1}^n (\complement G_i)$ is also finite.

Once we have chosen the open sets for a topological space $(X, \mathscr{T})$, we may say that a point x is a **limit** or **accumulation point** of a subset E iff every open set containing x contains a point of E different from x; i.e., if $x \in G \in \mathscr{T}$, then $E \cap G \setminus \{x\} \neq \emptyset$. The set of all limit points of a set E is called the **derived set** of E and is denoted by $\mathbf{d}(E)$.

If the set X has the discrete topology, then each point is an open set and so, by considering the equation $E \cap \{x\} \setminus \{x\} = \emptyset$, we see that the derived set of every set E is empty. On the other hand, if X has the indiscrete topology, the only open set containing a point x is X itself, and so we need only consider whether the set $E \cap X \setminus \{x\} = E \setminus \{x\}$ is empty. Clearly, the derived set of any set containing at least two points is the entire space; the derived set of a set consisting of exactly one point is the complement of that point, while the derived set of the empty set is empty.

Theorem 3.1.1. *If A, B, and E are subsets of the topological space $(X, \mathscr{T})$, then the derived set has the following properties*:

[D.1] $\mathbf{d}(\emptyset) = \emptyset$;

[D.2] *If* $A \subseteq B$, *then* $\mathbf{d}(A) \subseteq \mathbf{d}(B)$;

[D.3] *If* $x \in \mathbf{d}(E)$, *then* $x \in \mathbf{d}(E \setminus \{x\})$; *and*

[D.4] $\mathbf{d}(A \cup B) = \mathbf{d}(A) \cup \mathbf{d}(B)$.

Proof. **[D.1]** is true since $\emptyset \cap G \setminus \{x\} = \emptyset$ for any $x \in X$ and $G \in \mathscr{T}$. **[D.2]** follows from the fact that $A \subseteq B$ implies that $A \cap G \setminus \{x\} \subseteq B \cap G \setminus \{x\}$, and so if $A \cap G \setminus \{x\} \neq \emptyset$, then also $B \cap G \setminus \{x\} \neq \emptyset$. **[D.3]** is proven by considering the equation

$$\begin{aligned}(E \setminus \{x\}) \cap G \setminus \{x\} &= (E \cap \complement\{x\}) \cap G \cap \complement\{x\} \\ &= E \cap G \cap \complement\{x\} = E \cap G \setminus \{x\}.\end{aligned}$$

To prove **[D.4]**, we first note that $\mathbf{d}(A) \cup \mathbf{d}(B) \subseteq \mathbf{d}(A \cup B)$ by **[D.2]**, since $A \subseteq A \cup B$ and $B \subseteq A \cup B$. Now suppose that $x \notin \mathbf{d}(A) \cup \mathbf{d}(B)$, and so $x \notin \mathbf{d}(A)$ and $x \notin \mathbf{d}(B)$. From the definition, there must exist open sets G_A and G_B containing x and such that $G_A \cap A \setminus \{x\} = \emptyset$ and $G_B \cap B \setminus \{x\} = \emptyset$. Let $G = G_A \cap G_B$, which is an open set by **[0.2]**. Then $x \in G$, but $G \cap A \setminus \{x\} = G \cap B \setminus \{x\} = \emptyset$, and so $G \cap (A \cup B) \setminus \{x\} = \emptyset$, which implies that $x \notin \mathbf{d}(A \cup B)$. ∎

In our study of analysis we called a set of real numbers open iff it contained an open interval about each of its points. This family of open sets does satisfy the axioms, and so gives us a topology for the set of real numbers. This topology will be called the **usual** topology for the reals and will be understood to be the topology for them unless some other topology (like the discrete or indiscrete topology) is specifically mentioned. Of course the limit points we obtain with this topology are just those expected since our definition was just a rephrasing of the definition given in analysis.

Exercises

1. List all topologies for a set consisting of exactly three points and order them by inclusion.

2. Show that the union of two topologies for a set need not be a topology for the set, but the intersection of any family of topologies for a set will be a topology for that set. Prove that the family of all topologies for a fixed set forms a complete lattice when ordered by inclusion.

3. Let X be any uncountable set, and let $\mathscr{T}$ be the family consisting of $\varnothing$ and all complements of countable sets. Show that $\mathscr{T}$ is a topology for X.

4. Let $X = \mathbf{N}$, the set of positive integers, and let $\mathscr{T}$ be the family consisting of $\varnothing$, X, and all subsets of the form $\{1, 2, ..., n\}$. Show that $\mathscr{T}$ is a topology for X.

5. Let $X = \mathbf{N}$, and let $\mathscr{T}$ be the family consisting of $\varnothing$, X, and all subsets of the form $\{n, n+1, n+2, ...\}$. Show that $\mathscr{T}$ is a topology for X. Compare this topology with the topology for $\mathbf{N}$ formed by choosing $\varnothing$ and all complements of finite sets as the open sets.

6. Let $X = \{a, b, c\}$ and let $\mathscr{T} = \{\varnothing, \{a\}, \{b\}, \{a, b\}, X\}$. Show that $\mathbf{d}(\{a\}) = \{c\}$, $\mathbf{d}(\{c\}) = \varnothing$, and find the derived sets of the other subsets of X.

7. Let $X = \{a, b, c\}$ and let $\mathscr{T} = \{\varnothing, \{a\}, \{b, c\}, X\}$. Find the derived sets of all the subsets of X.

8. If x is a limit point of a subset E of a topological space $(X, \mathscr{T})$, what can be said about whether x is a limit point of E in the topological space $(X, \mathscr{T}^*)$ if $\mathscr{T} \geqslant \mathscr{T}^*$? What if $\mathscr{T} \leqslant \mathscr{T}^*$?

9. In the topologies of problems **4** and **5**, what are the derived sets of $\{1\}$?

3.2 Closed Sets and Closure

The concept of a topological space has been introduced in terms of the axioms for the open sets. Let us now introduce closed sets and show that they could have been used as the fundamental notion of topology. Following our motivating example of the real numbers, we shall say that a **closed set** is one which contains all of its limit points. Thus, a set F is closed iff $\mathbf{d}(F) \subseteq F$.

Theorem 3.2.1. *If $x \notin F$, where F is a closed subset of a topological space $(X, \mathscr{T})$, then there exists an open set G such that $x \in G \subseteq \complement F$.*

Proof. Suppose no such open set exists. Then $x \in G \in \mathscr{T}$ would imply that $G \cap F \neq \varnothing$. Since $x \notin F$, we would actually have $G \cap F \setminus \{x\} \neq \varnothing$, which means that $x \in \mathbf{d}(F)$ by the definition of limit point. F, however, is a closed set and so $\mathbf{d}(F) \subseteq F$, so that x must also belong to F. This contradiction shows that such an open set must exist. ▮

Corollary 1. *If F is a closed set, then $\complement F$ is an open set.*

Proof. If $x \in \complement F$, then $x \notin F$, where F is a closed set. By the theorem, there exists an open set G_x such that $x \in G_x \subseteq \complement F$. But then, $\complement F = \bigcup \{x : x \in \complement F\} \subseteq \bigcup \{G_x : x \in \complement F\} \subseteq \complement F$. Thus $\complement F = \bigcup \{G_x : x \in \complement F\}$ which is the union of open sets, and hence an open set by **[0.1]**. ▮

Corollary 2. *If $\complement F$ is an open set, then F is a closed set.*

Proof. If x were a limit point of F which did not belong to F, then $\complement F$ would be an open set containing x which would not intersect F. But then x could not be a limit point of F. ▮

Corollary 3. *A set is a closed subset of a topological space iff its complement is an open subset of the space.*

Proof. This follows immediately from the preceding corollaries. ▮

Corollary 4. *The family $\mathscr{F}$ of all closed subsets in a topological space has the following properties:*

[C.1] *The intersection of any number of members of $\mathscr{F}$ is a member of $\mathscr{F}$.* $(X \in \mathscr{F})$

[C.2] *The union of any finite number of members of $\mathscr{F}$ is a member of $\mathscr{F}$.* $(\varnothing \in \mathscr{F})$

Proof. Apply DeMorgan's laws to the axioms **[0.1]** and **[0.2]**. ▮

It is clear that any family $\mathscr{F}$ of subsets of a set X satisfying the properties **[C.1]** and **[C.2]** uniquely determines a topology for X in which the family $\mathscr{F}$ is the family of all closed sets. In particular, this topology is the family of all complements of members of $\mathscr{F}$.

The **closure** of a set E contained in a topological space $(X, \mathscr{T})$ is the intersection of all closed subsets of X containing E. It will be denoted by $\mathbf{c}(E)$ or $\bar{E}$. We see at once that $\mathbf{c}(E)$ is a closed set, by **[C.1]**, and so $\mathbf{c}(E)$ is the smallest closed set containing E. Obviously, a set is closed iff it equals its own closure. The following is a most important characterization of the closure.

Theorem 3.2.2. *For any set E in a topological space,* $\mathbf{c}(E) = E \cup \mathbf{d}(E)$.

Proof. Suppose $x \notin E \cup \mathbf{d}(E)$, so that $x \notin E$ and $x \notin \mathbf{d}(E)$. Since $x \notin \mathbf{d}(E)$, there exists an open set G_x containing x and such that $E \cap G_x \setminus \{x\} = \emptyset$. Since $x \notin E$, this actually means that $E \cap G_x = \emptyset$, so $G_x \subseteq \complement E$. Since G_x is an open set disjoint from E, no point of G_x can be a limit point of E; that is, $G_x \subseteq \complement\mathbf{d}(E)$. We now have $\complement(E \cup \mathbf{d}(E)) = \bigcup \{G_x : x \notin E \cup \mathbf{d}(E)\}$ which is an open set by **[0.1]**. By the above Corollary **2**, $E \cup \mathbf{d}(E)$ is a closed set which obviously contains E, and so $\mathbf{c}(E) \subseteq E \cup \mathbf{d}(E)$. Conversely, suppose $x \in E \cup \mathbf{d}(E)$, and suppose that F is any closed set containing E. If $x \in \mathbf{d}(E)$, then $x \in \mathbf{d}(F)$ by **[D.2]**, and so $x \in F$ since F is closed. But if $x \in E$, then again we have $x \in F$ since $E \subseteq F$. Thus x belongs to any closed set containing E and hence to the intersection of all such sets, which is the closure of E. Thus $E \cup \mathbf{d}(E) \subseteq \mathbf{c}(E)$. ∎

From this characterization of the closure of a set, which could have been chosen as the definition, we may now list the following elementary properties of the closure, which hold for any subsets A, B, E of a topological space.

Kuratowski Closure Axioms:

[K.1] $\mathbf{c}(\emptyset) = \emptyset$,

[K.2] $E \subseteq \mathbf{c}(E)$,

[K.3] $\mathbf{c}(\mathbf{c}(E)) = \mathbf{c}(E)$, and

[K.4] $\mathbf{c}(A \cup B) = \mathbf{c}(A) \cup \mathbf{c}(B)$.

We call the above properties "axioms," since we may now define a **closure operator** on a set X to be a mapping $\mathbf{c}$ of $\mathscr{P}(X)$ into itself which satisfies those four properties. The following theorem shows that a closure operator completely determines a topology, and that in this topology, the operator is the closure.

Theorem 3.2.3. Let $\mathbf{c}^*$ be a closure operator defined on a set X. Let $\mathscr{F}$ be the family of all subsets F of X for which $\mathbf{c}^*(F) = F$, and let $\mathscr{T}$ be the family of all complements of members of $\mathscr{F}$. Then $\mathscr{T}$ is a topology for X, and if $\mathbf{c}$ is the closure operator defined by the topology $\mathscr{T}$, then $\mathbf{c}^*(E) = \mathbf{c}(E)$ for all subsets $E \subseteq X$.

Proof. **[0.1]**: Suppose $G_\lambda \in \mathscr{T}$ for all λ. We must show that $\bigcup_\lambda G_\lambda \in \mathscr{T}$; that is, $\complement(\bigcup_\lambda G_\lambda) \in \mathscr{F}$. Thus we must show that $\mathbf{c}^*(\complement(\bigcup_\lambda G_\lambda)) = \complement(\bigcup_\lambda G_\lambda)$.

By **[K.2]**, $\complement(\bigcup_\lambda G_\lambda) \subseteq \mathbf{c}^*(\complement(\bigcup_\lambda G_\lambda))$ so we need only prove that $\mathbf{c}^*(\complement(\bigcup_\lambda G_\lambda) \subseteq \complement(\bigcup_\lambda G_\lambda)$. By DeMorgan's law, that is $\mathbf{c}^*(\bigcap_\lambda \complement G_\lambda) \subseteq \bigcap_\lambda \complement G_\lambda$. It is easy to show (problem **6**) that for any closure operator $\mathbf{c}^*$, $A \subseteq B$ implies that $\mathbf{c}^*(A) \subseteq \mathbf{c}^*(B)$. Using this result, we see that since $\bigcap_\lambda \complement G_\lambda \subseteq \complement G_\alpha$ for each particular α, $\mathbf{c}^*(\bigcap_\lambda \complement G_\lambda) \subseteq \mathbf{c}^*(\complement G_\alpha)$ for each α, and so $\mathbf{c}^*(\bigcap_\lambda \complement G_\lambda) \subseteq \bigcap_\lambda \mathbf{c}^*(\complement G_\lambda)$. But since $G_\lambda \in \mathscr{T}$, $\complement G_\lambda \in \mathscr{F}$, so $\mathbf{c}^*(\complement G_\lambda) = \complement G_\lambda$. Thus we have $\mathbf{c}^*(\bigcap_\lambda \complement G_\lambda) \subseteq \bigcap_\lambda \complement G_\lambda$, as desired. We may also note that $X \subseteq \mathbf{c}^*(X) \subseteq X$ by **[K.2]**, and so $X \in \mathscr{F}$ and $\varnothing \in \mathscr{T}$.

[0.2]: Suppose G_1 and G_2 belong to $\mathscr{T}$. Then, by definition, $\mathbf{c}^*(\complement G_1) = \complement G_1$ and $\mathbf{c}^*(\complement G_2) = \complement G_2$. We may now calculate that

$$\begin{aligned}\mathbf{c}^*(\complement(G_1 \cap G_2)) &= \mathbf{c}^*(\complement G_1 \cup \complement G_2) = \mathbf{c}^*(\complement G_1) \cup \mathbf{c}^*(\complement G_2)\\ &= \complement G_1 \cup \complement G_2 = \complement(G_1 \cap G_2).\end{aligned}$$

Hence $\complement(G_1 \cap G_2) \in \mathscr{F}$, and so $G_1 \cap G_2 \in \mathscr{T}$. We must also check that $X \in \mathscr{T}$, and this is true since, by **[K.1]**, $\mathbf{c}^*(\varnothing) = \varnothing$, and so $\varnothing \in \mathscr{F}$.

($\mathbf{c}^* = \mathbf{c}$): Before we prove this part, it is important to emphasize that $\mathbf{c}(E)$ is the intersection of all closed sets containing E, and that, since we have now shown that $\mathscr{T}$ is a topology for X, the closed sets are just the members of the family $\mathscr{F}$. By **[K.3]**, $\mathbf{c}^*(\mathbf{c}^*(E)) = \mathbf{c}^*(E)$, so $\mathbf{c}^*(E) \in \mathscr{F}$. By **[K.2]**, $E \subseteq \mathbf{c}^*(E)$. Thus $\mathbf{c}^*(E)$ is a closed set containing E, and hence $\mathbf{c}^*(E) \supseteq \mathbf{c}(E)$. On the other hand, by **[K.2]**, $E \subseteq \mathbf{c}(E) \in \mathscr{F}$, so $\mathbf{c}^*(E) \subseteq \mathbf{c}^*(\mathbf{c}(E)) = \mathbf{c}(E)$. Thus $\mathbf{c}^*(E) = \mathbf{c}(E)$ for any subset $E \subseteq X$. ▌

Exercises

1. If E is a subset of a topological space $(X, \mathscr{T})$, and if $\mathbf{d}(F) \subseteq E \subseteq F$ for some subset $F \subseteq X$, show that E is a closed set.

2. If $(X, \mathscr{T})$ and $(X, \mathscr{T}^*)$ are topological spaces, what can be said about the corresponding families $\mathscr{F}$ and $\mathscr{F}^*$ of closed sets if $\mathscr{T} \leqslant \mathscr{T}^*$?

3. What are the families of closed sets in the topological spaces given in problems **3** through **7** of Section **3.1**?

4. Prove the Kuratowski Closure Axioms.

5. Show that the four Kuratowski Closure Axioms may be replaced by the single condition:

$$A \cup \mathbf{c}(A) \cup \mathbf{c}(\mathbf{c}(B)) = \mathbf{c}(A \cup B) \setminus \mathbf{c}(\varnothing)$$

for all subsets $A, B \subseteq X$.

6. Show that any closure operator $\mathbf{c}$ has the property that $A \subseteq B$ implies that $\mathbf{c}(A) \subseteq \mathbf{c}(B)$.

7. If x is a point and E a subset of a topological space $(X, \mathscr{T})$, show that $x \in \mathbf{c}(E)$ iff every open set containing x has a nonempty intersection with E.

8. Completely define the closure operators in the topological spaces given in problems **3** through **7** of Section **3.1**.

9. Show that the closure operator in any topological space has the following properties:

(i) $\bigcup_\lambda \mathbf{c}(E_\lambda) \subseteq \mathbf{c}(\bigcup_\lambda E_\lambda)$,

(ii) $\bigcap_\lambda \mathbf{c}(E_\lambda) \supseteq \mathbf{c}(\bigcap_\lambda E_\lambda)$, and

(iii) $\mathbf{c}(A) \setminus \mathbf{c}(B) \subseteq \mathbf{c}(A \setminus B)$.

Give examples in which inequalities hold in each case.

10. If $\mathbf{c}$ and $\mathbf{c}^*$ are the closure operators in the topological spaces $(X, \mathscr{T})$ and $(X, \mathscr{T}^*)$, respectively, how are $\mathbf{c}(E)$ and $\mathbf{c}^*(E)$ related if $\mathscr{T} \leqslant \mathscr{T}^*$?

3.3 Operators and Neighborhoods

The closure operator is just one of a number of operators which may be used to define a topology. Let us first consider the "dual" operator. The **interior** of a set E contained in a topological space is the union of all open sets contained in E. It will be denoted by $\mathbf{i}(E)$ or $\mathring{E}$. We see at once that $\mathbf{i}(E)$ is an open set by [**0.1**], and so $\mathbf{i}(E)$ is the largest open set contained in E. Obviously a set E is open iff $E = \mathbf{i}(E)$.

Theorem 3.3.1. *For any set E in a topological space $(X, \mathscr{T})$, $\mathbf{i}(E) = \complement\mathbf{c}(\complement E)$.*

Proof. If $x \in \mathbf{i}(E)$, then $\mathbf{i}(E)$ is itself an open set containing x which is disjoint from $\complement E$, and so $x \notin \mathbf{d}(\complement E)$. But $x \notin \complement E$, so $x \notin (\complement E) \cup \mathbf{d}(\complement E) = \mathbf{c}(\complement E)$. Thus $x \in \complement\mathbf{c}(\complement E)$ and $\mathbf{i}(E) \subseteq \complement\mathbf{c}(\complement E)$. Now suppose $x \in \complement\mathbf{c}(\complement E)$. Immediately, $x \notin \mathbf{c}(\complement E)$, and so $x \notin \complement E$ and $x \notin \mathbf{d}(\complement E)$. Thus $x \in E$, and there exists an open set G containing x such that $\complement E \cap G \setminus \{x\} = \varnothing$. Since $x \notin \complement E$, we actually have $\complement E \cap G = \varnothing$, so $G \subseteq E$. We now have $x \in G \subseteq E$ for some open set G, and so x belongs to the union of all open sets contained in E, which is $\mathbf{i}(E)$. Thus $\complement\mathbf{c}(\complement E) \subseteq \mathbf{i}(E)$. ∎

From this characterization of the interior, it is clear that if the notion of closure is chosen as the primitive one, it is possible to find the interior of sets without even finding the open sets first. Conversely, by taking complements in the previous theorem, the relation $\mathbf{c}(E) = \complement\mathbf{i}(\complement E)$ shows that if the interiors of all sets are known, the closure of any set may be found immediately. Using these relations we may obtain the following elementary properties analogous to the Kuratowski Closure Axioms.

Interior Axioms:

[I.1] $\mathbf{i}(X) = X$,

[I.2] $\mathbf{i}(E) \subseteq E$,

[I.3] $\mathbf{i}(\mathbf{i}(E)) = \mathbf{i}(E)$, and

[I.4] $\mathbf{i}(A \cap B) = \mathbf{i}(A) \cap \mathbf{i}(B)$.

We will define an **interior operator** on a set X to be a mapping of $\mathscr{P}(X)$ into itself which satisfies the Interior Axioms. As one might expect, a theorem analogous to **3.2.3** holds for the interior operator. Thus, an interior operator completely determines a topology (a set is open iff it equals its own interior), and in that topology, the operator is the interior.

The **exterior** of a set E is the set of all points interior to the complement of E, and will be denoted by $\mathbf{e}(E)$. Thus we have $\mathbf{e}(E) = \mathbf{i}(\complement E)$. From this it follows that $\mathbf{i}(E) = \mathbf{e}(\complement E)$ so that the exterior may also be chosen as the primitive notion of topology. Analogous to the Kuratowski Closure Axioms we have:

Exterior Axioms:

[E.1] $\mathbf{e}(\emptyset) = X$,

[E.2] $\mathbf{e}(E) \subseteq \complement E$,

[E.3] $\mathbf{e}(E) = \mathbf{e}(\complement \mathbf{e}(E))$, and

[E.4] $\mathbf{e}(A \cup B) = \mathbf{e}(A) \cap \mathbf{e}(B)$.

The **boundary** of a set E is the set of all points interior to neither E nor $\complement E$. It will be denoted by $\mathbf{b}(E)$. Note that this set is sometimes described in the literature as the **frontier** of E, while some authors refer to the frontier as the set of all points of the set which are not interior to the set. To avoid confusion, we will not use the frontier operator at all.

From this definition we have $\mathbf{b}(E) = \complement(\mathbf{i}(E) \cup \mathbf{i}(\complement E))$. Using DeMorgan's laws and the definitions of **c** and **i**, we see immediately that $\mathbf{b}(E) = \mathbf{b}(\complement E) = \mathbf{c}(E) \cap \mathbf{c}(\complement E) = \mathbf{c}(E) \setminus \mathbf{i}(E)$. That the boundary may be chosen as the primitive notion of topology follows from the fact that if we know $\mathbf{b}(E)$, we may immediately find $\mathbf{c}(E) = E \cup \mathbf{b}(E)$ or $\mathbf{i}(E) = E \setminus \mathbf{b}(E)$.

Another primitive notion which may be used to define a topology is that of a neighborhood of a point, which is often more convenient than our open set notion. A **neighborhood** of a point is any set which contains an open set containing the point. Clearly E is a neighborhood of x iff $x \in \mathbf{i}(E)$. From this it follows that a set is open iff it is a neighborhood of each of its points. In order to determine a topology from a knowledge of the neighborhoods of the points of a set, we should call those sets open which are neighborhoods of each of their points. The conditions which we must place upon the association of neighborhoods to points so that the open sets chosen in this way actually form a topology are given in the next theorem.

Theorem 3.3.2. *Let there be associated with each point x of a set X a collection $\mathcal{N}_x{}^*$ of subsets, called neighborhoods, subject to the conditions:*

[N.1] *Every point of X is contained in at least one neighborhood, and is contained in each of its neighborhoods.*

[N.2] *The intersection of any two neighborhoods of a point is a neighborhood of that point.*

[N.3] *Any set which contains a neighborhood of a point is itself a neighborhood of that point.*

[N.4] *If N is a neighborhood of a point x, then there exists a neighborhood N^* of x such that N is a neighborhood of each point of N^*.*

Let $\mathcal{T}$ be the family of all subsets of X which are neighborhoods of each of their points; i.e., $G \in \mathcal{T}$ iff $x \in G$ implies that $G \in \mathcal{N}_x{}^*$. Then $\mathcal{T}$ is a topology for X, and if $\mathcal{N}_x$ is the collection of all neighborhoods of x defined by the topology $\mathcal{T}$, then $\mathcal{N}_x{}^* = \mathcal{N}_x$ for every $x \in X$.

Proof. **[0.1]**: Suppose $G_\lambda \in \mathcal{T}$ for all λ. If $x \in \bigcup_\lambda G_\lambda$, then $x \in G_\alpha$ for some α. By the definition of $\mathcal{T}$, G_α is a neighborhood of each of its points, so $G_\alpha \in \mathcal{N}_x{}^*$. By **[N.3]**, since $G_\alpha \subseteq \bigcup_\lambda G_\lambda$, $\bigcup_\lambda G_\lambda \in \mathcal{N}_x{}^*$. Thus $\bigcup_\lambda G_\lambda$ is a neighborhood of each of its points, and hence belongs to $\mathcal{T}$. Of course $\varnothing \in \mathcal{T}$ since it is vacuously a neighborhood of each of its points.

[0.2]: Suppose G_1 and G_2 belong to $\mathcal{T}$. If $x \in G_1 \cap G_2$, then $x \in G_1$ and $x \in G_2$. By the definition of $\mathcal{T}$, G_1 and G_2 are both neighborhoods of each of their points, so $G_1 \in \mathcal{N}_x{}^*$ and $G_2 \in \mathcal{N}_x{}^*$. By **[N.2]**, $G_1 \cap G_2 \in \mathcal{N}_x{}^*$, so $G_1 \cap G_2$ is a neighborhood of each of its points and hence is an open set. We also note that, for any $x \in X$, x is contained in at least one neighborhood by **[N.1]**, and this neighborhood is contained in X, so X is a neighborhood of x by **[N.3]**. Thus X is a neighborhood of each of its points, and so $X \in \mathcal{T}$.

($\mathcal{N}_x^* = \mathcal{N}_x$): If $N \in \mathcal{N}_x$, then there exists an open set G such that $x \in G \subseteq N$. From the definition of $\mathcal{T}$, $x \in G$ implies that $G \in \mathcal{N}_x^*$, and so $N \in \mathcal{N}_x^*$ by **[N.3]**. Thus $\mathcal{N}_x \subseteq \mathcal{N}_x^*$. Now suppose $N \in \mathcal{N}_x^*$. Let us define the set G to be all points which have N as a neighborhood. Clearly x is one of these points, so $x \in G$, while, by **[N.1]**, every point with N as a neighborhood is in N, so $G \subseteq N$. We will show that $G \in \mathcal{T}$; that is, G is in $\mathcal{N}_y^*$ for every $y \in G$. Let $y \in G$, so that $N \in \mathcal{N}_y^*$. By **[N.4]**, there exists a set N^* such that $N^* \in \mathcal{N}_y^*$, and if $z \in N^*$ then $N \in \mathcal{N}_z^*$. The definition of G shows that $N \in \mathcal{N}_z^*$ implies that $z \in G$, hence, $N^* \subseteq G$ and, by **[N.3]**, $G \in \mathcal{N}_y^*$. ▮

Exercises

1. Prove that the interior and exterior axioms are satisfied in any topological space.

2. State and prove a theorem analogous to **3.2.3** for the interior operator. Do the same for the exterior operator.

3. Verify the following properties of **i**, **e**, and **b** for any sets A, B, and E:

(i) $\mathbf{c}(E) = E \cup \mathbf{b}(E)$, $\mathbf{i}(E) = E \setminus \mathbf{b}(E)$,

(ii) $X = \mathbf{i}(E) \cup \mathbf{b}(E) \cup \mathbf{e}(E)$ where $\mathbf{i}(E) \cap \mathbf{b}(E) \cap \mathbf{e}(E) = \emptyset$,

(iii) $\mathbf{b}(\mathbf{i}(E)) \subseteq \mathbf{b}(E)$, $\mathbf{b}(\mathbf{c}(E)) \subseteq \mathbf{b}(E)$ (give an example where these sets are not equal),

(iv) $\mathbf{b}(A \cup B) \subseteq \mathbf{b}(A) \cup \mathbf{b}(B)$, $\mathbf{i}(A \cup B) \supseteq \mathbf{i}(A) \cup \mathbf{i}(B)$ (give an example where these sets are not equal),

(v) $\mathbf{b}(E) = \emptyset$ iff E is both open and closed,

(vi) If A and B are open, $\mathbf{i}(\mathbf{c}(A \cap B)) = \mathbf{i}(\mathbf{c}(A)) \cap \mathbf{i}(\mathbf{c}(B))$.

4. Verify the following properties of the operator **b** and see if they are equivalent to the Kuratowski Closure Axioms. (See [28].)

[B.1] $\mathbf{b}(\emptyset) = \emptyset$,

[B.2] $\mathbf{b}(E) = \mathbf{b}(\complement E)$,

[B.3] $\mathbf{b}(\mathbf{b}(E)) \subseteq \mathbf{b}(E)$,

[B.4] $A \cap B \cap \mathbf{b}(A \cap B) = A \cap B \cap (\mathbf{b}(A) \cup \mathbf{b}(B))$.

5. Rephrase the definitions of limit points and closures in terms of neighborhoods alone.

3.4 Bases and Relative Topologies

In order to completely determine a topological space, one must specify both the points and the open sets in the space. In many cases we have specified the open sets by listing all of them. In problem **6** of Section **3.1**, for example, the topology for the set $X = \{a, b, c\}$ was the family $\mathscr{T} = \{\emptyset, \{a\}, \{b\}, \{a, b\}, X\}$. Note that it was not really necessary to list the set $\{a, b\}$ to specify this topology, since that set must be open, by **[0.1]**, as soon as we know that $\{a\}$ and $\{b\}$ are open.

In the same way, it is clear that the discrete topology is determined for a set as soon as it is known that each set consisting of a single point is an open set. We shall say that a subfamily $\mathscr{B}$ of a topology $\mathscr{T}$ is a **base** for $\mathscr{T}$ iff each member of $\mathscr{T}$ is the union of members of $\mathscr{B}$. Equivalently, if $x \in G \in \mathscr{T}$, then there exists a $B \in \mathscr{B}$ such that $x \in B \subseteq G$. Thus, for example, the family of all open intervals is a base for the usual topology for the reals. Note that it is not necessary to include the empty set in a base for a topology, since $\emptyset = \bigcup \{B_\lambda : \lambda \in \emptyset\}$.

It is clear that not every family of subsets of a set X is a base for a topology for X. For example, if $X = \{a, b, c\}$ and the sets $\{a, b\}$ and $\{a, c\}$ belong to a base $\mathscr{B}$, then the set $\{a\}$ must also belong to $\mathscr{B}$ since $\{a, b\}$ and $\{a, c\}$ are open sets and by **[0.2]** their intersection $\{a\}$ must be open and hence be a member of $\mathscr{B}$. Necessary and sufficient conditions for a family of subsets to be a base for a topology are given in the following theorem.

Theorem 3.4.1. *A family $\mathscr{B}$ of sets is a base for a topology for the set $X = \bigcup \{B : B \in \mathscr{B}\}$ iff for every $B_1, B_2 \in \mathscr{B}$ and every $x \in B_1 \cap B_2$, there exists a $B \in \mathscr{B}$ such that $x \in B \subseteq B_1 \cap B_2$; that is, the intersection of any two members of $\mathscr{B}$ is a union of members of $\mathscr{B}$.*

Proof. If the family $\mathscr{B}$ is a base for a topology, then the members of the base are open sets, and the intersection of two open sets is an open set and hence the union of members of $\mathscr{B}$. Now suppose $\mathscr{B}$ is a family of sets satisfying the condition of the theorem, and we let $\mathscr{T}$ be the collection of all subsets of X which are unions of members of $\mathscr{B}$. We shall show that $\mathscr{T}$ is a topology for X. Since each member of $\mathscr{T}$ is a union of members of $\mathscr{B}$, the union of any number of members of $\mathscr{T}$ is a union of members of $\mathscr{B}$ and so belongs to $\mathscr{T}$. Thus **[0.1]** is satisfied. In order to prove that **[0.2]** is satisfied, we first note that the set X was defined to be the union of all members of $\mathscr{B}$ and so is a member of $\mathscr{T}$. Now suppose that G_1 and G_2 belong to $\mathscr{T}$. If $x \in G_1 \cap G_2$, then $x \in G_1$ and $x \in G_2$. By the definition of $\mathscr{T}$, G_1 and G_2 are unions of members of $\mathscr{B}$, and so there exist sets B_1 and B_2 belonging to $\mathscr{B}$ such that $x \in B_1 \subseteq G_1$ and $x \in B_2 \subseteq G_2$. Now $x \in B_1 \cap B_2$, and so, by hypothesis, there exists a $B \in \mathscr{B}$ such that $x \in B \subseteq B_1 \cap B_2$. Since $B_1 \cap B_2 \subseteq G_1 \cap G_2$, we have shown that every point of $G_1 \cap G_2$ is contained in a member of

$\mathscr{B}$ which is itself contained in $G_1 \cap G_2$. Thus $G_1 \cap G_2$ is the union of members of $\mathscr{B}$ and so belongs to $\mathscr{T}$. ▮

Clearly the definition of a base was chosen so that axiom **[0.1]** would be automatically satisfied if we started with any family of sets. It seems natural to give a method for obtaining the open sets of a topological space which automatically satisfies both of the open set axioms. We shall say that a subfamily $\mathscr{S}$ of a topology $\mathscr{T}$ is a **subbase** for $\mathscr{T}$ iff each member of $\mathscr{T}$ is the union of finite intersections of members of $\mathscr{S}$; that is, the family of all finite intersections of members of $\mathscr{S}$ is a base for $\mathscr{T}$.

It is clear from the previous theorem that every family of sets is a subbase for a topology for their union. Note that it is not necessary to include X in a subbase for a topology, since $X = \bigcap \{S_\lambda : \lambda \in \emptyset\}$.

The collection of all open intervals of real numbers satisfies the condition of the above theorem and so forms a base for a topology for the reals. This topology, of course, is the usual topology. Another base for the usual topology would be the collection of all open intervals with rational endpoints. It will be important later that this is a base with only a countable number of elements. As an example of a subbase we could choose all sets which are either of the form $\{x : x > a\}$ or the form $\{x : x < a\}$ for some real number a. Again it is sufficient to let a be an arbitrary rational number.

A topology for a set X which is linearly ordered by an irreflexive ordering $<$ (i.e., $x \nless x$ for any $x \in X$) may be chosen in a way analogous to that used for the real numbers. If we want the topology to be related to the ordering and not just be using the points of X as an abstract set, we may use the **order topology** for X which is obtained by choosing as a subbase all sets which are either of the form $\{x : x > a\}$ or of the form $\{x : x < a\}$ for some $a \in X$. As with the real numbers, it is possible to topologize an ordered set in many ways, but this topology is the one which is naturally associated with the ordering and will be understood whenever we have an ordered set unless the contrary is specifically stated.

If X^* is a subset of a topological space $(X, \mathscr{T})$, we may topologize it in many ways, but we will be most interested in some topology for it which is naturally associated with the topology for X so that we will not just be considering X^* as an abstract collection of points. The **induced** or **relative topology** for X^* is the collection $\mathscr{T}^*$ of all sets which are intersections of X^* with members of $\mathscr{T}$. We will call $(X^*, \mathscr{T}^*)$ a **subspace** of $(X, \mathscr{T})$ iff $\mathscr{T}^*$ is the induced topology. We must first show that $\mathscr{T}^*$ is, indeed, a topology for X^*.

Theorem 3.4.2. *$\mathscr{T}^*$ is a topology for X^*.*

Proof. **[0.1]**: If $G_\lambda{}^*$ belongs to $\mathscr{T}^*$ for all λ, then there exist sets G_λ belonging to $\mathscr{T}$ such that $G_\lambda{}^* = X^* \cap G_\lambda$ for each λ. Since $\bigcup_\lambda G_\lambda$ also belongs to $\mathscr{T}$, $\bigcup_\lambda G_\lambda{}^* = \bigcup_\lambda (X^* \cap G_\lambda) = X^* \cap (\bigcup_\lambda G_\lambda)$ belongs to $\mathscr{T}^*$.

[0.2]: We note that $X^* \in \mathscr{T}^*$ since $X^* = X^* \cap X$ and $X \in \mathscr{T}$. Now suppose $G_1{}^*$ and $G_2{}^*$ belong to $\mathscr{T}^*$. There must exist sets G_1 and G_2 belonging to $\mathscr{T}$ such that $G_1{}^* = X^* \cap G_1$ and $G_2{}^* = X^* \cap G_2$. Since $G_1 \cap G_2$ also belongs to $\mathscr{T}$, $G_1{}^* \cap G_2{}^* = (X^* \cap G_1) \cap (X^* \cap G_2) = X^* \cap (G_1 \cap G_2)$ belongs to $\mathscr{T}^*$. ∎

If $(X^*, \mathscr{T}^*)$ is a subspace of $(X, \mathscr{T})$, then a subset of X^* may be open or closed when considered as a subset of the topological space $(X^*, \mathscr{T}^*)$, but not when considered as a subset of $(X, \mathscr{T})$. To avoid ambiguity, sets which are open with respect to the subspace $(X^*, \mathscr{T}^*)$ will be called **relatively** open sets. We will also refer to them as $\mathscr{T}^*$-open, X^*-open, or open in X^*. The same convention will be used with respect to relatively closed sets and with our set operators. If we denote the closure operator in the topological space $(X, \mathscr{T})$ by $\mathbf{c}$, we will normally denote the closure operator in a subspace $(X^*, \mathscr{T}^*)$ by $\mathbf{c}^*$. Thus, $\mathbf{i}^*(E)$ would then mean the union of all relatively open sets contained in E.

Theorem 3.4.3. *If E is a subset of a subspace $(X^*, \mathscr{T}^*)$ of a topological space $(X, \mathscr{T})$, then $\mathbf{c}^*(E) = X^* \cap \mathbf{c}(E)$.*

Proof.

$$X^* \cap \mathbf{c}(E) = X^* \cap (\bigcap\{F : F \in \mathscr{F} \text{ and } E \subset F\}) = \bigcap\{X^* \cap F : F \in \mathscr{F} \text{ and } E \subseteq F\}$$

$$= \bigcap\{F^* : F^* \in \mathscr{F}^* \text{ and } E \subseteq F^*\} = \mathbf{c}^*(E). \blacksquare$$

Exercises

1. Show that two bases $\mathscr{B}$ and $\mathscr{B}^*$ generate the same topology for a set X iff (i) for every $x \in B \in \mathscr{B}$ there exists a $B^* \in \mathscr{B}^*$ such that $x \in B^* \subseteq B$, and (ii) for every $x \in B^* \in \mathscr{B}^*$ there exists a $B \in \mathscr{B}$ such that $x \in B \subseteq B^*$.

2. Show that the family of open disks in the plane forms a base for a topology for the Euclidean plane. This topology is the **usual** topology for the plane and will be understood unless another topology is specifically mentioned. Show also that the family of open rectangles is a base for the same topology.

3. Topologize the real numbers by chosing as a base the family of all half-open intervals of the form $[a, b) = \{x : a \leqslant x < b\}$ for any pair of real numbers a and b. Verify that this

is a base for a topology and describe the open sets. What is the closure of a set in this topology? How does this topology compare with the usual topology for the reals? This topology is called the **lower limit topology**. There is a similarly defined **upper limit topology**.

4. Topologize the real numbers by chosing as a base the family of all semi-infinite intervals of the form $(a, +\infty) = \{x : x > a\}$ for any real number a. Verify that this is a base for a topology and describe the open sets. What is the closure of a set in this topology? How does this topology compare with the usual, upper limit, and lower limit topologies for the reals? We will call this topology the **right-hand topology**. There is a similarly defined **left-hand topology** for the reals.

5. If $\mathscr{S}$ is a subbase for a topology $\mathscr{T}$, show that $\mathscr{T}$ is the intersection of all topologies containing the family $\mathscr{S}$.

6. Let X be an ordered set with the order topology, and let X^* be a subset of X. Since X^* is also ordered by the same ordering, there is an order topology for X^*. Since X^* is a subset of X, there is an induced topology for X^*. Give an example of a set X^* of real numbers in which the order topology for X^* is not the same as the induced topology for X^*.

7. Let $(X^*, \mathscr{T}^*)$ be a subspace of $(X, \mathscr{T})$ and let E be a subset of X^*. Show:

(i) The family of closed sets of $(X^*, \mathscr{T}^*)$ is the collection $\mathscr{F}^*$ of sets which are intersections of X^* with closed sets in $(X, \mathscr{T})$,

(ii) $\mathscr{T}^* \subseteq \mathscr{T}$ iff $X^* \in \mathscr{T}$,

(iii) $\mathscr{F}^* \subseteq \mathscr{F}$ iff $X^* \in \mathscr{F}$,

(iv) $\mathbf{e}^*(E) = X^* \cap \mathbf{e}(E)$,

(v) $\mathbf{b}^*(E) \subseteq X^* \cap \mathbf{b}(E)$ (give an example where these sets are not equal),

(vi) $\mathbf{i}(E) = \mathbf{i}^*(E) \cap \mathbf{i}(X^*)$.

CHAPTER 4

Connectedness, Compactness, and Continuity

4.1 Connected Sets and Components

Two subsets A and B form a **separation** or **partition** of a set E in a topological space $(X, \mathscr{T})$, written $E = A \mid B$, iff E is the union of A and B, and they are nonempty, disjoint sets, neither of which contains a limit point of the other. A set is called **connected** iff it has no separation.

Clearly an equivalent formulation of this definition is that a set is connected iff whenever it is written as the union of two nonempty, disjoint sets, at least one of them must contain a limit point of the other. The requirements that A and B be disjoint sets and neither contain a limit point of the other may be combined in the formula $[A \cap \mathbf{c}(B)] \cup [\mathbf{c}(A) \cap B] = \emptyset$, which is often called the **Hausdorff-Lennes Separation Condition**, and such subsets are called **separated.**

It is immediate from the definition that the empty set and every set consisting of exactly one point is a connected set. In a general topological space it is possible that these would be the only connected sets. An example of this would be in the case of the discrete topology on any set having at least two points. In the case of the real numbers, it is known (see Dieudonné [5, p. 64]) that the only connected sets are the intervals (with or without endpoints, degenerate, finite, semi-infinite, or infinite).

Theorem 4.1.1. *If E is a subset of a subspace $(X^*, \mathscr{T}^*)$ of a topological space $(X, \mathscr{T})$, then E is $\mathscr{T}^*$-connected iff it is $\mathscr{T}$-connected.*

Proof. In order to have a separation of E with respect to either topology, we must be able to write E as the union of two nonempty, disjoint sets. If A and B are two nonempty, disjoint sets whose union is E, then $A, B \subseteq X^* \subseteq X$.

Calculating with the Hausdorff-Lennes Separation Condition we find that

$$[A \cap \mathbf{c}(B)] \cup [\mathbf{c}(A) \cap B] = [A \cap X^* \cap \mathbf{c}(B)] \cup [\mathbf{c}(A) \cap X^* \cap B]$$

$$= [A \cap \mathbf{c}^*(B)] \cup [\mathbf{c}^*(A) \cap B].$$

Thus if the condition is satisfied with respect to one topology, it is satisfied with respect to the other. ▮

The above theorem leads us to say that connectedness is an **absolute property** of sets; that is, it does not depend on the space in which the set is contained except that the topology must, of course, be the relative topology. Because of this we may usually limit our considerations to the entire space when discussing connectedness.

It is clear that a separation of the entire topological space must be into two nonempty, disjoint sets which are both open and closed. We know that in any topological space, the sets ø and X are both open and closed sets. The question of whether there are any other sets which are both open and closed has now been answered (see problem **2**).

There are some very important properties of connected sets which follow from the next theorem.

Theorem 4.1.2. *If C is a connected subset of a topological space $(X, \mathscr{T})$ which has a separation $X = A \mid B$, then either $C \subseteq A$ or $C \subseteq B$.*

Proof. Clearly $C = C \cap X = C \cap (A \cup B) = (C \cap A) \cup (C \cap B)$. Since $X = A \mid B$, $[(C \cap A) \cap \mathbf{c}(C \cap B)] \cup [\mathbf{c}(C \cap A) \cap (C \cap B)] \subseteq [A \cap \mathbf{c}(B)] \cup [\mathbf{c}(A) \cap B] = ø$. Thus we see that if we assume that both $C \cap A$ and $C \cap B$ are nonempty, we have a separation for $C = (C \cap A) \mid (C \cap B)$. Hence, either $C \cap A$ is empty so that $C \subseteq B$, or $C \cap B$ is empty and $C \subseteq A$. ▮

Corollary 1. *If C is a connected set and $C \subseteq E \subseteq \mathbf{c}(C)$, then E is a connected set.*

Proof. If E is not a connected set, it must have a separation $E = A \mid B$. By the above theorem, C must be contained in A or contained in B; with no loss of generality let us suppose that $C \subseteq A$. From this it follows that $\mathbf{c}(C) \subseteq \mathbf{c}(A)$ and hence $\mathbf{c}(C) \cap B \subseteq \mathbf{c}(A) \cap B = ø$. On the other hand, $B \subseteq E \subseteq \mathbf{c}(C)$ and so $\mathbf{c}(C) \cap B = B$, so that we must have $B = ø$, which contradicts our hypothesis that $E = A \mid B$. ▮

Corollary 2. *If every two points of a set E are contained in some connected subset of E, then E is a connected set.*

Proof. If E is not connected, it must have a separation $E = A \mid B$. Since A and B must be nonempty, let us choose points $a \in A$ and $b \in B$. From the hypothesis we know that a and b must be contained in some connected subset C contained in E. The above theorem requires, however, that C be either a subset of A or a subset of B. Since A and B are disjoint, this is a contradiction. ∎

Corollary 3. *The union E of any family $\{C_\lambda\}$ of connected sets having a nonempty intersection is a connected set.*

Proof. If E is not connected, it must have a separation $E = A \mid B$. By hypothesis, we may choose a point $x \in \bigcap_\lambda C_\lambda$. The point x must belong to either A or B, and without loss of generality let us suppose $x \in A$. Since x belongs to C_λ for every λ, $C_\lambda \cap A \neq \emptyset$ for every λ. By the above theorem, however, each C_λ must be either a subset of A or a subset of B. Since A and B are disjoint sets we must have $C_\lambda \subseteq A$ for all λ, and so $E \subseteq A$. From this we obtain the contradiction that $B = \emptyset$. ∎

The structure of the connected subsets of the real line is deceptively simple. For example, if the removal of a single point x from a connected set C leaves a disconnected set, then $C \setminus \{x\}$ is the union of two disjoint connected sets. We cannot expect this simple behavior in a general topological space since Knaster and Kuratowski [47] have given an example of a connected subset of the plane with the property that the removal of a certain one of its points leaves no connected subsets bigger than the individual points of the remainder. Another geometrically reasonable property of connected sets is given in the following:

Theorem 4.1.3. *If a connected set C has a nonempty intersection with both a set E and the complement of E in a topological space $(X, \mathscr{T})$, then C has a nonempty intersection with the boundary of E.*

Proof. We will show that if we assume that C is disjoint from $\mathbf{b}(E)$, we obtain the contradiction that $C = (C \cap E) \mid (C \cap \complement E)$. From the equation $C = C \cap X = C \cap (E \cup \complement E) = (C \cap E) \cup (C \cap \complement E)$ we see that C is the union of the two sets. These two sets are nonempty by hypothesis. If we calculate $(C \cap E) \cap \mathbf{c}(C \cap \complement E) \subseteq [C \cap \mathbf{c}(E)] \cap \mathbf{c}(\complement E) = C \cap \mathbf{b}(E)$, we see that the assumption that $C \cap \mathbf{b}(E) = \emptyset$ leads to the conclusion that $(C \cap E) \cap \mathbf{c}(C \cap \complement E) = \emptyset$. In the same way we may show that $\mathbf{c}(C \cap E) \cap (C \cap \complement E) = \emptyset$, and we have a separation of C. ▮

When a topological space is not connected it is natural that we should attempt to obtain some information about the various "pieces" into which it can be separated. The maximal connected subsets of the space are particularly interesting. If x is a point of a subset E contained in a topological space $(X, \mathscr{T})$, then the union of all connected sets containing x and contained in E will be called the **component** of E corresponding to x, and will be denoted by $C(E, x)$.

By Corollary **3** above we know that each $C(E, x)$ is a connected set, hence $C(E, x)$ is the largest connected subset of E containing x. It is easy to show that the components corresponding to different points of E are either equal or disjoint, so that we may speak of the components of the set E without any reference to specific points. Every subset of a topological space has now been partitioned into disjoint subsets, its components.

Theorem 4.1.4. *The components of a topological space $(X, \mathscr{T})$ are closed subsets of X.*

Proof. If C is a component of X, choose a point $x \in C$ and suppose that $y \in \mathbf{c}(C)$. Since $\mathbf{c}(C)$ is a connected set by Corollary **1** above, y is in a connected subset of X which contains x. Hence $\mathbf{c}(C) \subseteq C$, and so C must be closed. ▮

This theorem may be rephrased, using **4.1.1**, so as to apply to subsets of a topological space. Thus, the components of any set E are closed in E. By problem **7**(iii) of Section **3.4**, this may again be rephrased to assert that the components of a closed set are closed sets in X. It seems natural to ask whether the components of open sets are open in X. An example shows that this is not true in general. If we choose as our space the rational numbers with the induced topology from the reals, then each point is a component of the entire space (an open set, certainly), but the individual points are not open sets in this topology.

The above example also shows that a component and its complement may not form a separation of a space. Let us now consider a type of topological space in which the components behave in a more natural way. A topological space $(X, \mathscr{T})$ will be said to be **locally connected** iff for every point $x \in X$ and every open set G containing x, there exists a connected open set G^* containing x and contained in G. Thus a space is locally connected iff the family of all open connected sets is a base for the topology for the space. A subset of a space will be called locally connected iff it is a locally connected space in its induced topology.

Note that a locally connected set need not be connected. For example, a set consisting of two disjoint open intervals is locally connected but not connected. The connected subsets of the real numbers are locally connected, but this implication need not hold in general. An example of a connected subset of the plane which is not locally connected may be constructed as follows. For each positive integer n, let us denote by $\mathbf{E}_n$ the line segment connecting the origin to the point $\langle 1, 1/n \rangle$. Each of these line segments is connected, and all contain the origin, so their union is connected. If we let $\mathbf{x}$ be the point $\langle 1, 0 \rangle$ and $\mathbf{y}$ be the point $\langle \frac{1}{2}, 0 \rangle$, then $\mathbf{x}$ and $\mathbf{y}$ are both limit points of the set consisting of all the $\mathbf{E}_n$'s. By Corollary **1** above, the set $\mathbf{E} = \{\mathbf{x}\} \cup \{\mathbf{y}\} \cup (\bigcup_n \mathbf{E}_n)$ is a connected set. This set is not locally connected, however, since an open set containing $\mathbf{x}$, if sufficiently small, will not contain a connected open set containing $\mathbf{x}$.

The above example also shows that if the removal of a point from a connected set leaves a set which is not connected, that point need not be a limit point of every component of the remainder. The sets $\{\mathbf{x}\}$ and $\{\mathbf{y}\}$ are both components of the set remaining after the removal of the origin, but the origin is not a limit point of either of these sets. Notice also that the points $\mathbf{x}$ and $\mathbf{y}$ do not lie in any connected subset of $\mathbf{E} \setminus \{\langle 0, 0 \rangle\}$, and so lie in different components of this remainder. Nevertheless, in any separation of this remainder they must both be in the same part. This is because one of the parts of the separation must contain an infinite number of the components $\mathbf{E}_n \setminus \{\langle 0, 0 \rangle\}$ and so also the points $\mathbf{x}$ and $\mathbf{y}$ which are limit points (see problem **9**).

The behavior of the points $\mathbf{x}$ and $\mathbf{y}$, above, leads us to define an equivalence relation on the points of a topological space $(X, \mathscr{T})$ by setting two points in this relation iff they must always belong to the same part of any separation of X. The equivalence classes under this equivalence relation will be called the **quasi components** of X. It is easy to see that each component of a space is contained in some quasi component, and these quasi components are also closed sets.

Exercises

1. Show that any separation of a topological space must be into two nonempty, disjoint sets which are both open and closed.

2. A topological space is connected iff it has no nonempty proper subsets which are both open and closed.

3. Which of the spaces given in problems **3** through **7** of Section **3.1** are connected? Which of the spaces given in problems **3** and **4** in Section **3.4** are connected?

4. The union of any family of connected sets, no pair of which are disjoint, is connected.

5. If $(X, \mathcal{T})$ is a connected topological space and $\mathcal{T}^* \leqslant \mathcal{T}$, show that $(X, \mathcal{T}^*)$ is connected.

6. If C is a connected subset of a topological space $(X, \mathcal{T})$ which is itself connected, and $X \setminus C = A \mid B$, then $A \cup C$ and $B \cup C$ are connected.

7. If E is a subset of a topological space $(X, \mathcal{T})$, prove that $\mathbf{c}(E)$ is connected iff E is not the union of any two nonempty sets A and B such that $\mathbf{c}(A) \cap \mathbf{c}(B) = \emptyset$.

8. In a connected topological space, every nonempty proper subset has a nonempty boundary.

9. If $E = A \mid B$ is closed, then A and B are closed.

10. Prove that the components of E corresponding to different points of E are either equal or disjoint.

11. Every open subset of a locally connected topological space is itself locally connected.

12. A topological space $(X, \mathcal{T})$ is locally connected iff every component of an open set is an open set in X.

13. If x and y are two points belonging to different components of a locally connected topological space $(X, \mathcal{T})$, then there exists a separation $X = A \mid B$ such that $x \in A$ and $y \in B$.

14. Show that each component of a space is contained in some quasi component, and these quasi components are closed sets.

15. If G is a connected open subset of the topological space X, then G is a component of $X \setminus \mathbf{b}(G)$.

16. A **dispersion point** of a topological space is a point which is contained in every connected subset of the space consisting of more than one point. Thus, the example of Knaster and Kuratowski [47] mentioned above has a dispersion point. Show that no connected topological space can have more than one dispersion point (see Kline [46]). Show also that there exists a topological space with no dispersion point which is not only connected but also cannot be written as the union of two nonempty, disjoint, connected subsets (see Miller [59]). For further information on this subject, the reader is referred to the article by Duda in [22].

4.2 Compact and Countably Compact Spaces

A **covering** of a set E is a collection of sets $\{A_\lambda\}$ such that $E \subseteq \bigcup_\lambda A_\lambda$. If all the sets of a covering are open sets, we say that we have an **open covering**. If some finite subcollection of a covering of a set E is also a covering of E, we say that the covering is **reducible to a finite subcovering**. Finally, a subset E of a topological space $(X, \mathcal{T})$ is **compact** iff every open covering of E is reducible to a finite subcovering of E. An older name for this property is **bicompact**.

The motivation for this concept is the famous **Heine-Borel Theorem**: A subset of the real line is compact iff it is closed and bounded. Unfortunately, the motivating theorem does not hold at all in general topological spaces. First of all, the entire concept of boundedness is missing since we have no notion of distance. Secondly, a compact subset need not be closed, as the example of any proper subset of an indiscrete space shows. Despite these problems, the concept of compactness is of fundamental importance in topology. Some of the properties which compact sets do possess are given in the following theorems.

Theorem 4.2.1. *If E is a subset of a subspace $(X^*, \mathscr{T}^*)$ of a topological space $(X, \mathscr{T})$, then E is $\mathscr{T}^*$-compact iff it is $\mathscr{T}$-compact.*

Proof. Suppose E is $\mathscr{T}^*$-compact and $\{G_\lambda\}$ is some $\mathscr{T}$-open covering of E. The family of sets $\{X^* \cap G_\lambda\}$ clearly forms a $\mathscr{T}^*$-open covering for E since $E = X^* \cap E \subseteq X^* \cap (\bigcup_\lambda G_\lambda) = \bigcup_\lambda (X^* \cap G_\lambda)$. Since E is $\mathscr{T}^*$-compact, there is a finite subcovering $E \subseteq \bigcup_{i=1}^n (X^* \cap G_i) \subseteq \bigcup_{i=1}^n G_i$ of E which yields a finite subcovering of E from $\{G_\lambda\}$.

Now suppose that E is $\mathscr{T}$-compact and $\{G_\lambda{}^*\}$ is some $\mathscr{T}^*$-open covering of E. From the definition of the induced topology, each $G_\lambda{}^* = X^* \cap G_\lambda$ for some $\mathscr{T}$-open set G_λ. The family $\{G_\lambda\}$ is clearly a $\mathscr{T}$-open covering of E, and so there must be some finite subcovering $E \subseteq \bigcup_{i=1}^n G_i$. But then we have $E = X^* \cap E \subseteq X^* \cap (\bigcup_{i=1}^n G_i) = \bigcup_{i=1}^n (X^* \cap G_i) = \bigcup_{i=1}^n G_i{}^*$, and so a finite subcovering of E from $\{G_\lambda{}^*\}$. ∎

The above theorem shows that compactness, like connectedness, is an absolute property of sets. For our next theorem, a sort of "dual" to the definition of compactness, we shall need the set-theoretic notion dual to that of having a finite cover. A family of sets will be said to have the **finite intersection property** iff every finite subfamily of the family has a nonempty intersection.

Theorem 4.2.2. *A topological space $(X, \mathscr{T})$ is compact iff any family of closed sets having the finite intersection property has a nonempty intersection.*

Proof. Let us suppose that $(X, \mathscr{T})$ is compact and $\{F_\lambda\}$ is a family of closed sets whose intersection is empty. Since $\bigcap_\lambda F_\lambda = \emptyset$, we may take the complement of each side of the equation and, using DeMorgan's Law, obtain $X = \mathbf{C}\emptyset = \mathbf{C}(\bigcap_\lambda F_\lambda) = \bigcup_\lambda \mathbf{C}F_\lambda$. Thus the family $\{\mathbf{C}F_\lambda\}$ is an open covering of the compact space X, and so there must exist some finite subcovering. But if $X = \bigcup_{i=1}^{n} \complement F_i$, then $\varnothing = \complement X = \complement(\bigcup_{i=1}^{n} \complement F_i) = \bigcap_{i=1}^{n} F_i$, so that the family $\{F_\lambda\}$ cannot have the finite intersection property.

Now suppose $(X, \mathscr{T})$ is not compact. From the definition this means that there must be some open covering $\{G_\lambda\}$ of X which has no finite subcovering. To say that there is no finite subcovering means that the complement of the union of any finite number of members of the cover is nonempty. By DeMorgan's Law, the family $\{\complement G_\lambda\}$ is then a family of closed sets with the finite intersection property. Since $\{G_\lambda\}$ is a covering of X, however, $\bigcap_\lambda \complement G_\lambda = \varnothing$ since $\varnothing = \complement X = \complement(\bigcup_\lambda G_\lambda) = \bigcap_\lambda \complement G_\lambda$. Thus this family of closed sets with the finite intersection property has an empty intersection. ▮

Theorem 4.2.3. *Every closed subset of a compact space is compact.*

Proof. If $\mathscr{G}$ is an open covering of a closed subset E of a compact space $(X, \mathscr{T})$, then $\mathscr{G}^* = \mathscr{G} \cup \{\complement E\}$ is an open covering of X. If we remove $\complement E$ from the finite subcovering of X, we will have a finite subcovering of E chosen from $\mathscr{G}$, as desired. ▮

A subset E of a topological space will be called **countably compact** iff every infinite subset of E has at least one limit point in E. At one time the name "compact" was given to this property, but that designation has gone out of style. The motivation for this concept is the famous **Bolzano-Weierstrass Theorem**, which we will rephrase with its converse as follows: A subset of the real line is compact iff it is countably compact. The following theorem shows that at least part of the Bolzano-Weierstrass Theorem holds for general topological spaces.

Theorem 4.2.4. *A compact subset of a topological space is countably compact.*

Proof. By **4.2.1**, we may assume that the topological space X is compact and show that every infinite subset of X has a limit point (in X). Now suppose that E is a set with no limit points. We know that each point $x \in X$ is not a limit point of E, so there must exist an open set G_x containing x such that $E \cap G_x \setminus \{x\} = \varnothing$. Clearly $E \cap G_x$ contains, at most, the one point x itself. Since the family $\{G_x\}_{x \in X}$ forms an open covering of the compact space X, there must be some finite subcovering $X = \bigcup_{i=1}^{n} G_{x_i}$. From this it follows that $E = E \cap X = E \cap (\bigcup_{i=1}^{n} G_{x_i}) = \bigcup_{i=1}^{n} (E \cap G_{x_i})$ is a finite union of sets, each containing, at most, one element, and so E is finite. Thus every infinite subset of X must have at least one limit point. ▮

The example of the space of all ordinals less than the first uncountable ordinal, given the order topology, shows that a space may be countably compact but not compact. Conditions under which these two notions are equivalent will be given in the next two chapters. In particular, they will be shown to be equivalent in all metric spaces.

Just as the notion of connectedness was localized in the last section, we may localize the notion of compactness as follows. A topological space $(X, \mathscr{T})$ will be called **locally compact** iff each point of X is contained in a compact neighborhood. Since a compact space is a compact neighborhood of each of its points, it is clear that every compact space is locally compact. It is easy to verify that a closed subset of a locally compact space is itself a locally compact space.

A slightly different definition of local compactness is also in use today, requiring that each point of the space be contained in a neighborhood whose closure is compact. In the problems, we will consider both of these properties and their relationships. Conditions under which the two notions are equivalent will be given in the next chapter.

Exercises

1. If $(X, \mathscr{T})$ is a compact topological space and $\mathscr{T}^* \leqslant \mathscr{T}$, show that $(X, \mathscr{T}^*)$ is compact.

2. Is a closed interval of the real line compact if it is given the lower limit topology of problem **3** of Section **3.4**? Is it compact with the right-hand topology of problem **4** of Section **3.4**?

3. Prove that a linearly ordered set with the order topology is a compact space iff it has both a least and a greatest member, and it cannot be written as the union of two nonempty sets A and B such that each element of A is less than each element of B, while A has no greatest member and B has no least member.

4. Show that the space of all ordinals less than the first uncountable ordinal, given the order topology, is countably compact but not compact.

5. Let $X = \mathbf{N}$ the positive integers, and let a base for a topology be the family of all sets of the form $\{2n - 1, 2n\}$. Show that this family is a base for a topology. Show that, with this topology, X is countably compact but not compact.

6. A closed subset of a countably compact space is countably compact.

7. The **one point compactification** of a topological space $(X, \mathscr{T})$ is the set $X^* = X \cup \{\infty\}$, where ∞ is any object not a member of X, with the topology $\mathscr{T}^*$ whose members are the open sets in X and all subsets G of X^* such that $X^* \setminus G$ is a closed and compact subset of X. Prove that $(X^*, \mathscr{T}^*)$ is a compact topological space and that $(X, \mathscr{T})$ is a subspace of it.

8. A closed subset of a locally compact space is locally compact.

9. Show that the space of problem **4** is locally compact. Consider the local compactness of the spaces in problem **2**.

10. Show that the following conditions are equivalent for any topological space $(X, \mathscr{T})$:

(i) Each point of X is contained in a neighborhood whose closure is compact.

(ii) There is a base for the topology consisting of sets with compact closures.

(iii) If $x \in G \in \mathscr{T}$, then there is an open set containing x and contained in G whose closure is compact.

Show further that each of these conditions implies local compactness, but, by giving an example, that the converse is not true.

4.3 Continuous Functions

A function $\mathfrak{f}$ mapping a topological space $(X, \mathscr{T})$ into a topological space $(X^*, \mathscr{T}^*)$ will be said to be **continuous at a point** $x \in X$ iff for every open set G^* containing $\mathfrak{f}(x)$ there is an open set G containing x such that $\mathfrak{f}(G) \subseteq G^*$. We say that $\mathfrak{f}$ is **continuous on a set** $E \subseteq X$ iff it is continuous at each point of E. It is easy to verify that this definition is just a rephrasing of the ordinary definition of continuity of a real-valued function of a real variable in terms of the open sets alone.

Theorem 4.3.1. *If* $\mathfrak{f} : X \to X^*$, *then the following conditions are each equivalent to the continuity of* $\mathfrak{f}$ *on* X:

(i) *The inverse of every open set in* X^* *is an open set in* X.

(ii) *The inverse of every closed set in* X^* *is a closed set in* X.

(iii) $\mathfrak{f}(\mathbf{c}(E)) \subseteq \mathbf{c}^*(\mathfrak{f}(E))$ for every $E \subseteq X$.

Proof. (i): Suppose that $\mathfrak{f}$ is continuous on X, and G^* is an open set in X^*. If x is any point of $\mathfrak{f}^{-1}(G^*)$, then $\mathfrak{f}$ is continuous at x, and there must exist an open set G containing x such that $\mathfrak{f}(G) \subseteq G^*$. Thus G is contained in $\mathfrak{f}^{-1}(G^*)$, and hence $\mathfrak{f}^{-1}(G^*)$ is an open set in X. Conversely, if the inverses of open sets are open, we may choose the set $\mathfrak{f}^{-1}(G^*)$ as the open set G required in the above definition.

(ii): This part follows immediately from part (i) since $\mathfrak{f}^{-1}(X^* \setminus E^*) = X \setminus \mathfrak{f}^{-1}(E^*)$ for any set $E^* \subseteq X^*$.

(iii): Suppose that $\mathfrak{f}$ is continuous on X, and E is a subset of X. Since $E \subseteq \mathfrak{f}^{-1}(\mathfrak{f}(E))$ for any function, $E \subseteq \mathfrak{f}^{-1}(\mathbf{c}^*(\mathfrak{f}(E)))$. But $\mathfrak{f}^{-1}(\mathbf{c}^*(\mathfrak{f}(E)))$ is the inverse under a continuous mapping of a closed set and hence is a closed set containing E. Therefore, $\mathbf{c}(E) \subseteq \mathfrak{f}^{-1}(\mathbf{c}^*(\mathfrak{f}(E)))$ and so $\mathfrak{f}(\mathbf{c}(E)) \subseteq \mathfrak{f}(\mathfrak{f}^{-1}(\mathbf{c}^*(\mathfrak{f}(E)))) \subseteq \mathbf{c}^*(\mathfrak{f}(E))$. Conversely, suppose the condition holds for all subsets $E \subseteq X$, and F^* is a closed subset of X^*. We may apply the condition with $E = \mathfrak{f}^{-1}(F^*)$ to obtain $\mathfrak{f}(\mathbf{c}(\mathfrak{f}^{-1}(F^*))) \subseteq \mathbf{c}^*(\mathfrak{f}(\mathfrak{f}^{-1}(F^*))) \subseteq \mathbf{c}^*(F^*) = F^*$. Thus $\mathbf{c}(\mathfrak{f}^{-1}(F^*)) \subseteq \mathfrak{f}^{-1}(F^*)$, and so the inverse of every closed set is a closed set. ∎

The **Darboux Theorem** of analysis states that a continuous function defined on an interval takes on all values between any two of its values. Since the intervals are the connected sets of real numbers, this may be rephrased to say that a continuous function takes connected sets of real numbers into connected sets of real numbers. In the following theorem we shall see that none of the special properties of the real numbers is necessary to prove that result.

Theorem 4.3.2. *If* $\mathfrak{f}$ *is a continuous mapping of* $(X, \mathscr{T})$ *into* $(X^*, \mathscr{T}^*)$, *then* $\mathfrak{f}$ *maps every connected subset of* X *onto a connected subset of* X^*.

Proof. Let E be a subset of X, and suppose that $E^* = \mathfrak{f}(E)$ is not connected. There must exist some separation $E^* = A^* \mid B^*$, where A^* and B^* are nonempty, disjoint sets which are both open (and hence both closed) subsets of E^*. Clearly, $A = \mathfrak{f}^{-1}(A^*) \cap E$ and $B = \mathfrak{f}^{-1}(B^*) \cap E$ are nonempty, disjoint sets which are both open (and hence both closed) subsets of E. Thus E must have the separation $E = A \mid B$, and so is not connected. ∎

An analogous theorem holds for compact sets.

Theorem 4.3.3. *If* $\mathfrak{f}$ *is a continuous mapping of* $(X, \mathscr{T})$ *into* $(X^*, \mathscr{T}^*)$, *then* $\mathfrak{f}$ *maps every compact subset of* X *onto a compact subset of* X^*.

Proof. Suppose E is a compact subset of X, and $\{G_\lambda^*\}$ is an open covering of $\mathfrak{f}(E)$. Since $E \subseteq \mathfrak{f}^{-1}(\mathfrak{f}(E)) \subseteq \mathfrak{f}^{-1}(\bigcup_\lambda G_\lambda^*) = \bigcup_\lambda \mathfrak{f}^{-1}(G_\lambda^*)$, the family $\{\mathfrak{f}^{-1}(G_\lambda^*)\}$ is an open covering of E by **4.3.1**. Since E is compact, there must be some finite subcovering of E, say $E \subseteq \bigcup_{i=1}^n \mathfrak{f}^{-1}(G_i^*)$. But then $\mathfrak{f}(E) \subseteq \mathfrak{f}(\bigcup_{i=1}^n \mathfrak{f}^{-1}(G_i^*)) = \bigcup_{i=1}^n \mathfrak{f}(\mathfrak{f}^{-1}(G_i^*)) \subseteq \bigcup_{i=1}^n G_i^*$, and we have a finite subcover for $\mathfrak{f}(E)$. ∎

The other properties of sets introduced in this chapter are not necessarily preserved by continuous transformations. For example, any nonlocally compact space $(X, \mathscr{T})$ is the continuous (one-to-one) image of the locally compact space consisting of the set X with the discrete topology, under the mapping which takes each point of X into itself. Another example is the countably compact space of problem **5** of

Section **4.2**, which may be mapped onto the noncountably compact space consisting of the positive integers with the discrete topology by the continuous function which takes the points $2n$ and $2n - 1$ into the point n for each integer n.

Although very few properties of sets are preserved by continuous transformations, many of the important properties are preserved if we put additional restrictions on the function. The following is an example of a property that is preserved if we merely add the restriction of one-to-oneness. We say that a subset E of a topological space is **dense-in-itself** iff every point of E is a limit point of E; that is, if $E \subseteq \mathbf{d}(E)$.

Theorem 4.3.4. *If $\mathfrak{f}$ is a one-to-one continuous mapping of $(X, \mathscr{T})$ into $(X^*, \mathscr{T}^*)$, then $\mathfrak{f}$ maps every dense-in-itself subset of X onto a dense-in-itself subset of X^*.*

Proof. Suppose E is a dense-in-itself subset of X. We must show that $\mathfrak{f}(E) \subseteq \mathbf{d}^*(\mathfrak{f}(E))$. If we let $x^* \in \mathfrak{f}(E)$, we must show that $x^* \in \mathbf{d}^*(\mathfrak{f}(E))$. Finally, if G^* is any open set containing x^*, we must show that $\mathfrak{f}(E) \cap G^* \setminus \{x^*\} \neq \varnothing$. Now since $x^* \in \mathfrak{f}(E)$, there must exist some point $x \in E$ such that $\mathfrak{f}(x) = x^*$. Thus $x \in \mathfrak{f}^{-1}(\{x^*\}) \subseteq \mathfrak{f}^{-1}(G^*)$ which is an open set since $\mathfrak{f}$ is continuous. But E is dense-in-itself, so $x \in E \subseteq \mathbf{d}(E)$. Thus x is a limit point of the set E which is contained in the open set $\mathfrak{f}^{-1}(G^*)$, and so, by the definition of limit point, $E \cap \mathfrak{f}^{-1}(G^*) \setminus \{x\} \neq \varnothing$. Since this set is nonempty, let us choose a point $z \in E \cap \mathfrak{f}^{-1}(G^*) \setminus \{x\}$. Since z is in this intersection, it is in each part. Thus, $z \in E$, and so $\mathfrak{f}(z) \in \mathfrak{f}(E)$, while $z \in \mathfrak{f}^{-1}(G^*)$, and so $\mathfrak{f}(z) \in \mathfrak{f}(\mathfrak{f}^{-1}(G^*)) \subseteq G^*$. Finally, $z \neq x$, and so $\mathfrak{f}(z) \neq \mathfrak{f}(x) = x^*$ since $\mathfrak{f}$ is one-to-one. This shows that $\mathfrak{f}(z) \in \mathfrak{f}(E) \cap G^* \setminus \{x^*\}$, and so $\mathfrak{f}(E) \cap G^* \setminus \{x^*\} \neq \varnothing$, as desired. ∎

The property of being dense-in-itself is interesting in its own right. It is easy to show that if D is a dense-in-itself set, $\mathbf{c}(D)$ is dense-in-itself, and any set E such that $D \subseteq E \subseteq \mathbf{d}(D)$ is also dense-in-itself. Furthermore, the union of any family of dense-in-itself sets is dense-in-itself. The **nucleus** of a set E is defined to be the union of all dense-in-itself subsets of E and is clearly the largest such subset. A set whose nucleus is empty is called **scattered**. A set which is both closed and dense-in-itself (so that $E = \mathbf{d}(E)$) is called **perfect**. Many additional properties of such sets may be found in the literature (see, e.g., [25]).

Exercises

1. Show that the definition of continuity for real-valued functions of a real variable agrees with our definition for topological spaces.

2. If $\mathfrak{f} : X \to X^*$, then the following condition is equivalent to the continuity of $\mathfrak{f}$ on X:

(iv) $\mathfrak{f}^{-1}(\mathbf{i}^*(E^*)) \subseteq \mathbf{i}(\mathfrak{f}^{-1}(E^*))$ for every $E^* \subseteq X^*$.

3. Show that the identity map $\mathfrak{i}_X$ of $(X, \mathscr{T})$ into $(X, \mathscr{T}^*)$, defined by setting $\mathfrak{i}_X(x) = x$ for every $x \in X$, is continuous on X iff $\mathscr{T}^* \leqslant \mathscr{T}$.

4. Give examples to show that the properties of being nonconnected and noncompact are not necessarily preserved by continuous transformations.

5. Show, by giving an example, that the converse of **4.3.2** is not valid. We shall call a function **connected** if it maps connected sets onto connected sets. Consider properties of connected mappings (see [68]).

6. Verify the statements made in the examples following **4.3.3**.

7. Give an example of a continuous function which maps a dense-in-itself set onto a nondense-in-itself set.

8. Verify the statements made about dense-in-itself subsets following **4.3.4**.

9. If $\mathfrak{f}$ is a mapping of the set X into the set X^*, and E is a subset of X, then the **restriction** of $\mathfrak{f}$ to E, denoted by $\mathfrak{f} \mid E$, is the mapping of E into X^* defined by setting $(\mathfrak{f} \mid E)(x) = \mathfrak{f}(x)$ for all $x \in E$. Prove that if $\mathfrak{f}$ is continuous on X, then $\mathfrak{f} \mid E$ is continuous on E.

10. As a special case of the above, if X^* is a subspace of X, the **inclusion mapping** is the restriction of the identity mapping to X^*. Prove that it is continuous.

11. If $\mathfrak{f} : X \to X^*$ and $\mathfrak{g} : X^* \to X^{**}$, then the **composition** of $\mathfrak{f}$ and $\mathfrak{g}$, denoted by $\mathfrak{g} \circ \mathfrak{f}$, is the mapping of X into X^{**} defined by setting $(\mathfrak{g} \circ \mathfrak{f})(x) = \mathfrak{g}(\mathfrak{f}(x))$ for all $x \in X$. Show that this definition agrees with the definition of composition of relations. Prove that if $\mathfrak{f}$ and $\mathfrak{g}$ are continuous, then $\mathfrak{g} \circ \mathfrak{f}$ is continuous.

12. The **characteristic function** of a subset E of a space X is the real-valued mapping $\mathfrak{f}$ of X defined by setting $\mathfrak{f}(x) = 1$ if $x \in E$, but $\mathfrak{f}(x) = 0$ if $x \notin E$. Prove that the characteristic function of a set E is continuous iff E is both open and closed. Note that the characteristic function of E is discontinuous on the boundary of E.

13. Show that a topological space $(X, \mathscr{T})$ is connected iff every continuous mapping of X into a discrete space is a constant (that is, $\mathfrak{f}(X)$ is a single point).

14. We shall say that $\mathfrak{f} : X \to X^*$ is **strongly continuous** iff $\mathfrak{f}(\mathbf{c}(E)) \subseteq \mathfrak{f}(E)$ for all $E \subseteq X$. Show that $\mathfrak{f}$ is strongly continuous iff the inverse of every subset of X^* is both open and closed. (See Levine [53].)

15. We shall call a topological space $(X, \mathscr{T})$ **pseudocompact** iff every real-valued continuous mapping $\mathfrak{f}$ of X is bounded; that is, the set $\mathfrak{f}(X)$ is a bounded set of real numbers. Show that every compact topological space is pseudocompact and give an example to show that the converse is not true.

16. Suppose the topological space $(X, \mathscr{T})$ is the union of the two closed subsets A and B, and $\mathfrak{f} : A \to X^*$ and $\mathfrak{g} : B \to X^*$ are continuous mappings into a topological space $(X^*, \mathscr{T}^*)$ such that $\mathfrak{f}(x) = \mathfrak{g}(x)$ for all $x \in A \cap B$. Show that the mapping $\mathfrak{h} : X \to X^*$, defined by setting $\mathfrak{h}(x) = \mathfrak{f}(x)$ for $x \in A$ and $\mathfrak{h}(x) = \mathfrak{g}(x)$ for $x \in B$, is continuous.

17. A real-valued mapping $\mathfrak{f}$ of a topological space $(X, \mathscr{T})$ is **upper-semicontinuous** (resp. **lower-semicontinuous**) iff the set $\{x : \mathfrak{f}(x) < a\} = \mathfrak{f}^{-1}((-\infty, a))$ (resp. $\{x : \mathfrak{f}(x) > a\} = \mathfrak{f}^{-1}((a, +\infty))$) is an open subset of X for each real number a.

(i) $\mathfrak{f}$ is upper-semicontinuous (lower-semicontinuous) iff it is continuous with respect to the left-(right-) hand topology for the reals (see problem **4** in Section **3.4**).

(ii) $\mathfrak{f}$ is continuous iff it is both upper-semicontinuous and lower-semicontinuous.

(iii) The characteristic function of a set E is upper-semicontinuous (lower-semicontinuous) iff E is closed (open).

(iv) Let $\mathfrak{f}$ be the real-valued function of a real variable defined as follows: $\mathfrak{f}(x) = 0$ for x irrational or zero; $\mathfrak{f}(p/q) = 1/q$ for each nonzero rational number p/q, written in lowest terms with $q > 0$. Show that $\mathfrak{f}$ is upper-semicontinuous but not lower-semicontinuous.

(v) If $\{\mathfrak{f}_\lambda\}$ is a collection of upper-semicontinuous mappings, then the function $\mathfrak{f}$ defined by setting $\mathfrak{f}(x) = \inf\{\mathfrak{f}_\lambda(x)\}$ (where we allow infinite values) is also upper-semicontinuous.

(vi) If $\mathfrak{f}$ is upper-semicontinuous on the compact space X, then $\mathfrak{f}$ takes on its maximum value on X; that is, there is a point $x_0 \in X$ such that $\mathfrak{f}(x_0) \geqslant \mathfrak{f}(x)$ for all $x \in X$.

(vii) Suppose X can be written as the union of the family $\{E_n\}_{n \in \mathbf{N}}$ of disjoint sets, and $\mathfrak{f}(E_{n+1}) = a_{n+1} > a_n$ for all $n \in \mathbf{N}$. Find necessary and sufficient conditions for the sets E_n such that $\mathfrak{f}$ will be upper-semicontinuous.

4.4 Homeomorphisms

Although the properties of connectedness and compactness are preserved by continuous transformations, the more basic properties of openness and closedness are not always preserved. For example, the identity mapping of $(X, \mathscr{T})$ onto $(X, \mathscr{T}^*)$ maps open sets onto open sets (and closed sets onto closed sets) iff $\mathscr{T}^* \geqslant \mathscr{T}$. We shall call a mapping **open** iff the image of every open set is an open set. Such mappings are also called **interior**. A mapping is **closed** iff the image of every closed set is a closed set.

Since there is no general containing relation between $\mathfrak{f}(\complement E)$ and $\complement\mathfrak{f}(E)$, we find that an open (closed) mapping need not be closed (open), even if continuous. For example, let $(X, \mathscr{T})$ be any topological space and let $(X^*, \mathscr{T}^*)$ be the space for which $X^* = \{a, b, c\}$ and $\mathscr{T}^* = \{\varnothing, \{a\}, \{a, c\}, X^*\}$. The transformation which takes each point of X into the point a is a continuous open map which is not closed. The transformation which takes each point of X into b is a continuous closed map which is not open.

Theorem 4.4.1. *A mapping* $\mathfrak{f}$ *of* X *into* X^* *is open iff* $\mathfrak{f}(\mathbf{i}(E)) \subseteq \mathbf{i}^*(\mathfrak{f}(E))$ *for every* $E \subseteq X$.

Proof. Suppose $\mathfrak{f}$ is open and $E \subseteq X$. Since $\mathbf{i}(E)$ is an open set and $\mathfrak{f}$ is an open function, $\mathfrak{f}(\mathbf{i}(E))$ is an open set in X^*. Since $\mathbf{i}(E) \subseteq E$, $\mathfrak{f}(\mathbf{i}(E)) \subseteq \mathfrak{f}(E)$. Thus $\mathfrak{f}(\mathbf{i}(E))$ is an open set contained in $\mathfrak{f}(E)$, and hence $\mathfrak{f}(\mathbf{i}(E)) \subseteq \mathbf{i}^*(\mathfrak{f}(E))$. Conversely, if G is an open set in X and $\mathfrak{f}(\mathbf{i}(E)) \subseteq \mathbf{i}^*(\mathfrak{f}(E))$ for all $E \subseteq X$, then $\mathfrak{f}(G) = \mathfrak{f}(\mathbf{i}(G)) \subseteq \mathbf{i}^*(\mathfrak{f}(G))$, and so $\mathfrak{f}(G)$ is an open set in X^*. ▮

There are a few results concerning continuous, open, and closed mappings which follow immediately from the definitions. We may suppose that $\mathfrak{f}$ is a given function mapping a set X into a set X^*, and consider the result of putting different topologies on the sets X and X^*. It is obvious that if $\mathfrak{f}$ is continuous with a certain choice of topologies for X and X^*, it would remain continuous with any larger topology for X or any smaller topology for X^*. On the other hand, if $\mathfrak{f}$ is open or closed with a certain choice of topologies for X and X^*, it would remain open or closed with any smaller topology for X or any larger topology for X^*.

If we fix the topology for X, it seems natural to inquire about the largest topology for X^* for which $\mathfrak{f}$ is continuous and the smallest topology for X^* for which $\mathfrak{f}$ is open or closed. If the topology for X^* is fixed, we might inquire about the smallest topology for X for which $\mathfrak{f}$ is continuous and the largest topology for X for which $\mathfrak{f}$ is open or closed. The student should find it fairly easy to describe the various topologies which satisfy the above conditions, where they exist. We shall return to these questions again in Sections **8.4** and **9.3**.

There are important relationships between open mappings and analytic functions of a complex variable. For example, every nonconstant analytic function is an open mapping. Open mappings have many of the properties of analytic functions. For a detailed investigation of this topic, the student should consult the treatise of G. T. Whyburn [27].

A mapping $\mathfrak{f}$ of X into X^* is a **homeomorphism** iff $\mathfrak{f}$ is one-to-one, onto, continuous, and open. Two topological spaces are **homeomorphic** iff there exists a homeomorphism of one space onto the other. This clearly sets up an equivalence relation between topological spaces, while the homeomorphism sets up a one-to-one correspondence between both the points and the open sets of the two spaces. A property of sets which is preserved by homeomorphisms is called a **topological property**.

We now have a number of examples of topological properties of sets. For example, the properties of a set being open, closed, connected, compact, or dense-in-itself are topological properties. Other properties will be considered in the exercises. We shall here consider the following property: A subset E of a topological space is **isolated** iff no point of E is a limit point of E; that is, if $E \cap \mathbf{d}(E) = \emptyset$.

Theorem 4.4.2. *If $\mathfrak{f}$ is a homeomorphism of X onto X^*, then $\mathfrak{f}$ maps every isolated subset of X onto an isolated subset of X^*.*

Proof. Suppose E is an isolated subset of X, and let $x^* \in \mathfrak{f}(E)$. There must then exist a point $x \in E$ such that $\mathfrak{f}(x) = x^*$. Since E is isolated, $x \notin \mathbf{d}(E)$, and so there must exist an open set G containing x such that $E \cap G \setminus \{x\} = \emptyset$. But $\mathfrak{f}$ is a homeomorphism, and so $\mathfrak{f}(G)$ is an open set in X^* which contains $\mathfrak{f}(x) = x^*$. From the fact that $\mathfrak{f}$ is one-to-one it follows that $\mathfrak{f}(E \cap G \setminus \{x\}) = \mathfrak{f}(E) \cap \mathfrak{f}(G) \setminus \{x^*\} = \emptyset$. Thus $x^* \notin \mathbf{d}(\mathfrak{f}(E))$, and $\mathfrak{f}(E)$ must be isolated. ∎

It should be noted that two topological spaces X and X^* may not be homeomorphic even if there is a one-to-one continuous mapping of X onto X^* and another one-to-one continuous mapping of X^* onto X. A simple example of such spaces has been given by Kuratowski [49]. Let X be the set of real numbers consisting of the open intervals of the form $(3n, 3n + 1)$ and the points $3n + 2$, where n is a nonnegative integer. Let $X^* = (X \setminus \{2\}) \cup \{1\}$; that is, X^* consists of exactly the same points as X except for the removal of the point 2 and the introduction of the point 1. It is clear that, with the induced topology, the spaces are not homeomorphic since no point of X corresponds to the point 1 in X^*. Nevertheless, the function $\mathfrak{f}$, defined by setting $\mathfrak{f}(x) = x$ for $x \neq 2$ and $\mathfrak{f}(2) = 1$, is a continuous one-to-one mapping of X onto X^*, while the function $\mathfrak{g}$, defined by setting $\mathfrak{g}(x) = x/2$ for $x \leqslant 1$, $\mathfrak{g}(x) = (x - 2)/2$ for $3 < x < 4$, and $\mathfrak{g}(x) = x - 3$ for $x \geqslant 5$, is a continuous one-to-one mapping of X^* onto X.

Exercises

1. Show that the identity mapping of $(X, \mathscr{T})$ onto $(X, \mathscr{T}^*)$ is open iff $\mathscr{T}^* \geqslant \mathscr{T}$.
2. Verify the statements made about the examples above **4.4.1**.
3. A mapping $\mathfrak{f}$ of X into X^* is closed iff $\mathfrak{f}(\mathbf{c}(E)) \supseteq \mathbf{c}^*(\mathfrak{f}(E))$ for every $E \subseteq X$.
4. Describe the topologies mentioned below **4.4.1**. Note that there is, in general, no largest topology for X making $\mathfrak{f}$ open.

5. If $\mathfrak{f}$ is a one-to-one mapping of X onto X^*, then $\mathfrak{f}$ is a homeomorphism iff $\mathfrak{f}(\mathbf{c}(E)) = \mathbf{c}^*(\mathfrak{f}(E))$ for every $E \subseteq X$.

6. If $\mathfrak{f}$ is a one-to-one mapping of X onto X^*, then $\mathfrak{f}$ is a homeomorphism iff $\mathfrak{f}(\mathbf{i}(E)) = \mathbf{i}^*(\mathfrak{f}(E))$ for every $E \subseteq X$.

7. Show that local compactness is a topological property.

8. Show that countable compactness is a topological property.

9. Show that scatteredness is a topological property.

4.5 Arcwise Connectivity

If E is a subset of a topological space X and we let $I = [0, 1]$, then a **path** in E joining two points x and y of E is a continuous mapping $\mathfrak{f}$ of I into E such that $\mathfrak{f}(0) = x$ and $\mathfrak{f}(1) = y$. The subset E is **arcwise connected** iff every two points in E may be joined by some path in E.

It is clear that the property of two points being joined by some path sets up an equivalence relation on the space, and so we may divide a topological space into equivalence classes which we will call the **arcwise connected components.** The relationship between these components and the connected components is made clear in the following theorem.

Theorem 4.5.1. *An arcwise connected space is connected, so that each arcwise connected component must be contained in a connected component, but a connected space need not be arcwise connected.*

Proof. Since I is connected, $\mathfrak{f}(I)$ is connected for any continuous mapping $\mathfrak{f}$. Thus any two points in an arcwise connected space belong to a connected subset $\mathfrak{f}(I)$ of the space, where $\mathfrak{f}$ is a path joining the two points. By Corollary 2 to **4.1.2**, any arcwise connected space must be connected. The example following **4.1.4** shows that a connected set need not be arcwise connected since **x** and **y** cannot be joined by a path in **E.** ▮

The property of a space being arcwise connected is a topological property. In fact, we may prove the following stronger result

Theorem 4.5.2. *If $\mathfrak{f}$ is a continuous mapping of X into X^*, then $\mathfrak{f}$ maps every arcwise connected subset of X onto an arcwise connected subset of X^*.*

Proof. Suppose E is an arcwise connected subset of X, and x^* and y^* are any two points of $\mathfrak{f}(E)$. There must exist points x and y in E such that $\mathfrak{f}(x) = x^*$ and $\mathfrak{f}(y) = y^*$. Since E is arcwise connected, there exists a path $\mathfrak{g}$ in E joining x and y; that is, a continuous mapping $\mathfrak{g}$ of I into E such that $\mathfrak{g}(0) = x$ and $\mathfrak{g}(1) = y$. By problem **11** of Section **4.3**, $\mathfrak{f} \circ \mathfrak{g}$ is a continuous mapping of I into $\mathfrak{f}(E)$ such that $(\mathfrak{f} \circ \mathfrak{g})(0) = x^*$ and $(\mathfrak{f} \circ \mathfrak{g})(1) = y^*$. Thus $\mathfrak{f} \circ \mathfrak{g}$ is a path in $\mathfrak{f}(E)$ joining x^* and y^*, and so $\mathfrak{f}(E)$ must be arcwise connected. ▮

Arcwise connectivity is particularly important in the study of functions of a complex variable. Although a region is defined to be an open, connected subset of the plane, most proofs use the arcwise connectivity of a region rather than its connectivity. That these two properties are equivalent for open subsets of the plane (and, indeed, for other Euclidean spaces) is shown in the following theorem.

Theorem 4.5.3. *An open connected subset of the plane is arcwise connected.*

Proof. Suppose $\mathbf{E}$ is an open connected subset of the plane, and $\mathbf{x}^*$ is a fixed point of $\mathbf{E}$. Let the set $\mathbf{A}$ be defined to be the set of all points of $\mathbf{E}$ which may be joined to $\mathbf{x}^*$ by a path in $\mathbf{E}$, and let $\mathbf{B}$ be the remaining points of $\mathbf{E}$. We may show that $\mathbf{A}$ is an open set as follows. Let $\mathbf{x}$ be a point of $\mathbf{A}$, and recall that $\mathbf{A}$ is a subset of the open set $\mathbf{E}$. Hence, there exists an open set $\mathbf{G}$ such that $\mathbf{x} \in \mathbf{G} \subseteq \mathbf{E}$, and we may pick the open set $\mathbf{G}$ to be a member of the basis of open disks. Since every point of $\mathbf{G}$ could then be connected to $\mathbf{x}$ by a straight line segment, every point of $\mathbf{G}$ can be joined to $\mathbf{x}$ by a path in $\mathbf{G}$. Since $\mathbf{x} \in \mathbf{A}$, there is a path joining $\mathbf{x}^*$ to $\mathbf{x}$, and so every point of $\mathbf{G}$ may be joined by a path to $\mathbf{x}^*$. Hence $\mathbf{G} \subseteq \mathbf{A}$, and $\mathbf{A}$ is open. By the same type of argument we may show that $\mathbf{B}$ must be open. Since $\mathbf{E}$ is connected and is the union of the two disjoint open sets $\mathbf{A}$ and $\mathbf{B}$, one of these sets must be empty. Since $\mathbf{x}^* \in \mathbf{A}$, $\mathbf{A} \neq \emptyset$, and so $\mathbf{B} = \emptyset$. Thus $\mathbf{E} = \mathbf{A}$, and every point of $\mathbf{E}$ may be joined to $\mathbf{x}^*$ by a path in $\mathbf{E}$. Thus, $\mathbf{E}$ is arcwise connected. ▮

Exercises

1. Show that the property of two points being joined by a path sets up an equivalence relation on a space.

2. If A is a connected component of X containing a point x, and B is an arcwise connected component of X containing x, what relationship is there between A and B?

3. If A and B are arcwise connected sets such that $A \cap B \neq \emptyset$, then $A \cup B$ is arcwise connected. Show also that this theorem cannot be proved with the weaker condition $A \cap c(B) \neq \emptyset$, even though this would be sufficient for connected sets.

CHAPTER **5**

Separation and Countability Axioms

5.1 T_0- and T_1-Spaces

The topological spaces we have been studying thus far have been generalizations of the real number system. We have obtained some interesting results, yet because of the degree of generalization many intuitive properties of the real numbers have been lost. We recall that all we required of our open sets was that they satisfy the two open set axioms **[0.1]** and **[0.2]**. We will now consider topological spaces which satisfy additional axioms that are motivated by elementary properties of the real numbers.

A topological space X is a $\boldsymbol{T_0}$**-space** iff it satisfies the following axiom of Kolomogorov:

[T$_0$] If x and y are two distinct points of X, then there exists an open set which contains one of them but not the other.

It is clear that every space homeomorphic to a T_0-space is a T_0-space. Another elementary result is that every subspace of a T_0-space is a T_0-space. In general, we call a property of a space **hereditary** iff every subspace of a space with the property must have the property. In the following theorem we will give a simple characterization of T_0-spaces.

Theorem 5.1.1. *A topological space X is a T_0-space iff the closures of distinct points are distinct.*

Proof. Suppose that $x \neq y$ implies that $\mathbf{c}(\{x\}) \neq \mathbf{c}(\{y\})$, and that x and y are distinct points of X. Since the sets $\mathbf{c}(\{x\})$ and $\mathbf{c}(\{y\})$ are not equal, there must exist some point z of X which is contained in one of them but not the other. Without loss of generality, let us suppose that $z \in \mathbf{c}(\{x\})$, but $z \notin \mathbf{c}(\{y\})$. If we had $x \in \mathbf{c}(\{y\})$, then we would have $\mathbf{c}(\{x\}) \subseteq \mathbf{c}(\mathbf{c}(\{y\})) = \mathbf{c}(\{y\})$, and so $z \in \mathbf{c}(\{x\}) \subseteq \mathbf{c}(\{y\})$, which is a contradiction. Hence, $x \notin \mathbf{c}(\{y\})$, and so $\mathbf{Cc}(\{y\})$ is an open set containing x but not y.

Conversely, let us suppose that X is a T_0-space, and that x and y are two distinct points of X. By **[T_0]**, there exists an open set G containing one of them but not the other. Without loss of generality, let us suppose that $x \in G$, but $y \notin G$. Clearly, $\complement G$ is a closed set containing y, but not x. From the definition of $\mathbf{c}(\{y\})$ as the intersection of all closed sets containing $\{y\}$, we see that $y \in \mathbf{c}(\{y\})$, but $x \notin \mathbf{c}(\{y\})$ because of $\complement G$. Hence, $\mathbf{c}(\{x\}) \neq \mathbf{c}(\{y\})$. ∎

A topological space X is a ***T_1*-space** iff it satisfies the following axiom of Fréchet:

[T_1] If x and y are two distinct points of X, then there exist two open sets, one containing x but not y, and the other containing y but not x.

The T_1 axiom is so important that some authors (e.g. Kuratowski [17], Sierpinski [20], and Pontrjagin [19]) use the term "topological space" only when it also is satisfied. It is clear that the property of being a T_1-space is both topological and hereditary. Although every T_1-space is obviously a T_0-space, the converse is not true. For example, the space of problem **4** of Section **3.1** is a T_0-space which is not a T_1-space. In the following theorem we will give a simple characterization of T_1-spaces.

Theorem 5.1.2. *A topological space X is a T_1-space iff every subset consisting of exactly one point is closed.*

Proof. If x and y are distinct points of a space X in which subsets consisting of exactly one point are closed, then $\complement\{x\}$ is an open set containing y but not x, while $\complement\{y\}$ is an open set containing x but not y. Thus X is a T_1-space.

Conversely, let us suppose that X is a T_1-space, and that x is a point of X. By **[T_1]**, if $y \neq x$, there exists an open set G_y containing y but not x; that is, $y \in G_y \subseteq \complement\{x\}$. But then $\complement\{x\} = \bigcup\{y : y \neq x\} \subseteq \bigcup\{G_y : y \neq x\} \subseteq \complement\{x\}$, and so $\complement\{x\}$ is the union of open sets, and hence is itself open. Thus $\{x\}$ is a closed set for every $x \in X$. ∎

From the above characterization of T_1-spaces we find that such spaces must have more of the properties one might expect from a generalization of the real number system. Thus, for example, no finite set can have a limit point, and every connected set containing more than one point must be infinite. These results follow directly from the following theorem.

Theorem 5.1.3. *In a T_1-space X, a point x is a limit point of a set E iff every open set containing x contains an infinite number of distinct points of E.*

Proof. The sufficiency of the condition is obvious. To prove the necessity, suppose there were an open set G containing x for which $G \cap E$ was finite. If we let $G \cap E \setminus \{x\} = \bigcup_{i=1}^{n} \{x_i\}$, then each set $\{x_i\}$ would be closed by the above theorem, and the finite union $\bigcup_{i=1}^{n} \{x_i\}$ would also be a closed set. But then $\complement(\bigcup_{i=1}^{n} \{x_i\}) \cap G$ would be an open set containing x with $[\complement(\bigcup_{i=1}^{n} \{x_i\}) \cap G] \cap E \setminus \{x\} = \complement(\bigcup_{i=1}^{n} \{x_i\}) \cap (\bigcup_{i=1}^{n} \{x_i\}) = \varnothing$. Thus x would not be a limit point of E. ▮

Countably compact spaces are more useful in T_1-spaces, since we may then characterize them in a way that is exactly analogous to that for compact spaces. The following theorem, in fact, explains why we chose the name "countably compact."

Theorem 5.1.4. *A T_1-space X is countably compact iff every countable open covering of X is reducible to a finite subcover.*

Proof. Suppose $\{G_n\}_{n \in \mathbf{N}}$ is a countable open covering of the countably compact space X which has no finite subcover. This means that $\bigcup_{i=1}^{n} G_i$ does not contain X for any $n \in \mathbf{N}$. If we let $F_n = \complement\bigcup_{i=1}^{n} G_i$, then each F_n is a nonempty closed set contained in the preceding one. From each F_n let us choose a point x_n, and let $E = \bigcup_{n \in \mathbf{N}} \{x_n\}$. The set E cannot be finite because there would then be some point in an infinite number, and hence all of the sets F_n, and this would contradict the fact that the family $\{G_n\}_{n \in \mathbf{N}}$ is a covering of X. Since E must be infinite, we may use the countable compactness of X to obtain a limit point x of E. By the above theorem, every open set containing x contains an infinite number of points of E, and so x must be a limit point of each of the sets $E_n = \bigcup_{i>n} \{x_i\}$. For each n, however, E_n is contained in the closed set F_n, and so x must belong to F_n for every $n \in \mathbf{N}$. This again contradicts the fact that the family $\{G_n\}_{n \in \mathbf{N}}$ is a covering of X. Hence, the condition is necessary.

Now let us suppose that E is an infinite subset of X and that E has no limit points. Since E is infinite, we may choose an infinite sequence of distinct points x_n from E. The set $A = \bigcup_{n \in \mathbf{N}} \{x_n\}$ has no limit points since it is a subset of E, and so, in particular, each point x_n is not a limit point of A. This means that for every $n \in \mathbf{N}$ there exists an open set G_n containing x_n such that $A \cap G_n \setminus \{x_n\} = \varnothing$. From the definition of A we see that $A \cap G_n = \{x_n\}$ for every $n \in \mathbf{N}$. Since A has no limit points, it is a closed set, and hence $\complement A$ is open. The collection $\{\complement A\} \cup \{G_n\}_{n \in \mathbf{N}}$ is then a countable open covering of X which has no finite subcover, since the set G_n is needed to cover the point x_n for every $n \in \mathbf{N}$. Thus, the condition is sufficient. ▮

Since we did not use the $[\mathbf{T}_1]$ axiom in the second part of the above proof, the condition given is sufficient for countable compactness in any topological space. From this characterization of countable compactness we may easily obtain the following result analogous to **4.2.2**.

Corollary 1. *A T_1-space X is countably compact iff every countable family of closed sets having the finite intersection property has a nonempty intersection.*

The following theorem of Cantor also follows easily if we define a countable collection of sets $\{E_n\}$ to be **monotone decreasing** iff $E_n \supseteq E_{n+1}$ for all n.

Corollary 2. *In a T_1-space, the intersection of a monotone decreasing countable collection of nonempty, closed sets, at least one of which is countably compact, is nonempty.*

Although countable compactness is a topological property, we noted below **4.3.3** that it may not be preserved by continuous mappings. With the aid of the above characterization, we may show that it is preserved by continuous mappings of T_1-spaces.

Theorem 5.1.5. *If $\mathfrak{f}$ is a continuous mapping of the T_1-space X into the topological space X^*, then $\mathfrak{f}$ maps every countably compact subset of X onto a countably compact subset of X^*.*

Proof. Suppose E is a countably compact subset of X and $\{G_n{}^*\}$ is a countable open covering of $\mathfrak{f}(E)$. We need only show that there is a finite subcovering of $\mathfrak{f}(E)$, since we noted above that the condition of **5.1.4** is always sufficient. Since $\mathfrak{f}$ is continuous, $\{\mathfrak{f}^{-1}(G_n{}^*)\}$ is a countable open covering of E. In the induced topology, $\{E \cap \mathfrak{f}^{-1}(G_n{}^*)\}$ is a countable open covering of the countably compact T_1-space E. By **5.1.4**, there exists some finite subcovering $\{E \cap \mathfrak{f}^{-1}(G_{n_i}^*)\}_{i=1}^k$, and clearly the family $\{G_{n_i}^*\}_{i=1}^k$ is the desired finite subcovering of $\mathfrak{f}(E)$. ▮

Exercises

1. The property of a space being a T_0-space is preserved by one-to-one, onto, open maps, and hence is a topological property.

2. Every subspace of a T_0-space is a T_0-space, and hence the property is hereditary.

3. If $(X, \mathscr{T})$ is a T_0-space and $\mathscr{T}^* \geqslant \mathscr{T}$, then $(X, \mathscr{T}^*)$ is also a T_0-space.

4. A topological space X is a T_0-space iff whenever x and y are two distinct points of X, either $x \notin \mathbf{c}(\{y\})$ or $y \notin \mathbf{c}(\{x\})$.

5. A reflexive partial ordering $\leqslant$ may be defined on any topological space X by setting $x \leqslant y$ iff $x \in \mathbf{c}(\{y\})$. Show that this ordering is antisymmetric iff X is a T_0-space.

6. The property of a space being a T_1-space is preserved by one-to-one, onto, open maps, and hence is a topological property.

7. Every subspace of a T_1-space is a T_1-space, and hence the property is hereditary.

8. If $(X, \mathscr{T})$ is a T_1-space and $\mathscr{T}^* \geqslant \mathscr{T}$, then $(X, \mathscr{T}^*)$ is also a T_1-space.

9. A topological space X is a T_1-space iff each point of X is the intersection of all open sets containing it.

10. Show that the spaces of problems **4** and **5** of Section **3.1** are T_0-spaces which are not T_1-spaces.

11. Show that, in a T_1-space, no finite set has a limit point.

12. Show that, in a T_1-space, every connected set containing more than one point is infinite. (Note however that Urysohn [79] has given an example of a countable connected space which satisfies the stronger axiom **[T$_2$]** introduced in the next section.)

13. A T_1-space X is countably compact iff any countable family of closed sets having the finite intersection property has a nonempty intersection.

14. In a T_1-space, the intersection of a monotone decreasing sequence of nonempty, closed sets, at least one of which is countably compact, is nonempty.

15. For any set X, there exists a unique smallest topology $\mathscr{T}$ such that $(X, \mathscr{T})$ is a T_1-space.

16. Every finite T_1-space has the discrete topology.

17. A T_1-space is countably compact iff every infinite open covering has a proper subcover.

5.2 T_2-Spaces and Sequences

A topological space X is a ***T*$_2$-space** or **Hausdorff space** iff it satisfies the following axiom of Hausdorff:

[T$_2$] If x and y are two distinct points of X, then there exist two disjoint open sets, one containing x and the other containing y.

It is clear that the property of being a T_2-space is both topological and hereditary. Although every T_2-space is obviously a T_1-space, the converse is not true. For example, the space of problem **3** of Section **3.1** is a T_1-space which is not a T_2-space.

Compact sets are more useful in T_2-spaces since we may prove a part of the Heine-Borel Theorem which does not hold in general topological spaces. In fact, many authors define a compact space to be a Hausdorff space which satisfies our definition of compactness.

Theorem 5.2.1. *Every compact subset E of a Hausdorff space X is closed.*

Proof. Let x be a fixed point in $\complement E$. By $[\mathrm{T}_2]$, for each point $y \in E$, there exist two disjoint open sets G_x and G_y such that $x \in G_x$ and $y \in G_y$. The family of sets $\{G_y : y \in E\}$ is an open covering of E. Since E is compact, there must be some finite subcovering $\{G_{y_i}\}_{i=1}^n$. Let $\{G_{x_i}\}_{i=1}^n$ be the corresponding open sets containing x, and let $G = \bigcap_{i=1}^n G_{x_i}$. Then G is an open set containing x since it is the intersection of a finite number of open sets containing x. Furthermore, we see that $G = \bigcap_{i=1}^n G_{x_i} \subseteq \bigcap_{i=1}^n \complement G_{y_i} = \complement \bigcup_{i=1}^n G_{y_i} \subseteq \complement E$. Thus each point in $\complement E$ is contained in an open set which is itself contained in $\complement E$. Hence $\complement E$ is an open set, and so E must be closed. ▮

Corollary. *If $\mathfrak{f}$ is a one-to-one continuous mapping of the compact topological space X onto the T_2-space X^*, then $\mathfrak{f}$ is also open, and so $\mathfrak{f}$ is a homeomorphism.*

Proof. Let G be open in X, so that $X \setminus G$ is closed. By **4.2.3**, $X \setminus G$ is compact. By **4.3.3**, $\mathfrak{f}(X \setminus G)$ is compact. By the above theorem, $\mathfrak{f}(X \setminus G)$ is closed. Thus $X^* \setminus \mathfrak{f}(X \setminus G)$ is open. Since $\mathfrak{f}$ is one-to-one and onto, $X^* \setminus \mathfrak{f}(X \setminus G) = \mathfrak{f}(G)$ which is open. ▮

The following theorem of Aleksandrov concerning the one point compactification introduced in problem **7** of Section **4.2** may now be proved.

Theorem 5.2.2. *The one point compactification X^* of a topological space X is a Hausdorff space iff X is a locally compact Hausdorff space.*

Proof. Suppose X is a locally compact Hausdorff space, and x and y are distinct points of X^*. If neither x nor y is equal to the "ideal" point ∞, then they both belong to X, and there must be disjoint sets containing them which are open in X and so open in X^*, as desired. We must then consider the case where one of the points, say y, is ∞, while the other is in X. By the local compactness of X and problem **5**, there must be some open set G containing x such that $\mathbf{c}(G)$ is compact and hence also closed by our first theorem. Thus $X \setminus \mathbf{c}(G)$ is an open set in X whose complement is closed and compact in X. By the definition of the one point compactification, $\{\infty\} \cup (X \setminus \mathbf{c}(G))$ is an open set in X^* containing ∞ which is disjoint from G, an open set in X^* containing x.

Now let us suppose that X^* is a Hausdorff space. Since X is a subspace of X^*, X is a Hausdorff space by problem **2**. Let x be a fixed point of X. Since x and ∞ are distinct points of the Hausdorff space X^*, there must exist disjoint open sets $G_x{}^*$ and $G_\infty{}^*$ in X^* such that $x \in G_x{}^*$ and $\infty \in G_\infty{}^*$. However, an open set containing ∞ must be of the form $G_\infty{}^* = \{\infty\} \cup G$ where G is an open set in X whose complement (in X) is compact. Since $\infty \notin G_x{}^*$, $G_x{}^*$ is an open set in X containing x whose closure is contained in $X \setminus G$ and hence is compact. Thus X is locally compact. ▮

In a Hausdorff space there must be a large number of open sets, as shown by the following result.

Theorem 5.2.3. *An infinite Hausdorff space X contains an infinite sequence of nonempty, disjoint, open sets.*

Proof. If X has no limit points, then X must have the discrete topology, and any infinite sequence of distinct points of X would serve as the desired sequence. Suppose, then, that x is a limit point of X. Choose x_1 to be any point of X different from x. By $[\mathbf{T}_2]$, there exist two disjoint open sets G_1 and V_1 such that $x_1 \in G_1$ and $x \in V_1$. Since x is a limit point of X belonging to the open set V_1, there exists some point $x_2 \in X \cap V_1 \setminus \{x\}$. By $[\mathbf{T}_2]$, there exist two disjoint open sets $G_2{}^*$ and $V_2{}^*$ such that $x_2 \in G_2{}^*$ and $x \in V_2{}^*$. If we let $G_2 = G_2{}^* \cap V_1$ and $V_2 = V_2{}^* \cap V_1$, then G_2 and V_2 are two disjoint open sets contained in V_1 (and hence disjoint from G_1) containing x_2 and x, respectively.

We will now proceed by using an inductive argument. Suppose we have already defined the points $\{x_k\}$ and the open sets $\{G_k\}$ and $\{V_k\}$ with the properties that $x_k \in G_k \subseteq V_{k-1}$, $x \in V_k \subseteq V_{k-1}$, and $G_k \cap V_k = \varnothing$ for all $k \leqslant n$. Now x is a limit point of X belonging to the open set V_n, and so there exists some point $x_{n+1} \in X \cap V_n \setminus \{x\}$. By $[\mathbf{T}_2]$, there exist two disjoint open sets G_{n+1}^* and V_{n+1}^* such that $x_{n+1} \in G_{n+1}^*$ and $x \in V_{n+1}^*$. If we let $G_{n+1} = G_{n+1}^* \cap V_n$ and $V_{n+1} = V_{n+1}^* \cap V_n$, then G_{n+1} and V_{n+1} are two disjoint open sets contained in V_n (and hence disjoint from G_n) containing x_{n+1} and x, respectively. Since the sets $\{V_n\}$ are monotone decreasing, we see that G_{n+1} is not only disjoint from G_n but is also disjoint from every G_k for $k \leqslant n$. Since $x_n \in G_n$, the infinite sequence $\langle G_n \rangle$, defined by induction, is the desired sequence of nonempty, disjoint, open sets. ▮

Since the notion of a convergent sequence of real numbers plays such a basic role in the study of the real number system, we might expect that the equivalent notion for topological spaces would be as primitive a concept as the closure. Although convergence has been used as the primitive notion for abstract spaces, we will see below that some of the natural properties fail to hold in more general spaces than Hausdorff spaces.

If x is a point and $\langle x_n \rangle$ a sequence of points in a topological space X, then the sequence has **limit** x or **converges** to x, written $\lim x_n = x$ or $x_n \to x$, iff for every open set G containing x there exists an integer $N(G)$ such that $x_n \in G$ whenever $n > N(G)$. If we rephrase the ordinary definition for limits of sequences of real numbers in terms of open sets alone, it is clear that we obtain the above definition for topological spaces. A sequence will be called **convergent** iff there is at least one point to which it converges.

It is obvious from the definition that every subsequence of a convergent sequence is also convergent and has the same limits. The convergence of a sequence and its limits are not affected by a finite number of alterations in the sequence, including the adding or removing of a finite number of terms of the sequence. Another trivial result is that a sequence $\langle x_n \rangle$ for which $x_n = x$ for all n converges to x. These three simple properties have been used to define limit spaces (see Kuratowski [17, pp. 83 ff] for a discussion of $\mathscr{L}^*$ spaces).

It is the failure of limits of sequences to be unique that makes this concept unsatisfactory in general topological spaces. An example of a T_1-space in which limits of sequences need not be unique was given in problem **5** of Section **3.1**. In particular, the sequence $\langle x_n \rangle$ for which $x_n = n$ for all n converges to every point of that space. The following result shows that this anomalous behavior cannot occur in a Hausdorff space.

Theorem 5.2.4. *In a Hausdorff space, a convergent sequence has a unique limit.*

Proof. Suppose a sequence $\langle x_n \rangle$ converged to two distinct points x and x^* in a Hausdorff space X. By **[T₂]**, there exist two disjoint open sets G and G^* such that $x \in G$ and $x^* \in G^*$. Since $x_n \to x$, there exists an integer N such that $x_n \in G$ whenever $n > N$. Since $x_n \to x^*$, there exists an integer N^* such that $x_n \in G^*$ whenever $n > N^*$. If m is any integer greater than both N and N^*, then x_m must be in both G and G^*, which contradicts the fact that G and G^* are disjoint. ▮

The converse of this theorem is not true. An example of a non-Hausdorff space in which every convergent sequence has a unique limit was given in problem **3** of Section **3.1**. A relationship between the limit points of sets and the limit points of sequences of points is given in the following theorem.

Theorem 5.2.5. *If $\langle x_n \rangle$ is a sequence of distinct points of a subset E of a topological space X which converges to a point $x \in X$, then x is a limit point of the set E.*

Proof. If x belongs to an open set G, then there exists an integer $N(G)$ such that $x_n \in G$ for all $n > N(G)$. Since the points x_n are distinct, at most one of them equals x, and so $E \cap G \setminus \{x\} \neq \emptyset$. ∎

The converse of this theorem is not true, even in a Hausdorff space. Let X be the set of all ordinal numbers less than or equal to the first uncountable ordinal Ω with the order topology. Although Ω is obviously a limit point of its complement, no (countable) sequence of distinct ordinals can converge to Ω by **2.4.6**. A relationship between continuity of functions and convergent sequences of points is given in the following theorem.

Theorem 5.2.6. *If $\mathfrak{f}$ is a continuous mapping of the topological space X into the topological space X^*, and $\langle x_n \rangle$ is a sequence of points of X which converges to the point $x \in X$, then the sequence $\langle \mathfrak{f}(x_n) \rangle$ converges to the point $\mathfrak{f}(x) \in X^*$.*

Proof. If $\mathfrak{f}(x)$ belongs to the open set G^* in X^*, then $\mathfrak{f}^{-1}(G^*)$ is an open set in X containing x, since $\mathfrak{f}$ is continuous. There must then exist an integer N such that $x_n \in \mathfrak{f}^{-1}(G^*)$ whenever $n > N$. Thus we have $\mathfrak{f}(x_n) \in G^*$ whenever $n > N$, and so $\mathfrak{f}(x_n) \to \mathfrak{f}(x)$. ∎

The converse of this theorem is also not true, even in a Hausdorff space. That is, a mapping $\mathfrak{f}$ for which $x_n \to x$ implies $\mathfrak{f}(x_n) \to \mathfrak{f}(x)$ may not be continuous. For example, let X be the Hausdorff space of ordinals described above. The real valued function $\mathfrak{f}$, defined by setting $\mathfrak{f}(\alpha) = 0$ if $\alpha < \Omega$ and $\mathfrak{f}(\Omega) = 1$, is not continuous at Ω, even though it does preserve convergent sequences.

The failure of the converses of the preceding three theorems to hold shows that the notion of limit for sequences of points is not completely satisfactory, even if the space satisfies the axiom $[\mathbf{T_2}]$. In the next section we will introduce another axiom for the open sets of a topological space with which we may prove these converses. Another way to obtain these results is to generalize the notion of a sequence. This leads to the idea of a **Moore-Smith sequence** or **net**. This method is used by Kelley [14, pp. 62 ff]. Still another approach is to consider the notion of a **filter**, which we shall do in Section **8.5**.

Exercises

1. The property of a space being a T_2-space is preserved by one-to-one, onto, open maps and hence is a topological property.

2. Every subspace of a T_2-space is a T_2-space, and hence the property is hereditary.

3. If $(X, \mathscr{T})$ is a T_2-space and $\mathscr{T}^* \geqslant \mathscr{T}$, then $(X, \mathscr{T}^*)$ is also a T_2-space.

4. Show that the space of problem **3** of Section **3.1** is a T_1-space which is not a T_2-space.

5. Show that the conditions of problem **10** of Section **4.2** are equivalent to local compactness for Hausdorff spaces.

6. If $(X, \mathscr{T}_1)$ is a Hausdorff space, $(X, \mathscr{T}_2)$ is compact, and $\mathscr{T}_1 \leqslant \mathscr{T}_2$, then $\mathscr{T}_1 = \mathscr{T}_2$.

7. If $(X, \mathscr{T})$ is a compact Hausdorff space, then X is not compact with any topology larger than and different from $\mathscr{T}$, and X is not a Hausdorff space with any topology smaller than and different from $\mathscr{T}$.

8. If $\mathfrak{f}$ and $\mathfrak{g}$ are continuous mappings of a topological space X into a Hausdorff space, then the set of points at which $\mathfrak{f}$ and $\mathfrak{g}$ are equal is a closed subset of X.

9. If $\mathfrak{f}$ is a continuous mapping of a Hausdorff space X into itself, show that the set of fixed points; i.e., $\{x : \mathfrak{f}(x) = x\}$, is closed.

10. In the space of problem **3** of Section **3.1**, what sequences converge to what points?

11. Let X be the set of all real numbers with the topology consisting of $\varnothing$ and all sets whose complements are countable. If E is the subset consisting of the irrationals, then every rational is a limit point of E, even though no rational is a limit point of a sequence of irrationals. Show also that the identity map of this space onto the reals with the usual topology is not continuous, even though it does preserve convergent sequences.

12. Let X be the set of all ordinal numbers less than or equal to the first uncountable ordinal Ω. Show that Ω is a limit point of its complement, but no sequence of distinct ordinals can converge to Ω (see problem **4** of Section **4.2**). Show also that the real valued function $\mathfrak{f}$ defined by setting $\mathfrak{f}(\alpha) = 0$ if $\alpha < \Omega$ and $\mathfrak{f}(\Omega) = 1$ is not continuous at Ω, even though it does preserve convergent sequences.

13. Every infinite Hausdorff space contains an infinite isolated set.

14. We shall call a subset E of a topological space X **sequentially compact** iff every sequence of points of E contains a subsequence which converges to a point of E. Show that every sequentially compact set is countably compact. Give examples to show that a compact set need not be sequentially compact, and a sequentially compact set need not be compact.

5.3 Axioms of Countability

A topological space X is a **first axiom space** iff it satisfies the following **first axiom of countability**:

[C$_{\text{I}}$] For every point $x \in X$, there exists a countable family $\{B_n(x)\}$ of open sets containing x such that whenever x belongs to an open set G, $B_n(x) \subseteq G$ for some n.

We will call the family $\{B_n(x)\}$ a **countable open base at** x. It is clear that at any point x of a first axiom space we may form a monotone decreasing countable open base at x by defining $B_n{}^*(x) = \bigcap \{B_k(x) : k \leqslant n\}$. The real number system is an example of a first axiom space since we may choose the open interval $(x - 1/n,\ x + 1/n)$ as $B_n(x)$ for each point x and integer n. On the other hand, Fort [40] has given an example of a compact Hausdorff space which does not satisfy the first axiom of countability.

Theorem 5.3.1. *Let X be a uncountable set, and let ∞ be a fixed point of X. Let $\mathscr{T}$ be the family of subsets G such that either* (i) $\infty \notin G$, *or* (ii) $\infty \in G$ and $\complement G$ *is finite. Fort's space $(X, \mathscr{T})$ is a compact, nonfirst axiom, Hausdorff topological space.*

Proof. It is an easy exercise to show that $(X, \mathscr{T})$ is a compact, Hausdorff topological space. Suppose there is a countable open base $\{B_n(\infty)\} = \{B_n\}$ at ∞. Since each B_n contains ∞, $\complement B_n$ must be finite for each n. Hence $\bigcup_n \complement B_n = \complement \bigcap_n B_n$ must be countable. Since X is uncountable, there must exist some point x in $\bigcap_n B_n$ other than ∞. But $\complement\{x\}$ is an open set containing ∞, and, by the definition of the base, $B_n \subseteq \complement\{x\}$ for some n. But then $x \notin B_n$, which is a contradiction. ▮

In the next three important theorems, we will show that the notion of sequences introduced in the previous section is quite satisfactory in spaces which satisfy the first axiom of countability.

Theorem 5.3.2. *A topological space X satisfying the first axiom of countability is a Hausdorff space iff every convergent sequence has a unique limit.*

Proof. The condition is necessary by **5.2.4**. Now suppose that X is not a Hausdorff space. There must exist two points x and y such that every open set containing x has a nonempty intersection with every open set containing y. If $\{B_n(x)\}$ and $\{B_n(y)\}$ are monotone decreasing countable open bases at x and y, respectively, we must have $B_n(x) \cap B_n(y) \neq \varnothing$ for every n, so we may choose a point x_n belonging to this intersection for each n. If G_x and G_y are arbitrary open sets containing x and y respectively, there must exist some integer N such that $B_n(x) \subseteq G_x$ and $B_n(y) \subseteq G_y$ for all $n > N$ by the definition of a monotone decreasing base. Hence $x_n \to x$ and $x_n \to y$, so that we have a convergent sequence without a unique limit. ▮

Theorem 5.3.3. *If x is a point and E a subset of a T_1-space X satisfying the first axiom of countability, then x is a limit point of E iff there exists a sequence of distinct points in E converging to x.*

Proof. The condition is sufficient by **5.2.5**. Now suppose $x \in \mathbf{d}(E)$, and let $\{B_n(x)\} = \{B_n\}$ be a monotone decreasing countable open base at x. Since x belongs to the open set B_n, the set $B_n \cap E \setminus \{x\}$ must be infinite by **5.1.3**. By induction we may choose a point x_n in this set different from each previously chosen x_k with $k < n$. Clearly, $x_n \to x$ since the sets $\{B_n\}$ form a monotone decreasing base at x. ▮

Theorem 5.3.4. *If $\mathfrak{f}$ is a mapping of the first axiom space X into the topological space X^*, then $\mathfrak{f}$ is continuous at $x \in X$ iff for every sequence $\langle x_n \rangle$ of points in X converging to x we have the sequence $\langle \mathfrak{f}(x_n) \rangle$ converges to the point $\mathfrak{f}(x) \in X^*$.*

Proof. The condition is necessary by **5.2.6**. Now suppose $\mathfrak{f}$ is not continuous at x, so that there must exist an open set G^* containing $\mathfrak{f}(x)$ such that $\mathfrak{f}(G) \cap \complement G^* \neq \emptyset$ for any open set G containing x. Let $\{B_n\}$ be a monotone decreasing countable open base at x. Then $\mathfrak{f}(B_n) \cap \complement G^* \neq \emptyset$ for each n, and we may pick $x_n^* \in \mathfrak{f}(B_n) \cap \complement G^*$. Since $x_n^* \in \mathfrak{f}(B_n)$, we may choose a point $x_n \in B_n$ such that $\mathfrak{f}(x_n) = x_n^*$. We now have $x_n \to x$ since the sets $\{B_n\}$ form a monotone decreasing base at x. The sequence $\langle \mathfrak{f}(x_n) \rangle = \langle x_n^* \rangle$ cannot converge to $\mathfrak{f}(x)$, however, since $x_n^* \in \complement G^*$ for all n. ▮

A topological space $(X, \mathscr{T})$ is a **second axiom space** iff it satisfies the following **second axiom of countability**:

[$\mathbf{C_{II}}$] There exists a countable base for the topology $\mathscr{T}$.

The existence of a countable base is clearly both a topological and a hereditary property. Although it is clear that every second axiom space is a first axiom space, the converse is not true. The discrete topology on any uncountable set, for example, has no countable base, since each set consisting of exactly one point must belong to any base, even though there is a countable open base at each point x, obtained by letting $B_n(x) = \{x\}$. The real number system is an example of a second axiom space since we may choose the family of all open intervals with rational endpoints as our countable base.

In constructing the Lebesgue measure for subsets of the reals, it is important to have a detailed description of the structure of the open sets. The result used is that every open set in the line is the union of a countable number of disjoint open intervals. The following theorem shows that this result depends only on the fact that the real numbers form a second axiom space.

Theorem 5.3.5. *In a second axiom space, every collection of nonempty disjoint, open sets is countable.*

Proof. Suppose $\mathscr{G}$ is a collection of nonempty, disjoint, open sets in the second axiom space X which has $\{B_n\}$ as a countable base of nonempty open sets. Since the sets $\{B_n\}$ form a base, for each set G in the collection $\mathscr{G}$ there must exist at least one integer n such that $B_n \subseteq G$. Let us associate with G the smallest integer n such that $B_n \subseteq G$. Since the members of the collection $\mathscr{G}$ are disjoint, different integers will be associated with different members. If we order the collection $\mathscr{G}$ according to the order of the associated integers for each member, we obtain a (possibly finite) sequence which contains all the members of $\mathscr{G}$. ∎

The relationship between compact and countably compact sets is made clearer by application of the following theorem due to Lindelöf. Indeed, it shows that the two notions are equivalent in second axiom T_1-spaces.

Theorem 5.3.6. *In a second axiom space, every open covering of a subset is reducible to a countable subcovering.*

Proof. Suppose $\mathscr{G}$ is an open covering of the subset E of the second axiom space X which has $\{B_n\}$ as a countable base. Let $N(\mathscr{G})$ be the countable collection of integers n such that $B_n \subseteq G$ for some $G \in \mathscr{G}$. With each integer $n \in N(\mathscr{G})$ we may then associate a set $G_n \in \mathscr{G}$ such that $B_n \subseteq G_n$. The family $\{G_n : n \in N(\mathscr{G})\}$ is clearly a countable subcollection of $\mathscr{G}$, and we assert that it is a covering of E. Let $x \in E$. Since $\mathscr{G}$ is a covering of E, $x \in G$ for some $G \in \mathscr{G}$. From the definition of a base we have $x \in B_n \subseteq G$ for some integer n. This, means, however, that $n \in N(\mathscr{G})$, and so $x \in B_n \subseteq G_n$, thus proving that $E \subseteq \bigcup \{G_n : n \in N(\mathscr{G})\}$. ∎

The condition introduced in the Lindelöf theorem is quite interesting in its own right. We will call a topological space a **Lindelöf space** iff every open covering of the space is reducible to a countable subcovering. Although the property of a space being Lindelöf is topological, it is not hereditary. It is clear that every compact space is a Lindelöf space. Fort's space, however, is compact even though the subspace $X \setminus \{\infty\}$ is not a Lindelöf space. Closed subspaces of Lindelöf spaces are Lindelöf spaces, however, as is easy to prove in a manner similar to that used in **4.2.3**.

For a topological space $(X, \mathscr{T})$, satisfying the second axiom of countability, it is possible to obtain restrictions on the cardinalities of X and $\mathscr{T}$. For a Hausdorff second axiom space, we may obtain the exact cardinality of the family of open sets.

Theorem 5.3.7. *If $(X, \mathscr{T})$ is a second axiom T_1-space, then $\bar{\bar{X}} \leqslant c$.*

Proof. Let $x \in X$, and suppose $\{B_n\}$ is a countable base for $\mathscr{T}$. Let $N(x)$ be the set of all integers n such that $x \in B_n$. By problem **3**, $\{x\} = \bigcap\{B_n : n \in N(x)\}$. Thus each point of X is determined by the set of integers $N(x)$. Since the collection of all sets of integers has cardinal c, $\bar{\bar{X}} \leqslant c$. ∎

Theorem 5.3.8. *If $(X, \mathscr{T})$ is a second axiom space, then $\bar{\bar{\mathscr{T}}} \leqslant c$. If $(X, \mathscr{T})$ is, in addition, an infinite Hausdorff space, then $\bar{\bar{\mathscr{T}}} = c$.*

Proof. Let $G \in \mathscr{T}$, and suppose $\{B_n\}$ is a countable base for $\mathscr{T}$. Let $N(G)$ be the set of integers n such that $B_n \subseteq G$. By the definition of a base, $G = \bigcup\{B_n ; n \in N(G)\}$. Thus each open set G of X is determined by the set of integers $N(G)$. Hence, $\bar{\bar{\mathscr{T}}} \leqslant c$. If $(X, \mathscr{T})$ is also an infinite Hausdorff space, then, by **5.2.3**, there exists an infinite sequence of nonempty, disjoint, open sets. The union of each distinct finite or infinite sequence of these open sets is a different open set. Since an infinite sequence has c different subsequences, $\bar{\bar{\mathscr{T}}} \geqslant c$. Thus, $\bar{\bar{\mathscr{T}}} = c$. ∎

Since the real number system satisfies the conditions of the previous theorem, we know that there are exactly c open sets on the line. A property of the real numbers that we have not yet obtained is that every uncountable set of real numbers has a limit point. In fact, a stronger result holds. We shall call a point x a **condensation point** of a set E in a topological space iff every open set containing x contains an uncountable number of points of E. We know that every uncountable set of real numbers has a condensation point and we may obtain that result in any second axiom space.

Theorem 5.3.9. *Every uncountable subset of a second axiom space contains a condensation point.*

Proof. Suppose E is a subset with no condensation points in a second axiom space X with base $\{B_n\}$. For each point $x \in E$, x is not a condensation point of E, and hence there exists an open set G containing x such that $G \cap E$ is countable. By **[C$_{\text{II}}$]**, for some integer n_x we have $x \in B_{n_x} \subseteq G$, and so $B_{n_x} \cap E$ is also countable. But we may write $E = \bigcup\{x : x \in E\} \subseteq \bigcup\{B_{n_x} \cap E : x \in E\}$, and there can be at most a countable number of different indices, so E is at most a countable union of countable sets. ▮

Exercises

1. The property of being a first axiom space is a topological property.

2. The property of being a first axiom space is a hereditary property.

3. For each point x in a first axiom T_1-space, $\{x\} = \bigcap_{n \in \mathbf{N}} B_n(x)$.

4. Show that Fort's space is a compact, Hausdorff, topological space.

5. Compare Fort's space with the one point compactification of an uncountable discrete space.

6. The property of being a second axiom space is a topological property.

7. The property of being a second axiom space is a hereditary property.

8. Every second axiom space is a first axiom space.

9. In a second axiom T_1-space, a set is compact iff it is countably compact.

10. The continuous image of a Lindelöf space is a Lindelöf space, so the property of being a Lindelöf space is a topological property.

11. Show that the subspace $X \setminus \{\infty\}$ of Fort's space is not a Lindelöf space, so the property of being a Lindelöf space is not hereditary.

12. Every closed subset of a Lindelöf space is a Lindelöf space.

13. If E is a subset of a second axiom space, the subset of E consisting of those points which are not condensation points of E is countable.

14. The set of all condensation points of a subset of a second axiom space is both closed and dense-in-itself.

15. A first axiom T_1-space is countably compact iff it is sequentially compact (see problem **14** of Section **5.2**).

5.4 Separability and Summary

A subset E of a topological space X will be called **dense** in X iff $c(E) = X$. A topological space X will be called **separable** iff it satisfies the following condition:

[S] There exists a countable dense subset of X.

Although the property of a space being separable is topological, it is not hereditary. We shall call a space **hereditarily separable** iff each subspace of the space is separable. It is easy to show that there are separable topological spaces which are not hereditarily separable by showing that every topological space is a subspace of a separable topological space. Indeed, if $(X, \mathcal{T})$ is a topological space and ∞ is any object not a member of X, we may construct a separable topology for the set $X^* = X \cup \{\infty\}$ as follows. Let $\mathcal{T}^* = \{\emptyset\} \cup \{G^* : G^* = G \cup \{\infty\}$ for some $G \in \mathcal{T}\}$, and we see that $(X, \mathcal{T})$ is a subspace of $(X^*, \mathcal{T}^*)$, and $\{\infty\}$ is a countable dense subset of X^*.

Theorem 5.4.1. *Every second axiom space is hereditarily separable.*

Proof. Since each subspace of a second axiom space is also a second axiom space, we need only show that every second axiom space is separable. The set obtained by choosing a point from each nonempty member of a countable open base for the space is dense in the space, since every open set will contain at least one point of the set. ∎

A separable topological space need not satisfy the second axiom of countability, as the example of the lower limit topology for the reals (see problem **3** of Section **3.4**) shows. Another interesting example was given by Appert [1] of a separable Hausdorff space which does not even satisfy the first axiom of countability.

Theorem 5.4.2. *Let X be the positive integers, and let $N(n, E)$ be the number of integers in a set E which are less than or equal to n. Let $\mathcal{T}$ be the family of subsets G such that either* (i) $1 \notin G$, *or* (ii) $1 \in G$ *and* $\lim N(n, G)/n = 1$. *Appert's space $(X, \mathcal{T})$ is a separable, nonfirst axiom, Hausdorff, topological space.*

Proof. **[0.1]**: Suppose $G_\lambda \in \mathcal{T}$ for every λ. If $1 \notin \bigcup_\lambda G_\lambda$, then $\bigcup_\lambda G_\lambda \in \mathcal{T}$ immediately. Suppose, then, that $1 \in G_\beta$ for some β. Since $N(n, \bigcup_\lambda G_\lambda) \geqslant N(n, G_\beta)$, $\lim N(n, \bigcup_\lambda G_\lambda)/n \geqslant \lim N(n, G_\beta)/n = 1$, and so $\bigcup_\lambda G_\lambda \in \mathcal{T}$.

[0.2]: It is clear that $X \in \mathcal{T}$ since $N(n, X) = n$, and so $1 \in X$ and $\lim N(n, X)/n = 1$. Suppose that G_1 and G_2 belong to $\mathcal{T}$. If $1 \notin G_1 \cap G_2$, then $G_1 \cap G_2 \in \mathscr{T}$, immediately. Suppose, then, that $1 \in G_1 \cap G_2$. Since $N(n, G) + N(n, \complement G) = n$, it is clear that if $1 \in G \in \mathscr{T}$, then $\lim N(n, \complement G)/n = 0$. In particular, since $1 \in G_1$ and $1 \in G_2$, we must have $\lim N(n, \complement G_1)/n = 0$ and $\lim N(n, \complement G_2)/n = 0$. Now consider the equation

$$N(n, G_1 \cap G_2) + N(n, G_1 \cap \complement G_2) + N(n, \complement G_1 \cap G_2) + N(n, \complement G_1 \cap \complement G_2) = n$$

and the inequalities

$$N(n, G_1 \cap \complement G_2) \leqslant N(n, \complement G_2),$$

$$N(n, \complement G_1 \cap G_2) \leqslant N(n, \complement G_1),$$

$$N(n, \complement G_1 \cap \complement G_2) \leqslant N(n, \complement G_1).$$

We may now calculate that

$$\begin{aligned}
&\lim N(n, G_1 \cap G_2)/n \\
&\quad = \lim [n - N(n, G_1 \cap \complement G_2) - N(n, \complement G_1 \cap G_2) - N(n, \complement G_1 \cap \complement G_2)]/n \\
&\quad \geqslant \lim [n - N(n, \complement G_2) - N(n, \complement G_1) - N(n, \complement G_1)]/n \\
&\quad = 1 - 0 - 0 - 0 = 1.
\end{aligned}$$

Hence, $G_1 \cap G_2 \in \mathscr{T}$.

[T$_2$]: Suppose x and y are two distinct points of X. If neither point is equal to 1, then the sets $\{x\}$ and $\{y\}$ are two disjoint open sets containing x and y respectively. Suppose, then, that $x \neq 1 = y$. The sets $\{x\}$ and $\complement\{x\}$ will be the disjoint open sets desired.

Non-**[C$_\text{I}$]**: Suppose $\{B_n\}$ was a countable open base at 1. Since each B_n must be infinite, we may pick a point $x_n \in B_n$ such that $x_n > 10^n$. Let $G = \complement \bigcup_n \{x_n\}$. Since $N(n, G) \geqslant n - \log_{10} n$, we have $\lim N(n, G)/n \geqslant \lim (n - \log_{10} n)/n = 1$. Hence G is an open set which contains 1. Since $\{B_n\}$ is a base at 1, $1 \in B_n \subseteq G$ for some n. This, however, contradicts the fact that $x_n \in B_n$ but $x_n \notin G$. ▮

We will now summarize the implication relationships which exist between compactness and the properties of spaces introduced in this section. Since the real numbers are second axiom, Lindelöf, and separable, none of these three properties may imply compactness. Since every compact space is a Lindelöf space, Fort's space shows that neither compactness nor the Lindelöf property implies either separability or the second axiom of countability. Appert's space was an example of a separable space which was not second axiom. Note that all of the above examples are Hausdorff spaces, so that none of the implications ruled out may hold even in Hausdorff spaces.

By **5.3.6** and **5.4.1**, every second axiom space is both Lindelöf and separable. The only other implication not yet considered is whether every separable topological space must be a Lindelöf space. Note that Appert's space is not an example of a separable, non-Lindelöf space. In problems **7** and **8** we will give examples of separable Hausdorff spaces which are not Lindelöf spaces.

In the following diagram we denote by arrows the implications which hold in any topological space, while no other implications hold, even in a Hausdorff space.

Compact
↘
Separable ← Second Axiom → Lindelöf

Exercises

1. The continuous image of a separable space is a separable space, so the property of being a separable space is a topological property.

2. Show that the family $\mathscr{T}^*$, described above **5.4.1**, is a topology for X^*, and that $(X, \mathscr{T})$ is a subspace of $(X^*, \mathscr{T}^*)$.

3. Show that the real numbers with the lower limit topology is an example of a separable, Hausdorff, nonsecond axiom, first axiom space.

4. In a separable space, every collection of nonempty, disjoint, open sets is countable (see **5.3.5**).

5. Show that Fort's space is not separable.

6. Show that Appert's space is a Lindelöf space.

7. Let X be the set of real numbers, and define a topology for X by requiring that a neighborhood of a point x is any set containing x which contains all the rationals in an open interval around x. Show that the result is a separable, non-Lindelöf, Hausdorff, topological space.

8. Let X be the set of points in the Euclidean plane, and let a base for a topology be the family of all sets of the form $\{\langle x, y\rangle : a \leqslant x < b, c \leqslant y < d\}$ where a, b, c, and d are real numbers. By considering the subset $\{\langle x, y\rangle : y = -x\}$, show that the result is a separable, non-Lindelöf, Hausdorff, topological space. This example is due to Sorgenfrey [73].

9. For any topological space $(X, \mathscr{T})$, let Y be an infinite collection of objects which do not belong to X. Let $X^* = X \cup Y$, and define $\mathscr{T}^*$ to be the collection of subsets of X^* consisting of $\emptyset$ and all sets G^* which are of the form $G \cup Z$, where G is an open set in X and Z contains all but a finite number of elements of Y. Show that $\mathscr{T}^*$ is a topology for X^*, $(X, \mathscr{T})$ is a subspace of $(X^*, \mathscr{T}^*)$, and Y is a dense subset of X^*. Show also that the closure operator $\mathbf{c}^*$ in X^* may be described in terms of the closure operator $\mathbf{c}$ in X by the rule that $\mathbf{c}^*(E) = \mathbf{c}(X \cap E) \cup (Y \cap E)$ if E contains only a finite number of points of Y, and $\mathbf{c}^*(E) = X^*$ if E contains an infinite number of points of Y.

10. A topological space X is a Lindelöf space iff for any compact space X^* containing X and any closed subset F^* in $X^* \setminus X$, there exists a real-valued continuous mapping $\mathfrak{f}$ of X^* such that $\mathfrak{f}(F^*) = 0$ and $\mathfrak{f}(x) > 0$ for all $x \in X$.

5.5 Regular and Normal Spaces

A topological space X is **regular** iff it satisfies the following axiom of Vietoris:

[R] If F is a closed subset of X and x is a point of X not in F, then there exist two disjoint open sets, one containing F and the other containing x.

A $\boldsymbol{T_3}$**-space** is a regular space which is also a T_1-space. The reader is warned that some authors use exactly the opposite convention with respect to the words "regular" and "T_3," while others do not use either term unless the T_1 axiom is satisfied.

Although every T_3-space is obviously a T_2-space, a regular space need not be a T_2-space, and a T_2-space need not be a regular (T_3) space. For example, the space of problem **7** of Section **3.1** is regular but not Hausdorff. Problem **7** in Section **5.4** gives an example of a nonregular Hausdorff space since, in that space, the irrationals form a closed set which is contained in only one open set, X itself.

The example given of a regular, non-Hausdorff space is not even a T_0-space. It is not possible to improve on this example since it is easy to show that a regular T_0-space is a T_3-space. It is equally easy to show that the property of regularity is both topological and hereditary. In the following theorem we will give another characterization of regularity.

Theorem 5.5.1. *A topological space X is regular iff for every point $x \in X$ and open set G containing x there exists an open set G^* such that $x \in G^*$ and $\mathbf{c}(G^*) \subseteq G$.*

Proof. Suppose X is regular, and the point x belongs to the open set G. Then $F = X \setminus G$ is a closed set which does not contain x. By **[R]**, there exist two open sets G_F and G_x such that $F \subseteq G_F$, $x \in G_x$, and $G_F \cap G_x = \emptyset$. Since $G_x \subseteq \complement G_F$, $\mathbf{c}(G_x) \subseteq \mathbf{c}(\complement G_F) = \complement G_F \subseteq \complement F = G$. Thus, $x \in G_x$ and $\mathbf{c}(G_x) \subseteq G$, and G_x is the desired set. Now suppose the condition holds and x is a point not in the closed set F. Then x belongs to the open set $\complement F$, and by hypothesis there must exist an open set G^* such that $x \in G^*$ and $\mathbf{c}(G^*) \subseteq \complement F$. Clearly G^* and $\complement\mathbf{c}(G^*)$ are disjoint open sets containing x and F, respectively. ∎

A topological space X is **normal** iff it satisfies the following axiom of Urysohn:

[N] If F_1 and F_2 are two disjoint closed subsets of X, then there exist two disjoint open sets, one containing F_1 and the other containing F_2.

A ***T_4*-space** is a normal space which is also a T_1-space.

Although every T_4-space is obviously a T_3-space, the example of problem **6** of Section **3.1** shows that a normal space need not be regular. This normal space is not a Hausdorff space, of course, although it is a T_0-space. Niemytzki has given the classic example of a T_3-space (in fact a Tichonov space, see Section **5.6**) which is not normal (T_4). Let X consist of those points $\langle x, y \rangle$ of the Euclidean plane for which $y \geqslant 0$. As a base for the open sets at a point for which $y > 0$, we choose the interiors of circles around the point. For points $\langle x, 0 \rangle$ on the X-axis, we choose as a base sets consisting of the point $\langle x, 0 \rangle$ and the interior of a circle tangent to the X-axis at the point. X with this topology is a T_3-space. It is not normal since the set consisting of the rational points and the set consisting of the irrational points on the X-axis are disjoint and closed but do not have any disjoint open sets containing them.

Another characterization of normality, analogous to that for regularity given in **5.5.1**, is given in the following theorem.

Theorem 5.5.2. *A topological space X is normal iff for any closed set F and open set G containing F, there exists an open set G^* such that $F \subseteq G^*$ and $\mathbf{c}(G^*) \subseteq G$.*

Proof. Suppose X is normal and the closed set F is contained in the open set G. Then $K = X \setminus G$ is a closed set which is disjoint from F. By **[N]**, there exist two disjoint open sets G_F and G_K such that $F \subseteq G_F$ and $K \subseteq G_K$. Since $G_F \subseteq X \setminus G_K$, we have $\mathbf{c}(G_F) \subseteq \mathbf{c}(X \setminus G_K) = X \setminus G_K \subseteq X \setminus K = G$. Thus G_F is the desired set. Now suppose the condition holds, and let F_1 and F_2 be disjoint closed subsets of X. Then F_1 is contained in the open set $X \setminus F_2$, and, by hypothesis, there exists an open set G^* such that $F_1 \subseteq G^*$ and $\mathbf{c}(G^*) \subseteq X \setminus F_2$. Clearly, G^* and $X \setminus \mathbf{c}(G^*)$ are the desired disjoint open sets containing F_1 and F_2, respectively. ∎

Although the property of normality is topological, an example will be given at the end of this section to show that it is not hereditary. Another characterization of normality relates that concept to the number of real-valued continuous functions defined on the space.

Urysohn's Lemma. *A topological space X is normal iff for every two disjoint closed subsets F_1 and F_2 of X and closed interval $[a, b]$ of reals, there exists a continuous mapping $\mathfrak{f} : X \to [a, b]$ such that $\mathfrak{f}(F_1) = \{a\}$ and $\mathfrak{f}(F_2) = \{b\}$.*

We will prove this result in Section **10.1**, where it will be used as the basis for a metrization theorem. If the reader wishes, he may skip directly to that proof since it requires no additional background. The following result shows one very important application of Urysohn's Lemma.

Theorem 5.5.3 (Tietze Extension Theorem). *A topological space X is normal iff for every real-valued continuous mapping $\mathfrak{f}$ of a closed subset F of X into a closed interval $[a, b]$, there exists a real-valued continuous mapping $\mathfrak{f}^*$ of X into $[a, b]$ such that $\mathfrak{f}^* \mid F = \mathfrak{f}$.*

Proof. Suppose X satisfies the condition of the theorem, F_1 and F_2 are two disjoint closed subsets of X, and $[a, b]$ is any closed interval. The mapping $\mathfrak{f}$, defined by setting $\mathfrak{f}(x) = a$ if $x \in F_1$ and $\mathfrak{f}(x) = b$ if $x \in F_2$, is then a continuous mapping of the closed domain $F_1 \cup F_2$ into $[a, b]$. The mapping $\mathfrak{f}^*$ given by the condition will satisfy the condition in Urysohn's Lemma, so X will be normal.

Now suppose that X is normal and $\mathfrak{f}$ is a real-valued continuous mapping of the closed subset F into the closed interval $[a, b]$ which, for numerical convenience, we take to be $[-1, +1]$. For each integer n, let us denote the real numbers $(\frac{1}{3})(\frac{2}{3})^n$ by b_n and $-(\frac{1}{3})(\frac{2}{3})^n$ by $a_n = -b_n$, and let us define a mapping $\mathfrak{g}_0 : F \to [-1, +1] = [3a_0, 3b_0]$ by setting $\mathfrak{g}_0(x) = \mathfrak{f}(x)$ for all $x \in F$. Now let

$$A_0 = \mathfrak{g}_0^{-1}([3a_0, a_0]) \qquad \text{and} \qquad B_0 = \mathfrak{g}_0^{-1}([b_0, 3b_0]),$$

which are disjoint sets which are closed in F and so also closed in X. By Urysohn's Lemma, there exists a continuous mapping $\mathfrak{f}_0 : X \to [a_0, b_0]$

such that $\mathfrak{f}_0(A_0) = \{a_0\}$ and $\mathfrak{f}_0(B_0) = \{b_0\}$. We define a mapping $\mathfrak{g}_1 : F \to [3a_1, 3b_1]$ by setting $\mathfrak{g}_1(x) = \mathfrak{g}_0(x) - \mathfrak{f}_0(x)$ for all $x \in F$. Now let

$$A_1 = \mathfrak{g}_1^{-1}([3a_1, a_1]) \quad \text{and} \quad B_1 = \mathfrak{g}_1^{-1}([b_1, 3b_1]),$$

which are disjoint sets which are closed in F and so also closed in X. By Urysohn's Lemma, there exists a continuous mapping $\mathfrak{f}_1 : X \to [a_1, b_1]$ such that $\mathfrak{f}_1(A_1) = \{a_1\}$ and $\mathfrak{f}_1(B_1) = \{b_1\}$. We define a mapping $\mathfrak{g}_2 : F \to [-(\frac{2}{3})^2, +(\frac{2}{3})^2] = [3a_2, 3b_2]$ by setting $\mathfrak{g}_2(x) = \mathfrak{g}_1(x) - \mathfrak{f}_1(x) = \mathfrak{g}_0(x) - \mathfrak{f}_0(x) - \mathfrak{f}_1(x)$ for all $x \in F$.

We now continue this construction by induction. Let us suppose that, for $k = 0, 1, \ldots, n-1$, we have continuous mappings $\mathfrak{f}_k : X \to [a_k, b_k]$. We define a mapping $\mathfrak{g}_n : F \to [3a_n, 3b_n]$ by setting

$$\mathfrak{g}_n(x) = \mathfrak{g}_0(x) - \sum_{k=0}^{n-1} \mathfrak{f}_k(x) \quad \text{for all} \quad x \in F.$$

Now let

$$A_n = \mathfrak{g}_n^{-1}([3a_n, a_n]) \quad \text{and} \quad B_n = \mathfrak{g}_n^{-1}([b_n, 3b_n]),$$

which are disjoint sets which are closed in F and so also closed in X. By Urysohn's Lemma, there exists a continuous mapping $\mathfrak{f}_n : X \to [a_n, b_n]$ such that $\mathfrak{f}_n(A_n) = \{a_n\}$ and $\mathfrak{f}_n(B_n) = \{b_n\}$. We define a mapping $\mathfrak{g}_{n+1} : F \to [3a_{n+1}, 3b_{n+1}]$ by setting $\mathfrak{g}_{n+1}(x) = \mathfrak{g}_n(x) - \mathfrak{f}_n(x) = \mathfrak{g}_0(x) - \sum_{k=0}^{n} \mathfrak{f}_k(x)$ for all $x \in F$.

It is easy to verify that the range of $\mathfrak{g}_{n+1}$ is contained in $[3a_{n+1}, 3b_{n+1}]$ by the following reasoning. If $x \in A_n$, then $3a_n \leqslant \mathfrak{g}_n(x) \leqslant a_n$ while $\mathfrak{f}_n(x) = a_n$, so that

$$0 \geqslant \mathfrak{g}_n(x) - \mathfrak{f}_n(x) \geqslant 3a_n - a_n = -2(\tfrac{1}{3})(\tfrac{2}{3})^n = 3a_{n+1}.$$

Similarly, if $x \in B_n$, then $b_n \leqslant \mathfrak{g}_n(x) \leqslant 3b_n$ while $\mathfrak{f}_n(x) = b_n$, so that

$$0 \leqslant \mathfrak{g}_n(x) - \mathfrak{f}_n(x) \leqslant 3b_n - b_n = 3b_{n+1}.$$

Finally, if $x \notin A_n \cup B_n$, then $a_n < \mathfrak{g}_n(x) < b_n$ while $a_n \leqslant \mathfrak{f}_n(x) \leqslant b_n$, so that

$$3a_{n+1} = a_n - b_n < \mathfrak{g}_n(x) - \mathfrak{f}_n(x) < b_n - a_n = 3b_{n+1}.$$

Thus the induction is complete.

We now set $\mathfrak{f}^*(x) = \sum_{n=0}^{\infty}\mathfrak{f}_n(x)$ for every $x \in X$. Since $|\mathfrak{f}_n(x)| \leqslant b_n$,

$$\left|\sum_{n=0}^{\infty} \mathfrak{f}_n(x)\right| \leqslant \sum_{n=0}^{\infty} |\mathfrak{f}_n(x)| \leqslant \sum_{n=0}^{\infty} b_n = 1,$$

so that the infinite series which defines $\mathfrak{f}^*(x)$ is absolutely and uniformly convergent for all $x \in X$. By the usual advanced calculus argument (see, e.g., [18, p. 279]) $\mathfrak{f}^*$ is a continuous mapping of X into $[-1, +1] = [a, b]$. Lastly, we note that $|\mathfrak{g}_n(x)| \leqslant 3b_n$ which approaches zero as n increases, and $\mathfrak{g}_0(x) = \mathfrak{f}(x)$ for all $x \in F$. From the definition of $\mathfrak{g}_n$ it is clear that $\mathfrak{f}^*(x) = \mathfrak{f}(x)$ for all $x \in F$, so that $\mathfrak{f}^* | F = \mathfrak{f}$. ▮

The above characterization of normality was also given by Urysohn in his generalization of Tietze's result which concerned metric spaces. A more elementary application of Urysohn's Lemma is the following theorem.

Theorem 5.5.4. *If the open set G has a nonempty intersection with a connected set C in a T_4-space X, then either C consists of only one point or the set $C \cap G$ has cardinality greater than or equal to c.*

Proof. Let us choose a point $x \in C \cap G$. Now if $C \cap G = \{x\}$, then $C = \{x\} \mid C \setminus \{x\}$ would give a separation of C in the T_1-space X unless C consisted of only one point. Now if $y \in C \cap G \setminus \{x\}$, the sets $\{x\}$ and $F = \{y\} \cup \complement G$ would be disjoint, closed subsets of the normal space X. By Urysohn's Lemma, there exists a continuous mapping $\mathfrak{f} : X \to [0,1]$ such that $\mathfrak{f}(\{x\}) = \{0\}$ and $\mathfrak{f}(F) = \{1\}$. By the Darboux property (**4.3.2**), $\mathfrak{f}(C)$ is a connected subset of $[0,1]$. Since $\mathfrak{f}(x) = 0$ and $\mathfrak{f}(y) = 1$, $\mathfrak{f}(C)$ must be all of $[0,1]$, and so have cardinality c. Now $C \cap \complement G \subseteq F$, so $\mathfrak{f}(C \cap \complement G) = \{1\}$ has finite cardinality. However, $\mathfrak{f}(C) = \mathfrak{f}(C \cap X) = \mathfrak{f}(C \cap (G \cup \complement G)) = \mathfrak{f}((C \cap G) \cup (C \cap \complement G)) = \mathfrak{f}(C \cap G) \cup \mathfrak{f}(C \cap \complement G)$. Thus $\mathfrak{f}(C \cap G)$ must have cardinality c, and so $C \cap G$ must have cardinality greater than or equal to c. ▮

We will now give two sufficient conditions for a topological space to be normal.

Theorem 5.5.5. *Every compact Hausdorff space is normal* (T_4).

Proof. Let F and F^* be two disjoint, closed subsets of the compact Hausdorff space X. By **4.2.3**, F and F^* are compact since they are closed subsets of a compact space. By **[T_2]**, for each pair $\langle x, x^*\rangle$ of points with $x \in F$ and $x^* \in F^*$, there exist two disjoint open sets $G(x, x^*)$

and $G^*(x, x^*)$ containing x and x^*, respectively. For each fixed point $x \in F$, the collection $\{G^*(x, x^*) : x^* \in F^*\}$ forms an open covering of the compact set F^*. There must be a finite subcovering, which we denote by $\{G^*(x, x_i^*) : i = 1, ..., n\}$. If we let $G^*(x) = \bigcup_{i=1}^n G^*(x, x_i^*)$ and the finite intersection $\bigcap_{i=1}^n G(x, x_i^*) = G(x)$, then $G(x)$ and $G^*(x)$ are disjoint open sets containing x and F^*, respectively. Now the collection $\{G(x) : x \in F\}$ forms an open covering of the compact set F. There must be a finite subcovering, which we denote by $\{G(x_i) : i = 1, ..., m\}$. If we let $G = \bigcup_{i=1}^m G(x_i)$ and the finite intersection $\bigcap_{i=1}^m G^*(x_i) = G^*$, then G and G^* are two disjoint open sets containing F and F^*, respectively. ∎

Theorem 5.5.6. *Every regular Lindelöf space is normal.*

Proof. Let F and F^* be two disjoint closed subsets of the regular Lindelöf space X. By problem **12** of Section **5.3**, F and F^* are Lindelöf since they are closed subsets of a Lindelöf space. By **[R]**, for each point $x \in F$, there exists an open set $G(x)$ such that $x \in G(x) \subseteq \mathbf{c}(G(x)) \subseteq X \setminus F^*$. The collection $\{G(x) : x \in F\}$ forms an open covering of the Lindelöf set F. There must be a countable subcovering, which we denote by $\{G_i\}_{i \in \mathbf{N}}$. Similarly, for each point $x \in F^*$ there must exist an open set $G^*(x)$ such that $x \in G^*(x) \subseteq \mathbf{c}(G^*(x)) \subseteq X \setminus F$. The collection $\{G^*(x) : x \in F^*\}$ forms an open covering of the Lindelöf set F^*. There must be a countable subcovering, which we denote by $\{G_i^*\}_{i \in \mathbf{N}}$. The reader may show that the sets $G = \bigcup_{n \in \mathbf{N}} [G_n \setminus \bigcup_{i \leqslant n} \mathbf{c}(G_i^*)]$ and $G^* = \bigcup_{n \in \mathbf{N}} [G_n^* \setminus \bigcup_{i \leqslant n} \mathbf{c}(G_i)]$ are disjoint open sets containing F and F^*, respectively. ∎

A topological space X is **completely normal** iff it satisfies the following axiom of Tietze:

[CN] If A and B are two separated subsets of X, then there exist two disjoint open sets, one containing A and the other containing B.

A $\boldsymbol{T_5}$**-space** is a completely normal space which is also a T_1-space.

Since disjoint closed sets are separated, every completely normal space is normal, and hence every T_5-space is a T_4-space. Before giving an example which shows that the converse is not true, we will give another characterization of complete normality. It follows from this next result that complete normality might better have been called "hereditary normality."

Theorem 5.5.7. *A topological space X is completely normal iff every subspace of X is normal.*

Proof. Suppose X is completely normal and $X^* \subseteq X$. Let F_1 and F_2 be disjoint (relatively) closed subsets of X^*. Then $F_1 \cap \mathbf{c}(F_2) = \mathbf{c}^*(F_1) \cap \mathbf{c}(F_2) = X^* \cap \mathbf{c}(F_1) \cap \mathbf{c}(F_2) = \mathbf{c}^*(F_1) \cap \mathbf{c}^*(F_2) = F_1 \cap F_2 = \varnothing$ and, similarly, $\mathbf{c}(F_1) \cap F_2 = \varnothing$. Hence F_1 and F_2 are separated subsets of X. By **[CN]**, there exist disjoint open sets G_1 and G_2 containing F_1 and F_2, respectively. Then the sets $X^* \cap G_1$ and $X^* \cap G_2$ are disjoint (relatively) open subsets of X^* which contain F_1 and F_2, respectively, so X^* is normal.

Now let us suppose that every subspace of X is normal, and let A and B be separated subsets of X. Consider the open set $\mathbf{C}[\mathbf{c}(A) \cap \mathbf{c}(B)] = X^*$ as a subspace of X. By hypothesis, X^* is normal. The sets $X^* \cap \mathbf{c}(A)$ and $X^* \cap \mathbf{c}(B)$ will be disjoint, relatively closed subsets of X^*, and so there must exist two disjoint relatively open sets G_A and G_B containing $X^* \cap \mathbf{c}(A)$ and $X^* \cap \mathbf{c}(B)$, respectively. Since X^* is an open subset of X, G_A and G_B are actually open subsets of X (see problem **7** (ii) of Section **3.4**). Thus we have $A \subseteq X^* \cap \mathbf{c}(A) \subseteq G_A$ and $B \subseteq X^* \cap \mathbf{c}(B) \subseteq G_B$, so that X is completely normal. ∎

Tichonov has given the classic example of a T_4-space which is not completely normal. We will now give a slight modification of that example. Let $X_1^* = X_1 \cup \{\alpha\}$ be the one point compactification of the uncountable, discrete space X_1 (see problem **7** of Section **4.2**, Theorem **5.2.2**, Theorem **5.3.1**, and problem **5** in Section **5.3**). Let $X_2^* = X_2 \cup \{\beta\}$ be the one point compactification of the infinite, discrete space X_2. The set $X = X_1^* \times X_2^*$ will be given a topology $\mathscr{T}$ by using as a base the family of all sets of the form $G_1 \times G_2$, where G_1 is an open subset of X_1^*, and G_2 is an open subset of X_2^*. In Chapter 8 we will see that this is a base for a topology (the product topology), and that with this topology $(X, \mathscr{T})$ is a compact Hausdorff space. By **5.5.5**, $(X, \mathscr{T})$ is normal (T_4). The subspace $X \setminus \{\langle\alpha, \beta\rangle\}$ is not normal, however, since the sets $A = \{\langle\alpha, y\rangle : y \in X_2\}$ and $B = \{\langle x, \beta\rangle : x \in X_1\}$ are disjoint, closed sets which are not contained in any disjoint open sets in $X \setminus \{\langle\alpha, \beta\rangle\}$.

This last statement about A and B will be more clear if we describe carefully the neighborhoods of points in $X \setminus \{\langle\alpha, \beta\rangle\}$. It follows from our definition of $\mathscr{T}$ that each one point set $\{\langle x, y\rangle\}$ for which $x \neq \alpha$ and $y \neq \beta$ is itself open since it is the product of the two open sets $\{x\}$ and $\{y\}$. Furthermore, for each fixed $y \in X_2$, a neighborhood of the point $\langle\alpha, y\rangle$ must contain all but at most a finite number of the points $\langle x, y\rangle$ with $x \in X_1$. Similarly, for each fixed $x \in X_1$, a neighborhood of the point $\langle x, \beta\rangle$ must contain all but at most a finite number of the points $\langle x, y\rangle$ with $y \in X_2$. These statements follow from the nature of the one point compactification of a discrete space. In particular, a neighborhood of α in $X_1{}^*$ must contain all but a finite number of points of X_1, and a neighborhood of β in $X_2{}^*$ must contain all but a finite number of points of X_2. From this description of neighborhoods it is obvious that A and B are disjoint closed subsets of $X \setminus \{\langle\alpha, \beta\rangle\}$.

Now let us suppose that A and B are contained in two disjoint open sets G_A and G_B, respectively. Since X_2 is infinite, we may choose a sequence $\langle y_1, y_2, ...\rangle$ of distinct points from it. The points $\langle\alpha, y_1\rangle$, $\langle\alpha, y_2\rangle$, ... are then distinct points of A. The set G_A must then contain all but a finite number of points in each set $\{\langle x, y_i\rangle : x \in X_1\}$. We now consider the open set G_B containing B. We note that at most a finite number of sets of the form $\{\langle x, y\rangle : y \in X_2{}^*\}$ can be completely contained in G_B, for otherwise G_A would not contain all but a finite number of points in the set $\{\langle x, y_1\rangle : x \in X_1\}$. Next we see that at most a finite number of sets of the form $\{\langle x, y\rangle : y \in X_2{}^*\}$ can be contained, except for exactly one point each, in G_B, for otherwise G_A would not contain all but a finite number of points in both of the sets $\{\langle x, y_1\rangle : x \in x_1\}$ and $\{\langle x, y_2\rangle : x \in X_1\}$.

By induction we see that for each nonnegative integer n, only a finite number of sets of the form $\{\langle x, y\rangle : y \in X_2{}^*\}$ can be contained, except for exactly n points each, in G_B, for otherwise G_A would not contain all but a finite number of points in the sets $\{\langle x, y_i\rangle : x \in X_1\}$ for $i = 1, 2, ..., n + 1$. Thus, for only a countable number of points x in X_1 can G_B contain all but a finite number of points in each set $\{\langle x, y\rangle : y \in X_2{}^*\}$. However, in order to be an open set containing B, G_B would have to satisfy that condition for each point $\langle x, \beta\rangle$ in B, and there are uncountably many such points. This contradiction completes the example.

Exercises

1. Regularity is a topological property.
2. Regularity is a hereditary property.
3. Every regular T_0-space is a T_3-space.
4. Show that the space of problem **7** of Section **3.1** is regular but not Hausdorff.
5. Let X be the set of real numbers and define the closure $\mathbf{c}(E)$ of a set $E \subseteq X$ to be the union of E and its condensation points (see **5.3.9**). Show that X with this operator is a Hausdorff topological space which is not regular.

6. Normality is a topological property.

7. Show that the space of problem **6** of Section **3.1** is normal but not regular.

8. Show that Niemytzki's space is regular.

9. Suppose that for every closed subset F of a topological space X there exists a continuous (on F) mapping $\mathfrak{f}_F$ of X into F such that $\mathfrak{f}_F(x) = x$ for $x \in F$. Must X be normal?

10. Show that the sets G and G^* in the proof of **5.5.6** are disjoint open sets containing F and F^*, respectively.

11. Show that the real numbers with the lower limit topology are normal.

12. Complete normality is a topological property.

13. Every regular second axiom space is completely normal. [*Hint*: Use the method of proof in **5.5.6**.]

14. Every linearly ordered set with the order topology is a T_5-space.

15. Show that Appert's space (**5.4.2**) is a T_5-space.

16. An open cover $\{G_\lambda\}$ of a topological space is **shrinkable** iff there is an open cover $\{G_\lambda^*\}$ of the space such that $\mathfrak{c}(G_\lambda^*) \subseteq G_\lambda$ for each λ. Show that a topological space is normal iff every finite open cover is shrinkable.

5.6 Completely Regular Spaces

One final separation axiom, whose importance has increased rapidly in recent topological researches, was first introduced by Urysohn [79], and its basic properties were considered by Tichonov [77]. A topological space X is **completely regular** iff it satisfies the following axiom:

[CR] If F is a closed subset of X, and x is a point of X not in F, then there exists a continuous mapping $\mathfrak{f} : X \to [0, 1]$ such that $\mathfrak{f}(x) = 0$ and $\mathfrak{f}(F) = \{1\}$.

A **Tichonov space** is a completely regular space which is also a T_1-space.

It is obvious that the property of being a completely regular space is both topological and hereditary. It is also immediate that every completely regular space is regular, every Tichonov space is a T_3-space, and every T_4-space is a Tichonov space by Urysohn's Lemma. Because of these facts, we might be inclined to call a Tichonov space a $T_{3\frac{1}{2}}$-space. On the other hand, since a normal space need not be regular, it also need not be completely regular. The following implication does hold, however.

Theorem 5.6.1. *A normal space is completely regular iff it is regular.*

Proof. We need only show that any normal, regular space X is completely regular. Suppose F is a closed subset of X not containing the point x, so that x belongs to the open set $X \setminus F$. By **5.5.1**, there exists an open set G such that $x \in G$ and $\mathbf{c}(G) \subseteq X \setminus F$. Since F and $\mathbf{c}(G)$ are disjoint closed sets in the normal space X, by Urysohn's Lemma there exists a continuous mapping $\mathfrak{f} : X \to [0, 1]$ such that $\mathfrak{f}(F) = \{1\}$ and $\mathfrak{f}(\mathbf{c}(G)) = \{0\}$. Since $x \in G$, $\mathfrak{f}(x) = 0$, and so X is completely regular. ▮

We have already mentioned in the previous section Niemytzki's example of a Tichonov space which is not normal. The Tichonov example given at the end of the previous section is another example of such a space. In particular, the subspace $X \setminus \{\langle \alpha, \beta \rangle\}$, as defined there, is not normal, but it is a Tichonov space. It is a Tichonov space because it is a subset of the compact Hausdorff space X. Thus X is a T_4-space by **5.5.5** and so a Tichonov space, and this is a hereditary property. Indeed, the following result, whose proof requires the Tichonov product theorem given in Section **8.5**, is an important more general result.

Theorem 5.6.2. *A topological space is a Tichonov space iff it is homeomorphic to a subset of a compact Hausdorff space.*

Corollary. *Every locally compact Hausdorff space is a Tichonov space.*

Proof. Every locally compact Hausdorff space is homeomorphic to a subset of its one point compactification, which is a compact Hausdorff space by **5.2.2**. ▮

For any topological space X, we shall call a **compactification** of X any compact space X^* such that X is homeomorphic to a dense subset of X^*. Again considering the one point compactification of a space, we see that every space has some compactification. On the other hand, this compactification is somewhat unsatisfactory since, for example, the one point compactification of a Hausdorff, nonlocally compact space is not even a Hausdorff space. The existence of a Hausdorff compactification for a Hausdorff space is a more interesting question, and we see from the above theorem that it is exactly the Tichonov spaces which have Hausdorff compactifications.

The most interesting use of the family of completely regular spaces is in the study of spaces of real-valued continuous functions. In Chapter 9 we will study such spaces in more detail, but we may note here that it is the Tichonov spaces in which there are "enough" real-valued continuous functions. In particular, it has been shown by Hewitt [43] that there exist T_3-spaces on which every real-valued continuous function is constant; that is, the range of each mapping consists of a single point. This clearly cannot happen in a Tichonov space since, by the following simple result, one can even distinguish between points in a Tichonov space by continuous functions.

Theorem 5.6.3. *If x and y are two distinct points in a Tichonov space X, then there exists a real-valued continuous mapping $\mathfrak{f}$ of X such that $\mathfrak{f}(x) \neq \mathfrak{f}(y)$.*

Proof. Since X is a T_1-space, we may say that the point x does not belong to the closed set $\{y\}$. By **[CR]**, there exists a real-valued continuous mapping $\mathfrak{f}$ of X such that $\mathfrak{f}(x) = 0$ and $\mathfrak{f}(\{y\}) = \{1\}$. ∎

Finally, we may show the very close relationship between the collection of real-valued continuous functions on a Tichonov space and its topology. If $\mathfrak{f}$ is a real-valued continuous mapping of the topological space X, we will call the **cozero set** of $\mathfrak{f}$ the set of points of X at which the mapping $\mathfrak{f}$ is not equal to zero.

Theorem 5.6.4. *A Hausdorff space $(X, \mathscr{T})$ is completely regular (Tichonov) iff the family of all cozero sets of real-valued continuous mappings of X is a base for the topology $\mathscr{T}$.*

Proof. Suppose $(X, \mathscr{T})$ is a Tichonov space and $x^* \in G^* \in \mathscr{T}$. Then x^* does not belong to the closed set $X \setminus G^*$, so, by **[CR]**, there exists a real-valued continuous mapping $\mathfrak{f}$ of X such that $\mathfrak{f}(x^*) = 0$ and $\mathfrak{f}(X \setminus G^*) = \{1\}$. Letting $\mathfrak{f}^*$ be defined by setting $\mathfrak{f}^*(x) = 1 - \mathfrak{f}(x)$ for all $x \subset X$, we obtain a continuous mapping of X such that $\mathfrak{f}^*(x^*) = 1$ and $\mathfrak{f}^*(X \setminus G^*) = \{0\}$. Thus the cozero set of $\mathfrak{f}^*$ contains x^* and is a subset of G^*. Since each cozero set is open and their union is X, this family forms a base for $\mathscr{T}$.

Conversely, suppose the family of cozero sets is a base for $\mathscr{T}$, and suppose x^* is a point which does not lie in the closed set F. Then x^* does belong to the open set $X \setminus F$, and so there must be a cozero set E of some real-valued mapping $\mathfrak{f}$ of X such that $x^* \in E \subseteq X \setminus F$. Thus $\mathfrak{f}(x^*) \neq 0$, so we may define a mapping $\mathfrak{f}^*$ of X by setting $\mathfrak{f}^*(x) = \max \{0, \min\{1, 1 - \mathfrak{f}(x)/\mathfrak{f}(x^*)\}\}$ for all $x \in X$. Clearly $\mathfrak{f}^*(x^*) = 0$, $\mathfrak{f}^*(F) = \{1\}$, and $\mathfrak{f}^*$ is continuous, so that $(X, \mathscr{T})$ is completely regular. ∎

For a very complete discussion of the topic which we have just barely introduced above, the reader is refered to the monograph of Gillman and Jerison [7].

Exercises

1. Complete regularity is a topological property.

2. Complete regularity is a hereditary property.

3. If X is completely regular, then for every pair of disjoint subsets A and B such that A is compact and B is closed, there exists a real-valued continuous mapping $\mathfrak{f}$ of X such that $\mathfrak{f}(A) = \{0\}$ and $\mathfrak{f}(B) = \{1\}$.

4. A completely regular space X is compact iff any family $\mathfrak{E}$ of real-valued continuous functions on X, with the property that any finite subfamily of $\mathfrak{E}$ has a common zero, has a common zero.

5. If a Tichonov space X, consisting of more than one point, is connected, then every nonempty open subset of X is uncountable.

6. A topological space $(X, \mathscr{T})$ will be called **0-dimensional** iff there is a base for $\mathscr{T}$ consisting of sets which are at the same time open and closed. Prove the following results:

(i) Every 0-dimensional T_0-space is completely regular and, in fact, **totally disconnected** (that is, there are no components larger than the individual points).

(ii) The real numbers with the usual topology are not 0-dimensional, but with the lower limit topology of problem **3** in Section **3.4** they are both 0-dimensional and normal.

(iii) The space of problem **8** in Section **5.4** due to Sorgenfrey is 0-dimensional.

(iv) The space of all ordinals less than the first uncountable ordinal, with the order topology, is 0-dimensional.

(v) Any two disjoint closed subsets of a compact 0-dimensional space are contained in disjoint open subsets whose union is the entire space.

(vi) Any two disjoint closed subsets of a second axiom, 0-dimensional space are contained in disjoint open subsets whose union is the entire space.

(vii) Every locally compact, totally disconnected space is 0-dimensional.

(viii) A Hausdorff space is 0-dimensional iff it is totally disconnected and it has a base consisting of sets whose boundaries are compact (see the article by Flachsmeyer in [22]).

For a general discussion of the basic facts of dimension theory, the reader is referred to the text of Hurewicz and Wallman [12].

CHAPTER **6**

Metric Spaces

6.1 Metric Spaces as Topological Spaces

Thus far in our study of topological spaces we have not assumed that there was any notion of a distance between points of our space, merely some information concerning the open sets. We will now consider what properties we should expect from the notion of distance if it should be present. A **metric** for a set X is a mapping d of $X \times X$ into the non-negative reals satisfying, for all x, y, $z \in X$, the following axioms:

[M.1] $d(x, x) = 0$.

[M.2] $d(x, z) \leqslant d(x, y) + d(y, z)$.

[M.3] $d(x, y) = d(y, x)$.

[M.4] If $x \neq y$, then $d(x, y) > 0$.

We will call $d(x, y)$ the **distance** between x and y, and always thus abbreviate $d(\langle x, y\rangle)$.

For the real numbers it is natural to define the distance between two numbers x and y by setting $d(x, y) = | x - y |$. That this function is a metric follows from the elementary properties of the absolute value. For two points $\langle x_1, x_2\rangle$ and $\langle y_1, y_2\rangle$ in the plane, we would usually define distances by setting

$$d(\langle x_1, x_2\rangle, \langle y_1, y_2\rangle) = \sqrt{(x_1 - y_1)^2 + (x_2 - y_2)^2}.$$

In this case, only **[M.2]** is not obvious, and it may be interpreted as requiring that the length of one side of a triangle is always less than or equal to the sum of the lengths of the other two sides. For this reason, axiom **[M.2]** is usually called the "triangle inequality."

Although the natural definitions given above, which we call the **usual** metrics for the line and the plane, respectively, are the most often used and always assumed unless the contrary is stated, it is important to realize that other metrics can be used for these sets. For example, the function d, defined by setting $d(x, x) = 0$ and $d(x, y) = 1$ when $x \neq y$, is a metric for any set.

The importance of a metric for a set is that it gives us a very convenient way to define a topology for the set. If x is a point of a set X with metric d, and ϵ is any positive real number, then the set of all points $y \in X$ such that $d(x, y) < \epsilon$ will be called the **ball** with center x and radius ϵ and will be denoted by $B(x, \epsilon)$. The name "spherical neighborhood" is often used for ball.

Theorem 6.1.1. *The family of all balls of points in a set X with metric d forms a base for a topology for X.*

Proof. Since $X = \bigcup\{B(x, 1) : x \in X\}$, by **3.4.1** we must show that if $x \in B(x_1, \epsilon_1) \cap B(x_2, \epsilon_2)$, then there is a ball containing x which is contained in that intersection. For $i = 1, 2$ we have $x \in B(x_i, \epsilon_i)$, hence $d(x, x_i) < \epsilon_i$, and so $\epsilon_i - d(x, x_i) > 0$. Let $\epsilon = \min_i\{\epsilon_i - d(x, x_i)\} > 0$. We assert that $B(x, \epsilon)$ is the desired ball. Let $y \in B(x, \epsilon)$. Then

$$\begin{aligned} d(y, x_i) &\leqslant d(y, x) + d(x, x_i) = d(x, y) + d(x, x_i) < \epsilon + d(x, x_i) \\ &\leqslant [\epsilon_i - d(x, x_i)] + d(x, x_i) = \epsilon_i \end{aligned}$$

for each i, where we have used **[M.2]**, **[M.3]**, and the definition of ϵ. Thus $B(x, \epsilon) \subseteq B(x_1, \epsilon_1) \cap B(x_2, \epsilon_2)$. ∎

If X is a set with a metric d, the topology for X obtained by using as a base the family of all balls of points is said to be **induced** by the metric d. We will call the set X and metric d a **metric space** (X, d) iff the topology for X is that induced by d. Thus a metric space is a topological space whose topology is induced by a particular metric.

The usual metrics for the line and plane induce the usual topologies, so these will be understood unless some other metric is specifically mentioned. If X is an arbitrary set, and d is the metric defined by setting $d(x, x) = 0$ and $d(x, y) = 1$ when $x \neq y$, then we say that (X, d) is a metric space only when we consider X as a topological space with the discrete topology. This follows from the fact that $B(x, 1/2) = \{x\}$ for every $x \in X$, and so each point is an open set in the induced topology.

It is interesting to note that the discrete topology would also be induced on a set X by the metric d^* defined by setting $d^*(x, x) = 0$ and $d^*(x, y) = 2$ when $x \neq y$. For topological purposes we would not want to distinguish between these two metrics. In general, we will call two metrics for a set **equivalent** iff their induced topologies are the same. For example, the metrics defined by setting

$$d^*(\langle x_1, x_2\rangle, \langle y_1, y_2\rangle) = | x_1 - y_1 | + | x_2 - y_2 |$$

and

$$d^{**}(\langle x_1, x_2\rangle, \langle y_1, y_2\rangle) = \max\{|x_1 - y_1|, |x_2 - y_2|\}$$

are easily shown to be equivalent to the usual metric for the plane. If (X, d) is any metric space, the metric d^* defined by setting $d^*(x, y) = \min\{1, d(x, y)\}$ is equivalent to d and has the obvious property that no two points have d^*-distance of more than one.

The above examples show that there may be many metrics which induce the same topology. The question of whether for a given topology there is any metric which would induce that topology immediately arises. We shall call a topological space $(X, \mathscr{T})$ **metrizable** iff there exists a metric for X which induces $\mathscr{T}$. Sufficient conditions for metrizability will be given in Chapter 10. As we shall soon see, every metrizable space is a Hausdorff space, and so not all topological spaces are metrizable. For the sake of brevity, even when the particular metric is not important we will usually state our theorems for metric spaces rather than for metrizable spaces.

For spaces which are metrizable, the properties of limits and continuity assume a very familiar form when rephrased into metric notation. The necessary rephrasing for limits of sets, limits of sequences, and continuity will be given in the problems. Let us now consider what topological properties must be enjoyed by all metric (metrizable) spaces. The simplest are the following.

Theorem 6.1.2. *Every metric space is a Hausdorff space.*

Proof. Let x and y be distinct points of a metric space (X, d). By **[M.4]**, $d(x, y) > 0$. Let ϵ be a real number such that $0 < 2\epsilon < d(x,y)$. By problem **1**, $B(x, \epsilon)$ and $B(y, \epsilon)$ are open sets containing x and y, respectively. If they were not disjoint, then there would exist some point $z \in B(x, \epsilon) \cap B(y, \epsilon)$. By **[M.2]**, **[M.3]**, and the definition of ϵ, we would have

$$d(x, y) \leqslant d(x, z) + d(z, y) = d(x, z) + d(y, z) < \epsilon + \epsilon < d(x, y),$$

which is a contradiction. Hence the two open sets must be disjoint. ∎

Theorem 6.1.3. *Every metric space is completely normal.*

Proof. Let A and B be separated subsets of a metric space (X, d). For each $x \in A$ and $y \in B$, $x \notin \mathbf{c}(B)$ and $y \notin \mathbf{c}(A)$, and hence there must exist $\epsilon_x > 0$ and $\epsilon_y > 0$ such that $B(x, \epsilon_x) \cap B = \varnothing$ and $B(y, \epsilon_y) \cap A = \varnothing$

by problem **6**. Let $G_A = \bigcup \{B(x, \epsilon_x/2) : x \in A\}$ and $G_B = \bigcup\{B(y, \epsilon_y/2) : y \in B\}$. These are open sets containing A and B, respectively. If they were not disjoint, then there would be a point $z \in G_A \cap G_B$. From the definitions, there would exist points $x \in A$ and $y \in B$ such that $z \in B(x, \epsilon_x/2)$ and $z \in B(y, \epsilon_y/2)$; that is, $d(x, z) < \epsilon_x/2$ and $d(y, z) < \epsilon_y/2$. But, by **[M.2]** and **[M.3]**, $d(x, y) \leqslant d(x, z) + d(z, y) = d(x, z) + d(y, z) < \epsilon_x/2 + \epsilon_y/2$. Thus if $\epsilon_y \leqslant \epsilon_x$, we have $d(x, y) < \epsilon_x$, and so $y \in B(x, \epsilon_x)$; while if $\epsilon_x \leqslant \epsilon_y$, we have $d(x, y) < \epsilon_y$, and so $x \in B(y, \epsilon_y)$. In either case, we would have a contradiction to the definitions of ϵ_x and ϵ_y, so the two open sets are disjoint. ∎

Theorem 6.1.4. *Every metric space is a first axiom space.*

Proof. Let x be a point of a metric space (X, d). If, for each positive integer n, we let $B_n(x) = B(x, 1/n)$, it is clear that we obtain a countable collection $\{B_n(x)\}$ of open sets containing x. Now suppose that x is contained in some open set G. By the definition of the induced topology, there exists some positive number ϵ such that $B(x, \epsilon) \subseteq G$. But then, for each $n > 1/\epsilon$, we have $B_n(x) \subseteq G$, and so X satisfies **[C$_\text{I}$]**. ∎

From these three theorems we conclude that every metric space is a first axiom T_5-space. From this it follows, for example, that continuity for metric spaces is equivalent to sequential continuity by **5.3.4**. Other properties of metric spaces will be obtained in later sections. Corresponding to the isomorphisms between sets and the homeomorphisms between topological spaces, we have the isometries between metric spaces. Two metric spaces (X, d) and (X^*, d^*) will be called **isometric** iff there is a one-to-one mapping $\mathfrak{f}$ of X onto X^* which is distance preserving, that is, such that $d(x, y) = d^*(\mathfrak{f}(x), \mathfrak{f}(y))$ for all $x, y \in X$.

Exercises

1. In the induced topology, every ball in a metric space is an open set.

2. The metric d^* defined by setting

$$d^*(\langle x_1, x_2\rangle, \langle y_1, y_2\rangle) = |x_1 - y_1| + |x_2 - y_2|$$

is equivalent to the usual metric for the plane.

3. The metric d^{**} defined by setting

$$d^{**}(\langle x_1, x_2\rangle, \langle y_1, y_2\rangle) = \max\{|x_1 - y_1|, |x_2 - y_2|\}$$

is equivalent to the usual metric for the plane.

4. Compare the geometric shapes of balls of points in the plane with respect to the usual metric and the metrics given in the two preceding problems.

5. The metric d^* defined by setting $d^*(x, y) = \min\{1, d(x, y)\}$ is equivalent to d.

6. Let $\{x_n\}$ be a sequence of points, x a point, and E a subset of a metric space (X, d), and let $\mathfrak{f}$ be a mapping of X into the metric space (X^*, d^*).

(i) $x \in \mathbf{d}(E)$ iff for every $\epsilon > 0$, $B(x, \epsilon) \cap E \setminus \{x\} \neq \emptyset$.

(ii) $x_n \to x$ iff for every $\epsilon > 0$ there exists an integer $N(\epsilon)$ such that $x_n \in B(x, \epsilon)$ whenever $n > N(\epsilon)$; equivalently, iff $d(x_n, x) \to 0$.

(iii) $\mathfrak{f}$ is continuous at x iff for every $\epsilon > 0$ there exists a $\delta(\epsilon) > 0$ such that $\mathfrak{f}(B(x, \delta(\epsilon))) \subseteq B^*(\mathfrak{f}(x), \epsilon)$; equivalently, iff $x_n \to x$ implies that $\mathfrak{f}(x_n) \to \mathfrak{f}(x)$.

(iv) $x \notin \mathbf{c}(E)$ iff $B(x, \epsilon) \cap E = \emptyset$ for some $\epsilon > 0$.

7. If $x_n \to x$ and $y_n \to y$ in a metric space (X, d), then $d(x_n, y_n) \to d(x, y)$ in the reals.

8. Metrizability is a topological property.

9. Two metrics d and d^* are equivalent for X iff for every sequence $\langle x_n \rangle$ in X, $d(x_n, x) \to 0$ iff $d^*(x_n, x) \to 0$.

10. If X^* is a subset of the metric space (X, d), then the mapping d^* defined by setting $d^*(x, y) = d(x, y)$ for all $x, y \in X^*$ is a metric for X^*. Show that the topology induced on X^* by d^* is the relative topology for X^* as a subspace of X.

11. Compare $\mathbf{c}(B(x, \epsilon))$ with $\{y : d(x, y) \leqslant \epsilon\}$.

12. Let X be the set of all real-valued continuous functions defined on some fixed interval $[a, b]$. If d is the mapping defined by setting $d(\mathfrak{f}, \mathfrak{g}) = \int_a^b | \mathfrak{f}(t) - \mathfrak{g}(t) | \, dt$, then d is a metric for X. If X contains all integrable functions on $[a, b]$, does d remain a metric for X?

13. If E is a subset of a metric space (X, d), then the **diameter** of E, written $\delta(E)$, is defined as follows: $\delta(\emptyset) = 0$; $\delta(E) = \sup\{d(x, y) : x, y \in E\}$ when E is nonempty and the supremum exists; and $\delta(E) = \infty$, otherwise. Obtain the following properties of the diameter for any subsets $A, B, E \subseteq X$:

(i) $\delta(E) = 0$ iff E contains at most one point.

(ii) If $A \subseteq B$, then $\delta(A) \leqslant \delta(B)$.

(iii) $\delta(\mathbf{c}(E)) = \delta(E)$.

(iv) If $A \cap B \neq \emptyset$, then $\delta(A \cup B) \leqslant \delta(A) + \delta(B)$.

14. If A and B are subsets of a metric space (X, d), then the **distance** between A and B, denoted $d(A, B)$, is defined as follows: $d(A, B) = \inf\{d(x, y) : x \in A, y \in B\}$ when A and B are nonempty, and $d(A, B) = \infty$, otherwise. Obtain the following properties of this distance for any subsets $A, B, E \subseteq X$:

(i) If $x \in A$, and $y \in B$, then $d(A, B) \leqslant d(x, y) \leqslant \delta(A \cup B)$.

(ii) $x \in \mathbf{c}(E)$ iff $d(\{x\}, E) = 0$.

(iii) $d(\mathbf{c}(A), \mathbf{c}(B)) = d(A, B)$.

(iv) $\delta(A \cup B) \leqslant \delta(A) + d(A, B) + \delta(B)$.

15. Show that an isometry between metric spaces is a homeomorphism. Show also that the relation of being isometric is an equivalence relation between metric spaces.

16. A T_0-space is the open image of a metric space iff it is a first axiom space (see Ponomarev [69]).

6.2 Topological Properties

An uncountable set with a metric that induces the discrete topology is an example of a metric space which is neither separable, second axiom, nor Lindelöf. In Section **5.4** we saw that the second axiom of countability implied, but was not implied by, separability and the Lindelöf property. We will now show that these three properties are equivalent in a metric space.

Theorem 6.2.1. *Every separable metric space is second axiom.*

Proof. Let (X, d) be a separable metric space, and suppose $E = \{x_n\}$ is a countable dense subset. We assert that the family $\{B(x_n, 1/k) : n, k \in \mathbf{N}\}$ is a countable open base for the topology. As a countable collection of countable collections, the family is certainly countable. Since the members of the family are open (by problem **1** in Section **6.1**), we must show that for each point x contained in an open set G, there is a member of the family containing x and contained in G. By the definition of the induced topology, there exists some $\epsilon > 0$ such that $B(x, \epsilon) \subseteq G$, and let us choose an integer $k > 2/\epsilon$. Since $\mathbf{c}(E) = X$, there exists an integer n such that $x_n \in B(x, 1/k)$, that is, $d(x, x_n) < 1/k$. We assert that $B(x_n, 1/k)$ has the desired properties. Since $d(x, x_n) = d(x_n, x) < 1/k$, it is clear that x is contained in $B(x_n, 1/k)$. Now if $y \in B(x_n, 1/k)$, so that $d(y, x_n) < 1/k$, we have

$$d(x, y) \leqslant d(x, x_n) + d(x_n, y) < 2/k < \epsilon.$$

Thus $y \in B(x, \epsilon) \subseteq G$, and we have $B(x_n, 1/k) \subseteq G$. ∎

Theorem 6.2.2. *Every Lindelöf metric space is second axiom.*

Proof. Consider the open covering $\{B(x, 1) : x \in X\}$ of the Lindelöf metric space (X, d). By the Lindelöf property, there exists a countable subcovering : $\{B(x_n^{(1)}, 1) : n \in \mathbf{N}\}$. Proceeding by induction, we consider the open covering $\{B(x, 1/k) : x \in X\}$ and obtain a countable subcovering $\{B(x_n^{(k)}, 1/k) : n \in \mathbf{N}\}$ for each positive integer k. We assert that the family $\{B(x_n^{(k)}, 1/k) : n, k \in \mathbf{N}\}$ is a countable open base for the topology. It is certainly a countable family of open sets, so let us assume the point x is contained in the open set G. There must exist some $\epsilon > 0$ such that $B(x, \epsilon) \subseteq G$, and let us choose an integer $k > 2/\epsilon$. Since $\{B(x_n^{(k)}, 1/k) : n \in \mathbf{N}\}$ is a covering of X, there exists an integer n such that $x \in B(x_n^{(k)}, 1/k)$, and we assert that this is the desired member of the family. Suppose $y \in B(x_n^{(k)}, 1/k)$, then

$$d(x, y) \leqslant d(x, x_n^{(k)}) + d(x_n^{(k)}, y) < 2/k < \epsilon.$$

Thus $y \in B(x, \epsilon) \subseteq G$, and we have $B(x_n^{(k)}, 1/k) \subseteq G$. ∎

Since every compact space is Lindelöf, it is clear that the three equivalent properties must all be implied by compactness. On the other hand, the example of the noncompact real line shows that the reverse implication does not hold in general. In the following diagram we denote by arrows the implications which hold in any metric space, while no other implications hold (compare with Section **5.4**).

$$\begin{array}{ccccc} & & \text{Compact} & & \\ & \swarrow & \downarrow & \searrow & \\ \text{Separable} & \Leftrightarrow & \text{Second Axiom} & \Leftrightarrow & \text{Lindelöf} \end{array}$$

We will now obtain some additional results concerning compact subsets of metric spaces. When the concept of a compact set was first introduced, it was pointed out that the motivating Heine-Borel Theorem had no meaning in a topological space, since there was no notion of boundedness. In a metric space, however, it is easy to generalize that notion from the real numbers. We shall say that a subset E of a metric space (X, d) is **bounded** iff there exists a real number β such that $d(x, y) < \beta$ for all $x, y \in E$.

Since every metric space is a Hausdorff space, every compact subset of a metric space is closed. We will now show that such subsets are also bounded; in fact they have the following stronger property. If ϵ is a positive real number, an **ϵ-net** for a subset E of a metric space (X, d) is a finite subset F of E such that $E \subseteq \bigcup\{B(x, \epsilon) : x \in F\}$. A subset E will be called **totally bounded** or **precompact** iff it has an ϵ-net for every positive number ϵ.

Since an ϵ-net is a finite set of points, it is clear that every totally bounded set is bounded. Since every compact set is countably compact, we need only show that every countably compact metric space is totally bounded in order to also prove that every compact subset of a metric space is both closed and bounded.

Theorem 6.2.3. *Every countably compact metric space is totally bounded.*

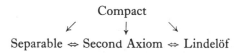

Proof. Suppose the countably compact metric space (X, d) is not totally bounded. Then, for some fixed positive number ϵ, X must have no ϵ-net. Let x_1 be any point of X. Then the finite set $\{x_1\}$ is not an ϵ-net for X, and so there exists a point $x_2 \notin B(x_1, \epsilon)$; that is, $d(x_1, x_2) \geqslant \epsilon$. Now the finite set $\{x_1, x_2\}$ is also not an ϵ-net for X, and so there exists a point $x_3 \notin \bigcup_{i=1}^{2} B(x_i, \epsilon)$; that is, $d(x_1, x_3) \geqslant \epsilon$ and $d(x_2, x_3) \geqslant \epsilon$. We now proceed by induction. If we have defined a set of points $\{x_1, x_2, ..., x_n\}$ such that $d(x_i, x_j) \geqslant \epsilon$ whenever $i \neq j$, then this finite set is not an ϵ-net for X, and so there exists a point $x_{n+1} \notin \bigcup_{i=1}^{n} B(x_i, \epsilon)$; that is, $d(x_i, x_j) \geqslant \epsilon$ whenever $i \neq j$. Now, by induction, we have defined a sequence $\langle x_n \rangle_{n \in \mathbf{N}}$ of distinct points in the countably compact space X such that $d(x_i, x_j) \geqslant \epsilon$ whenever $i \neq j$. Let $E = \bigcup_{n \in \mathbf{N}} \{x_n\}$. By countable compactness, E must have a limit point $x \in X$. But then $B(x, \epsilon/2)$ must contain an infinite number of the points of E, and this contradicts the fact that $d(x_i, x_j) \geqslant \epsilon$ whenever $i \neq j$. ∎

In the next section we will give an example of a metric space in which there are closed and bounded subsets which are not compact. We showed above that the properties of separability, second axiom, and Lindelöf, although distinct in general topological spaces, are equivalent in metric spaces. In the next theorem we shall show that the two properties of compactness and countable compactness, although distinct in general topological spaces, are equivalent in metric spaces.

Lemma. *Every countably compact metric space is separable.*

Proof. If (X, d) is a countably compact metric space, then by the previous theorem there exists a $(1/n)$-net for each $n \in \mathbf{N}$. Let us denote this net by $\{x_1^n, x_2^n, ..., x_{N(n)}^n\}$. Now let us define a set $E = \bigcup_{n \in \mathbf{N}} \bigcup_{i=1}^{N(n)} \{x_i^n\}$. This is clearly a countable subset of X, and we assert that it is dense in X. Let $B(x, \epsilon)$ be an arbitrary ball in the space. Let us choose an integer $n > 1/\epsilon$ and consider the $(1/n)$-net. There must be some integer $i \leqslant N(n)$ such that $x \in B(x_i^n, 1/n)$, and so $x_i^n \in B(x, 1/n) \subseteq B(x, \epsilon)$, as desired. ∎

Theorem 6.2.4. *In a metric space, a set is compact iff it is countably compact.*

Proof. By **4.2.4**, every compact set is countably compact, so let E be a countably compact set in a metric space. As a subspace, E is countably compact, and so, by the lemma, E is separable. By **6.2.1**, E is then second axiom. Since E is also T_1 by **6.1.2**, the Lindelöf Theorem **5.3.6** shows that E is compact (see problem **9** of Section **5.3**). ∎

It is also easy to show that, in a metric space, compactness and sequential compactness are equivalent. The notion of connectedness for metric spaces will be dealt with in the problems.

Exercises

1. Show that the lemma preceding **6.2.4** could be made stronger by stating that every totally bounded metric space is separable.

2. In the plane, define a new distance d^* in terms of the usual metric d by setting $d^*(\mathbf{x}, \mathbf{y}) = d(\mathbf{x}, \mathbf{y})$ if the line between $\mathbf{x}$ and $\mathbf{y}$ passes through the origin $\mathbf{0}$, while $d^*(\mathbf{x}, \mathbf{y}) = d(\mathbf{0}, \mathbf{x}) + (\mathbf{0}, \mathbf{y})$, otherwise. Show that d^* is a metric for the plane and that the resulting space is not separable.

3. If E is a compact subset of a metric space, then $\mathbf{d}(E)$ is compact. Give an example of a topological space which does not have this property.

4. A metric space is compact iff it is sequentially compact (see problem **15** of Section **5.3**).

5. A metric space is compact iff it is pseudocompact (see problem **15** of Section **4.3**).

6. If E is a nonempty compact subset of a metric space, then there exist points x and y in E such that $\delta(E) = d(x, y)$.

7. If x and y are two points of a set E in a metric space (X, d), and ϵ is a positive real number, then an **ϵ-chain** from x to y in E is a finite sequence $x_0, x_1, \ldots, x_n$ of points of E such that $x_0 = x$, $x_n = y$, and $d(x_{i-1}, x_i) < \epsilon$ for $i = 1, 2, \ldots, n$. The set E is **well-chained** iff for every two points x and y of E and any positive ϵ there exists an ϵ-chain from x to y in E. Prove:

(i) Every connected subset of a metric space is well-chained.

(ii) A well-chained subset of a metric space need not be connected.

(iii) A compact subset of a metric space is connected iff it is well-chained.

8. If A and B are compact subsets of a metric space, then there exist points $x \in A$ and $y \in B$ such that $d(A, B) = d(x, y)$.

9. If A is compact, B closed, and $A \cap B = \emptyset$ in a metric space, then $d(A, B) > 0$.

10. A subset of a topological space will be called an **$\mathbf{F}_\sigma$ set** (resp. a **$\mathbf{G}_\delta$ set**) iff it can be written as the countable union (resp. countable intersection) of closed (resp. open) sets. Prove:

(i) A set is an F_σ set (a G_δ set) iff its complement is a G_δ set (an F_σ set).

(ii) The countable union (countable intersection) of F_σ sets (G_δ sets) is an F_σ set (a G_δ set).

(iii) The finite intersection (finite union) of F_σ sets (G_δ sets) is an F_σ set (a G_δ set). Show, by examples, that this does not extend to infinite unions or intersections.

(iv) Every closed (open) subset of a metric space is a G_δ set (an F_σ set). Give an example of a closed subset of a topological space which is not a G_δ set.

(v) The union of any family of closed subsets of a metric space which is linearly ordered by inclusion is an F_σ set.

6.3 Hilbert (l_2) Space

The line and the plane are two examples of a very important type of metric space encountered early in the study of analysis. More generally, **Euclidean n-space** ($\mathbf{R}^n$, $d_E{}^n$) is the set $\mathbf{R}^n$ of all ordered n-tuples $\mathbf{x} = \langle x_1, x_2, ..., x_n \rangle$ of real numbers, with the metric $d_E{}^n$ defined by setting

$$d_E{}^n(\mathbf{x}, \mathbf{y}) = d_E{}^n(\langle x_1, ..., x_n \rangle, \langle y_1, ..., y_n \rangle)$$

$$= \sqrt{\textstyle\sum_{i=1}^n (x_i - y_i)^2}.$$

The real number x_i will be called the ith **coordinate** of $\mathbf{x}$. For a detailed investigation of the properties of $\mathbf{R}^n$, including a proof of the fact that $d_E{}^n$ is actually a metric for $\mathbf{R}^n$, the reader is referred to an advanced calculus text, such as Olmsted [18] or Fulks [6]. We will prove here only the following interesting result.

Theorem 6.3.1. *If, in* $\mathbf{R}^n$, *we let* $\mathbf{x}_k = \langle x_1{}^k, ..., x_n{}^k \rangle$ and $\mathbf{x} = \langle x_1, ..., x_n \rangle$, *then* $\lim_k \mathbf{x}_k = \mathbf{x}$ *iff* $\lim_k x_i{}^k = x_i$ *for every* $i = 1, ..., n$.

Proof. Since $0 \leqslant | x_i{}^k - x_i | \leqslant \sqrt{\sum_{i=1}^n (x_i{}^k - x_i)^2} = d_E{}^n(\mathbf{x}_k, \mathbf{x})$, it is clear that $\lim_k \mathbf{x}_k = \mathbf{x}$ implies that $\lim_k x_i{}^k = x_i$ for each i. Now suppose that $\lim_k x_i{}^k = x_i$ for each i, and let ϵ be an arbitrary positive number. For each i there must exist an integer $K(i, \epsilon)$ such that $| x_i{}^k - x_i | < \epsilon/\sqrt{n}$ whenever $k > K(i, \epsilon)$. Let $K(\epsilon) = \max_i\{K(i, \epsilon)\}$. For each $k > K(\epsilon)$ we must have

$$d_E{}^n(\mathbf{x}_k, \mathbf{x}) < \sqrt{\textstyle\sum_{i=1}^n (\epsilon/\sqrt{n})^2} = \epsilon. \blacksquare$$

It is natural to try to generalize the notion of Euclidean n-space from finite to infinite sequences of real numbers. Since the infinite series of squares might not converge, we may either use the analogous formula for distances and restrict the number of sequences allowed in the space, or else allow all infinite sequences of reals in the space but change the form of the distance formula. The former will be done in this section, while the latter will be done in the next section.

Hilbert space ($\mathbf{H}$, d_H) is the set $\mathbf{H}$ of all infinite sequences $\mathbf{x} = \langle x_1, x_2, ..., x_i, ... \rangle$ of real numbers for which $\sum_{i=1}^\infty x_i{}^2$ converges, with the metric d_H defined by setting

$$d_H(\mathbf{x}, \mathbf{y}) = d_H(\langle x_1, x_2, ...\rangle, \langle y_1, y_2, ...\rangle)$$
$$= \sqrt{\Sigma_{i=1}^{\infty} (x_i - y_i)^2}.$$

The name l_2 is often given to this space, and it is an example of a family of spaces of sequences of real numbers. For information about this family of spaces, the reader is referred to a text on functional analysis such as Kolmogorov and Fomin [16] or Taylor [23]. It should be noted that in modern works the term "Hilbert space" usually refers to a complete, infinite-dimensional, inner-product space. The classical prototype of this type of space is $\mathbf{H}$ and was first studied by Hilbert.

That d_H is a metric for $\mathbf{H}$ follows from the Schwarz inequality, and we thus have a generalization of $d_E{}^n$. It is interesting to note that the analogue of **6.3.1** does not hold in Hilbert space.

Theorem 6.3.2. *If, in* $\mathbf{H}$, we let $\mathbf{x}_k = \langle x_1{}^k, x_2{}^k, ...\rangle$ *and* $\mathbf{x} = \langle x_1, x_2, ...\rangle$, *then* $\lim_k \mathbf{x}_k = \mathbf{x}$ *implies that* $\lim_k x_i{}^k = x_i$ *for every* $i \in \mathbf{N}$, *but not conversely.*

Proof. Since $0 \leqslant | x_i{}^k - x_i | \leqslant \sqrt{\Sigma_{i=1}^{\infty}(x_i{}^k - x_i)^2} = d_H(\mathbf{x}_k, \mathbf{x})$, the above implication is obvious. On the other hand, if $x_i{}^k$ is defined to be equal to one if $i = k$ and equal to zero if $i \neq k$, then we have $\lim_k x_i{}^k = 0$ for each $i \in \mathbf{N}$. However, $\lim_k \mathbf{x}_k \neq \mathbf{0} = \langle 0, 0, ...\rangle$ since $d_H(\mathbf{x}_k, \mathbf{0}) = 1$ for each k. ▌

We will now obtain some properties of Hilbert space. In our first theorem we will give an example of a closed and bounded subset of Hilbert space which is not compact, so that we cannot hope to obtain the Heine-Borel Theorem in general metric spaces.

Theorem 6.3.3. *Hilbert space is not locally compact.*

Proof. If $\mathbf{H}$ were locally compact, then any point $\mathbf{x} \in \mathbf{H}$ would be contained in some compact neighborhood. Hence, for small enough $\epsilon > 0$, the closed and bounded closed ball $\bar{B}(\mathbf{x}, \epsilon) = \{\mathbf{y} : d_H(\mathbf{x}, \mathbf{y}) \leqslant \epsilon\}$ would be compact. Now if $\mathbf{x} = \langle x_1, x_2, ...\rangle$, we may define a sequence of points $\mathbf{x}_n = \langle x_1, ..., x_{n-1}, x_n + \epsilon, x_{n+1}, ...\rangle$ which are clearly in $\bar{B}(\mathbf{x}, \epsilon)$ and are such that $d_H(\mathbf{x}_i, \mathbf{x}_j) = \sqrt{2}\epsilon$ whenever $i \neq j$. Since the sequence $\langle \mathbf{x}_n \rangle$ can have no convergent subsequence, $\bar{B}(\mathbf{x}, \epsilon)$ is not compact. ▌

Although Hilbert space is not even locally compact, it does have some compact subsets of interest. One important such subset is the **Hilbert cube** consisting of all points of **H** with $0 \leqslant x_i \leqslant 1/i$ for every i. The following lemma, analogous to **6.3.1**, will allow us to prove this result.

Lemma. *Coordinatewise and pointwise convergence are equivalent in the Hilbert cube.*

Proof. In the notation of **6.3.2**, we need only show that $\lim_k \mathbf{x}_k = \mathbf{x}$ whenever $\lim_k x_i^k = x_i$ for all $i \in \mathbf{N}$, where the sequence of points $\langle \mathbf{x}_k \rangle$ belongs to the Hilbert cube. Since $0 \leqslant x_i^k \leqslant 1/i$, the compactness of the closed interval $[0, 1/i]$ implies that $0 \leqslant x_i \leqslant 1/i$, and so the point $\mathbf{x}$ must also belong to the Hilbert cube. Let $\epsilon > 0$ be given, and choose an integer $N = N(\epsilon)$ such that $\sum_{i=N+1}^{\infty}(1/i)^2 < \epsilon^2/2$. Now, for each $i = 1, ..., N$, there exists an integer $K(i, \epsilon)$ such that $| x_i^k - x_i | < \epsilon/\sqrt{2N}$ whenever $k > K(i, \epsilon)$. Let $K(\epsilon) = \max_i\{K(i, \epsilon)\}$. Then, for all $k > K(\epsilon)$, we have

$$d_H(\mathbf{x}_k, \mathbf{x}) = \sqrt{\textstyle\sum_{i=1}^{N} (x_i^k - x_i)^2 + \sum_{i=N+1}^{\infty} (x_i^k - x_i)^2}$$

$$\leqslant \sqrt{\textstyle\sum_{i=1}^{N} (\epsilon/\sqrt{2N})^2 + \sum_{i=N+1}^{\infty} (1/i)^2}$$

$$< \sqrt{N(\epsilon^2/2N) + \epsilon^2/2} = \epsilon.$$

Theorem 6.3.4. *The Hilbert cube is compact.*

Proof. We shall show that the Hilbert cube is sequentially compact and apply problem **4** of Section **6.2**. Let $\langle \mathbf{x}_n \rangle$ be a sequence of points in the Hilbert cube. The sequence of first coordinates consists of real numbers in the compact interval $[0, 1]$, and so there exists an infinite subsequence $\langle \mathbf{x}_n^{(1)} \rangle$ of the original sequence whose first coordinates converge to a number $x_1 \in [0, 1]$. In the same way, from this subsequence there must exist another subsequence $\langle \mathbf{x}_n^{(2)} \rangle$ whose second coordinates converge to a number $x_2 \in [0, \frac{1}{2}]$, while their first coordinates still converge to x_1. We may continue this process by induction. Finally, the "diagonal" subsequence $\langle \mathbf{x}_n^{(n)} \rangle$ of these subsequences will converge coordinatewise to the point $\langle x_1, x_2, ... \rangle$, which must also belong to the Hilbert cube. By the lemma, this subsequence will also converge pointwise as desired. ▮

Although not compact, Hilbert space does have the three equivalent properties of separability, second axiom, and Lindelöf.

Theorem 6.3.5. *Hilbert space is separable (second axiom, Lindelöf).*

Proof. Let **E** be the subset of **H** consisting of all points with rational coordinates and only a finite number of them nonzero; that is, each point of **E** has the form $\langle r_1, ..., r_n, 0, 0, 0, ...\rangle$ with each r_i rational. Clearly, the set **E** is countable, and we assert that it is dense in **H**. Let $B(\mathbf{x}, \epsilon)$ be an arbitrary ball in **H**, and suppose $\mathbf{x} = \langle x_1, x_2, ...\rangle$. Since $\mathbf{x} \in H$, there exists an integer $N = N(\epsilon)$ such that $\sum_{i=N+1}^{\infty} x_i^2 < \epsilon^2/2$. Now for each $i = 1, ..., N$, there exists a rational number r_i such that $| x_i - r_i | < \epsilon/\sqrt{2N}$. The point $\mathbf{r} = \langle r_1, ..., r_N, 0, 0, 0, ...\rangle$ then belongs to **E** and is such that

$$d_H(\mathbf{x}, \mathbf{r}) = \sqrt{\textstyle\sum_{i=1}^{N} (x_i - r_i)^2 + \sum_{i=N+1}^{\infty} (x_i - 0)^2}$$

$$< \sqrt{N(\epsilon/\sqrt{2N})^2 + \epsilon^2/2} = \epsilon. \blacksquare$$

Although a set is always a dense subset of itself (not dense-in-itself, however!), Hilbert space has a property that is almost the opposite of this. A subset E of a topological space X is called **nowhere dense** iff every nonempty open set in X contains a nonempty open set which is disjoint from E. An equivalent condition is that $\mathbf{i}(\mathbf{c}(E)) = \emptyset$. If E is nowhere dense in X, then $X \setminus E$ is dense in X. The converse of this is not true, however, as the example of the rationals shows.

Theorem 6.3.6. *Hilbert space is isometric to a nowhere dense subset of itself.*

Proof. Let **E** be the subset of **H** consisting of all points whose first coordinate is zero. Define a mapping $\mathfrak{f}$ of **H** into **E** by setting

$$\mathfrak{f}(\langle x_1, x_2, ...\rangle) = \langle 0, x_1, x_2, ...\rangle.$$

This is clearly a well-defined one-to-one mapping of **H** onto **E**, and it is an isometry since, for any $\mathbf{x}, \mathbf{y} \in \mathbf{H}$,

$$d_H(\mathbf{x}, \mathbf{y}) = \sqrt{\textstyle\sum_{i=1}^{\infty} (x_i - y_i)^2}$$

$$= \sqrt{0 + \textstyle\sum_{i=2}^{\infty} (x_{i-1} - y_{i-1})^2}$$

$$= d_H(\mathfrak{f}(\mathbf{x}), \mathfrak{f}(\mathbf{y})).$$

We assert that **E** is nowhere dense. Let $B(\mathbf{x}, \epsilon)$ be an arbitrary ball in **H**.

If $\mathbf{x} = \langle x_1, x_2, \ldots \rangle$, then we may choose a nonzero real number a such that $| x_1 - a | < \epsilon/2$, and let $\mathbf{y} = \langle a, x_2, x_3, \ldots \rangle$, which is certainly a point of $\mathbf{H}$. Let $\epsilon^* = \min\{| a |, \epsilon/2\}$. We assert that $B(\mathbf{y}, \epsilon^*) \subseteq B(\mathbf{x}, \epsilon)$ and $B(\mathbf{y}, \epsilon^*)$ is disjoint from $\mathbf{E}$. If $\mathbf{z} \in B(\mathbf{y}, \epsilon^*)$, then $d_H(\mathbf{x}, \mathbf{z}) \leqslant d_H(\mathbf{x}, \mathbf{y}) + d_H(\mathbf{y}, \mathbf{z}) < (\epsilon/2) + \epsilon^* \leqslant (\epsilon/2) + (\epsilon/2) = \epsilon$, so that $\mathbf{z} \in B(\mathbf{x}, \epsilon)$. Thus $B(\mathbf{y}, \epsilon^*) \subseteq B(\mathbf{x}, \epsilon)$. If $B(\mathbf{y}, \epsilon^*)$ was not disjoint from $\mathbf{E}$, then there would be a point $\mathbf{z}$ in both. But then the first coordinate of $\mathbf{z}$ would be zero, and $d_H(\mathbf{y}, \mathbf{z})$ would be at least as large as their difference in first coordinates, $| a |$. Thus $d_H(\mathbf{y}, \mathbf{z}) \geqslant | a | \geqslant \epsilon^* > d_H(\mathbf{y}, \mathbf{z})$, which is a contradiction. ∎

Exercises

1. Show that d_E^{n*} defined by setting $d_E^{n*}(\mathbf{x}, \mathbf{y}) = \sum_{i=1}^n | x_i - y_i |$ is a metric for $\mathbf{R}^n$ which is equivalent to d_E^n. Show also that $d_E^{n**}(\mathbf{x}, \mathbf{y}) = \max_i\{| x_i - y_i |\}$ is also equivalent to d_E^n.

2. Show that d_H is a metric for $\mathbf{H}$.

3. For every pair $\mathbf{x}, \mathbf{y}$ of points of $\mathbf{H}$, show that there exists a unique "midpoint" $\mathbf{z} \in \mathbf{H}$ such that $d_H(\mathbf{x}, \mathbf{z}) = d_H(\mathbf{y}, \mathbf{z}) = d_H(\mathbf{x}, \mathbf{y})/2$. From this show that although $\mathbf{R}^n$ is isometric to a subset of $\mathbf{H}$ for each n, there are metric spaces with just four points which are not isometric to any subset of $\mathbf{H}$.

4. Let $X = \{\mathbf{x} = \langle x_1, x_2, \ldots \rangle : 0 \leqslant x_i \leqslant 1\}$ with $d(\mathbf{x}, \mathbf{y})$ defined to be $\sum_{i=1}^\infty 2^{-i} | x_i - y_i |$. Prove that (X, d) is a metric space. Define a mapping $\mathfrak{f}$ of the Hilbert cube into X by setting $\mathfrak{f}(\langle x_1, x_2, \ldots, x_i, \ldots \rangle) = \langle x_1, 2x_2, \ldots, ix_i, \ldots \rangle$. Prove that $\mathfrak{f}$ is continuous. From this conclude that (X, d) is homeomorphic to the Hilbert cube.

5. Show that a set E is nowhere dense iff $\mathbf{i}(\mathbf{c}(E)) = \varnothing$. Show that if E is nowhere dense, then $X \setminus E$ is dense in X, while if E is open and dense in X, then $X \setminus E$ is nowhere dense.

6. Let $\mathfrak{c}$ be the family of all convergent sequences of real numbers with $d_{\mathfrak{c}}(\mathbf{x}, \mathbf{y}) = \sup_i\{| x_i - y_i |\}$. Prove that $(\mathfrak{c}, d_{\mathfrak{c}})$ is a metric space which is separable but not locally compact.

7. Let $\mathfrak{b}$ be the family of all bounded sequences of real numbers with $d_{\mathfrak{b}}(\mathbf{x}, \mathbf{y}) = \sup_i\{| x_i - y_i |\}$. Prove that $(\mathfrak{b}, d_{\mathfrak{b}})$ is a metric space which is neither separable nor locally compact.

8. Let $\mathbf{H}^*$ be the family of all sequences of complex numbers for which the series of squares of absolute values converges, with $d^*(\mathbf{x}, \mathbf{y}) = \sqrt{\sum_{i=1}^\infty | x_i - y_i |^2}$. Show that $(\mathbf{H}^*, d^*)$ is a metric space which is isometric with $(\mathbf{H}, d_H)$ under the mapping taking $\langle x_1 + iy_1, x_2 + iy_2, \ldots \rangle$ into $\langle x_1, y_1, x_2, y_2, \ldots \rangle$.

6.4 Fréchet Space

In this section we will generalize the notion of Euclidean n-space to all infinite sequences of real numbers by changing the form of the metric.

Fréchet space $(\mathbf{F}, d_F)$ is the set $\mathbf{F}$ of all infinite sequences $\mathbf{x} = \langle x_1, x_2, \ldots \rangle$ of real numbers, with the metric d_F defined by setting

$$d_F(\mathbf{x}, \mathbf{y}) = d_F(\langle x_1, x_2, \ldots \rangle, \langle y_1, y_2, \ldots \rangle)$$
$$= \Sigma_{i=1}^{\infty} 2^{-i} \mid x_i - y_i \mid / (1 + \mid x_i - y_i \mid).$$

That d_F is a metric for $\mathbf{F}$ follows from the inequality

$$\frac{\mid \alpha + \beta \mid}{1 + \mid \alpha + \beta \mid} \leqslant \frac{\mid \alpha \mid}{1 + \mid \alpha \mid} + \frac{\mid \beta \mid}{1 + \mid \beta \mid},$$

which holds for all real numbers α and β. Unlike Hilbert space, in Fréchet space, pointwise and coordinatewise convergence are equivalent.

Theorem 6.4.1. *If, in* $\mathbf{F}$, *we let* $\mathbf{x}_k = \langle x_1{}^k, x_2{}^k, \ldots \rangle$ *and* $\mathbf{x} = \langle x_1, x_2, \ldots \rangle$, *then* $\lim_k \mathbf{x}_k = \mathbf{x}$ *iff* $\lim_k x_i^k = x_i$ *for every* $i \in \mathbf{N}$.

Proof. Since $0 \leqslant 2^{-i} \mid x_i^k - x_i \mid / (1 + \mid x_i^k - x_i \mid) \leqslant d_F(\mathbf{x}_k, \mathbf{x})$ for each i, if $\lim_k \mathbf{x}_k = \mathbf{x}$, then

$$\lim_k 2^{-i} \mid x_i^k - x_i \mid / (1 + \mid x_i^k - x_i \mid) = 0$$

for each i. But i is a constant and the denominator is at least one, so for each i, $\lim_k \mid x_i^k - x_i \mid = 0$, as desired.

Now suppose that $\lim_k x_i^k = x_i$ for each i, and ϵ is any positive number. Choose $N = N(\epsilon)$ such that $\Sigma_{i=N+1}^{\infty} 2^{-i} < \epsilon/2$. For each $i = 1, \ldots, N$ there exists a $K(i, \epsilon)$ such that $\mid x_i^k - x_i \mid < \epsilon/2N$ whenever $k > K(i, \epsilon)$. Let $K(\epsilon) = \max_i \{K(i, \epsilon)\}$. Then, for all $k > K(\epsilon)$, we have

$$d_F(\mathbf{x}_k, \mathbf{x}) \leq \Sigma_{i=1}^{N} \mid x_i^k - x_i \mid + \Sigma_{i=N+1}^{\infty} 2^{-i}$$
$$< N(\epsilon/2N) + \epsilon/2 = \epsilon. \blacksquare$$

In addition to being an interesting generalization of $\mathbf{R}^n$, Fréchet space is important in that it may be considered as the topological prototype of all separable metric spaces. The next theorem shows that the study of separable metric spaces may be considered as the study of topological properties of subsets of Fréchet space.

Theorem 6.4.2. *Every separable metric space is homeomorphic to some subset of Fréchet space.*

Proof. Let (X, d) be a separable metric space, and let $\{x_n\}$ be a denumerable dense subset of X. We define a mapping $\mathfrak{f}$ of X into $\mathbf{F}$ by setting $\mathfrak{f}(x) = \langle d(x, x_1), d(x, x_2), \ldots\rangle$ for each $x \in X$. This is clearly a well-defined mapping of X onto the subset $\mathfrak{f}(X)$ of $\mathbf{F}$, and we assert that it is a homeomorphism. Suppose x and y are two distinct points of X. Since $d(x, y) > 0$, and the set $\{x_n\}$ is dense in X, there must exist an integer n such that $d(x, x_n) < d(x, y)/2$. Hence,

$$2d(x, x_n) < d(x, y) \leqslant d(x, x_n) + d(x_n, y),$$

and so $d(x, x_n) < d(x_n, y) = d(y, x_n)$. But these two distances are the nth coordinates of $\mathfrak{f}(x)$ and $\mathfrak{f}(y)$, so that $\mathfrak{f}(x) \neq \mathfrak{f}(y)$ and $\mathfrak{f}$ is one-to-one. To prove that $\mathfrak{f}$ is continuous we need only show, by problem **6** of Section **6.1**, that $y_k \to y$ always implies that $\mathfrak{f}(y_k) \to \mathfrak{f}(y)$. But in $\mathbf{F}$ pointwise and coordinatewise convergence are equivalent, so we need only consider the ith coordinates; that is, does $y_k \to y$ imply that $d(y_k, x_i) \to d(y, x_i)$ for each i? But this was shown in problem **7** of Section **6.1**. Finally, to show that $\mathfrak{f}$ is open (that is, $\mathfrak{f}^{-1}$ is also continuous), we will suppose that $\mathfrak{f}(y_k) \to \mathfrak{f}(y)$ and show that $y_k \to y$. Let ϵ be an arbitrary positive number. Since the set $\{x_n\}$ is dense in X, there must exist an integer n such that $d(y, x_n) < \epsilon/2$. But $\mathfrak{f}(y_k) \to \mathfrak{f}(y)$ implies that the nth coordinates converge, so

$$d(y_k, x_n) \to d(y, x_n) < \epsilon/2.$$

There must then exist an integer $K(\epsilon)$ such that $d(y_k, x_n) < \epsilon/2$ whenever $k > K(\epsilon)$. Thus we have

$$d(y_k, y) \leqslant d(y_k, x_n) + d(x_n, y) < \epsilon/2 + \epsilon/2 = \epsilon$$

whenever $k > K(\epsilon)$. ∎

Exercises

1. Show that d_F is a metric for $\mathbf{F}$.

2. Give a direct proof of the separability of Fréchet space by finding a countable dense subset.

3. Show that Fréchet space is homeomorphic to a subset of the Hilbert cube (see Sierpinski [20], p. 138).

4. Let (X, d) be a fixed bounded metric space. Let $\mathscr{F}^*$ denote the family of all nonempty, closed subsets of X and define d^* by setting

$$d^*(A, B) = \max\{\sup_{x\in A} \inf_{y\in B} d(x, y), \sup_{y\in B} \inf_{x\in A} d(x, y)\}$$

for every pair A and B in $\mathscr{F}^*$. Show that d^* is a metric (called the **Hausdorff metric**) for $\mathscr{F}^*$. Prove that if X is totally bounded (compact, separable and compact), then so is $\mathscr{F}^*$. For further information on this subject, see Kelley [44] and Michael [58].

6.5 Space of Continuous Functions

In advanced analysis an important subject is the study of spaces whose points are themselves functions, the so-called "function spaces." In this section we will study one standard example of a function space, which will illustrate some of the general ideas behind this subject.

The space $(\mathfrak{C}, d_{\mathfrak{C}})$ is the set $\mathfrak{C}$ of all real-valued continuous functions defined on $I = [0,1]$ with the metric $d_{\mathfrak{C}}$ defined by setting

$$d_{\mathfrak{C}}(\mathfrak{f}, \mathfrak{g}) = \sup\{| \mathfrak{f}(t) - \mathfrak{g}(t) | : t \in I\}.$$

We will call this space the **space of continuous functions** on I. It is easy to see that $d_{\mathfrak{C}}$ actually is a metric for $\mathfrak{C}$; in fact, by the compactness of I, there exists some point $t^* \in I$ at which $| \mathfrak{f}(t^*) - \mathfrak{g}(t^*) | = d_{\mathfrak{C}}(\mathfrak{f}, \mathfrak{g})$. It is important to note that the convergence of a sequence of points of $\mathfrak{C}$ corresponds to the uniform convergence of the sequence of functions considered in the usual sense of analysis.

It is easy to see that the space $\mathfrak{C}$ is not compact since the sequence of points (that is, real-valued functions) $\langle \mathfrak{f}_n \rangle$ defined by setting $\mathfrak{f}_n(t) = n$ for all $t \in I$ has no convergent subsequence. Actually, the following stronger result holds.

Theorem 6.5.1. *$(\mathfrak{C}, d_{\mathfrak{C}})$ is not locally compact.*

Proof. Let $B(\mathfrak{z}, \epsilon)$ be an arbitrary ball about the point $\mathfrak{z} \in \mathfrak{C}$ defined by setting $\mathfrak{z}(t) = 0$ for all $t \in I$. By definition, $B(\mathfrak{z}, \epsilon) = \{\mathfrak{f} : \mathfrak{f} \in \mathfrak{C}$ and $| \mathfrak{f}(t) | < \epsilon$ for all $t \in I\}$. We now define a sequence $\langle \mathfrak{f}_n \rangle$ of points of $\mathfrak{C}$ as follows:

$$\begin{aligned} \mathfrak{f}_n(t) &= -\epsilon/2 \qquad \text{if} \qquad 0 \leqslant t \leqslant 1/(n+1), \\ &= +\epsilon/2 \qquad \text{if} \qquad 1/n \leqslant t \leqslant 1, \\ &= (\epsilon/2)\,[2n(n+1)\,t - (2n+1)] \\ &\qquad\qquad\quad \text{if} \qquad 1/(n+1) \leqslant t \leqslant 1/n. \end{aligned}$$

It is easy to verify that $\mathfrak{f}_n \in B(\mathfrak{z}, \epsilon)$ for every n, and that $d_{\mathfrak{C}}(\mathfrak{f}_i, \mathfrak{f}_j) = \epsilon$ whenever $i \neq j$. Thus we have a sequence of points in $B(\mathfrak{z}, \epsilon)$ which has no convergent subsequence. ∎

For many purposes it is the uniform continuity of a continuous function defined on I that is important. The notion of uniform continuity may be generalized to metric spaces. A mapping $\mathfrak{f}$ of a metric space (X, d) into a metric space (X^*, d^*) is **uniformly continuous** on X iff for every $\epsilon > 0$ there exists a $\delta(\epsilon) > 0$ such that $d^*(\mathfrak{f}(x), \mathfrak{f}(y)) < \epsilon$ whenever $d(x, y) < \delta(\epsilon)$. As in the case of real functions, continuous functions on compact sets are uniformly continuous.

Theorem 6.5.2. *If $\mathfrak{f}$ is a continuous mapping of the compact metric space (X, d) into the metric space (X^*, d^*), then $\mathfrak{f}$ is uniformly continuous on X.*

Proof. Let ϵ be an arbitrary positive number. Since $\mathfrak{f}$ is continuous on X, it is continuous at each point of X. Thus, for each $x \in X$, there exists a $\delta(\epsilon, x) > 0$ such that $d^*(\mathfrak{f}(x), \mathfrak{f}(y)) < \epsilon/2$ whenever $d(x, y) < \delta(\epsilon, x)$. Since the family $\{B(x, \delta(\epsilon, x)/2) : x \in X\}$ forms an open covering of the compact space X, there must exist some finite subcovering $\{B(x_i, \delta(\epsilon, x_i)/2) : i = 1, ..., n\}$. Now let $\delta(\epsilon) = \min_i\{\delta(\epsilon, x_i)/2\}$. It is easy to verify that this $\delta(\epsilon)$ satisfies the conditions for uniform continuity. ▮

The final result we shall prove about $\mathfrak{C}$ is that it is separable (second axiom, Lindelöf).

Theorem 6.5.3. $(\mathfrak{C}, d_{\mathfrak{C}})$ *is separable.*

Proof. For each $n \in \mathbf{N}$, let $\mathfrak{E}_n$ be the set of points in $\mathfrak{C}$ (that is, real-valued functions) which take on rational values at the points k/n $(k = 0, 1, ..., n)$ and are linear in each of the intervals $((k-1)/n, k/n)$ for $k = 1, 2, ..., n$. Since each of the sets $\mathfrak{E}_n$ is countable, it is clear that their union $\mathfrak{E} = \bigcup_{n \in \mathbf{N}} \mathfrak{E}_n$ is a countable subset of $\mathfrak{C}$. We assert that it is dense in $\mathfrak{C}$. Let $B(\mathfrak{f}, \epsilon)$ be an arbitrary ball in $\mathfrak{C}$. By the previous theorem, $\mathfrak{f}$ is uniformly continuous on I, and so there exists a $\delta(\epsilon) > 0$ such that $|\mathfrak{f}(t_1) - \mathfrak{f}(t_2)| < \epsilon/5$ whenever $|t_1 - t_2| < \delta(\epsilon)$. We choose a positive integer n such that $1/n < \delta(\epsilon)$, and then for each $k = 0, 1, ..., n$ we choose a rational number r_k such that $|\mathfrak{f}(k/n) - r_k| < \epsilon/5$. Let $\mathfrak{g}$ be the function which takes on the value r_k at the point k/n $(k = 0, 1, ..., n)$ and is linear in each of the intervals $((k-1)/n, k/n)$ for $k = 1, 2, ..., n$. Clearly, $\mathfrak{g} \in \mathfrak{E}$. Now for each $t \in I$ there exists an integer k such that $k/n \leqslant t < (k+1)/n$. Since $\mathfrak{g}$ is linear, $|\mathfrak{g}(k/n) - \mathfrak{g}(t)| \leqslant |\mathfrak{g}(k/n) - \mathfrak{g}((k+1)/n)|$, and so, by the triangle inequality,

$$\begin{aligned}
| \mathfrak{f}(t) - \mathfrak{g}(t) | &\leqslant | \mathfrak{f}(t) - \mathfrak{g}(k/n) | + | \mathfrak{g}(k/n) - \mathfrak{g}(t) | \\
&\leqslant | \mathfrak{f}(t) - \mathfrak{g}(k/n) | + | \mathfrak{g}(k/n) - \mathfrak{g}((k+1)/n) | \\
&\leqslant | \mathfrak{f}(t) - \mathfrak{f}(k/n) | + | \mathfrak{f}(k/n) - \mathfrak{g}(k/n) | \\
&\quad + | \mathfrak{g}(k/n) - \mathfrak{f}(k/n) | + | \mathfrak{f}(k/n) - \mathfrak{f}((k+1)/n) | \\
&\quad + | \mathfrak{f}((k+1)/n) - \mathfrak{g}((k+1)/n) | \\
&< 5(\epsilon/5) = \epsilon.
\end{aligned}$$

Since this inequality holds for all $t \in I$, and the supremum of $| \mathfrak{f}(t) - \mathfrak{g}(t) |$ is actually taken on, $d_{\mathfrak{C}}(\mathfrak{f}, \mathfrak{g}) < \epsilon$, as desired. ▌

Another interesting property of $(\mathfrak{C}, d_{\mathfrak{C}})$, similar to **6.4.2**, is given in the famous **Banach-Mazur Theorem**: *Every separable metric space is isometric to some subset of* $(\mathfrak{C}, d_{\mathfrak{C}})$. For a proof of this theorem, the reader is referred to the text of Sierpinski [20].

Exercises

1. Show that $d_{\mathfrak{C}}$ is a metric for $\mathfrak{C}$.

2. Define uniform convergence for sequences of mappings of metric spaces and prove that the uniform limit of continuous mappings is continuous.

3. Show that $\mathfrak{f}_n \in B(\mathfrak{z}, \epsilon)$ for all n in **6.5.1**.

4. Suppose $\mathfrak{f}$ is a mapping of the subset E of the metric space X into the metric space X^*. The **oscillation** of $\mathfrak{f}$ at a point $x \in X$ is defined to be $\inf\{\delta(\mathfrak{f}(E \cap G)) : G \text{ open containing } x\}$. Prove that $\mathfrak{f}$ is continuous at $x \in E$ iff the oscillation of $\mathfrak{f}$ at x is zero. Prove also that if $\mathfrak{f}$ is uniformly continuous on E then the oscillation of $\mathfrak{f}$ is zero at every point of X.

5. Verify that $\delta(\epsilon)$ as defined in the proof of **6.5.2** does satisfy the conditions for uniform continuity.

6. If $\mathfrak{f}$ is a continuous mapping of the metric space (X, d) into the metric space Y, then there exists a metric d^* for X equivalent to d such that $\mathfrak{f}$ is uniformly continuous relative to d^* and the metric for Y. (See Levine [52].)

7. Give an example of a set which is not compact but which possesses the property that every real-valued continuous mapping of the space is uniformly continuous on the set. (For an investigation of sets which have this property, see Levine and Saunders [54] and Mrówka [60].)

8. Let $\mathfrak{B}$ be the set of all bounded real-valued functions defined on I with the metric $d_{\mathfrak{B}}$ defined by setting $d_{\mathfrak{B}}(\mathfrak{f}, \mathfrak{g}) = \sup\{| \mathfrak{f}(t) - \mathfrak{g}(t) | : t \in I\}$. Prove that $(\mathfrak{B}, d_{\mathfrak{B}})$ is a metric space which is neither separable nor locally compact.

9. For the set $\mathfrak{C}$ define another metric $d_{\mathfrak{C}}^*$ by setting $d_{\mathfrak{C}}^*(\mathfrak{f}, \mathfrak{g}) = \int_0^1 | \mathfrak{f}(t) - \mathfrak{g}(t) | \, dt$. Prove that this is a metric for $\mathfrak{C}$. Is it equivalent to $d_{\mathfrak{C}}$? What properties does it have?

10. Suppose $\mathfrak{f}$ is a mapping of the metric space (X, d) into the metric space (X^*, d^*), then $\mathfrak{f}$ is uniformly continuous iff $d^*(\mathfrak{f}(A), \mathfrak{f}(B)) = 0$ whenever $d(A, B) = 0$. (See Efremovich [39].)

CHAPTER **7**

Complete Metric Spaces

7.1 Cauchy Sequences

The notion of a Cauchy sequence plays a very important role in the study of the real numbers and may be generalized to metric spaces immediately. A sequence $\langle x_n \rangle$ of points in a metric space (X, d) will be called a **Cauchy sequence** iff for every positive number ϵ there exists an integer $N(\epsilon)$ such that $d(x_m, x_n) < \epsilon$ whenever $m, n > N(\epsilon)$.

The property of being a Cauchy sequence depends strongly on the particular metric for the space, in the sense that equivalent metrics may not have the same Cauchy sequences. For example, let X be the set of all real numbers of the form $1/n$ for some $n \in \mathbf{N}$. With the metric induced by the usual metric for the reals, X has the discrete topology, as it would with the metric for which distinct points have distance one. With the usual metric the sequence $\langle 1/n \rangle$ is a Cauchy sequence, while it is not a Cauchy sequence with the equivalent other metric.

One direct application of the notion of a Cauchy sequence is the following characterization of total boundedness (**6.2.3**).

Theorem 7.1.1. *A metric space (X, d) is totally bounded iff every sequence in X contains a Cauchy subsequence.*

Proof. Suppose X is totally bounded and $\langle x_n \rangle$ is a sequence of points in X. Since X contains an ϵ-net for $\epsilon = \frac{1}{2}$, it is contained in the union of a finite number of balls of radius $\frac{1}{2}$. One of these balls must contain a subsequence $\langle x_n^{(1)} \rangle$ of the original sequence, and the distance between any two points of this subsequence is less than 1. Now with $\epsilon = \frac{1}{4}$, we obtain a subsequence $\langle x_n^{(2)} \rangle$ of $\langle x_n^{(1)} \rangle$ in which the distance between any two points is less than $\frac{1}{2}$. Proceeding by induction, for $\epsilon = 1/2\,k$ we obtain a subsequence $\langle x_n^{(k)} \rangle$ of $\langle x_n^{(k-1)} \rangle$ in which the distance between any two points is less than $1/k$. We assert that the diagonal sequence $\langle x_n^{(n)} \rangle$ is a Cauchy subsequence of $\langle x_n \rangle$. This is clear since for any $\epsilon > 0$ we may choose $N(\epsilon) > 1/\epsilon$, and then $d(x_m^{(m)}, x_n^{(n)}) < \epsilon$ whenever $m, n > N(\epsilon)$. Conversely, if X is not totally bounded, there exists an $\epsilon > 0$ such that X has no ϵ-net. By the construction in **6.2.3** we may obtain a sequence $\langle x_n \rangle$ such that $d(x_i, x_j) \geqslant \epsilon$ whenever $i \neq j$. It is clear that this sequence can have no Cauchy subsequence. ▮

Although it is obvious that every convergent sequence is a Cauchy sequence, the converse is not true. For example, the sequence $\langle 1/n \rangle$ in the space consisting of the open interval (0, 1) does not converge even though it is a Cauchy sequence. We shall call a metric space **complete** iff every Cauchy sequence in the space converges to some point of the space.

By the classic Cauchy Theorem proved in advanced calculus, we know that $\mathbf{R}^n$ is complete. This shows that completeness is not a topological property since $\mathbf{R}$ and (0,1) are homeomorphic! Although not a topological property, completeness is of interest to a topologist since it is closely related to many topological properties. For example, every compact metric space is complete. This result will be proven later, but it may be proved directly, as may the fact that every closed subset of a complete space is complete. We shall now show that the spaces introduced in Sections **6.3–6.5** are complete.

Theorem 7.1.2. *Hilbert space is complete.*

Proof. Let $\langle \mathbf{x}_n = \langle x_1{}^n, x_2{}^n, \ldots \rangle \rangle$ be a Cauchy sequence in $\mathbf{H}$, and let ϵ be an arbitrary positive number. There exists an integer $N(\epsilon)$ such that $d_H(\mathbf{x}_m, \mathbf{x}_n) < \epsilon$ whenever $m, n > N(\epsilon)$. But then, for $m, n > N(\epsilon)$, $| x_i{}^m - x_i{}^n | \leqslant d_H(\mathbf{x}_m, \mathbf{x}_n) < \epsilon$, so the ith coordinates $\langle x_i{}^n \rangle$ form a Cauchy sequence of real numbers which must converge to some real number x_i. If we let $\mathbf{x} = \langle x_1, x_2, \ldots \rangle$, then we assert that $\mathbf{x}_n \to \mathbf{x} \in \mathbf{H}$. For each fixed integer J,

$$\sqrt{\textstyle\sum_{i=1}^{J} (x_i{}^m - x_i{}^n)^2} < \epsilon$$

for all $m, n > N(\epsilon)$. If we fix n and let m increase, we obtain

$$\sqrt{\textstyle\sum_{i=1}^{J} (x_i - x_i{}^n)^2} \leqslant \epsilon,$$

and since this was for each J,

$$\sqrt{\textstyle\sum_{i=1}^{\infty} (x_i - x_i{}^n)^2} = d_H(\mathbf{x}, \mathbf{x}_n) \leqslant \epsilon.$$

Thus $\mathbf{x}_n \to \mathbf{x}$, if the point $\mathbf{x}$ does indeed belong to $\mathbf{H}$. Now let us note that

$$(x_i)^2 = (x_i - x_i^n + x_i^n)^2$$
$$= (x_i - x_i^n)^2 + (x_i^n)^2 + 2(x_i - x_i^n)(x_i^n)$$
$$\leqslant 2(x_i - x_i^n)^2 + 2(x_i^n)^2$$

since $2\alpha\beta \leqslant \alpha^2 + \beta^2$. Since $\mathbf{x}_n \in \mathbf{H}$, $\sum_{i=1}^{\infty}(x_i^n)^2$ converges for every n. On the other hand, if $n > N(\epsilon)$, we have shown above that $\sum_{i=1}^{\infty}(x_i - x_i^n)^2 \leqslant \epsilon^2$. Thus, by choosing a fixed large value of n we show that $\sum_{i=1}^{\infty} (x_i)^2$ converges, and $\mathbf{x} \in \mathbf{H}$. ▮

Theorem 7.1.3. *Fréchet space is complete.*

Proof. Let $\langle \mathbf{x}_n = \langle x_1^n, x_2^n, \ldots\rangle\rangle$ be a Cauchy sequence in $\mathbf{F}$, and let ϵ be an arbitrary positive number. There exists an integer $N(\epsilon)$ such that $d_F(\mathbf{x}_m, \mathbf{x}_n) < \epsilon$ whenever $m, n > N(\epsilon)$. But then, for m, $n > N(\epsilon)$, $2^{-i} \mid x_i^m - x_i^n \mid /(1 + \mid x_i^m - x_i^n \mid) \leqslant d_F(\mathbf{x}_m, \mathbf{x}_n) < \epsilon$ for each i. It is easy to see that, for small ϵ, we have $\mid x_i^m - x_i^n \mid < 2^{1+i}\epsilon$ for all $m, n > N(\epsilon)$, so the ith coordinates form a Cauchy sequence of real numbers which must converge to some real number x_i. If we let $\mathbf{x} = \langle x_1, x_2, \ldots\rangle$, then it is obvious that $\mathbf{x} \in \mathbf{F}$. Since we have coordinatewise convergence, $\mathbf{x}_n \to \mathbf{x}$ by **6.4.1.** ▮

Theorem 7.1.4. *The space $\mathfrak{C}$ is complete.*

Proof. Let $\langle \mathfrak{f}_n\rangle$ be a Cauchy sequence in $\mathfrak{C}$, and let ϵ be an arbitrary positive number. There exists an integer $N(\epsilon)$ such that $d_{\mathfrak{C}}(\mathfrak{f}_m, \mathfrak{f}_n) < \epsilon$ whenever $m, n > N(\epsilon)$. That is,

$$\mid \mathfrak{f}_m(t) - \mathfrak{f}_n(t) \mid \leqslant d_{\mathfrak{C}}(\mathfrak{f}_m, \mathfrak{f}_n) < \epsilon$$

for all $m, n > N(\epsilon)$ and all $t \in I$. For each fixed $t \in I$, this shows that $\langle \mathfrak{f}_n(t)\rangle$ is a Cauchy sequence of reals which must converge to some number $\mathfrak{f}(t)$. We assert that $\mathfrak{f}_n \to \mathfrak{f} \in \mathfrak{C}$. For all $m, n > N(\epsilon)$ and all $t \in I$, we have $-\epsilon < \mathfrak{f}_m(t) - \mathfrak{f}_n(t) < +\epsilon$, and so

$$\mathfrak{f}_n(t) - \epsilon < \mathfrak{f}_m(t) < \mathfrak{f}_n(t) + \epsilon.$$

Letting m increase while holding n and t fixed gives us

$$\mathfrak{f}_n(t) - \epsilon \leqslant \mathfrak{f}(t) \leqslant \mathfrak{f}_n(t) + \epsilon$$

or

$$| \mathfrak{f}_n(t) - \mathfrak{f}(t) | \leqslant \epsilon$$

for all $n > N(\epsilon)$ and all $t \in I$. Taking the supremum over $t \in I$ we have $d_{\mathfrak{C}}(\mathfrak{f}_n, \mathfrak{f}) \leqslant \epsilon$ for $n > N(\epsilon)$. Thus $\mathfrak{f}_n \to \mathfrak{f}$, and we know that $\mathfrak{f} \in \mathfrak{C}$ by problem **2** of Section **6.5** since this convergence is uniform in the sense of analysis. ∎

The above proof may be generalized very easily to a somewhat more interesting class of spaces. We may let $\mathfrak{C}^*(X)$ be the set of all bounded, real-valued, continuous functions defined on the (topological) space X. The metric $d_{\mathfrak{C}}{}^*$ will be taken to be that given by setting $d_{\mathfrak{C}}{}^*(\mathfrak{f}, \mathfrak{g}) = \sup\{| \mathfrak{f}(t) - \mathfrak{g}(t) | : t \in X\}$. It is easy to see that $d_{\mathfrak{C}}{}^*$ is always a metric for $\mathfrak{C}^*(X)$, and we could describe the space $\mathfrak{C}$ as $\mathfrak{C}^*(I)$. It is clear that the above proof shows that $\mathfrak{C}^*(X)$ is complete for any space X.

Exercises

1. If a Cauchy sequence has a convergent subsequence, then it is itself convergent.

2. Every closed subset of a complete metric space is complete.

3. Every compact metric space is complete.

4. Show that the space $(\mathfrak{b}, d_{\mathfrak{b}})$ of bounded sequences defined in problem **7** of Section **6.3** is complete.

5. Show that the space $(\mathfrak{c}, d_{\mathfrak{c}})$ of convergent sequences defined in problem **6** of Section **6.3** is complete.

6. Show that the space $(\mathfrak{B}, d_{\mathfrak{B}})$ of bounded functions defined in problem **8** of Section **6.5** is complete.

7. Let $\mathfrak{C}^*(X, Y)$ be the set of all bounded, continuous functions of the topological space X into the metric space Y. Define a metric for $\mathfrak{C}^*(X, Y)$ in the obvious way, and show that if Y is complete, so is $\mathfrak{C}^*(X, Y)$ with that metric.

8. Let X be the set of all sequences $\langle x_n \rangle$ of positive integers with $d(\langle x_n \rangle, \langle y_n \rangle) = 1/n$ where n is the smallest integer for which $x_n \neq y_n$. Prove that this defines a metric for X, which we call the **Baire metric**. Prove that X with this metric is a complete space.

9. A mapping $\mathfrak{f}$ of a metric space (X, d) into itself is said to be a **contraction** iff there exists a real number $\alpha < 1$ such that $d(\mathfrak{f}(x), \mathfrak{f}(y)) \leqslant \alpha d(x, y)$ for all $x, y \in X$. Prove that every contraction mapping is continuous. Prove that every contraction mapping in a complete metric space has one and only one **fixed point**; that is, a point x such that $\mathfrak{f}(x) = x$. (For applications of this result, the reader is referred to the text of Kolmogorov and Fomin [16].)

10. Prove that completeness is an isometric invariant; that is, if two metric spaces are isometric and one is complete, then so is the other.

11. If $\mathfrak{f}^*$ is a uniformly continuous mapping of the dense subset X^* of the metric space X into the complete metric space Y, then there exists a unique uniformly continuous mapping $\mathfrak{f}$ of X into Y such that $\mathfrak{f} \mid X^* = \mathfrak{f}^*$.

7.2 Completions

If a metric space (X, d) is not complete, we may wish to find a complete metric space which contains it. By using the space $\mathfrak{C}^*(X)$ introduced in the last section, we may show directly that this is always possible.

Theorem 7.2.1. *Every metric space is isometric to a dense subset of a complete metric space.*

Proof. Let us fix a point z in the metric space (X, d). We will define a mapping $\mathfrak{f}$ of X into $\mathfrak{C}^*(X)$ by setting, for every $x \in X$, $\mathfrak{f}(x)$ equal to the real-valued function defined by setting $[\mathfrak{f}(x)](t) = d(t, x) - d(t, z)$ for every $t \in X$. Since d is a continuous function of one of its variables (see problem **7** of Section **6.1**), $\mathfrak{f}(x)$ is continuous. By the triangle inequality we may show that $| [\mathfrak{f}(x)](t) | \leqslant d(x, z)$ for all $t \in X$, so that $\mathfrak{f}(x)$ is bounded. Thus $\mathfrak{f}(x) \in \mathfrak{C}^*(X)$, and we assert that X and $\mathfrak{f}(X)$ are isometric; that is, $d_{\mathfrak{C}}(\mathfrak{f}(x), \mathfrak{f}(y)) = d(x, y)$ for all $x, y \in X$. Now

$$d_{\mathfrak{C}}(\mathfrak{f}(x), \mathfrak{f}(y)) = \sup_{t \in X} \{| [\mathfrak{f}(x)] (t) - [\mathfrak{f}(y)] (t) |\}$$

$$= \sup_{t \in X} \{| d(t, x) - d(t, y) |\}.$$

By letting $t = y$, we have $d_{\mathfrak{C}}(\mathfrak{f}(x), \mathfrak{f}(y)) \geqslant d(x, y)$ since the supremum is not less than any element. On the other hand, suppose that, for some $t \in X$, we had

$$d(t, x) - d(t, y) > d(x, y).$$

Then, by the triangle inequality,

$$d(t, x) > d(t, y) + d(x, y) \geqslant d(t, x)$$

which is a contradiction. Furthermore, if for some $x \in X$ we had

$$d(t, x) - d(t, y) < -d(x, y),$$

then

$$d(y, t) \leqslant d(x, y) + d(t, x) < d(t, y),$$

another contradiction. Hence, for every $t \in X$, we must have $| d(t, x) - d(t, y) | \leqslant d(x, y)$, and so, when we take the supremum, $d_{\mathfrak{C}}(\mathfrak{f}(x), \mathfrak{f}(y)) \leqslant d(x, y)$. We now have X isometric to the subset $\mathfrak{f}(X)$ of the complete metric space $\mathfrak{C}^*(X)$. The closure of $\mathfrak{f}(X)$ in $\mathfrak{C}^*(X)$ will be complete, and $\mathfrak{f}(X)$ will be dense in it. ∎

It should be noted that the above proof depends on the completeness of $\mathfrak{C}^*(X)$, which in turn depends on the fact that the reals are complete. In the development of the real numbers from the rationals, there is used a construction which may be generalized to any metric space and is quite interesting in itself. We will now outline this constructive proof of the above theorem.

In a metric space (X, d) we will say that two Cauchy sequences $\langle x_n \rangle$ and $\langle y_n \rangle$ are equivalent iff $\lim d(x_n, y_n) = 0$. One can show that this is an equivalence relation. This relation divides up the set of all Cauchy sequences in X into equivalence classes. The equivalence classes of Cauchy sequences will be taken to be the points of a new space X^*. We define a metric for X^* in the following way. For any two points (equivalence classes of Cauchy sequences in X) x^* and y^* in X^*, we choose any representatives $\langle x_n \rangle \in x^*$ and $\langle y_n \rangle \in y^*$ of these points and put $d^*(x^*, y^*) = \lim d(x_n, y_n)$. One can show that this limit always exists and is independent of the representatives chosen from x^* and y^*. One can also show that d^* is a metric for X^*. We may now define a mapping $\mathfrak{f}$ of X into X^* which takes each point $x \in X$ into the equivalence class of all Cauchy sequences which converge to x (one representative of this class is the sequence $\langle x_n \rangle$ with $x_n = x$ for all n). One can show that $\mathfrak{f}$ is an isometry of X onto the subset $\mathfrak{f}(X)$ of X^*.

To prove that $\mathfrak{f}(X)$ is dense in X^*, we choose $x^* \in X^*$ and $\epsilon > 0$ arbitrarily. There exists an integer N such that $d(x_m, x_n) < \epsilon$ whenever $m, n \geqslant N$ where $\langle x_n \rangle \in x^*$. The point represented by the constant sequence $\langle x_N \rangle$ has the property that $\lim_n d(x_n, x_N) \leqslant \epsilon$ and belongs to $\mathfrak{f}(X)$, as desired. Finally, we may show that X^* is complete. Let $\langle x_n^* \rangle$ be a Cauchy sequence in X^*, and let $\epsilon > 0$ be arbitrary. Choose representatives $\langle x_n^k \rangle \in x_k^*$ where, since these are Cauchy sequences in X and we may omit a finite number of terms from each, we may assume that $d(x_m^k, x_n^k) < 1/k$. Now choose $N(\epsilon) > 3/\epsilon$ such that

$$d^*(x_i^*, x_j^*) = \lim_n d(x_n^i, x_n^j) < \epsilon/3$$

for all $i, j > N(\epsilon)$. Thus, for sufficiently large n and all $i, j > N(\epsilon)$, we have $d(x_n{}^i, x_n{}^j) < \epsilon/3$. Now, by the triangle inequality,

$$\begin{aligned} d(x_i{}^i, x_j{}^j) &\leqslant d(x_i{}^i, x_n{}^i) + d(x_n{}^i, x_n{}^j) + d(x_n{}^j, x_j{}^j) \\ &< \epsilon/3 + \epsilon/3 + \epsilon/3 \\ &= \epsilon \end{aligned}$$

for all $i, j > N(\epsilon)$. Thus the diagonal sequence $\langle x_i{}^i \rangle$ is a Cauchy sequence in X and so determines a point $x^* \in X^*$. Clearly, $d^*(x_n{}^*, x^*) = \lim_i d(x_i{}^n, x_i{}^i) < \epsilon$, and so $\lim x_n{}^* = x^*$.

The space X^* constructed above is sometimes called the **complete enclosure** of X. In general, a **completion** of a metric space X is any complete metric space which contains a dense subset to which X is isometric. The two constructions used above give rise to the question of how many essentially different completions a metric space may have. It turns out that the completion of a space is unique up to an isometry.

Theorem 7.2.2. *All completions of a metric space are isometric.*

Proof. Let (X, d) be a metric space, and suppose (X^*, d^*) and (X^{**}, d^{**}) are both completions of it. In particular, we may assume that X^* and X^{**} both contain X as a dense subset and are complete. We will now define an isometry $\mathfrak{f}$ between X^* and X^{**}. For each $x^* \in X^*$, since X is dense in X^*, there exists some sequence $\langle x_n \rangle$ of points of X converging to x^*. But we may also consider $\langle x_n \rangle$ as a Cauchy sequence in X^{**} and, since X^{**} is complete, it must converge to some point $x^{**} \in X^{**}$. Define $\mathfrak{f}(x^*) = x^{**}$ by this construction. One can show that this construction is independent of the particular sequence $\langle x_n \rangle$ converging to x^* and gives a one-to-one mapping of X^* onto X^{**}. Clearly, $\mathfrak{f}(x) = x$ for all $x \in X$. Now if $x_n \to x^*$ in X^* and $x_n \to x^{**}$ in X^{**}, while $y_n \to y^*$ in X^* and $y_n \to y^{**}$ in X^{**}, then both $d^*(x^*, y^*) = \lim d(x_n, y_n)$ and $d^{**}(x^{**}, y^{**}) = \lim d(x_n, y_n)$. Thus we must have $d^{**}(\mathfrak{f}(x^*), \mathfrak{f}(y^*)) = d^*(x^*, y^*)$, and so $\mathfrak{f}$ is an isometry. ∎

Exercises

1. Fill in the missing details of the construction of the complete enclosure.

2. Show that the mapping $\mathfrak{f}$ defined in the proof of **7.2.2** is well-defined, one-to-one, and onto.

3. The completion of a metric space is separable iff the space is separable.

7.3 Equivalent Conditions

In this section we will give a few conditions which are equivalent to completeness. The first result gives an application of the completion theorem of the last section. We will say that a metric space (X, d) is **embedded** in a metric space (X^*, d^*) iff X is isometric to a subset of X^*. A metric space is **absolutely closed** iff its image is a closed subset of any space in which it can be embedded.

Theorem 7.3.1. *A metric space is complete iff it is absolutely closed.*

Proof. Suppose the complete space (X, d) is embedded by the isometry $\mathfrak{f}$ in the metric space (X^*, d^*). Let x^* be a d^*-limit point of $\mathfrak{f}(X)$. There must be some sequence $\langle \mathfrak{f}(x_n) \rangle$ in $\mathfrak{f}(X)$ whose d^*-limit is x^*. Since this sequence is convergent, and $\mathfrak{f}$ is an isometry, the sequence $\langle x_n \rangle$ must be a Cauchy sequence in X. Since X is complete, there must exist some d-limit point $x \in X$. Clearly, $\langle \mathfrak{f}(x_n) \rangle$ must converge to $\mathfrak{f}(x) \in \mathfrak{f}(X)$, and since limits are unique, we must have $x^* = \mathfrak{f}(x) \in \mathfrak{f}(X)$. Thus $\mathfrak{f}(X)$ must be a closed subset of X^*.

Conversely, suppose (X, d) is absolutely closed. By **7.2.1**, (X, d) has a completion, and so there must be an isometry $\mathfrak{f}$ of X onto a dense subset of a complete metric space (X^*, d^*). We thus have X embedded in X^*, and, by assumption, $\mathfrak{f}(X)$ is closed in X^*. But then $\mathfrak{f}(X)$ is a closed subset of a complete space and hence complete. Since $\mathfrak{f}$ is an isometry, X is also complete. ▮

For the next result we recall that a sequence $\langle E_n \rangle$ of sets is called **monotone decreasing** or **nested** iff $E_n \supseteq E_{n+1}$ for all n. We denote by $\bar{B}(x, \epsilon)$ the **closed ball** $\{y : d(x, y) \leqslant \epsilon\}$ with center at x and radius ϵ (see problem **11** in Section **6.1**).

Theorem 7.3.2. *A metric space is complete iff the intersection of every nested sequence of nonempty closed balls with radii tending to zero is nonempty.*

Proof. Suppose (X, d) is complete, and let $\langle \bar{B}(x_n, \epsilon_n) \rangle$ be a nested sequence of closed balls with $\epsilon_n \to 0$. The sequence $\langle x_n \rangle$ is a Cauchy sequence in X since if $m > n$, then $d(x_m, x_n) < \epsilon_n \to 0$. Since X is complete, there exists a point $x \in X$ such that $x_n \to x$. Now if $x \notin \bar{B}(x_N, \epsilon_N)$ for some N, then $d(\{x\}, \bar{B}(x_N, \epsilon_N)) > \epsilon$ for some $\epsilon > 0$. Since the balls are nested, we would have $d(x, x_n) > \epsilon$ for all $n \geqslant N$ which would contradict the fact that $x_n \to x$. Therefore, $x \in \bar{B}(x_n, \epsilon_n)$ for all n.

Now suppose (X, d) satisfies the condition of the theorem, and let $\langle x_n \rangle$ be a Cauchy sequence in X. For each integer k, there is a least integer n_k such that $d(x_{n_k}, x_n) < 1/2^k$ for all $n > n_k$. Consider the sequence $\langle \bar{B}(x_{n_k}, 1/2^{k-1}) \rangle$ of closed balls. It is clear that these are nonempty and their radii tend to zero. In order to use the condition of the theorem, we must show that they are nested. Now if $x \in \bar{B}(x_{n_{k+1}}, 1/2^k)$, then $d(x, x_{n_{k+1}}) \leq 1/2^k$, and so we have

$$\begin{aligned} d(x, x_{n_k}) &\leqslant d(x, x_{n_{k+1}}) + d(x_{n_{k+1}}, x_{n_k}) \\ &< 1/2^k + 1/2^k \\ &= 1/2^{k-1}, \end{aligned}$$

or $x \in \bar{B}(x_{n_k}, 1/2^{k-1})$. By our hypothesis, there is a point x belonging to all these balls. By considering the distance $d(x, x_n) \leqslant d(x, x_{n_k}) + d(x_{n_k}, x_n)$, it is clear that $x_n \to x$, and so the sequence $\langle x_n \rangle$ converges. ▮

It is very interesting to note that even in a complete space the intersection of a nested sequence of nonempty closed balls may be empty. An example of such a space is given by Sierpinski [20]. He calls the condition of this theorem the **Ascola Condition**. Our final characterization of complete metric spaces leads to an interesting relationship between compact and complete spaces.

Theorem 7.3.3. *A metric space is complete iff every infinite totally bounded subset has a limit point.*

Proof. Suppose X is complete and E is an infinite totally bounded subset of X. Since E is infinite, we may choose a sequence of distinct points from E, and then, by **7.1.1**, there is a Cauchy subsequence which must converge to some point x, since X is complete. Since the sequence was composed of distinct points of E, x is a limit point of E.

Now suppose every infinite totally bounded subset of X has a limit point, and $\langle x_n \rangle$ is a Cauchy sequence in X. The set $E = \bigcup_n \{x_n\}$ is totally bounded since, for any $\epsilon > 0$, there exists an integer $N(\epsilon)$ such that $d(x_m, x_n) < \epsilon$ whenever $m, n \geqslant N(\epsilon)$, and so $E \subseteq \bigcup_{n=1}^{N(\epsilon)} B(x_n, \epsilon)$; that is, the set $\{x_n\}_{n=1}^{N(\epsilon)}$ forms an ϵ-net for E. If E is *finite*, one of the terms in the sequence $\langle x_n \rangle$ must be repeated infinitely often, and the Cauchy sequence certainly converges to that point. On the other hand, if E is infinite, we may apply the hypothesis and find a limit point x of E. Clearly the point x would also be the limit of the sequence $\langle x_n \rangle$. ▮

Corollary. *A metric space is compact iff it is both complete and totally bounded.*

Proof. A compact space is totally bounded by **6.2.3** and is complete by any of the above theorems. Conversely, if X is complete and totally bounded, and if E is an infinite subset of X, then E is also totally bounded and has a limit point by the above theorem, which is sufficient by **6.2.4.** ▮

Exercises

1. A metric space is complete iff the intersection of every nested sequence of nonempty, closed sets with diameters tending to zero is exactly one point.
2. Give an example to show that the intersection of a nested sequence of nonempty, closed sets in a complete metric space may be empty.
3. A metric space is compact iff every homeomorphic image of it is complete (see Niemytski and Tichonov [63]).
4. A metric space is compact iff it is complete in every equivalent metric.
5. A metric space is compact iff it is bounded in every equivalent metric (see Levine [51]).
6. If every closed ball in a metric space is compact, then the space is complete, locally compact, and separable.

7.4 Baire Theorem

In applying topology to analysis, one of the most useful applications of completeness is the **Baire Category Theorem**. In this section we will first state and prove one form of the Baire Theorem, then introduce some terminology which is usually used to describe this result.

Theorem 7.4.1. *In a complete metric space, the intersection of a countable number of dense, open sets is itself dense.*

Proof. Let $\{G_n\}_{n\in\mathbf{N}}$ be a collection of dense, open sets in the complete metric space X, and suppose G is an arbitrary nonempty open set in X. We must find some point of $\bigcap_{n\in\mathbf{N}} G_n$ in G. Now $G \cap G_1$ is open and, by the denseness of G_1, nonempty. We may then find a point x_1 and, by the regularity of the metric space X, an $\epsilon_1 < 1$ such that the closed ball $\bar{B}(x_1, \epsilon_1)$ is contained in $G \cap G_1$. Now $B(x_1, \epsilon_1) \cap G_2$ is open and, by the denseness of G_2, nonempty. We may then find a point x_2 and an $\epsilon_2 < \frac{1}{2}$ such that $\bar{B}(x_2, \epsilon_2)$ is contained in $B(x_1, \epsilon_1) \cap G_2$. Proceeding by induction, we may obtain for each integer n, a point x_n and a real number $\epsilon_n < 1/n$ such that $\bar{B}(x_n, \epsilon_n) \subseteq B(x_{n-1}, \epsilon_{n-1}) \cap G_n$. The sequence $\langle \bar{B}(x_n, \epsilon_n) \rangle$ consists of nonempty, nested closed balls with radii tending to zero, and so, by **7.3.2**, it has a nonempty intersection consisting of exactly one point, say x. For each $n \geqslant 2$, we have

$$x \in \bar{B}(x_n, \epsilon_n) \subseteq B(x_{n-1}, \epsilon_{n-1}) \cap G_n \subseteq G_n,$$

while $x \in \bar{B}(x_1, \epsilon_1) \subseteq G \cap G_1$, so that x is a point of $\bigcap_{n \in \mathbf{N}} G_n$ in G. ▮

From the restatements of the Baire Theorem given in the problems, it is clear that we are interested in sets with empty interiors. We recall (see Section **6.3**) that a set E is **nowhere dense** iff $\mathbf{i}(\mathbf{c}(E)) = \varnothing$. The following terminology is very useful in considering the Baire Theorem. A set is said to be of the **first category** or **meager** iff it can be written as the union of a countable number of nowhere dense sets. A set which is not of the first category is said to be of the **second category**. In this terminology the Baire Theorem states that every complete metric space is of the second category.

Exercises

1. In a complete metric space, the union of a countable number of closed sets with empty interiors has an empty interior.

2. If a complete metric space is the union of a countable number of closed sets, then at least one of them must contain a nonempty open set.

3. (**Baire Category Theorem.**) In a locally compact regular topological space, the intersection of a countable number of dense, open sets is itself dense.

4. Every point of a dense-in-itself complete metric space is a condensation point (see **5.3.9**) of the space.

5. Every subset of a first category set is a first category set, and the countable union of first category sets is a first category set. Give an example of an uncountable first category set.

6. Every complete metric space is of the second category; in fact, the complement of each first category subset is dense in the space.

7. Every denumerable complete metric space contains an infinite number of isolated points.

CHAPTER **8**

Product Spaces

8.1 Finite Products

We have defined the Cartesian product of two sets X and Y to be the family of all ordered pairs $\langle x, y\rangle$ with $x \in X$ and $y \in Y$. If the sets X and Y have topologies associated with them, it is natural to try to find a topology to associate with their product that is related to these topologies. All of the results of this section have an obvious generalization to the product of a finite number of spaces, which we will not bother to state explicitly.

Theorem 8.1.1. *If X and Y are topological spaces, the family of all sets of the form $V \times W$ with V open in X and W open in Y is a base for a topology for $X \times Y$.*

Proof. Since the set $X \times Y$ is itself of the required form, $X \times Y$ is the union of all the members of the family. Now let $\langle x, y\rangle \in (V_1 \times W_1) \cap (V_2 \times W_2)$ with V_1 and V_2 open in X and W_1 and W_2 open in Y. Then $\langle x, y\rangle \in (V_1 \cap V_2) \times (W_1 \cap W_2) = (V_1 \times W_1) \cap (V_2 \times W_2)$ with $V_1 \cap V_2$ open in X and $W_1 \cap W_2$ open in Y. Thus, by **3.4.1**, the family is a base for a topology for $X \times Y$. ∎

The **product topology** for $X \times Y$ is that obtained by using the base described above. It is easy to see that the sets V and W need only be chosen from some bases for the respective topologies to obtain the same product topology. It is easy to show (see problem **1**) that the topological product is, up to a homeomorphism, a well-defined, commutative, and associative operation. We will now show that this topology is natural in the sense that it agrees with a natural metric for the product of two metric spaces.

Theorem 8.1.2. *If (X, d_X) and (Y, d_Y) are metric spaces, then the function d defined by setting*

$$d(\langle x_1, y_1\rangle, \langle x_2, y_2\rangle) = \sqrt{d_X^2(x_1, x_2) + d_Y^2(y_1, y_2)}$$

is a metric for $X \times Y$ which induces the product topology.

Proof. It is clear that d is a metric, so we must compare the induced topology with the product topology. Suppose **E** is a subset of $X \times Y$ which is open with respect to the metric d, and let $\langle x, y \rangle \in \mathbf{E}$. Since $\langle x, y \rangle$ is an interior point of **E**, there must exist an $\epsilon > 0$ such that $B(\langle x, y \rangle, \epsilon) \subseteq \mathbf{E}$. Let $V = B(x, \epsilon/\sqrt{2})$ and $W = B(y, \epsilon/\sqrt{2})$, which are certainly open sets containing x and y, respectively. We assert that $V \times W \subseteq \mathbf{E}$, and this will show that **E** is open in the product topology. Now if $\langle x^*, y^* \rangle \in V \times W$, then $x^* \in V$ and $y^* \in W$; that is, $d_X(x, x^*) < \epsilon/\sqrt{2}$ and $d_Y(y, y^*) < \epsilon/\sqrt{2}$. Thus

$$\begin{aligned} d(\langle x, y \rangle, \langle x^*, y^* \rangle) &= \sqrt{d_X{}^2(x, x^*) + d_Y{}^2(y, y^*)} \\ &< \sqrt{(\epsilon/\sqrt{2})^2 + (\epsilon/\sqrt{2})^2} \\ &= \epsilon, \end{aligned}$$

and so $\langle x^*, y^* \rangle \in B(\langle x, y \rangle, \epsilon) \subseteq \mathbf{E}$, as desired.

Now suppose that **E** is a subset of $X \times Y$ which is open with respect to the product topology, and let $\langle x, y \rangle \in \mathbf{E}$. By definition of the product topology, there must exist open sets V and W such that $\langle x, y \rangle \in V \times W \subseteq \mathbf{E}$. Thus $x \in V$ and $y \in W$, so there must exist ϵ_x, $\epsilon_y > 0$ such that $x \in B(x, \epsilon_x) \subseteq V$ and $y \in B(y, \epsilon_y) \subseteq W$. Let $\epsilon = \min\{\epsilon_x, \epsilon_y\}$. We assert that

$$B(\langle x, y \rangle, \epsilon) \subseteq B(x, \epsilon_x) \times B(y, \epsilon_y),$$

which will show that **E** is open with respect to the metric d since $\langle x, y \rangle \in B(\langle x, y \rangle, \epsilon)$ and $B(x, \epsilon_x) \times B(y, \epsilon_y) \subseteq V \times W \subseteq \mathbf{E}$. Now if $\langle x^*, y^* \rangle \in B(\langle x, y \rangle, \epsilon)$, then

$$d_X(x, x^*) \leqslant d(\langle x, y \rangle, \langle x^*, y^* \rangle) < \epsilon \leqslant \epsilon_x$$

and

$$d_Y(y, y^*) \leqslant d(\langle x, y \rangle, \langle x^*, y^* \rangle) < \epsilon \leqslant \epsilon_y,$$

so $\langle x^*, y^* \rangle \in B(x, \epsilon_x) \times B(y, \epsilon_y)$, as desired. ▮

Closely associated with the product of sets is the notion of the projection mappings onto the coordinate sets. The **projections**, π_X and π_Y, of the product of two sets X and Y are the mappings of $X \times Y$ onto X and Y, respectively, defined by setting $\pi_X(\langle x, y \rangle) = x$ and $\pi_Y(\langle x, y \rangle) = y$. The projections will play an important role in the definition of the product topology for arbitrary products, but their continuity is useful immediately.

Theorem 8.1.3. *The projections π_X and π_Y are continuous and open mappings (but not necessarily closed), and so the product topology is the smallest topology for which the projections are continuous.*

Proof. If V is an open set in X, then $\pi_X^{-1}(V) = V \times Y$, which is a basic open set in $X \times Y$, so π_X is continuous. Similarly, π_Y is continuous. If $\mathbf{G}$ is an open subset of $X \times Y$, then it is the union of basic elements $V \times W$ for which $\pi_X(V \times W) = V$. Thus $\pi_X(\mathbf{G})$ is the union of the open sets V, and hence π_X is an open mapping. Similarly, π_Y is open. The example of the closed subset $\{\langle x, y\rangle : xy = 1\}$ of the plane $\mathbf{R}^2$ which is projected onto the nonclosed set $\{x : x \neq 0\}$ shows that projections need not be closed. Finally, suppose that $\mathscr{T}$ is a topology for $X \times Y$ in which the projections are continuous. Then for each pair of open sets V and W in X and Y, respectively, the set $V \times W = (V \times Y) \cap (X \times W) = \pi_X^{-1}(V) \cap \pi_Y^{-1}(W)$ must be open in $\mathscr{T}$ since the projections are continuous in $\mathscr{T}$. Thus every set which is open in the product topology must be open in $\mathscr{T}$. ▮

The definition given above of a metric for the product of two metric spaces allows us to give another unusual property of Hilbert space.

Theorem 8.1.4. $\mathbf{H} \times \mathbf{H}$ is isometric to $\mathbf{H}$.

Proof. For each point $\langle \mathbf{x}, \mathbf{y}\rangle \in \mathbf{H} \times \mathbf{H}$, let $\mathfrak{f}(\langle \mathbf{x}, \mathbf{y}\rangle) = \mathfrak{f}(\langle\langle x_1, x_2, \ldots\rangle, \langle y_1, y_2, \ldots\rangle\rangle) = \langle x_1, y_1, x_2, y_2, \ldots\rangle$. Since the sum of the squares of the coordinates converges, the image is a point of $\mathbf{H}$, and so $\mathfrak{f}$ is a well-defined mapping of $\mathbf{H} \times \mathbf{H}$ into $\mathbf{H}$. For each point $\mathbf{z} = \langle z_1, z_2, \ldots\rangle \in \mathbf{H}$ we may let $\mathbf{x} = \langle z_1, z_3, z_5, \ldots\rangle$ and $\mathbf{y} = \langle z_2, z_4, z_6, \ldots\rangle$, and it is clear that $\langle \mathbf{x}, \mathbf{y}\rangle \in \mathbf{H} \times \mathbf{H}$ and $\mathfrak{f}(\langle \mathbf{x}, \mathbf{y}\rangle) = \mathbf{z}$, so that $\mathfrak{f}$ is onto. Finally, for any $\mathbf{x}, \mathbf{y}, \mathbf{z}, \mathbf{t} \in \mathbf{H}$,

$$d(\langle \mathbf{x}, \mathbf{y}\rangle, \langle \mathbf{z}, \mathbf{t}\rangle) = \sqrt{d_H{}^2(\mathbf{x}, \mathbf{z}) + d_H{}^2(\mathbf{y}, \mathbf{t})}$$

$$= \sqrt{\Sigma_{i=1}^{\infty} (x_i - z_i)^2 + \Sigma_{i=1}^{\infty} (y_i - t_i)^2}$$

$$= \sqrt{\Sigma_{i=1}^{\infty} [(x_i - z_i)^2 + (y_i - t_i)^2]}$$

$$= d_H(\mathfrak{f}(\langle \mathbf{x}, \mathbf{y}\rangle), \mathfrak{f}(\langle \mathbf{z}, \mathbf{t}\rangle)). \ ▮$$

Exercises

1. The topological product is, up to a homeomorphism, a well-defined, commutative, and associative operation; that is:

(i) If X is homeomorphic to X^*, and Y is homeomorphic to Y^*, then $X \times Y$ is homeomorphic to $X^* \times Y^*$.

(ii) $X \times Y$ is homeomorphic to $Y \times X$.

(iii) $X \times (Y \times Z)$ is homeomorphic to $(X \times Y) \times Z$.

2. If $A \subseteq X$ and $B \subseteq Y$, then:

(i) $\mathbf{i}_X(A) \times \mathbf{i}_Y(B) = \mathbf{i}_{X\times Y}(A \times B)$.

(ii) $\mathbf{c}_X(A) \times \mathbf{c}_Y(B) = \mathbf{c}_{X\times Y}(A \times B)$.

(iii) $[\mathbf{b}_X(A) \times \mathbf{c}_Y(B)] \cup [\mathbf{c}_X(A) \times \mathbf{b}_Y(B)] = \mathbf{b}_{X\times Y}(A \times B)$.

3. Show that d as defined in **8.1.2** is a metric for $X \times Y$. Show also that $d_X(x_1, x_2)+d_Y(y_1, y_2)$ and $\max\{d_X(x_1, x_2), d_Y(y_1, y_2)\}$ are equivalent to it.

4. A mapping $\mathfrak{f} : Z \to X \times Y$ is continuous iff $\pi_X \circ \mathfrak{f} : Z \to X$ and $\pi_Y \circ \mathfrak{f} : Z \to Y$ are continuous.

5. A space X is a Hausdorff space iff $\mathfrak{i}_X$ (the diagonal) is a closed subset of $X \times X$. Also, show that $\mathfrak{i}_X$ is homeomorphic to X.

6. If $\mathfrak{f} : X \to Y$ is continuous and Y is Hausdorff, then $\mathfrak{f}$ is a closed subset of $X \times Y$. If $\mathfrak{f}$ is a closed subset of $X \times Y$ and Y is compact, then $\mathfrak{f}$ is continuous.

7. If Y is compact, then π_X is a closed mapping of $X \times Y$ onto X.

8. If $\mathfrak{f} : X \to Y$ is continuous, then so is $\mathfrak{f}_2 : X \times X \to Y \times Y$ where $\mathfrak{f}_2(\langle x_1, x_2\rangle) = \langle \mathfrak{f}(x_1), \mathfrak{f}(x_2)\rangle$.

9. Show that the space of problem **8** in Section **5.4** is the product of the space of problem **3** in Section **3.4** with itself.

10. If d is a metric for X, then d is a continuous mapping of $X \times X$ into $\mathbf{R}$ (see also problem **7** in Section **6.1**).

8.2 Product Invariant Properties

In this section we will consider when the product of two spaces (or a finite number of spaces) with a certain property must also have that property. Such properties may be said to be **invariant under finite products**. The proofs of the invariance of many properties will be left to the exercises.

Theorem 8.2.1. *$X \times Y$ is connected iff X and Y are connected.*

Proof. Since the projection mappings are continuous and onto, if $X \times Y$ is connected then so are X and Y. Now suppose X and Y are connected. Let $\langle x, y\rangle$ and $\langle x^*, y^*\rangle$ be any two points of $X \times Y$.

By problem **1**, $\{x\} \times Y$ and $X \times \{y^*\}$ are homeomorphic to Y and X, respectively, and hence are connected. They intersect in the point $\langle x, y^* \rangle$, so their union is a connected set which contains the two points $\langle x, y \rangle$ and $\langle x^*, y^* \rangle$. Thus $X \times Y$ is connected. ∎

Theorem 8.2.2. *$X \times Y$ is compact iff X and Y are compact.*

Proof. Since the projection mappings are continuous and onto, if $X \times Y$ is compact then so are X and Y. Now suppose X and Y are compact. If $\mathscr{G}$ is any open covering of $X \times Y$, then each member of $\mathscr{G}$ is a union of basis elements of the form $V \times W$ with V open in X and W open in Y. We may restrict our attention to the covering $\{V_\lambda \times W_\lambda\}$ of $X \times Y$ by these basis elements where each $V_\lambda \times W_\lambda$ is contained in some member of $\mathscr{G}$, since any finite subcovering of this basic open cover will lead immediately to a finite subcovering chosen from the original cover $\mathscr{G}$. For each $x \in X$, let $Y_x = \{x\} \times Y$ which, by problem **1**, is homeomorphic to Y and hence compact. Since $\{V_\lambda \times W_\lambda\}$ also covers Y_x, there must exist a finite subcovering $\{V_{x,\lambda_i} \times W_{x,\lambda_i}\}_{i=1}^{n(x)}$ of Y_x by sets which have a nonempty intersection with Y_x. Letting $G_x = \bigcap_{i=1}^{n(x)} V_{x,\lambda_i}$ we see that G_x is an open set containing x, and the above finite subcover actually covers $G_x \times Y$. Now $\{G_x : x \in X\}$ covers X, and so there is a finite subcover $\{G_{x_j}\}_{j=1}^{N}$. But then $\{\{V_{x_j,\lambda_i} \times W_{x_j,\lambda_i}\}_{i=1}^{n(x_j)}\}_{j=1}^{N}$ covers $X \times Y$. ∎

Although the separation axioms **[T₀]**, **[T₁]**, **[T₂]**, **[R]**, and **[CR]** are all easily shown to give product invariant properties, it is very interesting to note that the product of normal spaces need not be normal. The space of problem **8** in Section **5.4** is not normal (the subsets $\{\langle x, y \rangle : y = -x,\ x \text{ rational}\}$ and $\{\langle x, y \rangle : y = -x,\ x \text{ irrational}\}$ are disjoint and closed but not contained in any disjoint open sets) but is the product of the space of problem **3** in Section **3.4** with itself (see problem **9** in Section **8.1**), and this space is normal (problem **11** in Section **5.5**).

The countability axioms and separability, in addition to such properties as isolatedness, are all examples of product invariant properties which have the stronger requirement that $X \times Y$ will have the property if and only if both X and Y have the property. As our final example, we will consider the dense-in-itself property (**4.3.4**) which satisfies the following slightly different requirement.

Theorem 8.2.3. *$X \times Y$ is dense-in-itself iff at least one of the spaces X and Y is dense-in-itself.*

Proof. Suppose neither X nor Y is dense-in-itself. There must exist points $x \in X$ and $y \in Y$ such that $x \notin \mathbf{d}(X)$ and $y \notin \mathbf{d}(Y)$, which can only occur if the points x and y are themselves open sets in X and Y, respectively. The point $\langle x, y \rangle = \{x\} \times \{y\}$ will then be an open set, and so $X \times Y$ would not be dense-in-itself.

Conversely, suppose X (for example) is dense-in-itself, and let $\langle x, y \rangle$ be an arbitrary point of $X \times Y$ contained in an open set $\mathbf{G}$. By the definition of the product topology, $\langle x, y \rangle \in V \times W \subseteq \mathbf{G}$ for some open sets V in X and W in Y. Since X is dense-in-itself and $x \in V$, there must exist some point x^* of X in V different from x. Then $\langle x^*, y \rangle$ is a point of $V \times W$ and hence of $\mathbf{G}$ different from $\langle x, y \rangle$ since their first coordinates differ. Thus $X \times Y$ is dense-in-itself. ∎

We must emphasize that throughout this section we have been concerned with finite products, and many properties that are invariant under finite products are not product invariant in general.

Exercises

1. If $\langle x, y \rangle$ is any point of $X \times Y$, then $\{x\} \times Y$ is homeomorphic to Y, and $X \times \{y\}$ is homeomorphic to X.

2. Show that $X \times Y$ has each of the properties listed below iff both X and Y have the same property:

(i) local connectivity,
(ii) arcwise connectivity,
(iii) local compactness,
(iv) T_0,
(v) T_1,
(vi) T_2,
(vii) regularity,
(viii) complete regularity,
(ix) first axiom,
(x) second axiom,
(xi) separability,
(xii) isolatedness.

3. Give the details of the example which shows that the product of normal spaces need not be normal (see [14], p. 134). Note that this example also shows that the Lindelöf property is not product invariant.

4. Show that the product of the space of all ordinals less than the first uncountable ordinal with the space of all ordinals less than or equal to the first uncountable ordinal is not normal (see [14], p. 131).

5. Show that, for metric spaces, the following properties are invariant under finite products:

(i) boundedness,

(ii) total boundedness,

(iii) completeness.

8.3 Metric Products

Generalizing the notion of the product of a finite number of sets to a countable number of sets, in accordance with Section **1.4**, we shall let the product $\Pi_{i=1}^{\infty} X_i$ of a denumerable number of sets $\{X_i\}_{i=1}^{\infty}$ be the family of all sequences $\mathbf{x} = \langle x_1, x_2, ..., x_i, ...\rangle$ where $x_i \in X_i$. If each set X_i has a metric d_i associated with it, we may metrize the product by the mapping d defined by setting

$$d(\mathbf{x}, \mathbf{y}) = d(\langle x_1, x_2, ...\rangle, \langle y_1, y_2, ...\rangle)$$

$$= \sum_{i=1}^{\infty} 2^{-i} d_i(x_i, y_i)/(1 + d_i(x_i, y_i)).$$

We note that if each space $X_i = \mathbf{R}$, then we just obtain Fréchet space $\mathbf{F}$ (see Section **6.4**). The fact that d is a metric, and that pointwise and coordinatewise convergence are equivalent follow from the proofs of the corresponding theorems about Fréchet space.

Although we could consider countably product invariant properties of metric spaces in detail at this time, we will return to the study of product invariant properties in the next section. Here we will only concern ourselves with one special example of the countable product of metric spaces. For each positive integer i, let X_i be the set consisting of the two real numbers zero and two with the usual metric, and denote by $\mathscr{D}$ their product metric space.

It follows from our above remarks that $\mathscr{D}$ is a subset of Fréchet space. It is easy to show that this space is compact by showing that every infinite sequence has a convergent subsequence. This follows from the fact that each coordinate must be either zero or two, and we may apply the method used in **6.3.4**. We recall that a set is perfect iff it is closed and dense-in-itself.

Theorem 8.3.1. *$\mathscr{D}$ is perfect.*

Proof. Since a compact subset of a metric space is closed, we must show that each point $\mathbf{x} = \langle x_1, x_2, ...\rangle$ of $\mathscr{D}$ is a limit point of $\mathscr{D}$. Let

$\mathbf{x}_n = \langle x_1, ..., x_n, 2, 0, 0, 0, ...\rangle$. Obviously this gives us a sequence $\langle \mathbf{x}_n \rangle$ of distinct points of $\mathscr{D}$ which converges coordinatewise, and hence pointwise to $\mathbf{x}$. ▌

In the study of analysis, the most interesting perfect set we find is the **Cantor discontinuum**, K, consisting of real numbers x of the form $x = \Sigma_{i=1}^{\infty} x_i/3^i$ where each x_i equals zero or two. Since every such series converges, K is a collection of real numbers which we may metrize by the usual metric. We first note that the series expression for each member of K is unique.

Lemma. *For any* $x = \Sigma_{i=1}^{\infty} x_i/3^i$ *and* $y = \Sigma_{i=1}^{\infty} y_i/3^i$ *in* K, $x = y$ *iff* $x_i = y_i$ *for all* i.

Proof. Obviously, if $x_i = y_i$ for all i, then $x = y$. Suppose, then, that $x_i \neq y_i$ for some i, and let j be the smallest such index. For definiteness we may suppose that $x_j = 0$, $y_j = 2$, and $x_i = y_i$ if $i < j$. By considering the geometric series $\Sigma_{i=j+1}^{\infty} 2/3^i = 1/3^j$, we see that

$$\begin{aligned} y = \sum_{i=1}^{\infty} y_i/3^i &\geqslant \sum_{i=1}^{j} y_i/3^i \\ &= \sum_{i=1}^{j-1} y_i/3^i + 2/3^j \\ &= \sum_{i=1}^{j-1} x_i/3^i + 2/3^j \\ &> \sum_{i=1}^{j-1} x_i/3^i + 1/3^j \\ &= \sum_{i=1}^{j-1} x_i/3^i + 0 + \sum_{i=j+1}^{\infty} 2/3^i \geqslant x, \end{aligned}$$

and so $x \neq y$. ▌

Theorem 8.3.2. $\mathscr{D}$ *is homeomorphic to* K.

Proof. For each $\mathbf{x} = \langle x_1, x_2, ..., x_i, ...\rangle \in \mathscr{D}$, we let $\mathfrak{f}(\mathbf{x}) = \Sigma_{i=1}^{\infty} x_i/3^i$, as might be expected. By the previous lemma, $\mathfrak{f}$ is a one-to-one mapping of $\mathscr{D}$ onto K. Since $\mathscr{D}$ is compact, by the Corollary to **5.2.1** we need only prove that $\mathfrak{f}$ is continuous, since $\mathfrak{f}$ will then automatically be open and hence a homeomorphism. Suppose $\langle \mathbf{x}_k \rangle$ is a sequence of points of $\mathscr{D}$ converging to a point $\mathbf{x} \in \mathscr{D}$. We will show that $\mathfrak{f}(\mathbf{x}_k) \to \mathfrak{f}(\mathbf{x})$. Let ϵ be an arbitrary positive number and choose an integer j such that $\Sigma_{i=j+1}^{\infty} 2/3^i < \epsilon/2$. Since $\mathbf{x}_k \to \mathbf{x}$, $x_i^k \to x_i$ for each i, and so there exists an integer $N(i)$ such that $| x_i^k - x_i | < 2$ whenever $k \geqslant N(i)$. Because of the fact that these coordinates are either zeros or twos, this inequality requires that $x_i^k = x_i$ whenever $k \geqslant N(i)$. Let $N = \max\{N(i) : i = 1, ..., j\}$. We may now calculate that, for $k \geqslant N$,

$$| \mathfrak{f}(\mathbf{x}_k) - \mathfrak{f}(\mathbf{x}) | = \left| \sum_{i=1}^{\infty} x_i^k/3^i - \sum_{i=1}^{\infty} x_i/3^i \right|$$

$$= \left| \sum_{i=1}^{j} (x_i^k - x_i)/3^i + \sum_{i=j+1}^{\infty} x_i^k/3^i - \sum_{i=j+1}^{\infty} x_i/3^i \right|$$

$$< 0 + \epsilon/2 + \epsilon/2 = \epsilon. \blacksquare$$

The usual description of the Cantor discontinuum is by "middle thirds." Take the closed unit interval [0,1] and remove the open middle third (1/3, 2/3). From the remaining two closed intervals, we remove their open middle thirds (1/9, 2/9) and (7/9, 8/9). By induction we may continue this process, and the remainder is the Cantor discontinuum. It is now clear that K is a nowhere dense, perfect set.

Exercises

1. Show that d^* defined by setting $d^*(\mathbf{x}, \mathbf{y}) = \Sigma_{i=1}^{\infty} 2^{-i} \min\{d_i(x_i, y_i), 1\}$ is equivalent to the metric d for the product defined in this section. From this conclude that if each space $X_i = I = [0, 1]$, the product is homeomorphic to the Hilbert cube (see problem **4** in Section **6.3**).

2. Show that $\mathscr{D}$ is compact and K is nowhere dense.

3. For each $x \in K$, define $\mathfrak{f}$ by setting $\mathfrak{f}(x) = \mathfrak{f}(\Sigma_{i=1}^{\infty} x_i/3^i) = \Sigma_{i=1}^{\infty} x_i/2^{i+1}$. Show that $\mathfrak{f}$ is a continuous mapping of K onto I.

4. If each space $X_i = K$, then $\Pi_i X_i$ is homeomorphic to K.

5. Show that the properties of being totally bounded, complete, and of the first category are countably productive for metric spaces.

6. A metric space is compact iff it is the continuous image of $\mathscr{D}$ (see Aleksandrov and Urysohn [31]).

8.4 Tichonov Topology

Let us recall that the **Cartesian product** $\prod_{\lambda \in \Lambda} X_\lambda$ of a collection of sets $\{X_\lambda\}_{\lambda \in \Lambda}$ is the collection of all mappings $\mathfrak{f}$ of Λ into $\bigcup_{\lambda \in \Lambda} X_\lambda$ such that $\mathfrak{f}(\lambda) \in X_\lambda$ for every $\lambda \in \Lambda$. We will denote an individual mapping in this collection by $\mathbf{x} = \langle x_\lambda \rangle_{\lambda \in \Lambda}$ where x_λ is the point of X_λ which is the image of λ. For each $\beta \in \Lambda$, the **projection mapping** π_β is the mapping of $\prod_\lambda X_\lambda$ onto X_β defined by setting $\pi_\beta(\langle x_\lambda \rangle_\lambda) = x_\beta$ for every point $\langle x_\lambda \rangle_\lambda$ of $\prod_\lambda X_\lambda$.

If, for each λ, Y_λ is a subset of X_λ, then the product $\prod_\lambda Y_\lambda$ is a subset of $\prod_\lambda X_\lambda$. It would seem natural to topologize the product of topological spaces $\{X_\lambda\}$ by using as a base the family of all sets of the form $\prod_\lambda G_\lambda$ where each G_λ is an open subset of X_λ. This does yield a topology for $\prod_\lambda X_\lambda$, in fact one in which the projection mappings are continuous and open. It turns out, however, that instead of choosing the largest topology for which the projections are continuous and open, it is more useful to choose the smallest topology having these properties. Tichonov [78] first defined this topology and proved the basic theorems concerning it.

We may now construct the smallest topology for which the projections are all continuous. In order for the projections to be continuous, it is necessary and sufficient that every set of the form $\pi_\beta^{-1}(G_\beta)$ be open, where G_β is any open subset of X_β. We note that $\pi_\beta^{-1}(G_\beta) = \prod_\lambda Y_\lambda$ where $Y_\beta = G_\beta$ and $Y_\lambda = X_\lambda$ whenever $\lambda \neq \beta$. We must now use the family of all sets of this form as a subbase in order to obtain the smallest topology for which all of these sets are open. The family of all finite intersections of these subbase elements would then form the base for the topology.

By taking finite intersections, we obtain the **Tichonov** or **product topology** for the product $\prod_\lambda X_\lambda$ of topological spaces by using as a base the family of all subsets of the form $\prod_\lambda Y_\lambda$ where each Y_λ is an open subset of X_λ, and $Y_\lambda = X_\lambda$ for all but a finite number of indices λ. From the above construction it is clear that the projection mappings are continuous and open with the Tichonov topology, and that it is the smallest topology for which they are continuous.

We will now consider some properties of topological spaces which may properly be called **product invariant**. Many similar results will be left to the exercises.

Theorem 8.4.1. *$\prod_\lambda X_\lambda$ is Hausdorff iff each space X_λ is Hausdorff.*

Proof. Suppose each space X_λ is Hausdorff, and let $\mathbf{x} = \langle x_\lambda \rangle_\lambda$ and $\mathbf{y} = \langle y_\lambda \rangle_\lambda$ be two distinct points of $\prod_\lambda X_\lambda$. Since $\mathbf{x}$ and $\mathbf{y}$ are distinct, there must exist some index β such that $x_\beta \neq y_\beta$. Since X_β is a Hausdorff space, there must exist disjoint open subsets G_x and G_y containing x_β and y_β, respectively. Clearly, the sets $\pi_\beta^{-1}(G_x)$ and $\pi_\beta^{-1}(G_y)$ are disjoint open sets in the product space containing $\mathbf{x}$ and $\mathbf{y}$, respectively.

Now suppose that $\prod_\lambda X_\lambda$ is Hausdorff. We shall show that each space X_λ is also Hausdorff by showing that each X_λ is homeomorphic to a certain subset of the product space and using the hereditary property of the T_2 axiom. Fix a point $\langle z_\lambda \rangle_\lambda$ in the product space, and for each β consider the subset $\mathbf{E}_\beta$ of the product space consisting of all points $\langle x_\lambda \rangle_\lambda$ such that $x_\lambda = z_\lambda$ if $\lambda \neq \beta$, while x_β may be any point of X_β. If we let $\mathfrak{f}$ be π_β restricted to $\mathbf{E}_\beta$ (see problem **9** of Section **4.3**), then $\mathfrak{f}$ is clearly a one-to-one, continuous mapping of $\mathbf{E}_\beta$ onto X_β since the projections are continuous. Now a base for the open sets in the subspace $\mathbf{E}_\beta$ is the family of intersections of $\mathbf{E}_\beta$ with the basis elements for the product topology. But $\mathbf{E}_\beta \cap \prod_\lambda Y_\lambda$ is either empty or consists of those points of $\mathbf{E}_\beta$ for which $x_\beta \in Y_\beta$. The image under $\mathfrak{f}$ is then either empty or Y_β, and so open in either case. Thus $\mathfrak{f}$ is a homeomorphism. ∎

The construction used in the above theorem is a generalization of problem **1** of Section **8.2**. It is clear that a similar argument would show that the set consisting of all points $\langle x_\lambda \rangle_\lambda$ such that $x_\lambda = z_\lambda$ if $\lambda \neq \beta_1, \beta_2$, which we could denote by $\mathbf{E}_{\beta_1} \times \mathbf{E}_{\beta_2}$, is homeomorphic to $X_{\beta_1} \times X_{\beta_2}$. We could extend this argument to any finite number of indices. An immediate application of these remarks is the following result.

Theorem 8.4.2. *$\prod_\lambda X_\lambda$ is connected iff each space X_λ is connected.*

Proof. If $\prod_\lambda X_\lambda$ is connected, then each space X_λ is also connected since the projections are continuous. Hence, suppose that each space X_λ is connected. Fix a point $\langle z_\lambda \rangle_\lambda$ in the product space, and let $\mathbf{C}$ be the component to which it belongs. We shall show that every point of $\prod_\lambda X_\lambda$ belongs to $\mathbf{C}$. Let $\prod_\lambda Y_\lambda$ be an arbitrary basic open set containing a point $\langle x_\lambda \rangle_\lambda$ where Y_λ is open in X_λ and $Y_\lambda = X_\lambda$ if $\lambda \neq \beta_1, \beta_2, \ldots, \beta_n$. By our above remarks, $\mathbf{E}_{\beta_1} \times \mathbf{E}_{\beta_2} \times \ldots \times \mathbf{E}_{\beta_n}$, that is, the set of all points $\langle t_\lambda \rangle_\lambda$ such that $t_\lambda = z_\lambda$ if $\lambda \neq \beta_1, \beta_2, \ldots, \beta_n$, is homeomorphic to $X_{\beta_1} \times X_{\beta_2} \times \ldots \times X_{\beta_n}$ and hence is connected by **8.2.1**. This set, then, lies completely in $\mathbf{C}$. But this set contains the point $\langle t_\lambda \rangle_\lambda$ for which $t_\lambda = z_\lambda$ if $\lambda \neq \beta_1, \beta_2, \ldots, \beta_n$, and $t_\lambda = x_\lambda$ for $\lambda = \beta_1, \beta_2, \ldots, \beta_n$. This point, however, lies in $\prod_\lambda Y_\lambda$, which was an arbitrary basic open set containing $\langle x_\lambda \rangle_\lambda$, so $\langle x_\lambda \rangle_\lambda$ is in the closure of **C**. Since **C**, as a component, is closed, $\langle x_\lambda \rangle_\lambda \in$ **C**, as desired. ▌

In problem 2(i) of Section **8.2** we saw that local connectivity has the property of being invariant under finite products. We will now see that it is not product invariant in general; indeed, it is not infinitely product invariant.

Theorem 8.4.3. *$\Pi_\lambda X_\lambda$ is locally connected iff each space X_λ is locally connected and all but a finite number are connected.*

Proof. Suppose $\Pi_\lambda X_\lambda$ is locally connected, and let $x_\beta \in X_\beta$ be contained in some open set Y_β. Choose some point $\mathbf{z} = \langle z_\lambda \rangle_\lambda$ with $z_\beta = x_\beta$, and we have **z** belonging to the open set $\pi_\beta^{-1}(Y_\beta)$. By local connectedness, there must exist a connected open set **G** containing **z** and contained in $\pi_\beta^{-1}(Y_\beta)$. Taking the βth projection, we see that $z_\beta = x_\beta$ is contained in the connected open set $\pi_\beta(\mathbf{G})$ which is itself contained in Y_β, and so X_β is locally connected. Furthermore, if **z** is any point of the product space, it must be contained in some connected open set **G**. By definition, $\mathbf{z} \in \Pi_\lambda Y_\lambda \subseteq \mathbf{G}$ where Y_λ is open in X_λ for all λ and $Y_\lambda = X_\lambda$ for all but a certain finite number of values of λ. But then the projections of **G** are connected and are equal to X_λ, except for that finite number of values of λ.

Now suppose that X_λ is locally connected for all λ and connected for $\lambda \neq \beta_1, \beta_2, \ldots, \beta_n$. Let $\mathbf{x} = \langle x_\lambda \rangle_\lambda$ be an arbitrary point of $\Pi_\lambda X_\lambda$ contained in an arbitrary basic open set $\Pi_\lambda Y_\lambda$ where Y_λ is open in X_λ for all λ and $Y_\lambda = X_\lambda$ for $\lambda \neq \beta_1^*, \beta_2^*, \ldots, \beta_k^*$. Since $x_\lambda \in Y_\lambda$ for all λ, there is a connected open set G_λ in X_λ such that $x_\lambda \in G_\lambda \subseteq Y_\lambda$. Consider the subset $\Pi_\lambda Z_\lambda$ where $Z_\lambda = G_\lambda$ if $\lambda = \beta_1, \ldots, \beta_n; \beta_1^*, \ldots, \beta_k^*$ and $Z_\lambda = X_\lambda$, otherwise. By the previous theorem, this set is connected. Hence we have found a connected open set containing **x** and contained in $\Pi_\lambda Y_\lambda$. ▌

We have now seen examples of a nonproduct invariant property (normality), a property which is invariant under finite products (local connectedness), and product invariant properties (Hausdorff, connectedness). In the last section we saw that the property of metrizability is at least countably product invariant. We will now give an example of a countably product invariant property that will show that metrizability is not product invariant.

Theorem 8.4.4. *$\Pi_\lambda X_\lambda$ is first axiom iff each space X_λ is first axiom and all but a countable number are indiscrete.*

Proof. Suppose $\Pi_\lambda X_\lambda$ is first axiom. Since each space X_β is homeomorphic to the set $\mathbf{E}_\beta$ defined above, and the first axiom of countability is both hereditary and topological, each space is first axiom. Now if the space X_λ is not indiscrete, we may choose a point $x_\lambda \in X_\lambda$ which is contained in an open set $G_\lambda \neq X_\lambda$. If X_λ is indiscrete, we choose any point $x_\lambda \in X_\lambda$. Let $\mathbf{x} = \langle x_\lambda \rangle_\lambda$, and suppose $\{\mathbf{B}_n\}_{n \in \mathbf{N}}$ is a countable open base at $\mathbf{x}$. For each integer n, the set $\mathbf{B}_n$ must contain a member of the Tichonov base of the form $\Pi_\lambda Y_\lambda$ where Y_λ is open in X_λ for all λ and $Y_\lambda = X_\lambda$ for all but a finite number of values of λ : $\lambda_1{}^n, \ldots, \lambda_{k_n}^n$. The collection of all the excepted values of λ : $\{\lambda_i{}^n : i = 1, \ldots, k_n$ and $n \in \mathbf{N}\}$ is countable. For any other value of λ, we chose $x_\lambda \in G_\lambda \neq X_\lambda$ if X_λ was not indiscrete, but $\pi_\lambda^{-1}(G_\lambda)$ would then be an open set containing $\mathbf{x}$ which would not contain any $\mathbf{B}_n$. Hence, for all other values of λ, X_λ must be indiscrete.

Now suppose that X_λ is first axiom for all λ and indiscrete for $\lambda \notin \{\lambda_i\}_{i \in \mathbf{N}}$. Let $\mathbf{x} = \langle x_\lambda \rangle_\lambda$ be an arbitrary point in $\Pi_\lambda X_\lambda$, and let $\{B_{n,\lambda}\}$ be a countable open base at x_λ. We note that $B_{n,\lambda} = X_\lambda$ for all n if $\lambda \notin \{\lambda_i\}$. The family $\{\pi_{\lambda_i}^{-1}(B_{n,\lambda_i}) : i,\ n \in \mathbf{N}\}$ is a countable collection of open sets in the product space. The set of all finite intersections of members of this collection is also countable, and it is clearly an open base at $\mathbf{x}$, as desired. ∎

Exercises

1. Show that the Tichonov topology agrees, in the case of a countable number of metric spaces, with the topology introduced in Section **8.3**.

2. If $E_\lambda \subseteq X_\lambda$, then $\Pi_\lambda\, \mathrm{c}(E_\lambda) = \mathrm{c}(\Pi_\lambda\, E_\lambda)$.

3. Show that $\mathbf{E}_{\beta_1} \times \mathbf{E}_{\beta_2}$ is homeomorphic to $X_{\beta_1} \times X_{\beta_2}$.

4. Show that $\Pi_\lambda X_\lambda$ has each of the properties listed below iff each space X_λ has the property:
   - (i) T_0,
   - (ii) T_1,
   - (iii) regularity,
   - (iv) complete regularity.

5. Each component of $\Pi_\lambda X_\lambda$ is of the form $\Pi_\lambda C_\lambda$ where C_λ is a component of X_λ for each λ.

6. Explain why metrizability is only a countably product invariant property.

7. $\Pi_\lambda X_\lambda$ is second axiom iff each space X_λ is second axiom and all but a countable number are indiscrete. (Note that separability does not behave this way, see Marczewski [55].)

8. Generalize problem **4** in Section **8.1** by showing that a mapping $\mathfrak{f}$ of a topological space X into a product $\prod_\lambda X_\lambda$ is continuous iff $\pi_\lambda \circ \mathfrak{f}$ is a continuous mapping of X into X_λ for every λ.

8.5 Tichonov Theorem

Before we can prove the **Tichonov Product Theorem** concerning the product of compact spaces, we must consider some further results in the theory of sets. A **filter** $\mathscr{F}$ in a set X is a family of subsets of X satisfying the following axioms:

[F.1] The intersection of any two members of $\mathscr{F}$ is in $\mathscr{F}$.

[F.2] Any set which contains a member of $\mathscr{F}$ is in $\mathscr{F}$.

[F.3] The empty set does not belong to $\mathscr{F}$.

We have already seen some examples of filters in our previous work. By **3.3.2**, the family of all neighborhoods of a fixed point x in a topological space X is a filter in X. Another filter would be the family of all subsets of X which contain a fixed point of X. More generally, the family of all subsets of X which contain a fixed nonempty subset of X is a filter in X. Still another example is the family of all sets with finite complements in an infinite set X.

One important way to obtain a filter is to start with any family $\mathscr{E}$ of subsets of X with the finite intersection property; that is, such that the intersection of any finite number of sets in $\mathscr{E}$ is nonempty. The family $\mathscr{F}$ of all subsets of X which contain the intersection of some finite number of members of $\mathscr{E}$ is easily seen to be a filter. We say that this filter is **generated** by $\mathscr{E}$.

Since filters in X are families of subsets of X, there is a natural partial ordering by inclusion between them; that is, $\mathscr{F} \leqslant \mathscr{F}^*$ iff $\mathscr{F} \subseteq \mathscr{F}^*$. It is important to consider whether there is a greatest filter, or at least maximal filters, in a set. It is easy to show that among families satisfying **[F.1]** and **[F.2]**, $\mathscr{P}(X)$, the family of all subsets of X, is the greatest, and it (and only it) is excluded by **[F.3]**. An **ultrafilter** in a set X is a filter in X which is maximal in the collection of all filters partially ordered by inclusion; that is, a filter which is not properly contained in any other filter. The filter consisting of all sets containing a fixed point of X is clearly an ultrafilter in X. The existence of other types of ultrafilters follows from the following application of Zorn's Lemma (see Section **2.5**).

Theorem 8.5.1. *Every filter is contained in an ultrafilter.*

Proof. Let $\mathscr{F}$ be a filter in X, and let Φ be the collection of all filters containing $\mathscr{F}$. Then Φ is nonempty, since it contains $\mathscr{F}$, and is partially ordered by inclusion. Now suppose Γ is a linearly ordered subset of Φ; that is, if $\mathscr{F}_1, \mathscr{F}_2 \in \Gamma$ then $\mathscr{F}_1 \subseteq \mathscr{F}_2$ or $\mathscr{F}_2 \subseteq \mathscr{F}_1$. Let $\mathscr{H}$ be the union of all sets in the filters in Γ; that is, $E \in \mathscr{H}$ iff there is a filter in Γ containing E. It is clear that $\mathscr{H}$ satisfies **[F.2]** and **[F.3]**. If $E_1, E_2 \in \mathscr{H}$, then $E_1 \in \mathscr{F}_1$ and $E_2 \in \mathscr{F}_2$ for some $\mathscr{F}_1, \mathscr{F}_2 \in \Gamma$. Since Γ is linearly ordered, both of the sets E_1 and E_2 must belong to either $\mathscr{F}_1$ or to $\mathscr{F}_2$, and in either case, their intersection belongs to $\mathscr{H}$. Thus $\mathscr{H}$ satisfies **[F.1]** and is a filter containing, and so no smaller than, all the filters in Γ. We have now shown that Φ is a partially ordered set which is nonempty and has the property that each linearly ordered subset has an upper bound. Thus we have satisfied the hypotheses of Zorn's Lemma and may conclude that Φ contains a maximal element. This maximal element is, by definition, an ultrafilter containing $\mathscr{F}$. ▮

In order to prove our main result, we need one more set-theoretic theorem.

Lemma. *If E is a subset of X which has a nonempty intersection with every member of an ultrafilter $\mathscr{F}$, then E must belong to $\mathscr{F}$.*

Proof. Let $\mathscr{E} = \{E\} \cup \mathscr{F}$. Clearly, the intersection of any finite number of elements of $\mathscr{E}$ is nonempty. The family $\mathscr{E}$ then generates a filter $\mathscr{F}^*$ containing all the sets of $\mathscr{E}$ and so, in particular E. But, since $\mathscr{F}$ is a maximal filter, $\mathscr{F} = \mathscr{F}^*$, and so $E \in \mathscr{F}$. ▮

Theorem 8.5.2. *$\prod_\lambda X_\lambda$ is compact iff each space X_λ is compact.*

Proof. If $\prod_\lambda X_\lambda$ is compact, then each space X_λ is compact since the projections are continuous. Hence, suppose each space X_λ is compact, and let $\mathscr{H}$ be a family of closed subsets of $\prod_\lambda X_\lambda$ with the finite intersection property. The family $\mathscr{H}$ generates a filter which, by the previous theorem, is contained in some ultrafilter $\mathscr{F}$. Consider the family $\{\mathbf{c}(\pi_\lambda \mathbf{F}) : \mathbf{F} \in \mathscr{F}\}$ of closed subsets of X_λ. This family has the finite intersection property because $\bigcap_{i=1}^n \mathbf{c}(\pi_\lambda \mathbf{F}_i) \supseteq \bigcap_{i=1}^n \pi_\lambda \mathbf{F}_i \supseteq \pi_\lambda(\bigcap_{i=1}^n \mathbf{F}_i)$ which is nonempty since $\mathscr{F}$ has the finite intersection property. Since X_λ is compact, there exists some point x_λ which belongs to $\mathbf{c}(\pi_\lambda \mathbf{F})$ for every $\mathbf{F} \in \mathscr{F}$. We shall let $\mathbf{x} = \langle x_\lambda \rangle_\lambda$ and show that $\mathbf{x}$ belongs to every set in $\mathscr{H}$.

Now let $\mathbf{S} = \Pi_\lambda Y_\lambda$ with $Y_\beta = G_\beta$ an open set in X_β, and $Y_\lambda = X_\lambda$ if $\lambda \neq \beta$, be an arbitrary member of the subbase for the product topology which contains $\mathbf{x}$. But then G_β is an open set containing the point x_β which is in the closure of $\pi_\beta \mathbf{F}$ for every $\mathbf{F} \in \mathscr{F}$. Hence, G_β must contain a point of $\pi_\beta \mathbf{F}$ for every $\mathbf{F} \in \mathscr{F}$. Then $\mathbf{S}$ must contain a point of $\mathbf{F}$ for every $\mathbf{F} \in \mathscr{F}$, and by the lemma this implies that $\mathbf{S} \in \mathscr{F}$.

Finally, let $\mathbf{x}$ be contained in an arbitrary open set $\mathbf{G}$. By definition, $\mathbf{x} \in \mathbf{S}_1 \cap \ldots \cap \mathbf{S}_n \subseteq \mathbf{G}$ for some finite number of sets $\mathbf{S}_i$ in the subbase. We have just shown that each $\mathbf{S}_i \in \mathscr{F}$, and so, by **[F.1]**, $\mathbf{S}_1 \cap \ldots \cap \mathbf{S}_n \in \mathscr{F}$, and hence, by **[F.2]**, $\mathbf{G} \in \mathscr{F}$. Going back to our original family $\mathscr{H}$ of closed sets with the finite intersection property, we note that each member of $\mathscr{H}$ is also a member of $\mathscr{F}$, and so $\mathbf{H} \cap \mathbf{G} \in \mathscr{F}$ for every $\mathbf{H} \in \mathscr{H}$ by **[F.1]**, and then $\mathbf{H} \cap \mathbf{G} \neq \emptyset$ for every $\mathbf{H} \in \mathscr{H}$ by **[F.3]**. Thus we have shown that $\mathbf{x} \in \mathbf{c}(\mathbf{H}) = \mathbf{H}$ for every $\mathbf{H} \in \mathscr{H}$, as desired. ∎

The dependence of the above proof upon **8.5.1**, which explicitly used the Zorn's Lemma form of the Axiom of Choice, is natural since, as Kelley [45] has shown, the two are essentially equivalent. One important application of this theorem is to the construction of a (Hausdorff) compactification of any Tichonov space. This will finally prove Theorem **5.6.2** and complete the discussion following that theorem concerning compactifications.

The compactification problem was solved by Tichonov [77] in 1930 when he showed that it is just the spaces which we have called Tichonov spaces which can be topologically embedded in compact Hausdorff spaces, indeed, in the product space of closed intervals. In 1937, Čech [33] showed that Tichonov's method led to a maximal compactification which was completely characterized by an additional extension property. At the same time Stone [75] also demonstrated this maximality and uniqueness, so that today this compactification of a Tichonov space X is universally known as the **Stone-Čech compactification**: βX.

Theorem 8.5.3. *Every Tichonov space X is homeomorphic to a dense subset $\hat{X}$ of a compact Hausdorff space βX which has the property that for every bounded, continuous, real-valued mapping $\mathfrak{f}$ defined on $\hat{X}$ there is a continuous extension to βX; that is, a continuous mapping $\mathfrak{f}^\beta$ of βX into $\mathbf{R}$ such that $\mathfrak{f}^\beta \mid \hat{X} = \mathfrak{f}$.*

Proof. Let $\{\mathfrak{f}_\lambda\}$ be the collection of all real-valued, bounded, continuous functions defined on X. Since these functions are bounded, we may let I_λ be a closed interval of real numbers containing the range of $\mathfrak{f}_\lambda$.

The product space $\prod_\lambda I_\lambda$ is then, by the Tichonov Product Theorem, compact, and it is Hausdorff by **8.4.1**. Let us define a mapping $\mathfrak{h}$ of X into $\prod_\lambda I_\lambda$ by setting $\mathfrak{h}(x) = \langle \mathfrak{f}_\lambda(x) \rangle$ for every $x \in X$. We will denote $\mathfrak{h}(X)$, the range of X, by $\hat{X}$, and its closure $\mathbf{c}(\mathfrak{h}(X))$ in $\prod_\lambda I_\lambda$ by βX. Since βX is a closed subset of a compact Hausdorff space, we have immediately that $\hat{X}$ is a dense subset of the compact Hausdorff space βX. We assert that $\mathfrak{h}$ is a homeomorphism between X and $\hat{X}$.

The mapping $\mathfrak{h}$ is clearly continuous since $\pi_\lambda \circ \mathfrak{h} = \mathfrak{f}_\lambda$ which is continuous (see problem **8** in Section **8.4**). If x and y are two distinct points of X, then there must exist some index λ such that $\mathfrak{f}_\lambda(x) = 0 \neq 1 = \mathfrak{f}_\lambda(y)$ since X is a Tichonov space. From this it follows that $\mathfrak{h}(x) \neq \mathfrak{h}(y)$ since their λth coordinates differ. Finally, let us suppose that G is an open subset of X, and we will show that $\mathfrak{h}(G)$ is open in $\hat{X}$. Fix any point $x \in G$, and, since X is a Tichonov space, there must be an index λ such that $\mathfrak{f}_\lambda(x) = 0$ and $\mathfrak{f}_\lambda(X \setminus G) = \{1\}$. Clearly, $\hat{X} \cap \pi_\lambda^{-1}((-\infty, 1))$ is an open subset of $\hat{X}$ containing $\mathfrak{h}(x)$. Furthermore, if $\mathbf{x} \in \hat{X} \cap \pi_\lambda^{-1}((-\infty, 1))$, then $\mathfrak{h}^{-1}(\mathbf{x}) \subseteq G$, so that $\mathbf{x} \in \mathfrak{h}(G)$. Thus $\hat{X} \cap \pi_\lambda^{-1}((-\infty, 1)) \subseteq \mathfrak{h}(G)$, so that $\mathfrak{h}(G)$ is open in X.

Lastly, suppose $\mathfrak{f}$ is a bounded, continuous, real-valued mapping defined on $\hat{X}$. We must have $\mathfrak{f} \circ \mathfrak{h} = \mathfrak{f}_{\lambda_0}$ for some index λ_0. Let $\mathfrak{f}^\beta$ be the mapping of βX into I_{λ_0} defined by setting $\mathfrak{f}^\beta(\langle x_\lambda \rangle) = \pi_{\lambda_0}(\langle x_\lambda \rangle) = x_{\lambda_0}$. Since the projections are continuous, $\mathfrak{f}^\beta$ is certainly continuous. Now if $\mathbf{x} = \langle \mathfrak{f}_\lambda(x) \rangle$, then $\mathfrak{f}^\beta(\mathbf{x}) = \mathfrak{f}_{\lambda_0}(x)$, while $\mathfrak{f}(\mathbf{x}) = \mathfrak{f}(\langle \mathfrak{f}_\lambda(x) \rangle) = \mathfrak{f}(\mathfrak{h}(x)) = (\mathfrak{f} \circ \mathfrak{h})(x) = \mathfrak{f}_{\lambda_0}(x)$, so that $\mathfrak{f}^\beta \mid \hat{X} = \mathfrak{f}$. ∎

Exercises

1. Show that:

(i) The family of all sets with finite complements is a filter in an infinite set.

(ii) A filter can be generated by a family of sets with the finite intersection property.

(iii) Among families satisfying **[F.1]** and **[F.2]**, $\mathscr{P}(X)$ is the greatest, and it (and only it) is excluded by **[F.3]**.

2. A family $\mathscr{B}$ is said to be a **base** for a filter $\mathscr{F}$ iff $\mathscr{F} = \{E : E \supseteq B$ for some $B \in \mathscr{B}\}$. Show that a family $\mathscr{B}$ is a base for some filter iff $\varnothing \notin \mathscr{B}$ and whenever $B_1, B_2 \in \mathscr{B}$, $B \subseteq B_1 \cap B_2$ for some $B \in \mathscr{B}$. A family $\mathscr{S}$ is a **subbase** for a filter $\mathscr{F}$ iff $\mathscr{F}$ consists of all subsets which contain the intersection of some finite number of members of $\mathscr{S}$; that is, the family of all finite intersections of members of $\mathscr{S}$ is used as a base. Under what conditions is a family of subsets a subbase for a filter?

3. Let $\langle x_n \rangle$ be a sequence of points in a set X. For each integer n, let $B_n = \{x_i : i \geqslant n\}$. Show that the family $\{B_n\}$ is a base for a filter in X. This filter is called the **Fréchet filter** associated with the sequence $\langle x_n \rangle$.

4. Let $\mathscr{F}$ be an ultrafilter in X. Show that the intersection of all the sets in $\mathscr{F}$ contains at most one point, and if that intersection is the set $\{x\}$, then $\mathscr{F}$ is the family of all subsets of X containing x. Are there any ultrafilters which are not of this form?

5. A filter $\mathscr{F}$ is an ultrafilter iff either of the following equivalent conditions is satisfied:

(i) If $A \cup B \in \mathscr{F}$, then $A \in \mathscr{F}$ or $B \in \mathscr{F}$.

(ii) If $E \subseteq X$, then $E \in \mathscr{F}$ or $X \setminus E \in \mathscr{F}$.

6. $\prod_\lambda X_\lambda$ is locally compact iff each space X_λ is locally compact and all but a finite number are compact.

7. A filter $\mathscr{F}$ in a topological space X **converges** to a point $x \in X$, called a **limit point** of $\mathscr{F}$, iff every neighborhood of x belongs to $\mathscr{F}$. A point x is an **adherence point** of a filter $\mathscr{F}$ iff x belongs to the closure of each member of $\mathscr{F}$. Prove:

(i) Every limit point of $\mathscr{F}$ is an adherence point of $\mathscr{F}$.

(ii) A point x is an adherence point of a filter $\mathscr{F}$ iff x is a limit point of some filter which contains $\mathscr{F}$.

(iii) A set E is closed iff it contains any adherence point of any filter containing E.

(iv) X is Hausdorff iff every convergent filter has a unique limit.

(v) X is compact iff every filter in X has at least one adherence point.

(vi) X is compact iff every ultrafilter in X converges.

8. Show that a Hausdorff space has a smallest (Hausdorff) compactification iff it is locally compact (see **5.2.2**). [An explicit partial order for compactifications is given in Kelley [14], p. 151].

9. Show that the space of all ordinal numbers less than the first uncountable ordinal has a unique (Hausdorff) compactification.

10. Describe the Stone-Čech compactification of the positive integers, the rationals, and the reals (see Chapter 6 of the text by Gillman and Jerison [7]).

CHAPTER 9

Function and Quotient Spaces

9.1 Topology of Pointwise Convergence

The results of the previous chapter lead immediately to a topology for general function spaces. We will designate by $\mathfrak{F}(X, Y)$ the family of all functions from X to Y. This set is also written Y^X since, by the definition of powers of cardinal numbers, its cardinality is $\overline{\overline{Y}}^{\overline{\overline{X}}}$. If for each $x \in X$ we let $Y_x = Y$, it is clear that $\mathfrak{F}(X, Y) = \prod\{Y_x : x \in X\}$. Thus if Y is a topological space, we obtain a topology for $\mathfrak{F}(X, Y)$ by considering it as this product with the product topology. This topology will be called the **point-open topology** or the **topology of pointwise convergence**.

The name "point-open" topology comes from the fact that a subbase for this topology is the family of all subsets of the form $\{\mathfrak{f} : \mathfrak{f}(x) \in G\}$ where $x \in X$ and G is an open subset of Y. This is clear since a subbase is known to be the collection of all sets of the form $\pi_x^{-1}(G) = \{\mathfrak{f} : \pi_x(\mathfrak{f}) = \mathfrak{f}(x) \in G\}$ for each $x \in X$ and G open in Y.

In the study of function spaces, there are certain natural mappings of interest. For each $x \in X$ we may define a map $\mathfrak{e}_x$ of $\mathscr{F}(X, Y)$ into Y by setting $\mathfrak{e}_x(\mathfrak{f}) = \mathfrak{f}(x)$. These mappings are called **evaluations**. It is easy to see that $\mathfrak{e}_x = \pi_x$, the projection map of $\mathfrak{F}(X, Y)$ into $Y_x = Y$, and so the point-open topology is the smallest for which all the evaluation maps $\mathfrak{e}_x$ are continuous.

From our study of product spaces in the previous chapter it is easy to tell which topological properties $\mathfrak{F}(X, Y)$ will inherit from Y.

Theorem 9.1.1. *$\mathfrak{F}(X, Y)$ with the point-open topology is connected, compact, T_0, T_1, T_2, regular, or completely regular iff Y has the same property.*

Proof. Each of these properties is product invariant. ∎

Although the topology of X, if it has one, has no effect on the point-open topology for $\mathfrak{F}(X, Y)$, its cardinality may matter, as the next theorem shows.

Theorem 9.1.2. *If X is infinite, $\mathfrak{F}(X, Y)$ with the point-open topology is locally connected (locally compact) iff Y is locally connected (locally compact) and connected (compact), in which case $\mathfrak{F}(X, Y)$ is also connected (compact).*

Proof. If $\mathfrak{F}(X, Y)$ is locally connected (locally compact), then $Y_x = Y$ is locally connected (locally compact) for all $x \in X$ and connected (compact) for all but a finite number of x's by **8.4.3** (**8.5.3**). With X infinite we have Y both locally connected (locally compact) and connected (compact). Conversely, if $Y = Y_x$ is locally connected (locally compact) and connected (compact) for all $x \in X$, then $\mathfrak{F}(X, Y)$ is locally connected (locally compact) by **8.4.3** (**8.5.3**) and also connected (compact) by **8.4.2** (**8.5.2**). ∎

Theorem 9.1.3. *If X is uncountable, $\mathfrak{F}(X, Y)$ satisfies* **[C$_{\text{I}}$]** (or **[C$_{\text{II}}$]**) *iff Y is indiscrete.*

Proof. This follows from **8.4.4** by the same reasoning as in the above theorem. ∎

The set $\mathfrak{C}^*(X)$, consisting of all bounded continuous mappings of X into $\mathbf{R}$, defined in Section **7.1**, is a subset of $\mathfrak{F}(X, \mathbf{R})$, but it is important to note that we did not assign to it the topology induced by the point-open topology on $\mathfrak{F}(X, \mathbf{R})$. Recalling that convergence in $\mathfrak{C}^*(X)$ was equivalent to the uniform convergence of the sequence of functions, the following theorem shows the essential difference between these topologies and explains the name "pointwise convergence."

Theorem 9.1.4. *If $\langle \mathfrak{f}_n \rangle$ is a sequence of points in $\mathfrak{F}(X, Y)$ with the topology of pointwise convergence, then* $\lim \mathfrak{f}_n = \mathfrak{f}$ iff $\lim \mathfrak{f}_n(x) = \mathfrak{f}(x)$ *for every* $x \in X$.

Proof. Let $\lim \mathfrak{f}_n(x) = \mathfrak{f}(x)$ for every $x \in X$, and suppose that $\mathfrak{f} \in \pi_x^{-1}(G)$; i.e., $\mathfrak{f}(x) \in G$, for some $x \in X$ and G open in Y. Then there exists an index N such that $\mathfrak{f}_n(x) \in G$ for all $n > N$; i.e., $\mathfrak{f}_n \in \pi_x^{-1}(G)$ for $n > N$. Hence $\lim \mathfrak{f}_n = \mathfrak{f}$.

Now suppose $\lim \mathfrak{f}_n = \mathfrak{f}$ and $\mathfrak{f}(x) \in G$; i.e., $\mathfrak{f} \in \pi_x^{-1}(G)$, for $x \in X$ and some G open in Y. Then there exists an index N such that $\mathfrak{f}_n \in \pi_x^{-1}(G)$ for all $n > N$; i.e., $\mathfrak{f}_n(x) \in G$ for $n > N$. Hence $\lim \mathfrak{f}_n(x) = \mathfrak{f}(x)$ for every $x \in X$. ∎

9.2 Topology of Compact Convergence

The example of $\mathfrak{C}^*(X)$ given in the last section shows that we may be interested in larger topologies than the point-open topology for $\mathfrak{F}(X, Y)$. One class of topologies may be found by generalizing the subbase $\{\mathfrak{f} : \mathfrak{f}(x) \in G\}$. If we let $\mathscr{E}$ be an arbitrary family of subsets of X, then the family of all sets of the form $\{\mathfrak{f} : \mathfrak{f}(E) \subseteq G\}$ for $E \in \mathscr{E}$ and G open in Y is a subbase for some topology for $\mathfrak{F}(X, Y)$, and we say that this topology is **induced** by $\mathscr{E}$.

In general, the evaluations $\mathfrak{e}_x$ will not be continuous, and, in fact, since the point-open topology is the smallest topology for which all the evaluations are continuous, they will be continuous iff $\mathscr{E}$ induces a topology which is larger than the point-open topology. This will clearly be the case if $\mathscr{E}$ contains every set consisting of exactly one point. We may now consider the point-open topology as that topology which is induced on $\mathfrak{F}(X, Y)$ by the family of all finite subsets of X.

Since compact sets have many of the nice properties of finite sets, we would naturally be led to consider the topology induced by the family of all compact subsets of X. This topology for $\mathfrak{F}(X Y)$ will be called the **compact-open topology** or the **topology of compact convergence** and has as a subbase the family of all subsets of the form $\{\mathfrak{f} : \mathfrak{f}(K) \subseteq G\}$ with K compact in X and G open in Y.

Since every set consisting of exactly one point is compact, our above remarks show that the compact-open topology is larger than the point-open topology, and all the evaluations will be continuous in it. On the other hand, if X is discrete, then the compact-open topology is the same as the point open topology. This shows that even if Y is normal, first axiom, second axiom, or separable, we cannot expect $\mathfrak{F}(X, Y)$, with the compact-open topology, to have the same property.

Such properties as regularity, connectedness, and compactness are also not inherited from Y in the case of the compact-open topology. In fact, if Y is a compact Hausdorff space, then $\mathfrak{F}(X, Y)$ will be a compact Hausdorff space with the point-open topology and, by problem **7** of Section **5.2**, will not be compact with any strictly larger topology. Almost the only properties which are inherited from Y are the separation axioms $[\mathbf{T}_0]$, $[\mathbf{T}_1]$, and $[\mathbf{T}_2]$.

Most of the interest in function spaces centers around the subspace $\mathfrak{C}(X, Y)$ of $\mathfrak{F}(X, Y)$ consisting of all continuous mappings of X into Y. In this subspace it is possible to prove, for example, that regularity is inherited from Y.

Theorem 9.2.1. *If Y is regular, then $\mathfrak{C}(X, Y)$, with the compact-open topology, is regular.*

Proof. Suppose Y is regular, and let $\mathfrak{f}^*$ be a point of $\mathfrak{C}(X, Y)$ contained in the subbasic open set $\{\mathfrak{f} : \mathfrak{f}(K) \subseteq G\}$ with K compact in X and G open in Y. Thus, in particular, $\mathfrak{f}^*(K) \subseteq G$. By regularity, for each $y \in \mathfrak{f}^*(K)$, there exists an open set V_y such that $y \in V_y$ and $\mathbf{c}(V_y) \subseteq G$. Since $\mathfrak{f}^*$ is continuous, $\mathfrak{f}^*(K)$ is compact, and the open covering $\{V_y : y \in \mathfrak{f}^*(K)\}$ must have a finite subcover, the union of whose members, denoted by V, will have the properties that $\mathfrak{f}^*(K) \subseteq V$ and $\mathbf{c}(V) \subseteq G$. We note that we now have $\mathfrak{f}^* \in \{\mathfrak{f} : \mathfrak{f}(K) \subseteq V\}$. However, if $\mathfrak{g} \notin \{\mathfrak{f} : \mathfrak{f}(K) \subseteq \mathbf{c}(V)\}$, then there exists an $x \in K$ such that $\mathfrak{g}(x) \notin \mathbf{c}(V)$. Thus, $\pi_x^{-1}(X \setminus \mathbf{c}(V))$ is an open set in the point-open topology, and hence also in the compact-open topology, which contains $\mathfrak{g}$ and is disjoint from $\{\mathfrak{f} : \mathfrak{f}(K) \subseteq V\}$. Therefore we now have

$$\mathbf{c}\{\mathfrak{f} : \mathfrak{f}(K) \subseteq V\} \subseteq \{\mathfrak{f} : \mathfrak{f}(K) \subseteq \mathbf{c}(V)\} \subseteq \{\mathfrak{f} : \mathfrak{f}(K) \subseteq G\}.$$

Finally, let $\mathfrak{f}^*$ be contained in a general open set $\mathscr{G}^*$, which then contains a basic open set

$$\{\mathfrak{f} : \mathfrak{f}(K_1) \subseteq G_1\} \cap \ldots \cap \{\mathfrak{f} : \mathfrak{f}(K_n) \subseteq G_n\}$$

where $\mathfrak{f}^*(K_i) \subseteq G_i$; that is, a basic open set containing $\mathfrak{f}^*$. By the above construction, the set $\mathscr{V}^*$, defined by setting

$$\mathscr{V}^* = \{\mathfrak{f} : \mathfrak{f}(K_1) \subseteq V_1\} \cap \ldots \cap \{\mathfrak{f} : \mathfrak{f}(K_n) \subseteq V_n\},$$

is an open set containing $\mathfrak{f}^*$ such that $\mathbf{c}(\mathscr{V}^*) \subseteq \mathscr{G}^*$. ∎

As an example of the importance of $\mathfrak{C}(X, Y)$, we note that the collection of all paths in Y (see Section **4.5**) is the space $\mathfrak{C}(I, Y)$, which, with the compact-open topology, is basic to the study of homotopy theory. For a complete treatment of that subject, the reader is referred to the text of Hu [11].

Our final result on function spaces will be based on a generalization of the fact that convergence in $\mathfrak{C} = \mathfrak{C}(I) = \mathfrak{C}^*(I, \mathbf{R})$ was equivalent to the uniform convergence of the sequence of functions. We recall that if Y is a bounded metric space, we may metrize $\mathfrak{F}(X, Y)$ by use of the metric d^* defined by setting

$$d^*(\mathfrak{f}, \mathfrak{g}) = \sup\{d(\mathfrak{f}(x), \mathfrak{g}(x)) : x \in X\}.$$

A basis for the neighborhoods of a point $\mathfrak{f} \in \mathfrak{F}(X, Y)$ would then be

$$B(\mathfrak{f}, \epsilon) = \{\mathfrak{g} : d^*(\mathfrak{f}, \mathfrak{g}) < \epsilon\}$$
$$= \{\mathfrak{g} : d(\mathfrak{f}(x), \mathfrak{g}(x)) < \epsilon \quad \text{for all} \quad x \in X\}$$

for every $\epsilon > 0$. We will call this topology the **topology of uniform convergence on** X.

The generalization proceeds in a manner similar to that used at the beginning of this section. If $\mathscr{E}$ is a family of subsets of X, the collection of all subsets of the form

$$B(\mathfrak{f}, \epsilon, E) = \{\mathfrak{g} : d(\mathfrak{f}(x), \mathfrak{g}(x)) < \epsilon \quad \text{for all} \quad x \in E\}$$

for $E \in \mathscr{E}$ and $\epsilon > 0$ is a subbase for the neighborhoods of a point $\mathfrak{f} \in \mathfrak{F}(X, Y)$. The topology thus obtained will be called the **topology of uniform convergence on members of** $\mathscr{E}$. We will be interested in this topology only in the case that the family $\mathscr{E}$ consists of all compact subsets of X. We call this topology the **topology of uniform convergence on compacta.**

Since each subset of X consisting of exactly one point is compact, it is clear that this topology is larger than the point-open topology. On the other hand, it is obviously smaller than the topology of uniform convergence on X but equal to it if X is compact (since $B(\mathfrak{f}, \epsilon, K) \supseteq B(\mathfrak{f}, \epsilon, X)$). Our final theorem will characterize this topology and explain the name "compact convergence."

Theorem 9.2.2. *The topology of uniform convergence on compacta is the same as the compact-open topology for the set* $\mathfrak{C}^*(X, Y)$ *of all bounded, continuous functions from the topological space* X *to the metric space* Y.

Proof. Let K be a compact subset of X and G an open subset of Y. The corresponding subbase element is $\{\mathfrak{f} : \mathfrak{f}(K) \subseteq G\}$ in the compact-open topology, and let us choose a point $\mathfrak{f}^*$ from it. We wish to find an $\epsilon > 0$ such that

$$B(\mathfrak{f}^*, \epsilon, K) \subseteq \{\mathfrak{f} : \mathfrak{f}(K) \subseteq G\},$$

thus showing that every neighborhood of $\mathfrak{f}^*$ in the compact-open topology is also a neighborhood in the topology of uniform convergence on K. Since $\mathfrak{f}^*$ is continuous, $\mathfrak{f}^*(K)$ is a compact subset of G, and so, by problem **9** in Section **6.2**, there exists an $\epsilon > 0$ such that

$d(\mathfrak{f}^*(K), Y \setminus G) = \epsilon$. Now if $\mathfrak{g} \in B(\mathfrak{f}^*, \epsilon, K)$, so that $d(\mathfrak{f}^*(x), \mathfrak{g}(x)) < \epsilon$ for all $x \in K$, we have $\mathfrak{g}(K) \subseteq G$, as desired. Thus the compact-open topology is smaller than the topology of uniform convergence on K, which itself is smaller than the topology of uniform convergence on compacta.

Now suppose a compact subset K of X, a point $\mathfrak{f}^* \in \mathfrak{C}^*(X, Y)$, and a positive number ϵ are given. The corresponding subbase element is $B(\mathfrak{f}^*, \epsilon, K)$ in the topology of uniform convergence on compacta. We wish to find a finite number of pairs $\{K_i, G_i\}_{i=1}^n$ of compact subsets K_i of X and open subsets G_i of Y such that

$$\mathfrak{f}^* \in \bigcap_{i=1}^{n} \{\mathfrak{f} : \mathfrak{f}(K_i) \subseteq G_i\} \subseteq B(\mathfrak{f}^*, \epsilon, K),$$

thus showing that every neighborhood in the topology of uniform convergence on compacta is a neighborhood in the compact-open topology. We must show, then, that $\mathfrak{f}^*(K_i) \subseteq G_i$, and if $\mathfrak{g}(K_i) \subseteq G_i$ for each i, then $d(\mathfrak{f}^*(x), \mathfrak{g}(x)) < \epsilon$ for all $x \in K$. Since $\mathfrak{f}^*$ is continuous. $\mathfrak{f}^*(K)$ is compact, and so we may choose a finite number of points $\{x_i\}_{i=1}^n$ in K such that the collection $\{B(\mathfrak{f}^*(x_i), \epsilon/3)\}_{i=1}^n$ covers $\mathfrak{f}^*(K)$. Let $K_i = K \cap \mathfrak{f}^{*-1}(\mathbf{c}(B(\mathfrak{f}^*(x_i), \epsilon/3)))$, and let $G_i = B(\mathfrak{f}^*(x_i), 2\epsilon/3)$. We may now show that these sets have the desired properties.

Since $\mathfrak{f}^*$ is continuous, each K_i is a closed subset of K and hence compact, while each G_i is obviously open. We calculate that

$$\mathfrak{f}^*(K_i) \subseteq \mathbf{c}(B(\mathfrak{f}^*(x_i), \epsilon/3)) \subseteq B(\mathfrak{f}^*(x_i), 2\epsilon/3) = G_i .$$

Finally, let us suppose that $\mathfrak{g}(K_i) \subseteq G_i$ for each i, and x is any point of K. By the covering property mentioned above, $K = \bigcup_{i=1}^n K_i$, so there exists an index i such that $x \in K_i$. Thus we have $d(\mathfrak{f}^*(x), \mathfrak{f}^*(x_i)) \leqslant \epsilon/3$. Hence,

$$\mathfrak{g}(x) \in \mathfrak{g}(K_i) \subseteq G_i = B(\mathfrak{f}^*(x_i), 2\epsilon/3);$$

that is, $d(\mathfrak{f}^*(x_i), \mathfrak{g}(x)) < 2\epsilon/3$. By the triangle inequality, $d(\mathfrak{f}^*(x), \mathfrak{g}(x)) < \epsilon$, as desired. ▮

Exercises

1. If Y is a T_i-space ($i = 0, 1, 2$), then so is $\mathfrak{F}(X, Y)$ with the compact-open topology.
2. If $\mathfrak{C}(X, Y)$, with the compact-open topology, is regular, then so is Y.

9.3 Quotient Topology

In Section **4.4** we considered the question of finding the largest topology for a set Y that would make a given mapping $\mathfrak{f}$ of a given topological space X onto Y continuous. We will call this topology the **quotient topology** for Y (relative to $\mathfrak{f}$ and the topology for X). The reason for the name will be given later, but it is easy to characterize the family of open sets in Y under this topology immediately.

Theorem 9.3.1. *A subset G of Y is open in the quotient topology (relative to $\mathfrak{f} : X \rightarrow Y$) iff $\mathfrak{f}^{-1}(G)$ is an open subset of X.*

Proof. The family of all subsets G of Y for which $\mathfrak{f}^{-1}(G)$ is open in X is clearly a topology for Y since it satisfies the axioms **[0.1]** and **[0.2]**. Furthermore, $\mathfrak{f}$ is obviously continuous with this topology for Y, since the inverse of every open set is open. Finally, this is the largest topology for which $\mathfrak{f}$ is continuous, since $\mathfrak{f}$ is continuous only if the inverse of every open set is open. ▮

In general, the mapping $\mathfrak{f}$ is not also open, and so the quotient topology does not coincide with the smallest topology for Y such that $\mathfrak{f}$ is open. The following theorem does give a relationship between these topologies.

Theorem 9.3.2. *If $\mathfrak{f}$ is a continuous, open mapping of the topological space X onto the topological space Y, then the topology for Y must be the quotient topology.*

Proof. Since the quotient topology is the largest for which $\mathfrak{f}$ is continuous, the topology for Y is smaller than the quotient topology. On the other hand, if G is a subset of Y for which $\mathfrak{f}^{-1}(G)$ is open, then $G = \mathfrak{f}(\mathfrak{f}^{-1}(G))$ is itself open in Y since $\mathfrak{f}$ is open. Hence the topology for Y is also larger than the quotient topology. ▮

The following basic topological properties are inherited by Y from X when we give Y the quotient topology.

Theorem 9.3.3. *If X is compact, connected, locally connected, separable, or Lindelöf, then so is Y with the quotient topology.*

Proof. Since $\mathfrak{f}$ is continuous, any property preserved by continuous mappings will naturally be inherited; hence the theorem is obvious for compact, connected, separable, and Lindelöf spaces. Now suppose that G^* is an open subset of Y, and let C^* be a component of G^*. Since Y has the quotient topology, the set $G = \mathfrak{f}^{-1}(G^*)$ will be an open subset of

X containing the set $C = \mathfrak{f}^{-1}(C^*)$. Let x be an arbitrary point of C, and denote by C_x the component of G containing x. Since $x \in C$ and $x \in C_x$, we have $\mathfrak{f}(x) \in \mathfrak{f}(\mathfrak{f}^{-1}(C^*)) = C^*$ and $\mathfrak{f}(x) \in \mathfrak{f}(C_x)$. Now C^* is connected, and so $\mathfrak{f}(C_x)$ is also connected, since $\mathfrak{f}$ is continuous. Furthermore, the sets C^* and $\mathfrak{f}(C_x)$ have a nonempty intersection which contains $\mathfrak{f}(x)$, and so, by Corollary **3** to **4.1.2**, their union, $C^* \cup \mathfrak{f}(C_x)$, is connected. By the maximality of components, it follows that $\mathfrak{f}(C_x) \subseteq C^*$, and so $C_x \subseteq C$. Assuming that X is locally connected, each component C_x must be open, and so C will be a neighborhood of x. This was the case for every point $x \in C$, and so C is open. Finally, since $C = \mathfrak{f}^{-1}(C^*)$ and Y has the quotient topology, C^* is open, and hence Y is locally connected. ▮

The separation and countability axioms are generally not preserved, as some simple examples will show. Thus, for example, if $X = [0,1]$, $Y = \{0,1\}$, and $\mathfrak{f}$ is the function which is zero on the irrationals and one on the rationals, then the quotient topology for Y is the indiscrete topology, which is not Hausdorff even though X is Hausdorff. We may easily characterize the case in which Y is a T_1-space.

Theorem 9.3.4. *Y, with the quotient topology, is a T_1-space iff $\mathfrak{f}^{-1}(y)$ is closed in X for every $y \in Y$.*

Proof. This follows immediately from **5.1.2** and problem **1**. ▮

Now let us consider the fact that an equivalence relation $\mathfrak{r}$ on X induces a mapping χ, called the **canonical map**, of X onto $X/\mathfrak{r}$ (see Section **1.3**) by setting $\chi(x) = [x]$, the equivalence class to which x belongs. We shall call $X/\mathfrak{r}$ a **quotient space** when we give this quotient set the quotient topology relative to χ.

Theorem 9.3.5. *χ is a continuous mapping of X onto $X/\mathfrak{r}$. A subset $\mathscr{E} \subseteq X/\mathfrak{r}$ is open iff $\bigcup\{E : E \in \mathscr{E}\}$ is open in X. If X is compact, connected, locally connected, separable, or Lindelöf, then so is $X/\mathfrak{r}$. $X/\mathfrak{r}$ is a T_1-space iff the equivalence classes in X by $\mathfrak{r}$ are closed.*

Proof. All these results follow immediately from the above theorems on quotient topologies. ▮

We have already seen an example of a quotient space of a Hausdorff space which is not a Hausdorff space. In particular, if $X = [0, 1]$ and $\mathfrak{r}$ is defined by the condition that $\langle x, y\rangle \in \mathfrak{r}$ iff x and y are either both rational or both irrational, then the quotient space $X/\mathfrak{r}$ is the indiscrete space with two points. Another equivalence relation for

$X = [0, 1]$ would be $\mathfrak{r} = \mathfrak{i}_X \cup \{\langle 0, 1\rangle, \langle 1, 0\rangle\}$, that is, the equivalence relation which identifies the endpoints of X. In this case the quotient space $X/\mathfrak{r}$ would be homeomorphic to a circle.

Another interesting example of a quotient space may be obtained from any topological space by identifying those points which are indistinguishable topologically; that is, points whose neighborhoods are exactly the same. The following theorem shows some of the expected results of this identification.

Theorem 9.3.6. *Let X be any topological space, and define $\mathfrak{r}$ by setting $\langle x, y\rangle \in \mathfrak{r}$ iff $\mathbf{c}(\{x\}) = \mathbf{c}(\{y\})$ (equivalently: iff $\mathcal{N}_x = \mathcal{N}_y$). Then $\mathfrak{r}$ is an equivalence relation, the canonical map χ is both open and closed, and $X/\mathfrak{r}$ is a T_0-space. If X is regular, then so is $X/\mathfrak{r}$.*

Proof. It is obvious that $\mathfrak{r}$ is an equivalence relation. We note immediately that if an open set has a nonempty intersection with one of the equivalence classes into which X is decomposed by $\mathfrak{r}$, then that open set must contain the entire equivalence class. From this it follows that every open set in X is a union of these equivalence classes, and so is the inverse of its image under χ. By the previous theorem, it follows that χ is an open mapping. In the same way it follows that χ is a closed map. Now suppose that $[x]$ and $[y]$ are distinct points of $X/\mathfrak{r}$ (that is, equivalence classes in X), and choose $x \in [x]$ and $y \in [y]$ as representatives. Since x and y are in different equivalence classes, their closures must be different. There must then exist some open set G containing one of them, say x, but not the other. As noted above, G must contain all of $[x]$ and be disjoint from $[y]$, so $\chi(G)$ is an open set in $X/\mathfrak{r}$ containing $[x]$ but not $[y]$. Thus $X/\mathfrak{r}$ is a T_0-space, Finally, suppose X is regular, and let x^* be a point of $X/\mathfrak{r}$ not contained in the closed set F^*. Then $\chi^{-1}(x^*) = [x]$ is disjoint from the closed set $\chi^{-1}(F^*)$. By the regularity of X, there exist disjoint open sets G_x and G_F containing x and $\chi^{-1}(F^*)$, respectively. Again we note that G_x must contain all of $[x]$, so $\chi(G_x)$ and $\chi(G_F)$ are the open sets desired. ∎

The obtaining of a metric space from a pseudometric space is still another important example of the use of quotient spaces. A **pseudometric** for a set X is a mapping d of $X \times X$ into the nonnegative reals satisfying the axioms **[M.1]**, **[M.2]**, and **[M.3]** for metrics (see Section **6.1**), but not necessarily axiom **[M.4]**. As in Section **6.1**, we may obtain a topology by using as a base the family of all balls in the set. With this topology, we say that we have a **pseudometric space**.

It is easy to show that every pseudometric space is a completely normal, first axiom space. The example of the pseudometric d, defined by setting $d(x, y) = 0$ for all $x, y \in X$, shows that the indiscrete topology on any set is pseudometrizable, and so we cannot obtain any of the separation axioms $[\mathbf{T}_i]$ $(i = 0, ..., 5)$ in general. It is natural to try to equate points in a pseudometric space which are zero distance apart. This identification does yield a metric space, as the next theorem shows.

Theorem 9.3.7. *If (X, d) is a pseudometric space, then the relation $\mathfrak{r}$, defined by setting $\langle x, y \rangle \in \mathfrak{r}$ iff $d(x, y) = 0$, is an equivalence relation, and the quotient space $X/\mathfrak{r}$ is metrizable.*

Proof. It is clear that $\mathfrak{r}$ is an equivalence relation. Let us define a mapping d^* of $(X/\mathfrak{r}) \times (X/\mathfrak{r})$ into the nonnegative reals by setting $d^*([x], [y]) = d(x, y)$ for some representatives $x \in [x]$ and $y \in [y]$. We must show that d^* is well defined (that is, it does not depend on the particular representatives chosen), and is a metric for $X/\mathfrak{r}$. Suppose we choose some other representatives $x' \in [x]$ and $y' \in [y]$. By axiom **[M.2]**, the triangle inequality,

$$d(x, y) \leqslant d(x, x') + d(x', y') + d(y', y) = d(x', y')$$

since $d(x, x') = d(y, y') = 0$ by the definition of $\mathfrak{r}$. In the same way, $d(x' y') \leqslant d(x, y)$, and so the two distances are equal. Hence d^* does indeed depend only on the equivalence classes $[x]$ and $[y]$, not on the particular representatives chosen. It is obvious that d^* is a metric for $X/\mathfrak{r}$. ∎

Exercises

1. A subset F of Y is closed in the quotient topology (relative to $\mathfrak{f} : X \to Y$) iff $\mathfrak{f}^{-1}(F)$ is a closed subset of X.

2. If $\mathfrak{f}$ is a continuous, closed mapping of X onto Y, then the topology for Y must be the quotient topology.

3. Give an example which shows that a mapping $\mathfrak{f} : X \to Y$ need not be either open or closed, even if Y has the quotient topology. Give examples to show that the separation and countability axioms need not be inherited by Y from X when we give Y the quotient topology.

4. If X is a countably compact T_1-space, then Y is countably compact with the quotient topology.

5. If X is completely regular or normal in **9.3.6**, then so is $X/\mathfrak{r}$.

6. Prove that χ is closed iff any one of the following conditions is satisfied:

(i) For any equivalence class $[x]$ in X mod $\mathfrak{r}$, and any open set G containing $[x]$, there exists an open set G^* containing $[x]$ and contained in G such that G^* is the union of equivalence classes in X mod $\mathfrak{r}$.

(ii) For any open set G in X, the union of all the equivalence classes which are subsets of G is open.

(iii) For any closed set F in X, the union of all equivalence classes which have nonempty intersections with F is closed.

7. If χ is closed and X is normal, then so is $X/\mathfrak{r}$; in fact, normality is preserved by any closed continuous map.

8. If χ is closed and the equivalence classes in X are compact subsets, then the properties of Hausdorff, regularity, second axiom, and local compactness are all inherited by $X/\mathfrak{r}$ from X.

9. A mapping $\mathfrak{f} : (X/\mathfrak{r}) \to Y$ is continuous iff $\mathfrak{f} \circ \chi : X \to Y$ is continuous.

10. If Y is a quotient space of X and Z is a quotient space of Y, then Z is homeomorphic to a quotient space of X. If $\mathfrak{r}_1 \subseteq \mathfrak{r}_2$, then $X/\mathfrak{r}_2$ is homeomorphic to a quotient space of $X/\mathfrak{r}_1$.

11. If $X/\mathfrak{r}$ is a Hausdorff space, then $\mathfrak{r}$ is a closed subset of $X \times X$. If $\mathfrak{r}$ is a closed subset of $X \times X$ and χ is open, then $X/\mathfrak{r}$ is a Hausdorff space. Give an example which shows that the requirement that χ be open cannot be omitted from this last result.

12. Give an example of a regular Hausdorff space X and a relation $\mathfrak{r}$ which is a closed subset of $X \times X$ such that $X/\mathfrak{r}$ is a Hausdorff space which is not regular. (*Hint*: Consider a nonnormal space.)

13. Let $\mathfrak{r}$ be the relation on the real numbers obtained by identifying all the integers. Show that χ is closed, $X/\mathfrak{r}$ is Hausdorff, but $X/\mathfrak{r}$ is neither locally compact, nor first axiom.

14. Let $\mathfrak{r}$ be the relation on the plane obtained by identifying all the points on the real axis. Show that χ is closed, $X/\mathfrak{r}$ is Hausdorff, but $X/\mathfrak{r}$ is neither locally compact, nor first axiom.

15. If $X = [0, 1]$ and $\mathfrak{r} = \mathfrak{i}_X \cup \{\langle 0, 1\rangle, \langle 1, 0\rangle\}$, then $X/\mathfrak{r}$ is homeomorphic to a circle.

16. Every pseudometric space is a completely normal first axiom space.

CHAPTER **10**

Metrization and Paracompactness

10.1 Urysohn's Metrization Theorem

In the case of separable metric spaces, Urysohn [80] found necessary and sufficient conditions for metrizability. The basis for the proof of his theorem is the classical lemma mentioned in Section **5.5**. We will now prove that lemma and the metrization theorem.

Urysohn's Lemma. *A topological space X is normal iff for every two disjoint closed subsets F_1 and F_2 of X and closed interval $[a, b]$ of reals, there exists a continuous mapping $\mathfrak{f} : X \to [a, b]$ such that $\mathfrak{f}(F_1) = \{a\}$ and $\mathfrak{f}(F_2) = \{b\}$.*

Proof. It is clear that if such a mapping $\mathfrak{f} : X \to [0, 1]$ exists, then X must be normal since $\mathfrak{f}^{-1}([0, \frac{1}{2}))$ and $\mathfrak{f}^{-1}((\frac{1}{2}, 1])$ would be disjoint open sets containing F_1 and F_2, respectively. Consequently, let us suppose that F_1 and F_2 are two disjoint closed subsets of the normal space X, and $[a, b]$ is a closed interval of reals. Since the mapping $\mathfrak{h}$ defined by setting $\mathfrak{h}(x) = (b - a)x + a$ is a continuous mapping of $[0, 1]$ onto $[a, b]$ (indeed, it is a homeomorphism if $[a, b]$ is nondegenerate), we need only construct a continuous mapping $\mathfrak{g} : X \to [0, 1]$ such that $\mathfrak{g}(F_1) = \{0\}$ and $\mathfrak{g}(F_2) = \{1\}$, and then $\mathfrak{f} = \mathfrak{h} \circ \mathfrak{g}$ will be the desired map.

We will first define a collection $\{G_r : r \text{ rational}\}$ of open sets such that $\mathbf{c}(G_r) \subseteq G_s$ whenever $r < s$ in the following way. For all $r < 0$ we let $G_r = \varnothing$, and for all $r > 1$ we let $G_r = X$. Next we define G_1 to be $X \setminus F_2$, which is an open set containing F_1 with the desired property. By the characterization of normality given in **5.5.2**, G_1 contains an open set G_0 containing F_1 whose closure is also contained in G_1. Now let $\{r_n\}_{n \in \mathbf{N}}$ be a listing of all the rationals in $[0, 1]$ with $r_1 = 0$ and $r_2 = 1$. For each $n \geqslant 3$ we will inductively define the open set G_{r_n} by taking the largest r_i and the smallest r_j such that $i, j < n$ and $r_i < r_n < r_j$, then using **5.5.2** to obtain the open set G_{r_n} with the property that $\mathbf{c}(G_{r_i}) \subseteq G_{r_n}$ and $\mathbf{c}(G_{r_n}) \subseteq G_{r_j}$.

We now define the desired mapping $\mathfrak{g}$ by setting $\mathfrak{g}(x) = \inf\{r : x \in G_r\}$.

Since every $x \in X$ belongs to some G_r, but not to all of them, $\mathfrak{g}(x)$ is a well-defined real number in [0, 1]. We note that $\mathfrak{g}(x) < q$ iff $x \in G_r$ for some $r < q$, and so

$$\{x : \mathfrak{g}(x) < q\} = \bigcup \{G_r : r < q\},$$

which is an open set. Furthermore, $\mathfrak{g}(x) > p$ iff $x \notin \mathbf{c}(G_r)$ for some $r > p$, and so

$$\{x : \mathfrak{g}(x) > p\} = \bigcup \{X \setminus \mathbf{c}(G_r) : r > p\},$$

which is again an open set. Thus $\mathfrak{g}^{-1}((p, q))$ is always an open set, and hence $\mathfrak{g}$ is continuous. Clearly, $\mathfrak{g}(F_1) = \{0\}$ and $\mathfrak{g}(F_2) = \{1\}$. ∎

Urysohn's Metrization Theorem. *Every second axiom T_3-space is metrizable.*

Proof. We shall show that any second axiom T_3-space X is homeomorphic to a subset of the Hilbert cube. Let $\{G_n\}_{n \in \mathbf{N}}$ be the nonempty sets in some denumerable base for X, made infinite by repetition if necessary. Now for each integer j, there is some point $x \in G_j$ and, by regularity, an open set G such that $x \in G \subseteq \mathbf{c}(G) \subseteq G_j$. Since the collection $\{G_n\}$ forms a base, there must be some integer i such that $x \in G_i \subseteq G$. Thus, for every integer j, there is an integer i such that $\mathbf{c}(G_i) \subseteq G_j$. The collection of all such pairs of elements from the base is denumerable, and suppose $\langle G_i, G_j \rangle$ is the nth pair in some fixed ordering. The sets $\mathbf{c}(G_i)$ and $X \setminus G_j$ are then disjoint closed subsets of X. By problem **13** in Section **5.5**, the regular second axiom space X is completely normal, and hence normal. Thus, by Urysohn's Lemma, there exists some continuous mapping $\mathfrak{f}_n : X \to [0, 1]$ such that $\mathfrak{f}_n(\mathbf{c}(G_i)) = \{0\}$ and $\mathfrak{f}_n(X \setminus G_j) = \{1\}$.

We may now define a mapping $\mathfrak{f}$ of X into the Hilbert cube by setting $\mathfrak{f}(x) = \langle 2^{-n}\mathfrak{f}_n(x) \rangle_{n \in \mathbf{N}}$ for every $x \in X$. Since $0 \leqslant \mathfrak{f}_n(x) \leqslant 1$ for all $x \in X$ and integers n, $\mathfrak{f}(x)$ is clearly a uniquely determined element of the Hilbert cube for each $x \in X$. We shall next show that $\mathfrak{f}$ is a homeomorphism of X onto $\mathfrak{f}(X)$.

Let x and y be two distinct points of X. Since X is a T_1-space, there exists some integer j such that $x \in G_j$ but $y \in X \setminus G_j$. As above, there exists some integer i such that $x \in G_i$ and $\mathbf{c}(G_i) \subseteq G_j$. Suppose $\langle G_i, G_j \rangle$ is the nth pair in our ordering. The nth coordinate of $\mathfrak{f}(x)$ is $2^{-n}\mathfrak{f}_n(x) = 0$ since $x \in \mathbf{c}(G_i)$, while the nth coordinate of $\mathfrak{f}(y)$ is $2^{-n}\mathfrak{f}_n(y) = 2^{-n} \neq 0$ since $y \in X \setminus G_j$. Thus, $\mathfrak{f}(x) \neq \mathfrak{f}(y)$, and $\mathfrak{f}$ is one-to-one.

Now let x^* be a fixed point of X, and let ϵ be an arbitrary positive number. Let us first choose an index $N = N(\epsilon)$ such that $\Sigma_{n=N+1}^{\infty} 2^{-2n} < \epsilon^2/2$. For each n such that $1 \leqslant n \leqslant N$, the mapping $\mathfrak{f}_n$ is continuous, and so there exists a basic open set G_n containing x^* such that $| \mathfrak{f}_n(x^*) - \mathfrak{f}_n(x) | < \epsilon/\sqrt{2N}$ whenever $x \in G_n$. Let $G = \bigcap_{n=1}^{N} G_n$, which is then an open set containing x^*. If $x \in G$, then $x \in G_n$ for each $n = 1, ..., N$, and so

$$d_H(\mathfrak{f}(x^*), \mathfrak{f}(x)) = \sqrt{\Sigma_{n=1}^{\infty} [2^{-n}\mathfrak{f}_n(x^*) - 2^{-n}\mathfrak{f}_n(x)]^2}$$

$$= \sqrt{\Sigma_{n=1}^{N} 2^{-2n} | \mathfrak{f}_n(x^*) - \mathfrak{f}_n(x) |^2 + \Sigma_{n=N+1}^{\infty} 2^{-2n} | \mathfrak{f}_n(x^*) - \mathfrak{f}_n(x) |^2}$$

$$\leqslant \sqrt{\Sigma_{n=1}^{N} | \mathfrak{f}_n(x^*) - \mathfrak{f}_n(x) |^2 + \Sigma_{n=N+1}^{\infty} 2^{-2n}}$$

$$< \sqrt{N(\epsilon/\sqrt{2N})^2 + \epsilon^2/2} = \epsilon.$$

Thus $\mathfrak{f}$ is continuous.

Finally, suppose G is an open subset of X and $\mathbf{y}$ is an arbitrary point of $\mathfrak{f}(G)$. Thus, $\mathbf{y} = \mathfrak{f}(x)$ for some point $x \in G$. As above, for some integer n, the nth pair $\langle G_i, G_j \rangle$ is such that $x \in G_i \subseteq \mathbf{c}(G_i) \subseteq G_j \subseteq G$. Hence $\mathfrak{f}_n(x) = 0$ and $\mathfrak{f}_n(X \setminus G) = \{1\}$. Thus for any $t \in X \setminus G$, $d_H(\mathfrak{f}(x), \mathfrak{f}(t)) \geqslant 2^{-n}$ because of the difference in their nth coordinates. That is,

$$\mathfrak{f}(X \setminus G) \cap B(\mathfrak{f}(x), 2^{-n}) = \varnothing.$$

Hence $\mathbf{y} \in B(\mathbf{y}, 2^{-n}) \cap \mathfrak{f}(X) \subseteq \mathfrak{f}(G)$, and so $\mathfrak{f}(G)$ is an open subset of $\mathfrak{f}(X)$. Since $\mathfrak{f}$ is then open, $\mathfrak{f}$ is a homeomorphism. ∎

Exercises

1. If E is an open F_σ set in a normal space X, then there exists a continuous mapping $\mathfrak{f} : X \to [0, 1]$ such that $\mathfrak{f}(x) > 0$ iff $x \in E$; thus, $X \setminus E = \mathfrak{f}^{-1}(0)$.

2. A compact Hausdorff space is metrizable iff it has a countable base. (This result is sometimes called Urysohn's second metrization theorem.)

10.2 Paracompact Spaces

Before introducing the topic of paracompact spaces, we will have to consider a number of basic set-theoretic and topological notions. The first new idea is a different relation on families of subsets of a space than inclusion. If $\mathscr{A}$ and $\mathscr{B}$ are two families of subsets of a set X, then $\mathscr{A}$ is a **refinement** of $\mathscr{B}$, or $\mathscr{A}$ **refines** $\mathscr{B}$, iff each member of $\mathscr{A}$ is a subset of some member of $\mathscr{B}$. It is clear that this is a transitive relation on the family of all subsets of X which is larger than inclusion; that is, if $\mathscr{A} \subseteq \mathscr{B}$, then $\mathscr{A}$ refines $\mathscr{B}$.

The most important use of the relation of inclusion was in the definition of compactness. We recall that a topological space X is compact iff for every open covering of X there is a finite open covering which is included in it. It is easy to show that X is also compact iff for every open covering of X there is a finite open covering which is a refinement of it. Thus we may shift our interest to refinements in any compactness argument.

The next notion will be a generalization of the finiteness property of compactness. A family $\mathscr{E}$ of subsets of a topological space X will be called **locally finite (discrete)** iff every point of the space has a neighborhood which has a nonempty intersection with at most a finite number (one) of the members of $\mathscr{E}$. The family $\mathscr{E}$ is **σ-locally finite** (**σ-discrete**) iff it is the countable union of locally finite (discrete) families. It is clear that every discrete family is locally finite but not conversely. We note that in a compact space, every locally finite or discrete family of subsets is finite. The following theorem gives one very important property of these systems.

Theorem 10.2.1. *If $\mathscr{E}$ is a locally finite (discrete) family of subsets of a topological space X, then the family of closures of members of $\mathscr{E}$ is also locally finite (discrete), and, in either case,* $\mathbf{c}(\bigcup\{E : E \in \mathscr{E}\}) = \bigcup\{\mathbf{c}(E) : E \in \mathscr{E}\}$.

Proof. By problem **9**(i) of Section **3.2**, we know that $\bigcup\{\mathbf{c}(E) : E \in \mathscr{E}\} \subseteq \mathbf{c}(\bigcup\{E : E \in \mathscr{E}\})$ for any family of subsets $\mathscr{E}$. Hence, suppose that $x \in \mathbf{c}(\bigcup\{E : E \in \mathscr{E}\})$. By our hypothesis, there must exist an open set G containing x which has a nonempty intersection with at most a finite number (one) of the members of $\mathscr{E}$. We see immediately that the openness of G implies that if $G \cap E = \varnothing$ then $G \cap \mathbf{c}(E) = \varnothing$, and so the family of closures of members of $\mathscr{E}$ is also locally finite (discrete). Let E_1, ..., E_n denote the finite number of members of $\mathscr{E}$ with which G has a nonempty intersection. Then, since $x \in \mathbf{c}(\bigcup\{E : E \in \mathscr{E}\})$, $x \in \mathbf{c}(E_1 \cup ... \cup E_n) = \mathbf{c}(E_1) \cup ... \cup \mathbf{c}(E_n) \subseteq \bigcup\{\mathbf{c}(E) : E \in \mathscr{E}\}$. ∎

Before we can prove the first major theorem concerning the occurrence of these systems, we must consider some preliminary definitions. For each subset E of a metric space (X, d) and each integer n, we may set

$B_n(E) = \{x : d(x, E) < 1/2^n\}$. This is essentially a ball about E of radius $1/2^n$ and could have been defined for any radius, but this is all we need for the next theorem. Clearly, $B_n(E)$ is an open set containing E which is nonempty whenever E is nonempty. We may also define a dual set $C_n(E) = \{x : B_n(x) = B(x, 1/2^n) \subseteq E\}$. It is easy to see that $C_n(E) = X \setminus B_n(X \setminus E)$, and so it is a closed set contained in E which may, however, be empty even if E is nonempty. We shall leave to the problems the verification of such properties as: $B_n(C_n(E)) \subseteq E$, $\mathbf{c}(B_m(E)) \subseteq B_n(E)$ whenever $m > n$, and $d(C_n(E), X \setminus E) \geqslant 1/2^n$ if both sets are nonempty. We shall use these properties, however, in proving the following theorem whose content was first shown by Stone [74]. We will follow the method of proof used by Smirnov [71].

Theorem 10.2.2. *For every open covering of a metric space, there is a locally finite open cover which refines it.*

Proof. Suppose that $\{G_\lambda\}_{\lambda \in \Lambda}$ is an open covering of the metric space (X, d), and let us assume that the indexing set Λ has been well-ordered. For each integer n, we will define by transfinite induction a collection $\{E_\lambda{}^n\}$ of closed subsets of X by setting $E_\lambda{}^n = C_n(G_\lambda \setminus \bigcup_{\beta<\lambda} E_\beta{}^n)$ for each $\lambda \in \Lambda$.

Since $\{G_\lambda\}$ is a covering of X and Λ is well-ordered, for each fixed point x in X we may let $\xi = \min\{\lambda : x \in G_\lambda\}$. Since G_ξ is open, there is an integer n such that $B_n(x) \subseteq G_\xi$. Now if $x \notin E_\xi{}^n$, then $B_n(x) \nsubseteq G_\xi \setminus \bigcup_{\beta<\xi} E_\beta{}^n$ by the definition of $E_\xi{}^n$. Since $B_n(x) \subseteq G_\xi$, we must have $B_n(x) \cap (\bigcup_{\beta<\xi} E_\beta{}^n) \neq \varnothing$, and so $B_n(x) \cap E_\alpha{}^n \neq \varnothing$ for some $\alpha < \xi$. For that α, however, we must then have

$$x \in B_n(E_\alpha{}^n) = B_n(C_n(G_\alpha \setminus \bigcup_{\beta<\alpha} E_\beta{}^n)) \subseteq G_\alpha \setminus \bigcup_{\beta<\alpha} E_\beta{}^n \subseteq G_\alpha .$$

This contradicts the definition of ξ as the minimum such α, and so we must have $x \in E_\xi{}^n$. This shows that the collection $\{E_\lambda{}^n\}$ is a covering of X.

For each $n \in \mathbf{N}$ and $\lambda \in \Lambda$, we may now define the sets $F_\lambda{}^n = \mathbf{c}(B_{n+3}(E_\lambda{}^n))$ and $G_\lambda{}^n = B_{n+2}(E_\lambda{}^n))$. As noted above, $F_\lambda{}^n \subseteq G_\lambda{}^n$. We shall prove that $d(G_\alpha{}^n, G_\beta{}^n) \geqslant 1/2^{n+1}$ whenever $\alpha \neq \beta$. In fact, it is clear that we need only prove that $d(E_\alpha{}^n, E_\beta{}^n) \geqslant 1/2^n$ whenever $\alpha \neq \beta$ and these sets are nonempty. This will be true if $B_n(E_\beta{}^n) \cap E_\alpha{}^n = \varnothing$ for all β and all $\alpha < \beta$. Finally, this follows from the calculation

$$B_n(E_\beta{}^n) = B_n(C_n(G_\beta \setminus \bigcup_{\alpha<\beta} E_\alpha{}^n)) \subseteq G_\beta \setminus \bigcup_{\alpha<\beta} E_\alpha{}^n \subseteq X \setminus E_\alpha{}^n$$

for $\alpha < \beta$. From the fact that there is a uniform distance between the closed sets $\{F_\lambda{}^n\}$, it follows that the sets $F^n = \bigcup_\lambda F_\lambda{}^n$ are closed.

We may now define the sets in our desired covering by setting $V_\lambda{}^n = G_\lambda{}^n \setminus \bigcup_{k<n} F^k$ for each $n \in \mathbf{N}$ and $\lambda \in \Lambda$. Since each F^k is a closed set, and we take only a finite union of them, it is clear that the sets $\{V_\lambda{}^n\}$ are open subsets of X. Suppose x is a fixed point of X. Since the collection $\{E_\lambda{}^n\}$ forms a covering of X, so does the collection $\{F_\lambda{}^n\}$, and hence there must exist a least integer n such that $x \in F_\lambda{}^n$ for some $\lambda \in \Lambda$. We then have

$$x \in F_\lambda{}^n \setminus \bigcup_{k<n} \bigcup_{\beta} F_\beta{}^k = F_\lambda{}^n \setminus \bigcup_{k<n} F^k \subseteq G_\lambda{}^n \setminus \bigcup_{k<n} F^k = V_\lambda{}^n.$$

Thus the collection $\{V_\lambda{}^n\}$ forms a covering of X. We note that

$$\begin{aligned} V_\lambda{}^n \subseteq G_\lambda{}^n &= B_{n+2}(E_\lambda{}^n) \subseteq B_n(E_\lambda{}^n) \\ &= B_n(C_n(G_\lambda \setminus \bigcup_{\beta<\lambda} E_\beta{}^n)) \subseteq G_\lambda \setminus \bigcup_{\beta<\lambda} E_\beta{}^n \subseteq G_\lambda , \end{aligned}$$

so that the collection $\{V_\lambda{}^n\}$ actually is a refinement of the original open covering $\{G_\lambda\}$.

Finally, we shall show that the collection $\{V_\lambda{}^n\}$ is locally finite. Let $x \in X$, and suppose that $x \in E_\lambda{}^n$. Then $B_{n+3}(x) \subseteq B_{n+3}(E_\lambda{}^n) \subseteq \mathbf{c}(B_{n+3}(E_\lambda{}^n)) = F_\lambda{}^n \subseteq F^n$, and so $B_{n+3}(x) \cap V_\lambda{}^k = \varnothing$ for all $k > n$ and all $\lambda \in \Lambda$, from the definition of $V_\lambda{}^k$. Since the diameter of $B_{n+3}(x)$ is less than $1/2^{n+1}$ and $d(G_\alpha{}^n, G_\lambda{}^n) \leqslant 1/2^{n+1}$, it follows that, for a fixed $k \leqslant n$, $B_{n+3}(x)$ can intersect at most one $G_\lambda{}^k$. Hence, for this fixed $k \leqslant n$, $B_{n+3}(x)$ can intersect at most one $V_\lambda{}^k$. This implies that $B_{n+3}(x)$ is an open set containing x which has a non-empty intersection with at most a finite number of members of the family $\{V_\lambda{}^n\}$. ∎

The property described in the conclusion of Stone's theorem is interesting in its own right and was first considered by Dieudonné [36]. We will call a topological space X **paracompact** iff for every open covering of X there is a locally finite open cover which refines it. Thus we have shown that every metric space is paracompact. Many authors require that the topological space also be either Hausdorff or regular. We shall not assume any separation axiom, but will immediately note the following relationship between paracompact spaces and Hausdorff or regular spaces in part proved by Dieudonné.

Theorem 10.2.3. *Every paracompact regular (resp. Hausdorff) space is normal (resp. T_4).*

Proof. Suppose X is a paracompact regular (Hausdorff) space and F is a closed subset of X. If $F^*(x^*)$ is a second closed set (a point) with $F \cap F^* = \emptyset$ ($x^* \notin F$), then, for each point $x \in F$, there exists an open set V_x containing x such that $\mathbf{c}(V_x) \cap F^* = \emptyset$ ($x^* \notin \mathbf{c}(V_x)$). The family of subsets $\{V_x : x \in F\} \cup \{X \setminus F\}$ is an open covering of X, and so there is a locally finite refinement of it. Suppose $\mathscr{G} = \{G_\lambda\}$ denotes the members of that family which have nonempty intersections with F. Let $G_F = \bigcup_\lambda G_\lambda$, which is clearly an open set containing F. Let $G^* = X \setminus \bigcup_\lambda \mathbf{c}(G_\lambda)$, which is an open set, since $\bigcup_\lambda \mathbf{c}(G_\lambda) = \mathbf{c}(\bigcup_\lambda G_\lambda)$ by **10.2.1**, and it is certainly disjoint from G_F. Since $\mathscr{G}$ is a refinement and each member of it intersects F, for each G_λ there must exist an $x \in F$ such that $G_\lambda \subseteq V_x$. Now, since $\mathbf{c}(G_\lambda) \subseteq \mathbf{c}(V_x) \subseteq X \setminus F^*$, $F^* \subseteq X \setminus \mathbf{c}(V_x) \subseteq X \setminus \mathbf{c}(G_\lambda)$ (since $\mathbf{c}(G_\lambda) \subseteq \mathbf{c}(V_x) \subseteq X \setminus \{x^*\}$, $\{x^*\} \subseteq X \setminus G_\lambda$) for every $G_\lambda \in \mathscr{G}$. Hence $F^* \subseteq G^*$ ($x^* \in G^*$), and so X is normal (and so X is regular; then, by the alternate statement of this theorem, X is also normal, and so T_4). ▮

As an indication of the usefulness of this new topological property, we may quote the great Russian mathematician P. S. Aleksandrov [30], who says: "The class of paracompact spaces is very likely the most important class of topological spaces defined in recent years." Indeed, since every compact space is clearly paracompact, this class of spaces includes every compact space and every metric space. Furthermore, study of paracompact spaces led to the solution of the metrization problem which we will give in the next section.

It is easy to show that the covering property of paracompactness is equivalent to some other similar covering properties.

Theorem 10.2.4. *In a regular topological space X, the following conditions are equivalent:*

[$\mathbf{PC_I}$] *For every open covering of X, there is a locally finite open cover which refines it.*

[$\mathbf{PC_{II}}$] *For every open covering of X, there is a locally finite cover which refines it.*

[$\mathbf{PC_{III}}$] *For every open covering of X, there is a locally finite closed cover which refines it.*

Proof. It is obvious that **[$\mathbf{PC_I}$]** implies **[$\mathbf{PC_{II}}$]**, so let us suppose that X is a regular space satisfying **[$\mathbf{PC_{II}}$]** and $\mathscr{G}$ is an open covering of X. Each point of X belongs to some open set in $\mathscr{G}$ and so, by regularity, to some open set whose closure is contained in that open set. Thus there is an open covering $\mathscr{G}^*$ of X such that the family of closures of members of $\mathscr{G}^*$ refines $\mathscr{G}$. By assumption, there is a locally finite cover $\mathscr{G}^{**}$ which refines $\mathscr{G}^*$, and the family of closures of members of $\mathscr{G}^{**}$ is the closed cover desired.

Now suppose that X is a regular space satisfying **[PC$_{\text{III}}$]** and $\mathscr{G}$ is an open covering of X. By hypothesis, there exists a locally finite covering $\mathscr{G}^*$ which refines $\mathscr{G}$. From the definition of local finiteness, each point of X is contained in an open set which intersects at most a finite number of members of $\mathscr{G}^*$. Let $\mathscr{H}$ be a covering of X by such sets and, by **[PC$_{\text{III}}$]** again, let $\mathscr{H}^*$ be a closed, locally finite refinement of $\mathscr{H}$ which covers X. Now for each set $E \in \mathscr{G}^*$, let $E^+ = \complement \bigcup \{H : H \in \mathscr{H}^*$ and $E \cap H = \varnothing\}$. Since the members of $\mathscr{H}^*$ are closed and locally finite, their union is also closed, and so E^+ is an open set which clearly contains E. Furthermore, a set in $\mathscr{H}^*$ intersects E^+ iff it intersects E. Since $\mathscr{G}^*$ refines $\mathscr{G}$, for each $E \in \mathscr{G}^*$ pick a set $G_E \in \mathscr{G}$ such that $E \subseteq G_E$. Finally, let $\mathscr{G}^{**} = \{E^+ \cap G_E : E \in \mathscr{G}^*\}$. Clearly, $\mathscr{G}^{**}$ is an open covering of X which is a refinement of $\mathscr{G}$. Since every member of the locally finite family $\mathscr{H}^*$ intersects at most a finite number of members of $\mathscr{G}^{**}$, $\mathscr{G}^{**}$ itself is locally finite. ▮

The above theorem is due to Michael [56], who also proved that, for regular spaces, paracompactness is equivalent to some properties which would seem to be much weaker than the definition. Before giving those results, we will introduce some notions used by Tukey [24]. If $\mathscr{E}$ is a family of subsets of a space X, then for each point $x \in X$, the **star** of x in $\mathscr{E}$, written $\text{St}(x, \mathscr{E})$, is the union of those members of $\mathscr{E}$ which contain x. The **star** of $\mathscr{E}$, written $\text{St}(\mathscr{E})$, is the family of all stars of points; that is, $\text{St}(\mathscr{E}) = \{\text{St}(x, \mathscr{E}) : x \in X\}$. We say that a collection $\mathscr{A}$ of sets is a **star refinement** of a collection $\mathscr{B}$ iff the star of $\mathscr{A}$ is a refinement of $\mathscr{B}$. Finally, a topological space X is called **fully normal** iff for every open covering of X there is an open cover which star refines it.

Theorem 10.2.5. *In a regular space X, the following conditions are equivalent to paracompactness*:

[PC$_{\text{IV}}$] *For every open covering of X, there is a σ-locally finite open cover which refines it.*

[PC$_{\text{V}}$] *For every open covering of X, there is a σ-discrete open cover which refines it.*

[FN] *For every open covering of X, there is an open cover which star refines it.*

Proof. We shall show the sequence of implications **[PC$_{\text{III}}$]** $\Rightarrow$ **[FN]** $\Rightarrow$ **[PC$_{\text{V}}$]** $\Rightarrow$ **[PC$_{\text{IV}}$]** $\Rightarrow$ [PC$_{\text{II}}$] which, by the previous theorem, will prove the theorem.

Suppose X is a topological space satisfying **[PC$_{\text{III}}$]** and $\mathscr{G}$ is an open covering of X. By hypothesis, we may let $\mathscr{H}$ be a closed, locally finite refinement of $\mathscr{G}$ which covers X. Thus, for each $H \in \mathscr{H}$ there exists a $G_H \in \mathscr{G}$ such that $H \subseteq G_H$. For each $x \in X$, we will set

$$V_x = \bigcap\{G_H : x \in H \in \mathscr{H}\} \cap (\bigcap\{\complement H : x \notin H \in \mathscr{H}\}).$$

Since $\mathscr{H}$ is locally finite, $\bigcup\{H : x \notin H \in \mathscr{H}\}$ is closed by **10.2.1**, and so $\complement\bigcup\{H : x \notin H \in \mathscr{H}\} = \bigcap\{\complement H : x \notin H \in \mathscr{H}\}$ is open. Also, $x \in H \in \mathscr{H}$ for at most a finite number of H's, so $\bigcap\{G_H : x \in H \in \mathscr{H}\}$ is open, and hence V_x is an open set. Since we must either have $x \in H$ or $x \notin H$, it is clear that $x \in V_x$, and so the family $\mathscr{V} = \{V_x : x \in X\}$ is an open cover of X. We shall show that the star of $\mathscr{V}$ refines $\mathscr{G}$. Let y be any fixed point of X. We shall show that $\text{St}(y, \mathscr{V})$ is a subset of some member of $\mathscr{G}$. Since $\mathscr{H}$ covers X, we may suppose that $y \in H$. We will show that $\text{St}(y, \mathscr{V}) \subseteq G_H \in \mathscr{G}$. Suppose $y \in V_x$ for some $x \in X$. If $x \notin H$, then we would have $y \in V_x \subseteq \complement H$ by the definition of V_x, and this is a contradiction. Hence we must have $x \in H$, and so $V_x \subseteq G_H$ since V_x is the intersection of such sets. Thus $\text{St}(y, \mathscr{V}) \subseteq G_H$, as desired.

The fact that **[FN]** implies **[PC$_{\text{V}}$]** was proven by Stone [74], and the reader is referred to his paper for a long but straightforward proof of this result. Since each σ-discrete system is σ-locally finite, the next implication is obvious.

Finally, suppose X is a topological space satisfying **[PC$_{\text{IV}}$]** and $\mathscr{G}$ is an open covering of X. By hypothesis, there exists a σ-locally finite open cover $\mathscr{H}$ which refines $\mathscr{G}$, which we may write as $\mathscr{H} = \bigcup_{n \in \mathbf{N}} \mathscr{H}_n$ with each $\mathscr{H}_n$ locally finite. Now for each $H \in \mathscr{H}$, $H \in \mathscr{H}_n$ for some smallest n, and we may let $V_H = H \setminus \bigcup\{H^* : H^* \in \mathscr{H}_i \text{ for } i < n\}$. Since $V_H \subseteq H$, the family $\mathscr{V} = \{V_H : H \in \mathscr{H}\}$ refines $\mathscr{H}$ and so also $\mathscr{G}$. For each $x \in X$, there is a smallest integer n such that there exists an $H_x \in \mathscr{H}_n$ containing x. Since $x \in V_{H_x}$, $\mathscr{V}$ covers X. We note that H_x is disjoint from each V_H for $H \in \mathscr{H}_i$ with $i > n$ (where we choose the smallest possible index i). Lastly, since each $\mathscr{H}_i$ is locally finite, for each $i = 1, 2, \ldots, n$ there exists an open set W_i containing x which intersects at most a finite number of members of $\mathscr{H}_i$. If we let $W = H_x \cap W_1 \cap \ldots \cap W_n$, then W is an open set containing x which intersects at most a finite number of members of $\mathscr{V}$, so that $\mathscr{V}$ is locally finite. ∎

The characterization **[PC$_V$]** allows us to state some simple sufficient conditions for paracompactness. We say that a topological space is **σ-compact** iff it is the union of a countable collection of compact sets.

Corollary. *Every regular Lindelöf space is paracompact. Every regular space which is either second axiom or σ-compact is paracompact.*

Proof. Every open covering of a Lindelöf space has a countable subcovering, and so, automatically, a σ-discrete refinement. Every σ-compact and every second axiom space is a Lindelöf space. ∎

The behavior of paracompact spaces with respect to products is of great interest today. The space of problem **8** in Section **5.4** due to Sorgenfrey [73], is an example of a product of regular Lindelöf spaces which is not normal (problem **3** in Section **8.2**), and so the product of paracompact spaces need not be paracompact. Dieudonné [36] showed that the product of a paracompact space with a compact space is paracompact. This result was strengthened by Michael [56] in the following theorem.

Theorem 10.2.6. *If X is a regular paracompact space and Y is a regular σ-compact space, then $X \times Y$ is paracompact.*

Proof. Let $Y = \bigcup_{n \in \mathbf{N}} Y_n$ with each Y_n compact, and suppose that $\mathscr{G}$ is an open cover of $X \times Y$. For each point $\mathbf{z} = \langle x, y \rangle$ in $X \times Y$, there are open sets $V_\mathbf{z}$ and $W_\mathbf{z}$ in X and Y, respectively, such that $\langle x, y \rangle \in V_\mathbf{z} \times W_\mathbf{z} \subseteq \mathbf{G}$ for some $\mathbf{G} \in \mathscr{G}$. Let us denote, for each $x \in X$ and $n \in \mathbf{N}$, the set $\{\langle x, y \rangle : y \in Y_n\} = \{x\} \times Y_n$ by $\mathbf{E}_x{}^n$. The family $\{W_\mathbf{z} : \mathbf{z} \in \mathbf{E}_x{}^n\}$ will then form an open cover of the compact set Y_n, and so there is a finite subset $\mathbf{F}_x{}^n$ of $\mathbf{E}_x{}^n$ such that $\{W_\mathbf{z} : \mathbf{z} \in \mathbf{F}_x{}^n\}$ covers Y_n. Let $V_x{}^n = \bigcap\{V_\mathbf{z} : \mathbf{z} \in \mathbf{F}_x{}^n\}$, and then $\mathscr{V}_n = \{V_x{}^n : x \in X\}$ will be an open cover of X. Since X is paracompact, $\mathscr{V}_n$ has an open, locally finite refinement $\mathscr{V}_n{}^*$ which covers X. By the definition of refinement, for each $V \in \mathscr{V}_n{}^*$, there exists a point $x_V \in X$ such that $V \subseteq V_{x_V}^n$. Hence,

$$\mathscr{G}_n{}^* = \{V \times W_\mathbf{z} : V \in \mathscr{V}_n{}^* \quad \text{and} \quad \mathbf{z} \in \mathbf{F}_{x_V}^n\}$$

is an open cover of $X \times Y_n$ which refines $\mathscr{G}$, and so $\mathscr{G}^* = \bigcup_{n \in \mathbf{N}} \mathscr{G}_n{}^*$ is an open cover of $X \times Y$ which refines $\mathscr{G}$. Finally, for each point $\langle x, y \rangle$ in $X \times Y$, there is an open set U containing x which has a non-empty intersection with at most a finite number of members $V \in \mathscr{V}_n{}^*$, since $\mathscr{V}_n{}^*$ is locally finite. Hence, $\pi_X^{-1}(U)$ is an open set containing

$\langle x, y\rangle$ which has a nonempty intersection with at most a finite number of sets $V \times W_z$ from $\mathscr{G}_n{}^*$, since $\mathbf{F}_x{}^n$ is finite. Thus, $\mathscr{G}^*$ is σ-locally finite, and $X \times Y$ is paracompact by **[$\mathbf{PC_{IV}}$]**. ∎

Corollary. *The product of a paracompact space with a compact space is paracompact.*

Proof. If $Y_n = Y$ for all n in the above proof, then we immediately obtain $\mathscr{G}_n{}^* = \mathscr{G}^*$, an open locally finite refinement of $\mathscr{G}$. Thus $X \times Y$ will be paracompact by **[$\mathbf{PC_I}$]**, and we do not have to require X to be regular. ∎

There are many unsolved problems concerning paracompact spaces. For example, it is not known whether the product of a paracompact space with the closed unit interval is even normal. Indeed, until recently it was not known whether the product of a normal space and a metric space is always normal. This problem has been solved negatively by Michael [57]. For a discussion of some of the unsolved problems in this field, the reader is referred to the article by Michael in [21]. A very complete survey of the field is also available in Katětov's appendix to the text by Čech [4].

Exercises

1. A topological space X is compact iff for every open covering of X there is a finite open covering which is a refinement of it.

2. For any subset E of a metric space (X, d):
   (i) $C_n(E) = X \setminus B_n(X \setminus E)$.
   (ii) $B_n(C_n(E)) \subseteq E$.
   (iii) $\mathbf{c}(B_m(E)) \subseteq B_n(E)$, whenever $m > n$.
   (iv) $d(C_n(E), X \setminus E) \geqslant 1/2^n$ if both sets are nonempty.

3. Paracompactness is a topological property.

4. Every F_σ subset of a regular paracompact space is paracompact.

5. If every open subset of a paracompact space is paracompact, then every subset is paracompact.

6. Every σ-compact space is Lindelöf.

7. Show that the set of all ordinal numbers less than or equal to the first uncountable ordinal, with the order topology, forms a paracompact space which has a nonparacompact subspace.

8. A family $\mathfrak{F}$ of continuous mappings $\mathfrak{f} : X \to [0, 1]$ will be called a **partition of unity** iff $\sum \{\mathfrak{f}(x) : \mathfrak{f} \in \mathfrak{F}\} = 1$. A partition of unity $\mathfrak{F}$ is called **locally finite** iff every

point of X is contained in an open set on which all but a finite number of members of $\mathfrak{F}$ are zero. A partition of unity $\mathfrak{F}$ is **subordinate** to a cover $\mathscr{G}$ of X iff every member of $\mathfrak{F}$ is zero on the complement of some member of $\mathscr{G}$. Prove that a Hausdorff or regular space is paracompact iff for every open covering of X there is a locally finite partition of unity subordinate to it. (See Michael [56].)

9. A topological space X will be called **countably paracompact** iff for every countable open covering of X there is a locally finite open cover which refines it. Prove that every closed subset of a countably paracompact space is countably paracompact. Prove that the product of a countably paracompact space and a compact space is countably paracompact. (See Dowker [38].)

10. If $\mathscr{G}$ is an open covering of a space X, then a **$\mathscr{G}$-mapping** is a continuous mapping $\mathfrak{f}$ of X into some space X^* such that for every $x^* \in X^*$, there exists an open set G^* containing x^* such that $\mathfrak{f}^{-1}(G^*)$ is contained in some element of $\mathscr{G}$. Show that a regular space X is paracompact (Lindelöf) iff for every open covering $\mathscr{G}$ of X there exists a $\mathscr{G}$-mapping of X onto a metric (separable metric) space. (See Dowker [38].)

11. In a regular paracompact space, every open cover is shrinkable (see problem **16** in Section **5.5**).

10.3 Nagata-Smirnov Metrization Theorem

Although Urysohn solved the metrization problem for separable metric spaces in 1924, the general metrization problem was not solved until 1950. Three mathematicians, J. Nagata [62], Yu. M. Smirnov [71], and R. H. Bing [32], gave independent solutions to this problem. The characterizations of Nagata and Smirnov are based on the existence of a σ-locally finite base, while that of Bing requires a σ-discrete base for the topology.

We will prove the first of these metrization theorems by Smirnov's method, which consists of showing that a topological space satisfying certain conditions is homeomorphic to a subset of a certain metrizable space which is a generalization of Hilbert space. We will first describe that metric space.

Let τ be a fixed, infinite cardinal number, and suppose that Λ is a fixed set of elements whose cardinality is τ. The **generalized Hilbert space** $(H^\tau, d_H{}^\tau)$ of weight τ is the set H^τ of all real-valued mappings $\mathfrak{f}$ defined on Λ such that each mapping is different from zero on at most a countable subset of Λ, and the series $\sum_{\lambda\in\Lambda} [\mathfrak{f}(\lambda)]^2$ converges, with the metric $d_H{}^\tau$ defined by setting

$$d_H{}^\tau(\mathfrak{f}, \mathfrak{g}) = \sqrt{\textstyle\sum_{\lambda\in\Lambda} [\mathfrak{f}(\lambda) - \mathfrak{g}(\lambda)]^2}.$$

Since the Hilbert space defined in Section **6.3** is clearly $H^{\aleph_0}$, it is easy to show, using the Schwarz inequality, that d_{H^τ} is a metric for H^τ. Before proving our metrization theorem, we need the following two lemmas.

Lemma 1. *In a T_3-space with a σ-locally finite base, every open set is an F_σ set.*

Proof. Let X be a T_3-space with the σ-locally finite base $\{B_{n,\lambda} : n \in \mathbf{N}, \lambda \in \Lambda_n\}$, and suppose G is an open subset of X. By regularity, for each $x \in G$ there exists an open set containing x whose closure is contained in G. Hence there is a member $B_{n(x),\lambda(x)}$ of the base containing x whose closure is contained in G. Since, for each fixed integer k the collection $\{B_{k,\lambda} : \lambda \in \Lambda_k\}$ is locally finite, if we let $B_k = \bigcup_{x \in G} B_{k,\lambda(x)}$, then $\mathbf{c}(B_k) = \bigcup_{x \in G} \mathbf{c}(B_{k,\lambda(x)}) \subseteq G$ by **10.2.1**. Thus we have $G = \bigcup_{k \in \mathbf{N}} \mathbf{c}(B_k)$, which is the countable union of closed sets. ▮

Lemma 2. *A T_3-space with a σ-locally finite base is normal.*

Proof. Let F and K be disjoint closed subsets of the T_3-space X with σ-locally finite base $\{B_{n,\lambda} : n \in \mathbf{N}, \lambda \in \Lambda_n\}$. As above, for each point $x \in F$, there exists a basic open set $B_{n(x),\lambda(x)}$ containing x whose closure is contained in $X \setminus K$, and for each $y \in K$, there exists a basic open set $B_{n(y),\lambda(y)}$ containing y whose closure is contained in $X \setminus F$. If we let $B_{k,F} = \bigcup_{x \in F} B_{k,\lambda(x)}$ and $B_{k,K} = \bigcup_{y \in K} B_{k,\lambda(y)}$, then, by the local finiteness of $\{B_{k,\lambda} : \lambda \in \Lambda_k\}$ and **10.2.1**,

$$\mathbf{c}(B_{k,F}) = \bigcup_{x \in F} \mathbf{c}(B_{k,\lambda(x)}) \subseteq X \setminus K$$

and

$$\mathbf{c}(B_{k,K}) = \bigcup_{y \in K} \mathbf{c}(B_{k,\lambda(y)}) \subseteq X \setminus F.$$

Thus the sets

$$G_{n,F} = B_{n,F} \setminus \bigcup_{k \leqslant n} \mathbf{c}(B_{k,K})$$

and

$$G_{n,K} = B_{n,K} \setminus \bigcup_{k \leqslant n} \mathbf{c}(B_{k,F})$$

are open sets with the property that $G_{n,F}$ contains every point $x \in F$ for which $n(x) = n$, and $G_{n,K}$ contains every point $y \in K$ for which $n(y) = n$. Finally, we may let $G_F = \bigcup_{n \in \mathbf{N}} G_{n,F}$ and $G_K = \bigcup_{n \in \mathbf{N}} G_{n,K}$, and we obtain two disjoint open sets containing F and K, respectively. ▮

We are now prepared to prove the main result of this section.

Nagata-Smirnov Metrization Theorem. *A topological space is metrizable iff it is a T_3-space with a σ-locally finite base.*

Proof. The necessity of this condition follows from Stone's theorem **10.2.2**. If we consider the open covering of a metric space X by balls $\{B(x, 1/n) : x \in X\}$, we may find, for each n, a locally finite open cover which refines it. The union of these covers is a σ-locally finite base for X.

Now suppose X is a T_3-space with a σ-locally finite base $\{B_{n,\lambda} : n \in \mathbf{N}, \lambda \in \Lambda_n\}$. We shall denote by Λ the collection of all pairs $\langle n, \lambda \rangle$, with $n \in \mathbf{N}$ and $\lambda \in \Lambda_n$, with which we have indexed the base, and suppose the cardinality of Λ is τ. We shall show that X is homeomorphic to a subset of H^τ. We note that, by the above lemmas, X is normal, and every open subset is an F_σ. Hence, by problem **1** in Section **10.1**, for each $\langle n, \lambda \rangle \in \Lambda$, there exists a continuous mapping $\mathfrak{f}_{n,\lambda} : X \to [0, 1]$ such that $\mathfrak{f}_{n,\lambda}(x) > 0$ iff $x \in B_{n,\lambda}$. For each fixed integer n, the family $\{B_{n,\lambda} : \lambda \in \Lambda_n\}$ is locally finite, and so, for each fixed point $x \in X$, $\mathfrak{f}_{n,\lambda}(x) \neq 0$ for at most a finite number of values of λ. Hence $1 + \Sigma_\beta \mathfrak{f}^2_{n,\beta}(x)$ is a well-defined continuous mapping of X which is never less than one. From this it follows that we may define a continuous mapping $\mathfrak{g}_{n,\lambda} : X \to [0,1]$ by setting

$$\mathfrak{g}_{n,\lambda}(x) = \mathfrak{f}_{n,\lambda}(x) \left[1 + \sum_\beta \mathfrak{f}^2_{n,\beta}(x)\right]^{-1/2}.$$

Again we see that $\mathfrak{g}_{n,\lambda}(x) > 0$ iff $x \in B_{n,\lambda}$, while, for a fixed integer n and fixed point $x \in X$, $\mathfrak{g}_{n,\lambda}(x) \neq 0$ for at most a finite number of values of λ. It is obvious that $\Sigma_\lambda \mathfrak{g}^2_{n,\lambda}(x) < 1$ and it is easy to verify that $\Sigma_\lambda[\mathfrak{g}_{n,\lambda}(x) - \mathfrak{g}_{n,\lambda}(y)]^2 < 2$ for all $x, y \in X$.

We may now set $\mathfrak{h}_{n,\lambda}(x) = 2^{-n/2}\mathfrak{g}_{n,\lambda}(x)$, and it is clear that $\Sigma_{\langle n,\lambda \rangle} \mathfrak{h}^2_{n,\lambda}(x) = \Sigma_n 2^{-n} \Sigma_\lambda \mathfrak{g}^2_{n,\lambda}(x) < \Sigma_n 2^{-n} = 1$. Thus, for each $x \in X$, $\mathfrak{h}_{n,\lambda}(x)$ is a real-valued mapping of Λ which is such that the mapping is different from zero on at most a countable subset of Λ, and is such that the series of squares converges. From the definition of generalized Hilbert space of weight τ, it follows that, for each $x \in X$, we have found a point $\mathfrak{f}(x) = \mathfrak{h}_{n,\lambda}(x)$ in H^τ. Thus we have defined a mapping $\mathfrak{f}$ of X into H^τ which is onto some subset $\mathfrak{f}(X)$. We shall show that $\mathfrak{f}$ is a homeomorphism.

If x and y are distinct points of X, then there exists a basic open set $B_{n,\lambda}$ containing x but not y since X is a T_1-space. It follows that $\mathfrak{h}_{n,\lambda}(x) > 0$, while $\mathfrak{h}_{n,\lambda}(y) = 0$, so $\mathfrak{f}(x) \neq \mathfrak{f}(y)$, and $\mathfrak{f}$ is one-to-one.

Now suppose that $x \in X$ and $\epsilon > 0$ are given. First choose an integer $N = N(\epsilon)$ such that $2^{-N} < \epsilon^2/4$. By the local finiteness property, there must exist an open set G containing x which has a nonempty intersection with at most a finite number of the sets $B_{n,\lambda}$ with $n \leqslant N$. Let us denote these sets by B_{n_i,λ_i}, where $n_i \leqslant N$ for $i = 1, ..., K$. Since each function $\mathfrak{h}_{n,\lambda}$ is continuous, we may find, for each $\langle n, \lambda \rangle \in \Lambda$, an open set $G_{n,\lambda}$ containing x such that

$$| \mathfrak{h}_{n,\lambda}(x) - \mathfrak{h}_{n,\lambda}(y) | < \epsilon/\sqrt{2K}$$

for every $y \in G_{n,\lambda}$. Let us set

$$G^* = G \cap \left(\bigcap_{i=1}^{K} G_{n_i,\lambda_i} \right),$$

which is an open set containing x. We now note that for $\langle n, \lambda \rangle \in \Lambda$ but not equal to some (n_i, λ_i), $\mathfrak{h}_{n,\lambda}(x) = \mathfrak{h}_{n,\lambda}(y) = 0$ for every $y \in G^*$. Thus we have, for $y \in G^*$,

$$\sum_{n \leqslant N, \lambda} [\mathfrak{h}_{n,\lambda}(x) - \mathfrak{h}_{n,\lambda}(y)]^2 < K(\epsilon/\sqrt{2K})^2 = \epsilon^2/2,$$

while

$$\begin{aligned} \sum_{n > N, \lambda} & [\mathfrak{h}_{n,\lambda}(x) - \mathfrak{h}_{n,\lambda}(y)]^2 \\ & = \sum_{n > N} 2^{-n} \sum_{\lambda} [\mathfrak{g}_{n,\lambda}(x) - \mathfrak{g}_{n,\lambda}(y)]^2 \\ & \leqslant 2 \sum_{n > N} 2^{-n} = 2(2^{-N}) < 2(\epsilon^2/4) = \epsilon^2/2. \end{aligned}$$

Thus we have shown that

$$d_H{}^\tau(\mathfrak{f}(x), \mathfrak{f}(y)) = \sqrt{\textstyle\sum_{n,\lambda} [\mathfrak{h}_{n,\lambda}(x) - \mathfrak{h}_{n,\lambda}(y)]^2} < \epsilon$$

for all $y \in G^*$, and so $\mathfrak{f}$ is continuous.

Finally, let G be an arbitrary open set in X, and choose a point $x \in G$. We must have $x \in B_{n,\lambda} \subseteq G$ for some $\langle n, \lambda \rangle \in \Lambda$. Let $\mathfrak{h}_{n,\lambda}(x)$, which is a positive real number, be denoted by δ. If $\mathfrak{f}(y)$ is a point of $\mathfrak{f}(X)$ such that $d_H{}^\tau(\mathfrak{f}(x),\mathfrak{f}(y)) < \delta$, then $\mathfrak{h}_{n,\lambda}(y)$ is also positive, and so $y \in B_{n,\lambda} \subseteq G$. Thus

$$\mathfrak{f}^{-1}(B(\mathfrak{f}(x), \delta)) \subseteq G$$

so that $\mathfrak{f}$ is open. From this it follows that $\mathfrak{f}$ is a homeomorphism. ∎

By a construction very similar to that used to prove Stone's theorem **10.2.2**, it is possible to show that for every open covering of a metric space, there is a σ-discrete open cover which refines it. Hence, every metric space is a T_3-space with a σ-discrete base. Since every σ-discrete family is a σ-locally finite family, we may state the following:

Bing Metrization Theorem. *A topological space is metrizable iff it is a T_3-space with a σ-discrete base.*

If the condition that the topological space be a T_1-space is removed, the above theorems yield pseudometrizable spaces (see **9.3.7**). Examples may be given, however, to show how the condition of regularity is essential.

Exercises

1. Show that $d_H{}^\tau$ is a metric for H^τ.

2. Show that Urysohn's metrization theorem is a corollary to Bing's metrization theorem.

3. Show that Urysohn's second metrization theorem (problem **2** in Section **10.1**) is a corollary to Bing's metrization theorem.

4. Give an example of a second axiom Hausdorff space which is not regular, and hence not metrizable (see Smirnov [71]).

5. A topological space is called **locally metrizable** iff every point is contained in an open set which is metrizable. *Prove*: If a normal space has a locally finite covering by metrizable subsets, then the entire space is metrizable. *Corollary*: A locally metrizable Hausdorff space is metrizable iff it is paracompact (see Smirnov [71]).

CHAPTER 11

Uniform Spaces

11.1 Quasi Uniformization

We have already discussed a few nontopological notions, such as uniform continuity, uniform convergence, and completeness. Although these concepts are valuable in the study of metric spaces, they are lost in the generalization to topological spaces. We will now consider another generalization of metric spaces in which these concepts are meaningful.

A **quasi-uniform space** $(X, \mathfrak{U})$ is a set X together with a nonempty family $\mathfrak{U}$ of subsets of $X \times X$ which satisfies the following axioms:

[U.1] For every $\mathfrak{u} \in \mathfrak{U}$, $\mathfrak{i}_X \subseteq \mathfrak{u}$.

[U.2] If $\mathfrak{v} \supseteq \mathfrak{u} \in \mathfrak{U}$, then $\mathfrak{v} \in \mathfrak{U}$.

[U.3] If $\mathfrak{u} \in \mathfrak{U}$ and $\mathfrak{v} \in \mathfrak{U}$, then $\mathfrak{u} \cap \mathfrak{v} \in \mathfrak{U}$.

[U.4] For every $\mathfrak{u} \in \mathfrak{U}$, there exists a $\mathfrak{v} \in \mathfrak{U}$ such that $\mathfrak{v} \circ \mathfrak{v} \subseteq \mathfrak{u}$.

The family $\mathfrak{U}$ is said to be a **quasi uniformity** for X. The quasi-uniform space $(X, \mathfrak{U})$ will always be considered to be a topological space, with the topology obtained by using as the family of all neighborhoods of a point $x \in X$ the sets of the form $\mathfrak{u}(x)$ with $\mathfrak{u} \in \mathfrak{U}$.

That the family of sets $\mathfrak{u}(x)$ may be chosen to be the neighborhoods of the point x follows from the fact that the above axioms are just uniform forms of the usual neighborhood axioms **[N.1]** through **[N.4]** of Section **3.3** (see [67]).

As generalizations of metric spaces, it should be possible to obtain a quasi-uniform space from any metric space in some natural way. Suppose d is a **quasi metric** for X; that is, a mapping of $X \times X$ into the nonnegative reals satisfying the axioms **[M.1]** and **[M.2]** for metrics (see Sections **6.1** and **9.3**). The family $\mathfrak{U}$ of all sets $\mathfrak{u}$ which contain a set of the form

$$\mathfrak{w}_\epsilon = \{\langle x, y\rangle : d(x, y) < \epsilon\}$$

for some $\epsilon > 0$ is a quasi uniformity for X. We call this quasi uniformity the **metric quasi uniformity** induced by d.

Since, by **[U.2]** and **[U.3]**, a quasi uniformity is a filter (see Section **8.5**) of sets containing $\mathfrak{i}_X$ (the diagonal) by **[U.1]**, we may discuss bases and subbases for a quasi uniformity (see problem **2** in Section **8.5**). Thus the ϵ-neighborhoods of the diagonal, which we have called $\mathfrak{w}_\epsilon$, form a base for the metric quasi uniformity. As one might expect, not every family of sets $\mathfrak{S}$ containing the diagonal is a subbase for a quasi uniformity, for it is required that for every $\mathfrak{u} \in \mathfrak{S}$ there exist a $\mathfrak{v} \in \mathfrak{S}$ such that $\mathfrak{v} \circ \mathfrak{v} \subseteq \mathfrak{u}$.

As with topological spaces, it would be useful to know when, for a given quasi-uniform space $(X, \mathfrak{U})$, there is a quasi metric for X which induces $\mathfrak{U}$; that is, under what conditions is a quasi-uniform space **quasi-metrizable**. The result is much simpler than that for topological spaces, as the following theorem shows.

Theorem 11.1.1. *A quasi-uniform space is quasi-metrizable iff its quasi-uniformity has a countable base.*

Proof. Clearly, if d is a quasi metric for X, then the family of sets of the form

$$\mathfrak{w}_{1/n} = \{\langle x, y\rangle : d(x, y) < 1/n\},$$

for each $n \in \mathbf{N}$, is a countable base for the metric quasi-uniformity. Now suppose that $(X, \mathfrak{U})$ is a quasi-uniform space with the countable base $\{\mathfrak{v}_n\}_{n\in\mathbf{N}}$ for its quasi-uniformity. We may define, by induction, a family of sets $\{\mathfrak{u}_n\}_{n\in\mathbf{N}}$ which forms a base for $\mathfrak{U}$ and is such that $\mathfrak{u}_n \subseteq \mathfrak{v}_n$ and $\mathfrak{u}_n \circ \mathfrak{u}_n \circ \mathfrak{u}_n \subseteq \mathfrak{u}_{n-1}$ for every $n \in \mathbf{N}$. We let $\mathfrak{u}_1 = \mathfrak{v}_1$, and suppose that $\mathfrak{u}_{n-1}$ has been defined. By **[U.4]** there exists a set $\mathfrak{u}_n{}^* \in \mathfrak{U}$ such that $\mathfrak{u}_n{}^* \circ \mathfrak{u}_n{}^* \subseteq \mathfrak{u}_{n-1}$, and then there must also exist a set $\mathfrak{u}_n^{**} \in \mathfrak{U}$ such that $\mathfrak{u}_n^{**} \circ \mathfrak{u}_n^{**} \subseteq \mathfrak{u}_n{}^*$. We will let $\mathfrak{u}_n = \mathfrak{u}_n^{**} \cap \mathfrak{v}_n$ so that $\mathfrak{u}_n \subseteq \mathfrak{v}_n$ immediately. Since $\mathfrak{i}_X \subseteq \mathfrak{u}_n$, by **[U.1]**, we have

$$\begin{aligned}
\mathfrak{u}_n \circ \mathfrak{u}_n \circ \mathfrak{u}_n &= \mathfrak{i}_X \circ \mathfrak{u}_n \circ \mathfrak{u}_n \circ \mathfrak{u}_n \\
&\subseteq \mathfrak{u}_n \circ \mathfrak{u}_n \circ \mathfrak{u}_n \circ \mathfrak{u}_n \\
&\subseteq (\mathfrak{u}_n^{**} \cap \mathfrak{v}_n) \circ (\mathfrak{u}_n^{**} \cap \mathfrak{v}_n) \circ (\mathfrak{u}_n^{**} \cap \mathfrak{v}_n) \circ (\mathfrak{u}_n^{**} \cap \mathfrak{v}_n) \\
&\subseteq (\mathfrak{u}_n^{**} \circ \mathfrak{u}_n^{**}) \circ (\mathfrak{u}_n^{**} \circ \mathfrak{u}_n^{**}) \subseteq \mathfrak{u}_n{}^* \circ \mathfrak{u}_n{}^* \subseteq \mathfrak{u}_{n-1}.
\end{aligned}$$

Next, we define a real-valued mapping φ on $X \times X$ by setting

$$\varphi(x, y) = \inf_n \{2^{-n} : \langle x, y\rangle \in \mathfrak{u}_n\}$$

for each $\langle x, y\rangle \in X \times X$. Finally, we define the desired quasi-metric d by letting

$$d(x, y) = \inf \sum_{i=1}^{k} \varphi(x_{i-1}, x_i)$$

where the infimum is taken over all finite sequences $\langle x_0, \ldots, x_k\rangle$ such that $x_0 = x$ and $x_k = y$. It is clear from the definition that d is a nonnegative function satisfying the triangle inequality **[M.2]**. Since $\langle x, x\rangle \in \mathfrak{i}_X \subseteq \mathfrak{u}_n$ for all n, $\varphi(x, x) = 0$, and so $d(x, x) = 0$ for all $x \in X$, so that d satisfies **[M.1]** and is a quasi metric.

We must now show that d induces $\mathfrak{U}$. For any positive number ϵ we may choose an integer $N = N(\epsilon)$ such that $2^{-N} < \epsilon$. If $\langle x, y\rangle \in \mathfrak{u}_N$, then $d(x, y) \leqslant \varphi(x, y) \leqslant 2^{-N} < \epsilon$, and so $\langle x, y\rangle \in \mathfrak{w}_\epsilon$. Thus, $\mathfrak{u}_N \subseteq \mathfrak{w}_\epsilon$, and so $\mathfrak{U}$ is finer than the quasi uniformity induced by d. In order to show the converse, we must first prove that the inequality

$$\varphi(x_0, x_k) \leqslant 2 \sum_{i=1}^{k} \varphi(x_{i-1}, x_i)$$

holds for all integers k (see Frink [42]). Using induction on k, we first note that the inequality holds for $k = 1$. Now suppose it holds for all integers less than k. Denoting $\sum_{i=1}^{k} \varphi(x_{i-1}, x_i)$ by S, we shall let j be the largest integer such that $\sum_{i=1}^{j} \varphi(x_{i-1}, x_i) \leqslant S/2$. Clearly, we also have $\sum_{i=j+2}^{k} \varphi(x_{i-1}, x_i) \leqslant S/2$ and $\varphi(x_j, x_{j+1}) \leqslant S$. By our induction hypothesis, $\varphi(x_0, x_j) \leqslant 2(S/2) = S$, and $\varphi(x_{j+1}, x_k) \leqslant 2(S/2) = S$. If we now let n be the smallest integer such that $2^{-n} \leqslant 2S$, it is clear that $\langle x_0, x_j\rangle$, $\langle x_j, x_{j+1}\rangle$, and $\langle x_{j+1}, x_k\rangle$ all belong to $\mathfrak{u}_{n+1}$. From the fact that $\mathfrak{u}_{n+1} \circ \mathfrak{u}_{n+1} \circ \mathfrak{u}_{n+1} \subseteq \mathfrak{u}_n$, it follows that $\langle x_0, x_k\rangle \in \mathfrak{u}_n$, and so

$$\varphi(x_0, x_k) \leqslant 2^{-n} \leqslant 2S = 2 \sum_{i=1}^{k} \varphi(x_{i-1}, x_i),$$

which is the desired inequality. Now suppose, for any fixed $n \in \mathbf{N}$, we have $\langle x, y\rangle \in \mathfrak{w}_{2^{-(n+1)}}$. Thus, $d(x, y) < 2^{-(n+1)}$, and so

$$\sum_{i=1}^{k} \varphi(x_{i-1}, x_i) < 2^{-(n+1)}$$

for some sequence $\langle x_0, ..., x_k \rangle$ such that $x_0 = x$ and $x_k = y$. By our inequality,

$$\varphi(x_0, x_k) \leqslant 2 \sum_{i=1}^{k} \varphi(x_{i-1}, x_i) < 2 \cdot 2^{-(n+1)} = 2^{-n}.$$

From the definition of φ it follows that $\langle x, y \rangle \in \mathfrak{u}_n$, and so $\mathfrak{w}_{2^{-(n+1)}} \subseteq \mathfrak{u}_n$. Thus the quasi uniformity induced by d is finer than $\mathfrak{U}$. ∎

Having seen that quasi-uniform spaces are generalizations of metric spaces, it would now be possible to introduce the various concepts mentioned at the beginning of this section and show that they are meaningful in quasi-uniform spaces. But rather than do that at this time, we shall first ask under what conditions on a topological space $(X, \mathscr{T})$ there is a quasi uniformity $\mathfrak{U}$ for X which generates $\mathscr{T}$. The answer is rather surprising.

Theorem 11.1.2. *Every topological space is quasi-uniformizable.*

Proof. If $(X, \mathscr{T})$ is any topological space, we may let $\mathfrak{s}_G = (G \times G) \cup (\complement G \times X)$ for each $G \in \mathscr{T}$. It is easy to verify (see [66]) that the family $\{\mathfrak{s}_G : G \in \mathscr{T}\}$ is a subbase for a quasi uniformity which, in turn, generates $\mathscr{T}$. ∎

As an example of a quasi-uniform space, let X be the set of real numbers, and let d be the quasi metric obtained by setting

$$d(x, y) = \max\{x - y, 0\}$$

for all $\langle x, y \rangle \in X \times X$. The metric quasi uniformity induced by d has the family $\{\mathfrak{w}_\epsilon : \epsilon > 0\}$ as a base. Clearly, the set $\mathfrak{w}_\epsilon$ consists of all points in the plane above the line $y = x - \epsilon$. In the topology induced by this quasi uniformity, a set is open iff it is of the form $\{x : x > a\}$ for some real number a. Thus we have the right hand topology for the reals (see problem **4** in Section **3.4**). We note that, in this example, the induced topology is neither regular nor Hausdorff (it is T_0 but not T_1), the members of the quasi uniformity are not neighborhoods of the diagonal in $X \times X$, and the quasi uniformity constructed in the above theorem is not even comparable to the metric quasi uniformity induced by d.

Exercises

1. If $\mathfrak{U}$ is a quasi uniformity for X, show that the family $\{\mathfrak{u}(x) : \mathfrak{u} \in \mathfrak{U}\}$ is the family of neighborhoods of the point x in some topology for X.

2. If d is a quasi metric for X, show that the family $\{\mathfrak{w}_\epsilon : \epsilon > 0\}$ is a base for a quasi uniformity for X.

3. If $(X, \mathscr{T})$ is a topological space, the family $\{\mathfrak{s}_G : G \in \mathscr{T}\}$ defined in **11.1.2** is a subbase for a quasi uniformity for X which generates $\mathscr{T}$.

4. Give the details of the example at the end of this section.

11.2 Uniformization

Rather than continue with the above generalization of quasi-metric spaces, let us now consider the equivalent structures obtained from pseudometric spaces. Since the difference is merely the requirement that the distance function be symmetric (**[M.3]**), it is clear that the metric quasi uniformity must have a symmetric base. Although it would be reasonable to call these spaces pseudouniform and reserve the term uniform space for those which are induced by metrics, and hence those which induce Hausdorff topologies, we will follow the standard nomenclature. A quasi-uniform space $(X, \mathfrak{U})$ is said to be a **uniform** space, and the family $\mathfrak{U}$ will be called a **uniformity** for X, iff the quasi uniformity satisfies the additional axiom:

[U.5] If $\mathfrak{u} \in \mathfrak{U}$, then $\mathfrak{u}^{-1} \in \mathfrak{U}$.

We may immediately reconsider the questions asked in the previous section as to pseudometrizability and uniformizability. The pseudometrization problem turns out to be no more difficult than the quasi-metrization problem. Let us first consider the following important lemma.

Lemma. *In a uniform space* $(X, \mathfrak{U})$, if $\mathfrak{u} \in \mathfrak{U}$, *then there exists a symmetric set* $\mathfrak{v} \in \mathfrak{U}$ such that $\mathfrak{v} \circ \mathfrak{v} \subseteq \mathfrak{u}$.

Proof. By **[U.4]**, there exists a set $\mathfrak{v}^* \in \mathfrak{U}$ such that $\mathfrak{v}^* \circ \mathfrak{v}^* \subseteq \mathfrak{u}$. By **[U.5]**, $\mathfrak{v}^{*-1} \in \mathfrak{U}$, and hence $\mathfrak{v} = \mathfrak{v}^* \cap \mathfrak{v}^{*-1} \in \mathfrak{U}$ by **[U.3]**. Clearly, $\mathfrak{v}$ is symmetric and $\mathfrak{v} \circ \mathfrak{v} \subseteq \mathfrak{u}$. ∎

Theorem 11.2.1. *A uniform space is pseudometrizable iff its uniformity has a countable base.*

Proof. By the above lemma, the family $\{\mathfrak{u}_n\}_{n\in\mathbf{N}}$ of sets defined in the proof of the quasi-metrization theorem **11.1.1** may be chosen to be symmetric. From this it follows that the function φ defined there is also symmetric, and finally, the quasi-metric d is symmetric, and so it is a pseudometric. ∎

The uniformization problem is much more complicated than the quasi-uniformization one, and the final result is that uniformizability is equivalent to complete regularity. We shall divide the proof of this into two rather long theorems, the first of which (see Weil [26, pp. 13–14]) shows that not all topological spaces are uniformizable.

Theorem 11.2.2. *Every uniform space is completely regular.*

Proof. Let $(X, \mathfrak{U})$ be a uniform space, and z a fixed point of X not in the closed set $F \subseteq X$. Since z is in the open complement of F, there exists a symmetric set $\mathfrak{u}_0 \in \mathfrak{U}$ such that $\mathfrak{u}_0(z) \subseteq X \setminus F$. By the above lemma, there exists a symmetric set $\mathfrak{u}_1 \in \mathfrak{U}$ such that $\mathfrak{u}_1 \circ \mathfrak{u}_1 \subseteq \mathfrak{u}_0$. Proceeding by induction we can find, for each $n \in \mathbf{N}$, a symmetric set $\mathfrak{u}_n \in \mathfrak{U}$ such that $\mathfrak{u}_n \circ \mathfrak{u}_n \subseteq \mathfrak{u}_{n-1}$.

For each dyadic rational number r in (0,1] expressed as a finite sum

$$r = \sum_{k=1}^{K} 2^{-n_k}$$

where $0 \leqslant n_1 < n_2 < \dots < n_K$, we let

$$\mathfrak{v}_r = \mathfrak{u}_{n_K} \circ \mathfrak{u}_{n_{K-1}} \circ \dots \circ \mathfrak{u}_{n_2} \circ \mathfrak{u}_{n_1}.$$

Since all of these sets contain $\mathfrak{i}_X$, it is convenient to define $\mathfrak{v}_0 = \mathfrak{i}_X$. We note that our definition gives $\mathfrak{v}_1 = \mathfrak{u}_0$. We assert that $r \leqslant r^*$ implies that $\mathfrak{v}_r \subseteq \mathfrak{v}_{r^*}$. This will follow from the inclusion

$$\mathfrak{u}_n \circ \mathfrak{v}_{m2^{-n}} \subseteq \mathfrak{v}_{(m+1)2^{-n}}$$

which we shall show holds for $n = 0, 1, \dots$ and $m = 0, 1, \dots, 2^n - 1$. We note that for $n = 0$ the inclusion states only that $\mathfrak{u}_0 \circ \mathfrak{v}_0 \subseteq \mathfrak{v}_1$, and this is true since

$$\mathfrak{u}_0 \circ \mathfrak{v}_0 = \mathfrak{u}_0 \circ \mathfrak{i}_X = \mathfrak{u}_0 = \mathfrak{v}_1 .$$

Now let us suppose the inclusion holds for $n - 1$. If m is an even number, say $2p$, then

$$m2^{-n} = (2p)\,2^{-n} = p2^{-(n-1)}$$

and

$$(m+1)\,2^{-n} = (2p+1)\,2^{-n} = p2^{-(n-1)} + 2^{-n},$$

so that, by definition,

$$\mathfrak{v}_{p2^{-(n-1)}+2^{-n}} = \mathfrak{u}_n \circ \mathfrak{v}_{p2^{-(n-1)}},$$

as required. Now suppose m is an odd number, say $2p+1$, so that

$$m2^{-n} = (2p+1)\,2^{-n} = p2^{-(n-1)} + 2^{-n}$$

and

$$(m+1)\,2^{-n} = (2p+2)\,2^{-n} = (p+1)\,2^{-(n-1)}.$$

By our induction hypothesis,

$$\mathfrak{u}_{n-1} \circ \mathfrak{v}_{p2^{-(n-1)}} \subseteq \mathfrak{v}_{(p+1)2^{-(n-1)}}.$$

Using the fact that $\mathfrak{u}_n \circ \mathfrak{u}_n \subseteq \mathfrak{u}_{n-1}$, we may now calculate

$$\begin{aligned}
\mathfrak{u}_n \circ \mathfrak{v}_{m2^{-n}} &= \mathfrak{u}_n \circ \mathfrak{v}_{p2^{-(n-1)}+2^{-n}} \\
&= \mathfrak{u}_n \circ \mathfrak{u}_n \circ \mathfrak{v}_{p2^{-(n-1)}} \\
&\subseteq \mathfrak{u}_{n-1} \circ \mathfrak{v}_{p2^{-(n-1)}} \\
&\subseteq \mathfrak{v}_{(p+1)2^{-(n-1)}} = \mathfrak{v}_{(m+1)2^{-n}},
\end{aligned}$$

as desired.

We may now define a real-valued function φ on X by setting $\varphi(z) = 0$, and, for $x \neq z$, setting

$$\varphi(x) = \sup\{r : x \notin \mathfrak{v}_r(z)\},$$

where the supremum is taken over all dyadic rationals in [0, 1]. Since $\mathfrak{v}_0 = \mathfrak{i}_X$, the set $\{r : x \notin \mathfrak{v}_r(z)\}$ will be non-empty, and so the supremum exists, and we certainly have $0 \leqslant \varphi(x) \leqslant 1$ for all $x \in X$. Since $\mathfrak{u}_0(z) \subseteq X \setminus F$, if $x \in F$, then $x \notin \mathfrak{u}_0(z) = \mathfrak{v}_1(z)$, so that $\varphi(x) = 1$, while $\varphi(z) = 0$ by definition.

We must show that φ is continuous, so let x be an arbitrary point of X, and let ϵ be any positive real number. If we choose $N = N(\epsilon)$ such that

$2^N > 2/\epsilon$, we may show that $\mathfrak{u}_N(x)$ is a neighborhood of x with the desired properties for continuity. Let y be any point in $\mathfrak{u}_N(x)$, so that $\langle x, y\rangle \in \mathfrak{u}_N$, and let us consider only the case when both $\varphi(x)$ and $\varphi(y)$ are less than 1. Let m and m^* be chosen so that $m2^{-N} > \varphi(x) \geqslant (m-1)2^{-N}$ and $m^*2^{-N} > \varphi(y) \geqslant (m^*-1)2^{-N}$. By the definition of φ, $x \in \mathfrak{v}_{m2^{-N}}(z)$ and $y \in \mathfrak{v}_{m^*2^{-N}}(z)$, so that $\langle z, x\rangle \in \mathfrak{v}_{m2^{-N}}$ and $\langle z, y\rangle \in \mathfrak{v}_{m^*2^{-N}}$. Using the symmetry of $\mathfrak{u}_N$, so that both $\langle x, y\rangle$ and $\langle y, x\rangle$ belong to $\mathfrak{u}_N$, we obtain

$$\langle z, y\rangle \in \mathfrak{u}_N \circ \mathfrak{v}_{m2^{-N}} \subseteq \mathfrak{v}_{(m+1)2^{-N}},$$

or $\varphi(y) \leqslant (m+1)2^{-N}$, and

$$\langle z, x\rangle \in \mathfrak{u}_N \circ \mathfrak{v}_{m^*2^{-N}} \subseteq \mathfrak{v}_{(m^*+1)2^{-N}},$$

or $\varphi(x) \leqslant (m^*+1)2^{-N}$. From these inequalities and our choices for m and m^*, we now have

$$|\varphi(x) - \varphi(y)| \leqslant 2 \cdot 2^{-N} < 2(\epsilon/2) = \epsilon. \blacksquare$$

We may now prove the converse of the above theorem by showing that there are enough continuous functions on a completely regular space to allow us to obtain a uniformity for it.

Theorem 11.2.3. *Every completely regular topological space is uniformizable.*

Proof. Let $(X, \mathscr{T})$ be a completely regular topological space. For every continuous function $\varphi : X \to [0, 1]$ and every $\epsilon > 0$, let us define

$$\mathfrak{u}_{\varphi,\epsilon} = \{\langle x, y\rangle : |\varphi(x) - \varphi(y)| < \epsilon\}.$$

The family of all such sets forms a subbase for some filter $\mathfrak{U}$ on $X \times X$ since the intersection of any two is nonempty. We assert that $\mathfrak{U}$ is a uniformity for X. Axiom **[U.1]** is satisfied, since each subbase element contains $\mathfrak{i}_X$, and so also any finite intersection of such elements. Axioms **[U.2]** and **[U.3]** merely require that $\mathfrak{U}$ be a filter. Axiom **[U.4]** follows from the inclusion $\mathfrak{u}_{\varphi,\epsilon} \circ \mathfrak{u}_{\varphi,\epsilon} \subseteq \mathfrak{u}_{\varphi,2\epsilon}$, which is obvious from the triangle inequality for the reals. Lastly, $\mathfrak{u}_{\varphi,\epsilon}^{-1} = \mathfrak{u}_{\varphi,\epsilon}$, and so **[U.5]** is satisfied.

We assert that $\mathfrak{U}$ induces the topology $\mathscr{T}$. If $\mathfrak{u}_{\varphi,\epsilon}(x)$ is a subbasic neighborhood of x in the topology induced by $\mathfrak{U}$, then, since φ is continuous, there must exist an open set $G \in \mathscr{T}$ containing x such that $\varphi(G) \subseteq B(\varphi(x), \epsilon)$ where the ball is taken in the reals. But then, $x \in G \subseteq \mathfrak{u}_{\varphi,\varepsilon}(x)$, and so the neighborhoods induced by $\mathscr{T}$ are finer than those induced by $\mathfrak{U}$. Conversely, if $x \in G \in \mathscr{T}$, then, by the complete regularity of $(X, \mathscr{T})$, there exists a continuous mapping $\varphi : X \rightarrow [0, 1]$ such that $\varphi(x) = 0$ and $\varphi(X \setminus G) = \{1\}$. Consider the neighborhood $\mathfrak{u}_{\varphi,1}(x)$ of x in the topology induced by $\mathfrak{U}$. If $y \in \mathfrak{u}_{\varphi,1}(x)$, then $\varphi(y) = | \varphi(x) - \varphi(y) | < 1$, and so $y \in G$. Thus the neighborhoods induced by $\mathfrak{U}$ are finer than those induced by $\mathscr{T}$, and the two must be the same. ▌

Since we have restricted our discussion to uniformizable (completely regular) spaces, there are more properties to be expected of uniformities than quasi-uniformities. In contrast to the example given at the end of the previous section, the members of a uniformity must be neighborhoods of the diagonal $\mathfrak{i}_X$. Indeed, the following stronger theorem holds.

Theorem 11.2.4. *The interior of every member of a uniformity belongs to the uniformity, so that every member of a uniformity is a neighborhood of the diagonal in the product topology induced by the uniformity. Furthermore, the family of closed symmetric members of the uniformity is also a base for the uniformity.*

Proof. Let $(X, \mathfrak{U})$ be a uniform space, and suppose that $\mathfrak{u} \in \mathfrak{U}$. By our earlier lemma, we may find a symmetric set $\mathfrak{v} \in \mathfrak{U}$ such that $\mathfrak{v} \circ \mathfrak{v} \circ \mathfrak{v} \subseteq \mathfrak{u}$. We shall show that $\mathfrak{v}$ is contained in the interior of $\mathfrak{u}$, so that the interior of $\mathfrak{u}$ must belong to $\mathfrak{U}$ by **[U.2]**. Suppose $\langle x, y\rangle \in \mathfrak{v}$. In the topology induced by $\mathfrak{U}$, the set $\mathfrak{v}(x) \times \mathfrak{v}(y)$ must be a neighborhood of the point $\langle x, y\rangle$ with the product topology for $X \times X$. We assert that this entire neighborhood is contained in $\mathfrak{u}$. Suppose $\langle x^*, y^*\rangle$ belongs to this neighborhood, so that $x^* \in \mathfrak{v}(x)$ and $y^* \in \mathfrak{v}(y)$. Thus $\langle x, x^*\rangle \in \mathfrak{v}$ and $\langle y, y^*\rangle \in \mathfrak{v}$, which, by the symmetry of $\mathfrak{v}$, also gives us $\langle x^*, x\rangle \in \mathfrak{v}$. Now we have $\langle x^*, y^*\rangle \in \mathfrak{v} \circ \mathfrak{v} \circ \mathfrak{v} \subseteq \mathfrak{u}$, as desired. Now suppose $\langle x, y\rangle$ is a point in the closure of $\mathfrak{v}$. Since $\mathfrak{v}(x) \times \mathfrak{v}(y)$ is a neighborhood of $\langle x, y\rangle$, there must be some point, say $\langle x^*, y^*\rangle$, in $(\mathfrak{v}(x) \times \mathfrak{v}(y)) \cap \mathfrak{v}$. Again using the triple composition property of $\mathfrak{v}$, we may show that $\langle x, y\rangle \in \mathfrak{u}$. Thus the closure of $\mathfrak{v}$ is contained in $\mathfrak{u}$, giving us a base consisting of closed symmetric members of $\mathfrak{U}$. ▌

Although every member of a uniformity is a neighborhood of the diagonal, the converse is not always true. In the usual (metric) uniformity for the reals, for example, not all neighborhoods of the diagonal belong to the uniformity. The following is a most interesting example of this phenomenon. Let X be the set of all ordinal numbers less than the first uncountable ordinal Ω. As a base for a uniformity for X, we may choose the family of all sets of the form

$$\mathfrak{b}_\tau = \mathfrak{i}_X \cup \{\langle \alpha, \beta \rangle : \alpha > \tau \quad \text{and} \quad \beta > \tau\}$$

for each ordinal $\tau < \Omega$. It is easy to see that this uniformity induces the discrete topology on X, and so this uniformity does not consist of all neighborhoods of the diagonal; that is, all sets containing the diagonal. Indeed, since $\mathfrak{i}_X$, itself, is a base for a uniformity which induces the same topology, there is a metrizable uniformity which induces the same topology. It is easy to see, however, that the original uniformity is not metrizable, since it can have no countable base.

The most interesting case in which the uniformity is uniquely determined by the topology, and does indeed consist of all neighborhoods of the diagonal, is when the topological space is compact. We shall say that a uniform space is **compact** when the topological space it induces is compact.

Theorem 11.2.5. *If a uniform space is compact, then the uniformity consists of all neighborhoods of the diagonal.*

Proof. Let $(X, \mathfrak{U})$ be a compact uniform space, and suppose $\mathfrak{g}$ is a subset of $X \times X$ containing the diagonal which is open in the topology induced by $\mathfrak{U}$. By the previous theorem, there is a base $\mathfrak{B}$ for $\mathfrak{U}$ consisting of closed sets. Now if a point $\langle x, y \rangle$ belongs to all the members of $\mathfrak{B}$, then y must belong to every neighborhood of x, so that $\langle x, y \rangle \in \mathfrak{g}$, in particular. Thus the family $\{\mathfrak{g}\} \cup \{\complement \mathfrak{b} : \mathfrak{b} \in \mathfrak{B}\}$ forms an open covering of the compact space $X \times X$. There must then exist a finite subcover. From this we see that $\mathfrak{g}$ must contain some finite intersection of members of $\mathfrak{B}$, and so $\mathfrak{g} \in \mathfrak{U}$, as desired. ∎

Exercises

1. If $(X, \mathfrak{U})$ is a uniform space, $E \subseteq X$, and $\mathfrak{e} \subseteq X \times X$, then $c_X(E) = \bigcap \{\mathfrak{u}(E) : \mathfrak{u} \in \mathfrak{U}\}$ and $c_{X \times X}(\mathfrak{e}) = \bigcap \{\mathfrak{u} \circ \mathfrak{e} \circ \mathfrak{u} : \mathfrak{u} \in \mathfrak{U}\}$.

2. Let X be the set of all ordinals less than the first uncountable ordinal. Choose as a base for a uniformity $\mathfrak{U}$ on X the family of all sets of the form $\mathfrak{b}_\tau = \mathfrak{i}_X \cup \{\langle \alpha, \beta \rangle : \alpha > \tau$ and $\beta > \tau\}$ for each ordinal $\tau < \Omega$. Show that $\mathfrak{U}$ is not metrizable.

3. Show that there is only one uniformity for the set of all ordinals less than the first uncountable ordinal that induces the order topology (see Dieudonné [35]). For information concerning conditions under which a space has a unique uniformity, see Doss [37].

4. Tukey [24] gave the following derivation of uniform spaces. Let Γ be a family of open covers of the space X satisfying the following properties: (1) If a cover $\mathscr{G} \in \Gamma$, then any cover which $\mathscr{G}$ refines belongs to Γ; and (2) Any two members of Γ have a common star refinement in Γ. Then the family $\cup \{G \times G : G \in \mathscr{G}\}$ for $\mathscr{G} \in \Gamma$ is a base for a uniformity $\mathfrak{U}$ for X. The neighborhoods of a point x in the induced topology are the members of the family $\{\mathrm{St}(x, \mathscr{G}) : \mathscr{G} \in \Gamma\}$. In the uniformity $\mathfrak{U}$, the family Γ has the property that each member $\mathscr{G}$ of Γ is a **uniform cover** of X; that is, there exists a set $\mathfrak{u} \in \mathfrak{U}$ such that $\{\mathfrak{u}(x) : x \in X\}$ refines $\mathscr{G}$. Conversely, the family Γ of all uniform covers of a uniform space satisfies the above properties (1) and (2).

11.3 Uniform Continuity

The first property of metric spaces which we shall introduce in the more general setting of uniform spaces is that of uniform continuity of functions. Recalling that it involves finding a distance which satisfies certain requirements for all points of the space simultaneously, we see that it is natural to consider this notion in uniform spaces since each member of a uniformity gives a particular neighborhood of each point of the space simultaneously. A mapping φ of a uniform space $(X, \mathfrak{U})$ into a uniform space $(Y, \mathfrak{V})$ is **uniformly continuous** iff for every $\mathfrak{v} \in \mathfrak{V}$ there exists a $\mathfrak{u} \in \mathfrak{U}$ such that $\langle \varphi(x_1), \varphi(x_2) \rangle \in \mathfrak{v}$ whenever $\langle x_1, x_2 \rangle \in \mathfrak{u}$.

For a mapping $\varphi : (X, d_X) \to (Y, d_Y)$ of metric spaces, it is clear that uniform continuity in the metric uniformities is equivalent to the requirement that for every $\epsilon > 0$ there exists a $\delta > 0$ such that $d_Y(\varphi(x_1), \varphi(x_2)) < \epsilon$ whenever $d_X(x_1, x_2) < \delta$. Thus we have really generalized the usual notion of uniform continuity for metric spaces.

The definition may be put in a more convenient form by using the function $\varphi_2 : X \times X \to Y \times Y$, which we associated with the mapping $\varphi : X \to Y$ by setting $\varphi_2(\langle x_1, x_2 \rangle) = \langle \varphi(x_1), \varphi(x_2) \rangle$ in problem **8** of Section **8.1**. With this notation, φ is uniformly continuous iff for every $\mathfrak{v} \in \mathfrak{V}$ there exists a $\mathfrak{u} \in \mathfrak{U}$ such that $\varphi_2(\mathfrak{u}) \subseteq \mathfrak{v}$. Equivalently, we must have $\varphi_2^{-1}(\mathfrak{v}) \supseteq \mathfrak{u}$, which, by **[U.2]**, may be written $\varphi_2^{-1}(\mathfrak{v}) \in \mathfrak{U}$. Thus, φ is uniformly continuous iff $\varphi_2^{-1}(\mathfrak{v}) \in \mathfrak{U}$ for every $\mathfrak{v} \in \mathfrak{V}$.

We may also define the uniform equivalent of a homeomorphism between topological spaces. If $\varphi : (X, \mathfrak{U}) \to (Y, \mathfrak{V})$ is a one-to-one and onto mapping such that both φ and φ^{-1} are uniformly continuous, we say that φ is a **uniform isomorphism.** Two uniform spaces are **uniformly isomorphic** iff there exists some uniform isomorphism of one of them onto the other. **Uniform invariants** are those properties of uniform spaces which must be possessed by every space uniformly isomorphic to a space with the property. The fact that every uniform isomorphism is a homeomorphism between the induced topological spaces follows from the following theorem.

Theorem 11.3.1. *If* $\varphi : (X, \mathfrak{U}) \to (Y, \mathfrak{V})$ *is uniformly continuous, then* φ *is continuous in the induced topologies.*

Proof. For any point $x \in X$, suppose $\varphi(x)$ is contained in some neighborhood which, by the definition of the induced topology, we may denote by $\mathfrak{v}(\varphi(x))$ for some $\mathfrak{v} \in \mathfrak{V}$. Since φ is uniformly continuous, there exists some set $\mathfrak{u} \in \mathfrak{U}$ such that $\varphi_2(\mathfrak{u}) \subseteq \mathfrak{v}$. Now if $y \in \varphi(\mathfrak{u}(x))$, then there exists some point $x^* \in \mathfrak{u}(x)$ such that $\varphi(x^*) = y$. Then $\langle x, x^* \rangle \in \mathfrak{u}$, so that $\langle \varphi(x), \varphi(x^*) \rangle = \langle \varphi(x), y \rangle \in \mathfrak{v}$ by the definition of $\mathfrak{u}$. Since we now have $y \in \mathfrak{v}(\varphi(x))$, we have proven that $\mathfrak{u}(x)$ is a neighborhood of x such that $\varphi(\mathfrak{u}(x)) \subseteq \mathfrak{v}(\varphi(x))$, and so φ is continuous. ▮

Of course the converse of this theorem is not true, since we have seen continuous mappings of metric spaces which were not uniformly continuous. In **6.5.2** we saw that, for compact metric spaces, every continuous mapping was uniformly continuous. The following theorem shows that this property carries over into uniform spaces.

Theorem 11.3.2. *If* φ *is a continuous mapping of the compact uniform space* $(X, \mathfrak{U})$ *into the uniform space* $(Y, \mathfrak{V})$, *then* φ *is uniformly continuous.*

Proof. By problem **8** in Section **8.1**, the associated mapping φ_2 is also continuous. Now if $\mathfrak{v} \in \mathfrak{V}$, $\mathfrak{v}$ is a neighborhood of the diagonal of Y by **11.2.4**. Then, by the continuity of φ_2, $\varphi_2^{-1}(\mathfrak{v})$ is a neighborhood of the diagonal of X. For compact X, however, all neighborhoods of the diagonal belong to the uniformity by **11.2.5**. Thus $\varphi_2^{-1}(\mathfrak{v}) \in \mathfrak{U}$, and φ is uniformly continuous. ▮

Following the discussion of Section **4.4**, we may suppose that φ is a mapping of a set X into a uniform space $(Y, \mathfrak{V})$, and we may consider the smallest uniformity for X such that φ is uniformly continuous. It is easy to verify that the family of all sets of the form $\varphi_2^{-1}(\mathfrak{v})$ for $\mathfrak{v} \in \mathfrak{V}$ is a base for this uniformity. We may also generalize this construction to the case where we have a family of mappings of X into various uniform spaces.

Suppose $\{\varphi_\lambda\}$ is a collection of mappings, where φ_λ maps X into a uniform space $(Y_\lambda, \mathfrak{V}_\lambda)$. It is easy to show that the family of all sets of the form $(\varphi_\lambda)_2^{-1}(\mathfrak{v}_\lambda)$ for $\mathfrak{v}_\lambda \in \mathfrak{V}_\lambda$ forms a subbase for a uniformity for X. Furthermore, this uniformity is the smallest such that each mapping φ_λ is uniformly continuous.

As a particular application of this construction, we may obtain a uniformity for the product of uniform spaces. It is natural to define the **product uniformity** for the product $\Pi_\lambda X_\lambda$ of uniform spaces $\{X_\lambda\}$ to be the smallest uniformity such that the projections π_λ are all uniformly continuous. It is easy to show that the product uniformity does, indeed, induce the product topology.

Another application of these ideas comes from considering the fact that a pseudometric on X is a mapping of the set $X \times X$ into the (uniform) space of real numbers. We may ask when this mapping is uniformly continuous.

Theorem 11.3.3. *If d is a pseudometric on $(X, \mathfrak{U})$, then d is uniformly continuous on $X \times X$ iff $\mathfrak{w}_\epsilon = \{\langle x, y\rangle : d(x, y) < \epsilon\} \in \mathfrak{U}$ for every $\epsilon > 0$.*

Proof. Suppose d is uniformly continuous on $X \times X$, and ϵ is a given positive number. From the above definition of the product uniformity, it follows that a subbase for the product uniformity for a product $\Pi_\lambda X_\lambda$ of uniform spaces $\{(X_\lambda, \mathfrak{U}_\lambda)\}$ is the family of all sets of the form

$$\{\langle \mathbf{x}, \mathbf{y}\rangle : \langle x_\lambda, y_\lambda\rangle \in \mathfrak{u}_\lambda\}$$

for $\mathfrak{u}_\lambda \in \mathfrak{U}_\lambda$ and all λ. In the case under consideration (only two spaces, each equal to X), the subbase would consist of all sets of the form

$$\{\langle\langle x_1, x_2\rangle, \langle y_1, y_2\rangle\rangle : \langle x_1, y_1\rangle \in \mathfrak{u}\}$$

or of the form

$$\{\langle\langle x_1, x_2\rangle, \langle y_1, y_2\rangle\rangle : \langle x_2, y_2\rangle \in \mathfrak{u}\}$$

for $\mathfrak{u} \in \mathfrak{U}$. Using the uniformity axioms, we see that a base for this product uniformity consists of the sets

$$\mathbf{b}_\mathfrak{u} = \{\langle\langle x_1, x_2\rangle, \langle y_1, y_2\rangle\rangle : \langle x_1, y_1\rangle \in \mathfrak{u}, \langle x_2, y_2\rangle \in \mathfrak{u}\}$$

for all $\mathfrak{u} \in \mathfrak{U}$. Corresponding to the positive real number ϵ, the member of the usual uniformity for the reals is $\{\langle \alpha, \beta\rangle : | \alpha - \beta | < \epsilon\}$. Since d is uniformly continuous, there must exist some set $\mathfrak{u} \in \mathfrak{U}$ such that

$$d_2(\mathbf{b}_\mathfrak{u}) \subseteq \{\langle \alpha, \beta\rangle : | \alpha - \beta | < \epsilon\}.$$

That is, if $\langle x_1, y_1\rangle \in \mathfrak{u}$ and $\langle x_2, y_2\rangle \in \mathfrak{u}$, then $| d(x_1, x_2) - d(y_1, y_2) | < \epsilon$.

If we now let $x_1 = x$ and $x_2 = y_1 = y_2 = y$, we have $\langle x, y\rangle \in \mathfrak{u}$ implies that $d(x, y) < \epsilon$. Thus $\mathfrak{u} \subseteq \mathfrak{w}_\epsilon$, so $\mathfrak{w}_\epsilon \in \mathfrak{U}$ for all $\epsilon > 0$.

Conversely, if $\mathfrak{w}_\epsilon \in \mathfrak{U}$ for every $\epsilon > 0$, then for any fixed $\epsilon > 0$, $\mathfrak{w}_{\epsilon/2} \in \mathfrak{U}$. Now if $\langle x_1, y_1\rangle \in \mathfrak{w}_{\epsilon/2}$ so that $d(x_1, y_1) < \epsilon/2$, and $\langle x_2, y_2\rangle \in \mathfrak{w}_{\epsilon/2}$ so that $d(x_2, y_2) < \epsilon/2$, it is clear that $| d(x_1, y_1) - d(x_2, y_2) | < \epsilon$. Thus $d_2(\mathbf{b}_{\mathfrak{w}_{\epsilon/2}}) \subseteq : \{\langle \alpha, \beta\rangle \mid \alpha - \beta \mid < \epsilon\}$, and d is uniformly continuous on $X \times X$. ▮

From this theorem it follows that the metric uniformity induced by d is the smallest such that d is uniformly continuous on $X \times X$. More generally, we may consider the smallest uniformity which makes each member of a family of pseudometrics uniformly continuous. If $\{d_\lambda : \lambda \in \Lambda\}$ is a family of pseudometrics on X, this uniformity must have a subbase consisting of all sets of the form $\mathfrak{w}_{\epsilon,\lambda} = \{\langle x, y\rangle : d_\lambda(x, y) < \epsilon\}$ where $\lambda \in \Lambda$ and $\epsilon > 0$. We shall say that the uniformity which is the smallest such that each member of a family of pseudometrics is uniformly continuous is **generated** by the family.

Theorem 11.3.4. *If* $(X, \mathfrak{U})$ *is a uniform space, then* $\mathfrak{U}$ *is generated by the family of all pseudometrics which are uniformly continuous on* $X \times X$.

Proof. By **11.3.3**, $\mathfrak{U}$ is larger than the uniformity generated by the family, since $\mathfrak{w}_{\epsilon,\lambda} \in \mathfrak{U}$ for every $\epsilon > 0$ and $\lambda \in \Lambda$. Conversely, if $\mathfrak{u} \in \mathfrak{U}$, then, by the pseudometrization theorem **11.2.1**, there exists a pseudometric d such that $\{\langle x, y\rangle : d(x, y) < \epsilon\} \in \mathfrak{u}$ and

$$\{\langle x, y\rangle : d(x, y) < \epsilon\} \subseteq \mathfrak{u}$$

for some $\epsilon > 0$. Now d is uniformly continuous in the uniformity it generates, and hence in any larger uniformity (such as $\mathfrak{U}$) as shown in the first part of this proof. Since $d = d_\lambda$ for some $\lambda \in \Lambda$, the uniformity generated by the family is larger than $\mathfrak{U}$. ▮

For a discussion of uniform spaces from the point of view of their uniformly continuous pseudometrics, the reader is referred to Chapter XV of the text by Gillman and Jerison [7].

Exercises

1. If $\varphi : X \to (Y, \mathfrak{B})$, then the family $\{\varphi_2^{-1}(\mathfrak{v}) : \mathfrak{v} \in \mathfrak{B}\}$ is a base for the smallest uniformity such that φ is uniformly continuous.

2. If $\varphi_\lambda : X \to (Y_\lambda, \mathfrak{B}_\lambda)$, then the family $\{(\varphi_\lambda)_2^{-1}(\mathfrak{v}_\lambda) : \mathfrak{v}_\lambda \in \mathfrak{B}_\lambda\}$ is a subbase for the smallest uniformity such that each φ_λ is uniformly continuous.

3. Let E be a subset of the uniform space $(X, \mathfrak{U})$. Show that $\mathfrak{U}_E = \{\mathfrak{u} \cap (E \times E) : \mathfrak{u} \in \mathfrak{U}\}$ is a uniformity for E. We call this the **subspace uniformity**. Show that $\mathfrak{U}_E$ is the smallest uniformity for E such that the inclusion mapping (see problem **10** in Section **4.3**) of E into X is uniformly continuous.

4. Show that the product uniformity induces the product topology.

5. A mapping $\varphi : X \to \prod_\lambda Y_\lambda$ is uniformly continuous iff $\pi_\lambda \circ \varphi : X \to Y_\lambda$ is uniformly continuous for every λ. (Compare with problem **8** in Section **8.4**.)

6. Show that the uniformity generated by a family $\{d_\lambda\}$ of pseudometrics is the smallest such that the identity mapping of X into (X, d_λ) is uniformly continuous for every λ.

7. A uniform space $(X, \mathfrak{U})$ will be called **uniformly connected** iff every uniformly continuous mapping of X into a discrete space (a space whose topology is discrete) is constant. Prove:

(i) The rational numbers with the subspace uniformity from the usual uniformity for the reals are uniformly connected but not connected.

(ii) Every connected uniform space is uniformly connected.

(iii) $(X, \mathfrak{U})$ is uniformly connected iff for every pair of points x and y in X and every $\mathfrak{u} \in \mathfrak{U}$, there exists a finite sequence $x_0, \ldots, x_n$ of points in X such that $x_0 = x$, $x_n = y$, and $\langle x_{i-1}, x_i \rangle \in \mathfrak{u}$ for $i = 1, \ldots, n$.

(iv) $(X, \mathfrak{U})$ is uniformly connected iff the range of every real-valued continuous mapping of X is dense in an interval (see [61]).

11.4 Completeness and Compactness

The most interesting nontopological notion we have considered is completeness, and we may now show that uniform spaces are a natural place in which to consider a generalization of this notion. One problem does arise immediately, however. In Sections **5.2** and **5.3** we saw that sequences are inadequate for a complete description of the topologies of spaces unless some additional restriction, such as **[C$_\text{I}$]**, is placed on the spaces. Although in Chapter 7 we considered only Cauchy sequences in metric spaces, in order to obtain the proper generality we must here consider some more general type of limit.

As mentioned in Section **5.2**, we may generalize the notion of a sequence to the idea of a Moore-Smith sequence, or net, and obtain the desired results. This method is used by Kelley [14], and the reader is referred to his text for a description of that approach. Another method is to consider the notion of a filter, which we have already introduced in Section **8.5**.

We recall that a **filter** is a family of nonempty sets which is closed under finite intersections and which contains every superset of every member of the family. In problem **7** in Section **8.5** we defined a **limit**

point of a filter $\mathscr{F}$ in a topological space $(X, \mathscr{T})$ to be a point $x \in X$ such that every neighborhood of x belongs to $\mathscr{F}$. Furthermore, a point x is an **adherence point** of the filter $\mathscr{F}$ iff x belongs to the closure of each member of $\mathscr{F}$. These are the main facts about filters needed for this discussion.

The basic notion behind the definition of a Cauchy sequence is that the points of the sequence must get near to each other. In terms of a uniformity this would require that pairs of points in the sequence must lie in some member of the uniformity. We may consider a similar notion for filters in uniform spaces. A filter $\mathscr{F}$ in a uniform space $(X, \mathfrak{U})$ will be said to be a **Cauchy filter** iff for every $\mathfrak{u} \in \mathfrak{U}$, $F \times F \subseteq \mathfrak{u}$ for some $F \in \mathscr{F}$. We note that the Fréchet filter associated with a sequence (see problem **3** in Section **8.5**) is a Cauchy filter iff the sequence is a Cauchy sequence. Corresponding to the equivalent results for metric spaces, we have the following elementary properties of Cauchy filters.

Theorem 11.4.1. *In a uniform space, every convergent filter is a Cauchy filter, and every Cauchy filter converges to each of its adherence points.*

Proof. Suppose $\mathscr{F}$ is a filter in the uniform space $(X, \mathfrak{U})$ which converges to the point x, and $\mathfrak{u} \in \mathfrak{U}$. By the lemma of the previous section, there exists some symmetric set $\mathfrak{v} \in \mathfrak{U}$ such that $\mathfrak{v} \circ \mathfrak{v} \subseteq \mathfrak{u}$. Since $\mathscr{F}$ converges to x, $\mathfrak{v}(x) \in \mathscr{F}$. We assert that $\mathfrak{v}(x) \times \mathfrak{v}(x) \subseteq u$. If $\langle p, q \rangle \in \mathfrak{v}(x) \times \mathfrak{v}(x)$, then $\langle x, p \rangle \in \mathfrak{v}$ and $\langle x, q \rangle \in \mathfrak{v}$, so that $\langle p, q \rangle \in \mathfrak{v} \circ \mathfrak{v}^{-1} = \mathfrak{v} \circ \mathfrak{v} \subseteq \mathfrak{u}$. Thus $\mathscr{F}$ is a Cauchy filter.

Now suppose $\mathscr{F}$ is a Cauchy filter with adherence point z; that is, $z \in \mathbf{c}(F)$ for every $F \in \mathscr{F}$. Let $\mathfrak{u}(z)$ be an arbitrary neighborhood of z in the induced topology. By **[U.4]**, there exists a set $\mathfrak{v} \in \mathfrak{U}$ such that $\mathfrak{v} \circ \mathfrak{v} \subseteq \mathfrak{u}$. Since $\mathscr{F}$ is a Cauchy filter, there exists some set $F \in \mathscr{F}$ such that $F \times F \subseteq \mathfrak{v}$. Now $z \in \mathbf{c}(F)$, and so there must exist some point $y \in \mathfrak{v}(z) \cap F$. Thus $y \in \mathfrak{v}(z)$, so that $\langle z, y \rangle \in \mathfrak{v}$. Furthermore, $y \in F$, so that for any point $x \in F$, $\langle y, x \rangle \in F \times F \subseteq \mathfrak{v}$, and so $\langle z, x \rangle \in \mathfrak{v} \circ \mathfrak{v} \subseteq \mathfrak{u}$, which means that $x \in \mathfrak{u}(z)$. Thus $F \subseteq \mathfrak{u}(z)$, which implies that $\mathfrak{u}(z) \in \mathscr{F}$, and $\mathscr{F}$ must converge to z. ▌

Perhaps a more important question about Cauchy filters is whether they are uniform invariants. This will follow from the following result.

Theorem 11.4.2. *If $\varphi : (X, \mathfrak{U}) \to (Y, \mathfrak{B})$ is uniformly continuous and $\mathscr{F}$ is a Cauchy filter (or the base of a Cauchy filter), then $\varphi(\mathscr{F}) = \{\varphi(F) : F \in \mathscr{F}\}$ is the base of a Cauchy filter.*

Proof. It is clear that $\varphi(\mathscr{F})$ is the base of some filter in Y, so suppose $\mathfrak{v} \in \mathfrak{V}$. There must exist some set $\mathfrak{u} \in \mathfrak{U}$ such that $\varphi_2(\mathfrak{u}) \subseteq \mathfrak{v}$, since φ is uniformly continuous, and there must exist some set $F \in \mathscr{F}$ such that $F \times F \subseteq \mathfrak{u}$, since $\mathscr{F}$ is a Cauchy filter (or the base of a Cauchy filter). We assert that $\varphi(F) \times \varphi(F) \subseteq \mathfrak{v}$, which will show that $\varphi(\mathscr{F})$ is the base of a Cauchy filter. Let $\langle y_1, y_2 \rangle \in \varphi(F) \times \varphi(F)$, so that y_1 and y_2 belong to $\varphi(F)$. There must exist points x_1 and x_2 in F such that $y_1 = \varphi(x_1)$ and $y_2 = \varphi(x_2)$. Since $\langle x_1, x_2 \rangle \in F \times F \subseteq \mathfrak{u}$, $\varphi_2(\langle x_1, x_2 \rangle) = \langle \varphi(x_1), \varphi(x_2) \rangle = \langle y_1, y_2 \rangle \in \mathfrak{v}$. ∎

It is now natural to define a uniform space $(X, \mathfrak{U})$ to be **complete** iff every Cauchy filter in X converges to a point of X. This is certainly a uniform invariant by the preceding theorem. Certain general results similar to those for complete metric spaces may now be proven. We will call a uniform space **Hausdorff** or **separated** iff the topological space it induces is Hausdorff.

Theorem 11.4.3. *Every closed subset of a complete uniform space is complete, and every complete subspace of a Hausdorff uniform space is closed.*

Proof. Let E be a closed subset of the complete uniform space $(X, \mathfrak{U})$, and suppose that $\mathscr{F}$ is a Cauchy filter in E. Then $\mathscr{F}$ is the base of a Cauchy filter in X which must then converge to some point $x \in X$. Since every limit point of a filter is certainly an adherence point of that filter and $E \in \mathscr{F}$, we must have $x \in \mathbf{c}(E) = E$, and so $\mathscr{F}$ converges to a point of E.

Now suppose E is a complete subspace of the Hausdorff uniform space $(X, \mathfrak{U})$, and let $x \in \mathbf{c}(E)$. In the induced topology, we must have $\mathfrak{u}(x) \cap E \neq \varnothing$ for all $\mathfrak{u} \in \mathfrak{U}$. Consider the family of sets $\mathscr{F} = \{\mathfrak{u}(x) \cap E : \mathfrak{u} \in \mathfrak{U}\}$, which is clearly a filter in E. If, for every $\mathfrak{u} \in \mathfrak{U}$, we choose a symmetric set $\mathfrak{v} \in \mathfrak{U}$ such that $\mathfrak{v} \circ \mathfrak{v} \subseteq \mathfrak{u}$, then

$$(\mathfrak{v}(x) \cap E) \times (\mathfrak{v}(x) \cap E) \subseteq \mathfrak{u} \cap (E \times E),$$

which is the form of the general element of the uniformity for E. Thus $\mathscr{F}$ is a Cauchy filter in the complete space E, and so it has a limit point $x^* \in E$. The filter $\mathscr{F}$ in E is a base for a filter $\mathscr{F}^*$ in X, and we must still have x^* a limit point of $\mathscr{F}^*$. On the other hand, x must be a limit point of $\mathscr{F}^*$ since $\mathfrak{u}(x) \in \mathscr{F}^*$ for every $\mathfrak{u} \in \mathfrak{U}$. By problem **7** (iv) in Section **8.5**, limits are unique in a Hausdorff space, and so $x = x^* \in E$, and E must be closed. ∎

We would expect that our definitions should agree with those given for metric spaces, and the following theorem shows that they do.

Theorem 11.4.4. *A pseudometric space is complete in its metric uniformity iff every Cauchy sequence in the space converges.*

Proof. It is clear that the Fréchet filter associated with a Cauchy sequence is a Cauchy filter. Hence, in a complete uniform space, every Cauchy sequence must converge. Now suppose that $\mathscr{F}$ is a Cauchy filter in the pseudometric space (X, d) in which every Cauchy sequence converges. Thus, for every $\epsilon > 0$ there exists a set $F \in \mathscr{F}$ such that

$$F \times F \subseteq \mathfrak{w}_\epsilon = \{\langle x, y \rangle : d(x, y) < \epsilon\}.$$

For each $n \in \mathbf{N}$ we may set $\epsilon = 1/n$ and obtain a monotone decreasing sequence of sets $F_n \in \mathscr{F}$ such that $F_n \times F_n \subseteq \mathfrak{w}_{1/n}$. Since each member of $\mathscr{F}$ is nonempty, we may choose a point $x_n \in F_n$ and obtain a sequence $\langle x_n \rangle$, which is clearly a Cauchy sequence in X. Let x be the limit point of the sequence, and suppose $\mathfrak{u}(x)$ is an arbitrary neighborhood of x. Then $x \in B(x, 1/n) \subseteq \mathfrak{u}(x)$ for some $n \in \mathbf{N}$. Choose an integer m such that $m > 2n$ and such that $x_m \in B(x, 1/2n)$, so that $d(x, x_m) < 1/2n$. Now for any $y \in F_m$, $d(x_m, y) < 1/m$ since $F_m \times F_m \subseteq w_{1/m}$, and so $d(x, y) < (1/2n) + (1/m) < 1/n$. Hence $y \in \mathfrak{u}(x)$, and so $F_m \subseteq \mathfrak{u}(x)$, which shows that $\mathfrak{u}(x) \in \mathscr{F}$. Thus $\mathscr{F}$ must converge to x. ▮

The equivalence given in the above theorem shows that the construction of the completion of a metric space given in Section **7.2** could be carried over to this more general setting for pseudometrizable uniform spaces. Furthermore, by **11.3.4**, a uniformity is determined by a family of pseudometrics, and so the following theorem is easy to establish.

Theorem 11.4.4. *Every uniform space is uniformly isomorphic to a dense subset of a complete uniform space. Furthermore, if a uniform space is a Hausdorff space, it must have a Hausdorff completion, and all of its Hausdorff completions are uniformly isomorphic.*

Proof. A detailed description of the necessary construction for the above results is given in the text by the Bourbaki [3]. ▮

The relationship between completeness and compactness is the same as that given for metric spaces in the corollary to **7.3.3**. We say that a uniform space $(X, \mathfrak{U})$ is **totally bounded** or **precompact** iff for every $\mathfrak{u} \in \mathfrak{U}$ there exists a finite set of points $x_1, \ldots, x_n \in X$ such that

$X = \bigcup_{i=1}^n \mathfrak{u}(x_i)$. It is clear that this definition agrees with that given for metric spaces. It is easy to show that $(X, \mathfrak{U})$ is totally bounded iff the pseudometric space (X, d) is totally bounded for every pseudometric d which is uniformly continuous on $X \times X$. Our main theorem will follow from the next lemma.

Lemma. *A uniform space is totally bounded iff every filter is contained in a Cauchy filter.*

Proof. Suppose $(X, \mathfrak{U})$ is totally bounded, and $\mathscr{F}$ is a filter in X. By **8.5.1**, $\mathscr{F}$ is contained in some ultrafilter $\mathscr{F}^*$. Let $\mathfrak{u} \in \mathfrak{U}$, and choose a symmetric set $\mathfrak{v} \in \mathfrak{U}$ such that $\mathfrak{v} \circ \mathfrak{v} \subseteq \mathfrak{u}$. By total boundedness, there exists a finite set $x_1, ..., x_n \in X$ such that $X = \bigcup_{i=1}^n \mathfrak{v}(x_i)$. If, for each $i = 1, ..., n$, there exists a set $F_i^* \in \mathscr{F}^*$ such that $\mathfrak{v}(x_i) \cap F_i^* = \emptyset$, then the set $F^* = \bigcap_{i=1}^n F_i^*$ belongs to $\mathscr{F}^*$, but

$$F^* \cap X = F^* \cap \left(\bigcup_{i=1}^n \mathfrak{v}(x_i)\right)$$

$$= \bigcup_{i=1}^n (F^* \cap \mathfrak{v}(x_i))$$

$$\subseteq \bigcup_{i=1}^n (F_i^* \cap \mathfrak{v}(x_i)) = \emptyset,$$

which is a contradiction. Hence, for some i, $\mathfrak{v}(x_i) \cap F^* \neq \emptyset$ for every $F^* \in \mathscr{F}^*$. Since $\mathscr{F}^*$ is an ultrafilter, $\mathfrak{v}(x_i) \in \mathscr{F}^*$ by **8.5.2**. Clearly, $\mathfrak{v}(x_i) \times \mathfrak{v}(x_i) \subseteq \mathfrak{u}$, and so $\mathscr{F}^*$ is a Cauchy filter containing $\mathscr{F}$.

Conversely, suppose every filter in $(X, \mathfrak{U})$ is contained in a Cauchy filter, and let $\mathfrak{u} \in \mathfrak{U}$. For every finite subset $E \subseteq X$, assume that $\mathfrak{u}(E) = \bigcup\{\mathfrak{u}(x) : x \in E\} \neq X$, so that $\complement\mathfrak{u}(E) \neq \emptyset$. The family $\{\complement\mathfrak{u}(E)\}$ for all finite subsets E is the base of a filter which, by hypothesis, is contained in a Cauchy filter $\mathscr{F}$. Thus, $F \times F \subseteq \mathfrak{u}$ for some $F \in \mathscr{F}$. For a fixed point $x \in F$, $F \subseteq \mathfrak{u}(x)$, and so $\mathfrak{u}(x) \in \mathscr{F}$. On the other hand, $\{x\}$ is a finite set, and so $\complement\mathfrak{u}(x) \in \mathscr{F}$, also. This gives us a contradiction since we now have $\mathfrak{u}(x) \cap \complement\mathfrak{u}(x) = \emptyset \in \mathscr{F}$. Thus, $\mathfrak{u}(E) = X$ for some finite subset $E \subseteq X$, and X is totally bounded. ▮

Theorem 11.4.5. *A uniform space is compact iff it is complete and totally bounded.*

Proof. If $(X, \mathfrak{U})$ is compact, then for every $\mathfrak{u} \in \mathfrak{U}$ the collection $\{\mathfrak{u}(x) : x \in X\}$ is a covering of X by neighborhoods, and so there must be some finite subcovering. This means that X is totally bounded. Furthermore, if $\mathscr{F}$ is a Cauchy filter, then, since every filter has some adherence point in a compact space (see problem **7**(v) in Section **8.5**), $\mathscr{F}$ must converge by **11.4.1**.

Conversely, if $(X, \mathfrak{U})$ is complete and totally bounded, then any filter $\mathscr{F}$ in X is contained in a Cauchy filter $\mathscr{F}^*$, by the lemma. Since X is complete, $\mathscr{F}^*$ must converge to a point which (see problem **7**(i) in Section **8.5**) will be an adherence point of $\mathscr{F}$. Thus (see problem **7**(v) in Section **8.5**) X is compact. ∎

Exercises

1. Give examples showing that a uniform space need not remain complete with either a larger or a smaller uniformity.

2. Show that the space of all ordinals less than the first uncountable ordinal, with its unique uniformity inducing the order topology (see problem **3** in Section **11.2**), is not complete.

3. Let $X = \mathbf{N}$, and let $\mathfrak{v}_n = \{\langle x, y\rangle : x \equiv y \pmod{n}\}$ for each $n \in \mathbf{N}$. Show that the family $\{\mathfrak{v}_n : n \in \mathbf{N}\}$ is a base for a uniformity $\mathfrak{U}$ for X. Show that $(X, \mathfrak{U})$ is not complete.

4. $\prod_\lambda X_\lambda$ is totally bounded iff each space X_λ is totally bounded.

5. $\prod_\lambda X_\lambda$ is complete iff each space X_λ is complete.

6. If φ^* is a uniformly continuous mapping of the dense subspace X^* of the uniform space $(X, \mathfrak{U})$ into the complete uniform space $(Y, \mathfrak{B})$, then there exists a uniformly continuous mapping φ of X into Y such that $\varphi \mid X^* = \varphi^*$. If $(Y, \mathfrak{B})$ is, in addition, a Hausdorff space, then φ is uniquely determined. (See problem **11** in Section **7.1**.)

11.5 Proximity Spaces

In this section we shall briefly consider another generalization of metric spaces in which the notions of uniform continuity and completeness may be considered. In 1941, Wallace [81], Krishna Murti [48], and Szymanski [76] independently used the notion of separation of sets as the primitive notion of topology. Later, Aleksandrov [29] and Freudenthal [41] introduced a subordination, or strong inclusion relation, in an attempt to find all compactifications of a topological space. Finally, a very similar relation was introduced by Efremovich [39] in 1952, and it is in terms of this relation that much of the Russian work on uniform spaces is stated. For a discussion of the relationship between these various structures, the reader is referred to [64].

A **proximity space** (X, δ) is a set X together with a relation δ satisfying the following axioms:

[P.1] $E\bar{\delta}\varnothing$ for every $E \subseteq X$, where $\bar{\delta}$ denotes the negation of δ.

[P.2] $\{x\}\delta\{x\}$ for every $x \in X$.

[P.3] $C\delta(A \cup B)$ iff $C\delta A$ or $C\delta B$.

[P.4] If $A\bar{\delta}B$, then there exists a set $C \subseteq X$ such that $A\bar{\delta}C$ and $X \setminus C\bar{\delta}B$.

[P.5] $A\delta B$ iff $B\delta A$.

The relation δ will be called a **proximity** for X, and we shall say that A is **near** B whenever $A\delta B$.

It is easy to show that the relation δ, defined by setting $A\delta B$ iff $d(A, B) = 0$ in a pseudometric space (X, d), is a proximity relation for X. The corresponding relation for a quasimetric space is discussed in [65]. Since $\mathbf{c}(E) = \{x : d(\{x\}, E) = 0\}$ (see problem **14** (ii) in Section **6.1**), it is natural to consider a proximity space (X, δ) as a topological space with the closure operator defined by setting

$$\mathbf{c}(E) = \{x : \{x\}\, \delta E\}.$$

More generally, for any uniform space $(X, \mathfrak{U})$ the relation δ, defined by setting $A\delta B$ iff for every $\mathfrak{u} \in \mathfrak{U}$ there exists a point $x \in A$ and a point $y \in B$ such that $\langle x, y\rangle \in \mathfrak{u}$, is a proximity relation for X. Conversely, for any proximity space (X, δ) we may set $\mathfrak{S} = \{\mathfrak{u}_{A,B} : A\bar{\delta}B\}$ where

$$\mathfrak{u}_{A,B} = \complement[(A \times B) \cup (B \times A)]$$

and obtain a subbase for a uniformity for X. Furthermore, the proximity derived from the uniformity thus obtained will be δ. Thus the topological spaces which may be derived from a proximity space are exactly the uniformizable (completely regular) spaces.

A mapping $\mathfrak{f}$ of a proximity space (X, δ) into a proximity space (X^*, δ^*) will be called **equicontinuous** or a δ**-mapping** iff $\mathfrak{f}(A)\delta^*\mathfrak{f}(B)$ whenever $A\delta B$. It is easy to see that an equicontinuous mapping is a continuous mapping with respect to the topologies on X and X^*. Also, a uniformly continuous mapping is equicontinuous with respect to the proximities on X and X^*. Efremovich [39] has shown (see problem **10** in Section **6.5**) that proximities are sufficiently general to allow consideration of all the properties of uniformly continuous mappings of metric spaces.

Although we will leave the verifications of most of the elementary properties of proximities to the problems, two important results will be proven here. The following are useful in suggesting an answer to the question of how proximity spaces may be constructed topologically.

Theorem 11.5.1. *For any two subsets A and B of the proximity space (X, δ), $A\delta B$ iff $\mathbf{c}(A)\delta\mathbf{c}(B)$.*

Proof. If A is near B, then the larger sets $\mathbf{c}(A)$ and $\mathbf{c}(B)$ are near, by problem **2**(i). Now suppose $A\bar{\delta}B$. By **[P.4]**, there exists a set $C \subseteq X$ such that $A\bar{\delta}C$ and $X \setminus C\bar{\delta}B$. If there were some point x in both $\mathbf{c}(A)$ and C, then we would have $\{x\}\delta A$ and $x \in C$. Thus, for the larger set C, we must have $C\delta A$, or, by **[P.5]**, $A\delta C$. This contradiction shows that $\mathbf{c}(A) \subseteq X \setminus C$. But since $X \setminus C\bar{\delta}B$, again by problem **2**(i), we must have $\mathbf{c}(A)\bar{\delta}B$. By the same method, $B\bar{\delta}\mathbf{c}(A)$ implies that $\mathbf{c}(B)\bar{\delta}\mathbf{c}(A)$, and so $\mathbf{c}(A)\bar{\delta}\mathbf{c}(B)$. ∎

Theorem 11.5.2. *For any two subsets A and B of a proximity space (X, δ) whose topology is compact, $A\delta B$ iff $\mathbf{c}(A) \cap \mathbf{c}(B) \neq \emptyset$.*

Proof. If $\mathbf{c}(A) \cap \mathbf{c}(B) \neq \emptyset$, then there exists some point x in each set. By **[P.2]**, $\{x\}\delta\{x\}$, and so we must have $\mathbf{c}(A)\delta\mathbf{c}(B)$, by problem **2**(i). By the previous theorem, this implies that $A\delta B$. Now suppose that $\mathbf{c}(A) \cap \mathbf{c}(B) = \emptyset$. For every point $x \in \mathbf{c}(A)$, we must then have $x \notin \mathbf{c}(B) = \mathbf{c}(\mathbf{c}(B))$. Thus $\{x\}\bar{\delta}\mathbf{c}(B)$, or, by **[P.5]**, $\mathbf{c}(B)\bar{\delta}\{x\}$. By **[P.4]**, there exists a set C_x such that $\mathbf{c}(B)\bar{\delta}C_x$ and $X \setminus C_x\bar{\delta}\{x\}$. It is clear that $x \in C_x$, for otherwise we would have $X \setminus C_x\delta\{x\}$ (see problem **2**(ii)). Furthermore, C_x is a neighborhood of x since $\{x\}\bar{\delta}X \setminus C_x$ means that $x \notin \mathbf{c}(X \setminus C_x)$. Thus the family $\{C_x : x \in \mathbf{c}(A)\}$ is a covering of $\mathbf{c}(A)$ by neighborhoods. As a closed subset of the compact space X, $\mathbf{c}(A)$ is compact, and so there must be some finite subcovering. Thus $\mathbf{c}(A) \subseteq \bigcup_{i=1}^{n} C_{x_i}$ for some finite number of points $x_i \in \mathbf{c}(A)$. We note, however, that $\mathbf{c}(B)\bar{\delta}C_{x_i}$ for each i, and so $\mathbf{c}(B)\bar{\delta}\bigcup_{i=1}^{n} C_{x_i}$, by **[P.3]**. But then, for the smaller set $\mathbf{c}(A)$, we must have $\mathbf{c}(B)\bar{\delta}\mathbf{c}(A)$, or, by **[P.5]**, $\mathbf{c}(A)\bar{\delta}\mathbf{c}(B)$. ∎

If we now restrict our attention to proximities which induce Hausdorff topological spaces, we may obtain a very interesting characterization of those spaces which have proximities defined on them. Since every proximity induces a completely regular topological space, it is clear that we are just discussing the Tichonov spaces again. By **8.5.3**, these are exactly the spaces which have (Hausdorff) compactifications, and, as just shown, in these compactifications the proximity is uniquely determined. The final result, proved by Smirnov [72], is the following:

Theorem 11.5.3. *Every Hausdorff proximity space* (X,δ) *is a dense subspace of a unique compact Hausdorff space* X^* *such that* $A\delta B$ *in* X *iff* $\mathbf{c}^*(A) \cap \mathbf{c}^*(B) \neq \varnothing$ *where the closure* $\mathbf{c}^*$ *is taken in* X^*.

Other interesting proofs of this theorem have been given by Leader [50], and by Császár and Mrówka [34]. For information concerning the dimension of proximity spaces, see Smirnov [70].

Exercises

1. The operator $\mathbf{c}$ defined by setting $\mathbf{c}(E) = \{x : \{x\}\ \delta E\}$ is a closure operator for any proximity space (X, δ).

2. In any proximity space (X, δ):

   (i) If $A \supseteq A^*$, $B \supseteq B^*$, and $A^*\ \delta\ B^*$, then $A\ \delta\ B$.

   (ii) If $A \cap B \neq \varnothing$, then $A\ \delta\ B$.

3. In any pseudometric space (X, d), the relation δ, defined by setting $A\ \delta\ B$ iff $d(A, B) = 0$, is a proximity relation.

4. In any uniform space $(X, \mathfrak{U})$, the relation δ, defined by setting $A\ \delta\ B$ iff for every $\mathfrak{u} \in \mathfrak{U}$ there exists a point $x \in A$ and a point $y \in B$ such that $\langle x, y\rangle \in \mathfrak{u}$, is a proximity relation for X which induces the same topology as $\mathfrak{U}$.

5. In any proximity space (X, δ), the family $\{\mathfrak{u}_{A,B} : A\ \bar{\delta}\ B\}$, as defined in the text, is a subbase for a uniformity for X which induces δ.

6. In any completely regular topological space $(X, \mathscr{T})$, the relation δ, defined by setting $A\ \delta\ B$ iff A and B cannot be functionally separated (i.e., there does not exist any continuous mapping $\mathfrak{f}$ of X into $[0, 1]$ such that $\mathfrak{f}(A) = \{0\}$ and $\mathfrak{f}(B) = \{1\}$), is a proximity relation which induces $\mathscr{T}$.

7. An equicontinuous mapping of proximity spaces is continuous with respect to the induced topologies. A uniformly continuous mapping of uniform spaces is equicontinuous with respect to the induced proximities.

8. Describe the proximity relations obtained for the real numbers by considering (i) the one point compactification, (ii) the two point compactification.

9. Describe the proximity relations obtained for the plane by considering (i) the one point compactification, (ii) the compactification obtained by adding two "ideal" points on each line with parallel lines having the same ideal points, (iii) the Stone-Čech compactification. What is the compactification corresponding to the metric proximity?

Bibliography

BOOKS

[1] A. Appert, "Propriétés des Espaces Abstraits les Plus Généraux." Actual. Sci. Ind. No. 146, Hermann, Paris, 1934.

[2] G. Birkhoff, "Lattice Theory," rev. ed. Amer. Math. Soc. Colloq. Publ. XXV, New York, 1948.

[3] N. Bourbaki, "Éléments de Mathématique: Livre III, Topologie Générale." Actual. Sci. Ind. Nos. 858-1142, 916-1143, 1029-1235, 1045, 1084, Hermann, Paris, 1939–1955.

[4] E. Čech, "Topologické Prostory." Czech. Akad., Praha, 1959.

[5] J. Dieudonné, "Foundations of Modern Analysis." Academic Press, New York, 1960.

[6] W. Fulks, "Advanced Calculus." Wiley, New York, 1961.

[7] L. Gillman and M. Jerison, "Rings of Continuous Functions." Van Nostrand, Princeton, New Jersey, 1960.

[8] K. Gödel, "The Consistency of the Axiom of Choice and of the Generalized Continuum Hypothesis with the Axioms of Set Theory" (Ann. of Math. Studies, No. 3). Princeton Univ. Press, Princeton, New Jersey, 1940.

[9] C. Goffman, "Real Functions." Holt, New York, 1953.

[10] P. R. Halmos, "Naive Set Theory." Van Nostrand, Princeton, New Jersey, 1960.

[11] S. Hu, "Homotopy Theory." Academic Press, New York, 1959.

[12] W. Hurewicz and H. Wallman, "Dimension Theory" (Princeton Math. Series, No. 4). Princeton Univ. Press, Princeton, New Jersey, 1948.

[13] E. Kamke, "Theory of Sets." Dover, New York, 1950.

[14] J. L. Kelley, "General Topology." Van Nostrand, Princeton, New Jersey, 1955.

[15] K. Knopp, "Theory and Application of Infinite Series." Blackie, London, 1951.

[16] A. N. Kolmogorov and S. V. Fomin, "Elements of the Theory of Functions and Functional Analysis, Vol. 1: Metric and Normed Spaces." Graylock Press, Rochester, New York, 1957.

[17] K. Kuratowski, "Topologie, I," 3rd ed. (Monografie Matematyczne, Tom XX). Warsaw, 1952.

[18] J. M. H. Olmsted, "Real Variables." Appleton, New York, 1959.

[19] L. Pontrjagin, "Topological Groups" (Princeton Math. Series, No. 2). Princeton Univ. Press, Princeton, New Jersey, 1939.

[20] W. Sierpinski, "General Topology." Univ. Toronto Press, Toronto, 1952.

[21] Summer Institute on Set Theoretic Topology, Madison, Wisconsin, 1955 (rev. 1957).

[22] "General Topology and Its Relations to Modern Analysis and Algebra" (Proceedings of the Symposium held in Prague, 1961). Academic Press, New York, 1962.

[23] A. E. Taylor, "Introduction to Functional Analysis." Wiley, New York, 1958.

[24] J. W. Tukey, "Convergence and Uniformity in Topology" (Ann. of Math. Studies, No. 2). Princeton Univ. Press, Princeton, New Jersey, 1940.

[25] R. Vaidyanathaswamy, "Set Topology," 2nd ed. Chelsea, New York, 1960.

[26] A. Weil, "Sur les Espaces a Structure Uniforme." Actual. Sci. Ind. No. 551, Hermann, Paris, 1937.

[27] G. T. Whyburn, "Analytic Topology." Amer. Math. Soc. Colloq. Publ. XXVIII, New York, 1942.

Papers

[28] J. Albuquerque, La notion de "frontière" en topologie. *Portugal. Math.* **2** (1941), 280–289.

[29] P. S. Aleksandrov, Bicompact extensions of topological spaces. *Mat. Sb.* (47) **5** (1939), 403–424 (in Russian).

[30] P. S. Aleksandrov, Some results in the theory of topological spaces, obtained within the last twenty-five years. *Russian Math. Surveys* **15** (1960), 23–84.

[31] P. S. Aleksandrov and P. Urysohn, Mémoire sur les espaces topologiques compactes. *Verh. Kon. Akad. Wetensch., Amsterdam* **14** (1929), 1–96.

[32] R. H. Bing, Metrization of topological spaces. *Canad. J. Math.* **3** (1951), 175–186.

[33] E. Čech, On bicompact spaces. *Ann. of Math.* **38** (1937), 823–844.

[34] A. Császár and S. Mrówka, Sur la compactification des espaces de proximité. *Fund. Math.* **46** (1958), 195–207.

[35] J. Dieudonné, Un exemple d'espace normal non susceptible d'une structure uniforme d'espace complet. *C. R. Acad. Sci.* **209** (1939), 145–147.

[36] J. Dieudonné, Une généralization des espaces compacts. *J. Math. Pures Appl.* **23** (1944), 65–76.

[37] R. Doss, On uniform spaces with a unique structure. *Amer. J. Math.* **71** (1949), 19–23.

[38] C. H. Dowker, An extension of Aleksandrov's mapping theorem. *Bull. Amer. Math. Soc.* **54** (1948), 386–391.

[39] V. A. Efremovich, Geometry of proximity, I. *Mat. Sb.* (73) **31** (1952), 189–200 (in Russian).

[40] M. K. Fort, Jr., Nested neighborhoods in a Hausdorff space (Solution to problem 4577). *Amer. Math. Monthly* **62** (1955), 372.

[41] H. Freudenthal, Neuaufbau der Endentheorie. *Ann. of Math.* **43** (1942), 261–279.

[42] A. H. Frink, Distance functions and the metrization problem. *Bull. Amer. Math. Soc.* **43** (1937), 133–142.

[43] E. Hewitt, On two problems of Urysohn. *Ann. of Math.* **47** (1946), 503–509.

[44] J. L. Kelley, Hyperspaces of a continuum. *Trans. Amer. Math. Soc.* **52** (1942), 22–36.

[45] J. L. Kelley, The Tychonoff product theorem implies the axiom of choice. *Fund. Math.* **37** (1950), 75–76.

[46] J. R. Kline, A theorem concerning connected point sets. *Fund. Math.* **3** (1922), 238–239.

[47] B. Knaster and K. Kuratowski, Sur les ensembles connexes. *Fund. Math.* **2** (1921), 206–255.

[48] S. B. Krishna Murti, A set of axioms for topological algebra. *J. Indian Math. Soc.* **4** (1940), 116–119.

[49] K. Kuratowski, Solution d'un problème concernant les images continues d'ensembles de points. *Fund. Math.* **2** (1921), 158–160.

[50] S. Leader, On clusters in proximity spaces. *Fund. Math.* **47** (1959), 205–213.

[51] N. Levine, A characterization of compact metric spaces. *Amer. Math. Monthly* **68** (1961), 657–658.

[52] N. Levine, Remarks on uniform continuity in metric spaces. *Amer. Math. Monthly* **67** (1960), 562–563.

[53] N. Levine, Strong continuity in topological spaces. *Amer. Math. Monthly* **67** (1960), 269.

[54] N. Levine and W. G. Saunders, Uniformly continuous sets in metric spaces. *Amer. Math. Monthly* **67** (1960), 153–156.

[55] E. Marczewski, Séparabilité et multiplication cartésienne des espaces topologiques. *Fund. Math.* **34** (1947), 127–143.

[56] E. A. Michael, A note on paracompact spaces. *Proc. Amer. Math. Soc.* **4** (1953), 831–838.

[57] E. A. Michael, The product of a normal space and a metric space need not be normal. *Notices Amer. Math. Soc.* **10** (1963), 258. See also: K. Morita, On the product of a normal space with a metric space. *Proc. Japan Acad.* **39** (1963), 148–150.

[58] E. A. Michael, Topologies on spaces of subsets. *Trans. Amer. Math. Soc.* **71** (1951), 152–182.

[59] E. W. Miller, Concerning biconnected sets. *Fund. Math.* **29** (1937), 123–133.

[60] S. G. Mrówka, On normal metrics. *Notices Amer. Math. Soc.* **10** (1963), 281.

[61] S. G. Mrówka and W. J. Pervin, On uniform connectedness. *Proc. Amer. Math. Soc.* **15** (1964), 446–449.

[62] J. Nagata, On a necessary and sufficient condition of metrizability. *J. Polytech. Inst. Osaka City Univ.* **1** (1950), 93–100.

[63] V. Niemytski and A. Tichonov, Beweis des Satzes, dass ein metrisierbarer Raum dann und nur dann kompakt ist, wenn er in jeder Metrik vollständig ist. *Fund. Math.* **12** (1928), 118–120.

[64] W. J. Pervin, On separation and proximity spaces. *Amer. Math. Monthly* **71** (1964), 158–161.

[65] W. J. Pervin, Quasi-proximities for topological spaces. *Math. Ann.* **150** (1963), 325–326.

[66] W. J. Pervin, Quasi-uniformization of topological spaces. *Math. Ann.* **147** (1962), 316–317.

[67] W. J. Pervin, Uniformization of neighborhood axioms. *Math. Ann.* **147** (1962), 313–315.

[68] W. J. Pervin and N. Levine, Connected mappings of Hausdorff spaces. *Proc. Amer. Math. Soc.* **9** (1958), 488–496.

[69] V. Ponomarev, Countability axioms and continuous mappings. *Bull. Acad. Polon. Sci.* **8** (1960), 127–133 (in Russian).

[70] Yu. M. Smirnov, On dimension of proximity spaces. *Mat. Sb.* (80) **38** (1956), 283–302 (in Russian). See also, *Amer. Math. Soc. Transl.* Ser. 2, No. 21.

[71] Yu. M. Smirnov, On metrization of topological spaces. *Uspekhi Mat. Nauk* (*N.S.*) **6** (1951), 100–111 (in Russian). See also, *Amer. Math. Soc. Transl.* No. 91.

[72] Yu. M. Smirnov, On proximity spaces. *Mat. Sb.* (73) **31** (1952), 543–574 (in Russian).

[73] R. H. Sorgenfrey, On the topological product of paracompact spaces. *Bull. Amer. Math. Soc.* **53** (1947), 631–632.

[74] A. H. Stone, Paracompactness and product spaces. *Bull. Amer. Math. Soc.* **54** (1948), 977–982.

[75] M. H. Stone, Applications of the theory of Boolean rings to general topology. *Trans. Amer. Math. Soc.* **41** (1937), 375–481.

[76] P. Szymanski, La notion des ensembles séparés terme primitif de la topologie. *Math. Timişoara* **17** (1941), 65–84.

[77] A. Tichonov, Über die topologische Erweiterung von Räumen. *Math. Ann.* **102** (1930), 544–561.
[78] A. Tichonov, Über einen Funktionenraum. *Math. Ann.* **111** (1935), 762–766.
[79] P. Urysohn, Über die Mächtigkeit der zusammenhängenden Mengen. *Math. Ann.* **94** (1925), 262–295.
[80] P. Urysohn, Über Metrization des kompakten topologischen Raumes. *Math. Ann.* **92** (1924), 275–293.
[81] A. D. Wallace, Separation spaces. *Ann. of Math.* **43** (1941), 687–697. See also: Separation spaces, II. *An. Acad. Brasileira Cien.* **14** (1942), 203–206.
[82] E. Zermelo, Beweis, dass jede Menge wohlgeordnet werden kann. *Math. Ann.* **59** (1904), 514–516. See also: Neuer Beweis für die Möglichkeit einer Wohlordnung. *Math. Ann.* **65** (1908), 107–128.

Index

M

N

O

S